Item	Description	URL
Macintosh P2P Technologies		
Carracho	P2P client, server, and tracker	www.carracho.com
Zombie	Real-time collaboration and file-sharing tool	zombie.badmoon.org
Newsgroups		
alt.2600	Hierarchy of newsgroups frequented by pirates, hackers, and wannabes	alt.2600
alt.binaries.mac.applications	Newsgroup frequented by Mac pirates, hackers, and wannabes	alt.binaries.mac.applications
Deja.com	Newsgroup archive	www.deja.com
Online Drives		
Freedrive	Online drive	www.freedrive.com
i-drive	Online drive	www.idrive.com
myplay, inc.	Online drive that offers 3GB per user	www.myplay.inc
Visto	Online drive	www.visto.com
Online E-mail Services		
HotMail	Online e-mail service	www.hotmail.com
HushMail	Online e-mail service that offers encryption	www.hushmail.com
Yahoo! Mail	Online e-mail service	mail.yahoo.com
Other P2P Technologies		
audioGnome	P2P technology for sharing MP3 files; links to the Napster network	www.audiognome.com
CuteMX	P2P technology	www.cutemx.com
Freenet	P2P technology	freenet.sourceforge.com
iMesh	P2P technology	www.imesh.com

Internet Piracy Exposed

Internet Pricay Exposed

Guy Hart-Davis

SYBEX®

San Francisco Paris
Düsseldorf Soest London

Associate Publisher: Dick Staron
Contracts and Licensing Manager: Kristine O'Callaghan
Acquisitions and Developmental Editors: Gary Masters, Maureen Adams
Editor: Brianne Hope Agatep
Production Editor: Leslie E.H. Light
Technical Editor: Eric Bell
Book Designer: Maureen Forys, Happenstance Type-O-Rama
Electronic Publishing Specialist: Maureen Forys, Happenstance Type-O-Rama
Proofreaders: Nelson Kim, Leslie E.H. Light, Laurie O'Connell, Nancy Riddiough
Indexer: Ted Laux
Cover Designer: Daniel Ziegler
Cover Illustrator/Photographer: Daniel Ziegler

Library of Congress Card Number: 20010807083

ISBN: 0-7821-2920-X

Manufactured in the United States of America

10 9 8 7 6 5 4 3 2 1

*This book is dedicated
to Edward.*

Acknowledgments

I would like to thank the following people for their help with this book:

- Gary Masters for frequent help and encouragement.
- Maureen Adams for developing the book.
- Brianne Agatep for editing the book with patience and good humor.
- Eric "Howling Dog" Bell for reviewing the manuscript for technical accuracy.
- Adrienne Crew for reviewing Chapter 2 and making valuable suggestions for improving it.
- Leslie Light for coordinating the production of the book.
- Maureen Forys for typesetting the manuscript.
- Nelson Kim, Leslie Light, Laurie O'Connell, and Nancy Riddiough for proofreading the book.
- Ted Laux for creating the index.

Contents at a Glance

Contents

Introduction

Take piracy, a traditional if not exactly honorable occupation since well before the Romans and Phoenicians took to the seas, and one that was continued with gusto into the 20th century and (in some of the more lively areas of the world) into the 21st century. Add the Internet, new file-sharing technologies, and ubiquitous computers powerful enough to deliver quality audio and video. Brew these ingredients together, and you get Internet piracy, the up-and-coming hobby of the new millennium.

What Is Internet Piracy?

Internet piracy is piracy conducted via the Internet.

As you know, the essence of piracy is taking something that doesn't belong to you without paying for it. For example, pirates used to halt ships on the high seas, board them, and relieve them of either any over-valuable items they happened to be carrying or (if the ship were heavily burdened with good stuff) of that part of the crew determined to guard the cargo and unwilling to change masters in pursuit of survival.

Now that computers have gained a foothold in many homes worldwide, piracy has gone digital. So instead of involving the stealing of physical property, Internet piracy involves the theft of intellectual property.

Because it's digital and involves intellectual rather than physical property, Internet piracy seems less harmful to most people than does physical piracy or plain theft. If someone steals your car, your wallet, or your pants, chances are that you'll notice the loss and want the item back. But if you create an original work, such as a story, a movie, a piece of music, or a software application and publish it, you're much less likely to notice when someone casually rips off a copy of it. For example, if they burn a copy of a CD or of a DVD containing your work, you're unlikely to know about it unless you happen to see the copy they made.

Internet piracy has been around for as long as the Internet itself, but it's increased monstrously in the last few years. This is because the tools for Internet piracy have become much more powerful, far easier to use, and, as a result, far more widely used.

Napster, perhaps the first protocol to become a household word within a year of its invention, has ushered in a new and relatively golden age of peer-to-peer (P2P) file-sharing, letting users share and download MP3 files—and other files disguised as MP3 files—with a minimum of effort and delay. And, as you'll see in the book, post-Napster technologies have sprung up that let you share any kind of file you happen to have.

Who Is This Book For?

This book is for anyone who wants to know how Internet piracy works—and how they can use the same tools that the pirates use, but for legitimate purposes.

This book assumes that you're a law-abiding citizen who wants to access files that are being shared legally on the Internet and perhaps share some files of your own—music you've created, stories you've written, movies or animations you've made, or even your teen-angst poetry.

So the book discusses what the pirates do, why they do it (and how they try to justify it), and how they do it. It tells you why piracy is wrong. It points out what the penalties for piracy are. And it explains how pirates can be caught.

More positively, this book tells you what the law is—what you can legally do, and what you can't—and how you can stay on the right side of it. None of the tools and techniques discussed in this book is illegal, but almost all of them can be used illegally, in much the same way that it's legal to use a knife to carve meat but illegal to use one to carve humans.

What Does This Book Cover?

This book covers everything you need to know about Internet piracy and the law in order to share files legally and easily.

Here's a chapter-by-chapter breakdown of what this book covers:

- Chapter 1, "Digital Piracy 101," covers the basics of Internet piracy: who the pirates are, what they do, why they do it, and the assorted justifications they offer for piracy. This chapter also discusses why piracy is wrong and tries to point out some of the effects it's having. (I say "tries to" because quantifying the effects of piracy is like trying to measure live eels.)

🕱 Chapter 2, "Crime and Punishment: Piracy and the Law, " examines how piracy and the law relate to each other, what you can and cannot legally do (and why), and the penalties that the law provides for those caught breaking it. This chapter covers intellectual property and copyright, the concepts of fair use and personal use; and what the public domain is. It also discusses some of the key pieces of legislation that affect P2P file-sharing, including the Betamax Decision, the Audio Home Recording Act, and the Digital Millennium Copyright Act.

🕱 Chapter 3, "The Pirate's Basic Tools," discusses the set of tools that digital pirates need, from computer through Internet connection, anti-virus software, and a healthy sense of paranoia. If you're an active user of the Internet, you've probably got most of these tools, with the possible exception of the paranoia.

🕱 Chapter 4, "The Early Days of Piracy," details tools and techniques pirates used to exchange files in the early days of piracy. These tools included e-mail, newsgroups, FTP sites, dial-up and direct connections, and some physical media—and almost all of them are still valuable nowadays when more modern tools and techniques fail.

🕱 Chapter 5, "The Pirate Community Grows," discusses how the pirate community grew in the early, mid, and almost-late 1990s. This chapter covers pirate Web sites, company networks and college networks, removable disks, and recordable CDs. It discusses the most effective physical and virtual media for transferring files asynchronously from one person to another.

Where this book covers software, it provides examples for Windows, Linux, and the Macintosh wherever possible. Where one example adequately covers what you need to know, the book uses a Windows example. This is because (however fervently many people hate Microsoft), Windows is still by far the most widely used operating system.

☠ Chapter 6, "Napster: Piracy for the Masses," discusses the phenomenon of Napster, the immensely popular P2P technology for finding and sharing MP3 files. With more than 50 million users worldwide in February 2001, and still growing like a prize turkey on steroids, Napster has been a force to be reckoned with. But (at this writing) Napster, Inc., is facing shutdown as the result of a February 12, 2001, ruling by the Ninth U.S. Circuit Court of Appeals that Napster must prevent its users from sharing copyrighted music. Napster, Inc., plans to appeal the ruling and is currently still operating. At the end of the chapter, you'll find coverage of using Wrapster and Wrapintosh to disguise other files as MP3 files so that you can share them via Napster, audioGnome, and other P2P technologies.

☠ Chapter 7, "Post-Napster Technologies," covers the best of the post-Napster P2P technologies. In July 2000, the skies darkened briefly when a San Francisco judge ordered Napster, Inc., to shut down. Forward sprang a number of P2P technologies—including audioGnome, Gnutella, Aimster, and Freenet—to fill the anticipated void; though Napster, Inc., is still in business, these three are going strong. This chapter discusses those four technologies, together with three others: iMesh, Spinfrenzy.com, and CuteMX.

☠ Chapter 8, "NetMeeting and HotLine—the Tools of the Pros," shows you the preferred tools of the pro pirates: NetMeeting for Windows and HotLine for the Mac. NetMeeting and HotLine let you implement secure, private file-sharing with your friends and are great for legitimate file exchange as well as piratical activities.

☠ Chapter 9, "The Future of Piracy, Digital Content, and P2P," wraps up the book by discussing where piracy, digital content, and P2P technologies are going. You might enjoy this chapter for a couple of reasons: First, it's good and short, and second, it contains predictions about the future that will doubtless turn out little more accurate than your horoscope for last month.

At the end of the book, there's a glossary of terms covering digital piracy and other areas touched on in the book.

"A Pirate Speaks" Sidebars

At the end of each chapter, you'll find a sidebar (one of these gray-background sections) giving the point of view of a particular pirate that I've run into on the Net. These sections are presented in the first person ("I do this" rather than "John does this"), but it's the pirate speaking, not me. I've edited what the pirates said for clarity and profanity, but apart from that, these sections are straight from the horse's, uh, mouth.

I've included these sidebars in the book to help illuminate the often murky world of digital piracy. It goes without saying that I don't necessarily endorse the sentiments expressed by the pirates—except for the sentiment about CDs and DVDs being viciously overpriced—and am *not* encouraging you to break the law.

Terminology and Conventions Used in This Book

To keep this book down to a manageable size, I've used a number of conventions to represent information concisely and accurately:

- ☠ The menu arrow, ➢, indicates selecting a choice from a menu or submenu. For example, "choose Edit ➢ Preferences" means that you should pull down the Edit menu and select the Preferences item from it.

- ☠ + signs indicate key combinations. For example, "press Ctrl+P" means that you should hold down the Ctrl key and press the P key; and "press Apple+Q" means that you should hold the Apple-symbol key on your Macintosh and press the Q key. Likewise, "Ctrl+click" and "Shift+click" indicate that you should hold down the key involved and then click.

- *Italics* mostly indicate new terms being introduced, but sometimes they simply indicate a word or sentence I wanted to emphasize.

- **Boldface** indicates text that you may need to type letter for letter. The exception is in the Glossary, in which boldface indicates glossary terms defined elsewhere.

- Unless I'm missing it, there's no really appropriate word in English for "chunk of audio." For example, a "song" is usually understood to have words, and a "track" is usually understood as meaning one piece of music (or speech, or noise) from a CD, a cassette, or a vinyl record. In the absence of a better word, I refer to a chunk of audio as a "track," because this word at least doesn't imply that the chunk of audio necessarily has words.

- Still on the subject of words, the words *folder* and *directory* mean the same thing for Windows-based computers. I've used them interchangeably, trying to follow the terminology that the application being discussed uses.

- URLs: I've left off the `http://` from each URL for brevity (and to prevent bad line breaks). For example, the URL `http://sound.media.mit.edu/mpeg4/` appears in the book as `sound.media.mit.edu/mpeg4/`. So you'll need to add the `http://` to each URL you use.

I've Got Those Evolution Blues...

You'll see the phrase "at this writing" appear frequently in this book. This book went to press in February 2001 and reflects the state of software and hardware at that time.

Because software and hardware is evolving more or less at Internet speed, you'll likely find that some things have changed by the time you read this book. For example, you may find that newer versions of software applications have more features than I describe in the book or that those features are implemented in a somewhat different way. However, the descriptions in this book should give you a good idea of how the applications work; if they're not the same feature for feature, they should at least be similar in enough ways for you to figure them out easily.

Be good. Be very good. But enjoy.

Chapter 1

Digital Piracy 101

Featuring

- Who are the new pirates?
- What do the pirates do?
- Why do they do it?
- How do they justify it?
- Why is piracy wrong?
- What effects is piracy having?

This chapter sets the scene for your understanding of piracy. It covers who the new pirates are, what they're doing, and why they're doing it. It then discusses how the pirates justify what they're doing, why none of those justifications holds water, and the effects that piracy is having. Then, once you're convinced that piracy is morally wrong, it's time for Chapter 2, which tells you what the law has to say about piracy. (Quick hint: It's not enthusiastic about it.)

This chapter is short, so even if you think you know everything about piracy, you might want to skim through it.

Who Are the Digital Pirates?

Piracy has evolved massively since the days of physical pirates such as the notorious Blackbeard. In those days, the ambitious pirate needed a fast, heavily armed boat; a crew of ruffians; as many barrels of rum, salt pork, and baccy as he could lay his bloodstained hands on; a boatload of attitude; and a lime or two to ward off the curse of scurvy and keep the men's teeth in their heads. Cat-o'-nine-tails in hand (or hook), the pirate would drive his crew to sail for months through spectacularly bad weather, shooting the occasional albatross, in pursuit of treasure or booty.

It was a hard life enlivened by pitched battles, loss of limbs or eyes, and a severe lack of wenching except for marauding forays and a drunken pit stop every year or two in a scummy port. Sport consisted of pillage and plunder, with a little keel-hauling reserved for slow days.

Okay, so you knew all that. (If you didn't, read *Treasure Island* or another pirate classic.) But things are different now.

Technology has changed piracy forever. Except in some of the more exciting areas of the world, physical piracy is passé. Piracy has moved into the modern age and become digital, and the computer has become the greatest tool of piracy ever.

Barring fetishes and fantasies, digital pirates have no need of eye patches, parrots, or prostheses made from dead trees. The only schooner a modern pirate needs is one full of ale—and if their favorite brew doesn't go with lime, they can pop a vitamin C pill and floss their teeth to keep their gums full. But attitude still helps.

In the days when computing used to be difficult and the Web was a twinkle in the eye of Tim Berners-Lee, digital piracy used to be difficult too. It was hard for pirates to find the material they wanted to steal. It was tricky for them to download it, because connectivity was poor, modem speeds were slow, and protocols were as hairy as a porcupine's butt. Even enjoying the pirated material was difficult, because the pirate typically had to decode and reassemble the files—and in those days, sound and video cards were primitive enough to make multimedia a chore for professionals.

Now that computing has become, if not easy, at least socially acceptable in most parts of the western world, piracy is easier too. The pirate no longer needs to be a hacker (though some modern pirates are crackers). All the pirate needs is a computer, an Internet connection, and a little software that's easy to come by.

As a result, more and more computer- and Internet-literate people are turning to digital piracy to find the material they want. Chances are, the digital pirates are all around you. (Hell, you may even be one yourself.)

What Do the Digital Pirates Do?

To put it simply: Pirates steal stuff. Digital pirates steal digital stuff by transferring files back and forth.

This stealing prefers other names to its own. Ripping off. Copying. Getting without paying. But whatever the pirate calls it, and no matter what justification they offer for it, it remains theft in the eyes of the law.

The files the digital pirates share with each other typically contain music, video, pictures, texts, and software. More specialized pirates share files containing sensitive material, such as any industrial secrets or classified government material they've managed to glean.

This book concentrates on the main categories of interest to the average pirate. The following subsections look at the categories in turn.

Music

At this writing, music files form the largest category of piracy on the Net. Much of the current bandwidth occupied by piracy is taken up by MP3 files being traded using peer-to-peer (P2P) technologies such as Napster and audioGnome, which together gave piracy a tremendous boost in 1999 and 2000.

MP3 has become huge for several reasons:

- First, music is ideal for enjoying via computer. Almost all computers sold since 1998 have acceptable-to-decent sound capabilities (and if your computer doesn't, you can upgrade it easily enough by adding a sound card). Unlike text, which many people find awkward to read on screen, music lends itself to being played on computer, either via a CD-ROM drive or as music files.

- Second, the MP3 file format has made it possible to transfer music files easily from one computer to another and to store a large number of high-quality tracks on a medium-sized hard drive. By compressing near–CD-quality audio to around a tenth of its original (uncompressed) size, MP3 makes music wieldy and portable. MP3 software is widely available for free or for a few dollars and is exceedingly easy to use.

- Third, Napster and post-Napster technologies have made it childishly simple to share your MP3 files with other users and download the MP3 files they're sharing.

Video

The next biggest footprint on the bandwidth scale belongs to video—video clips of anything from the latest DVDs to sports games to music videos to pornography.

Far fewer pirates are trading video than audio, because video files are so large as to tax even DSLs and cable Internet connections. Depending on the compression used, DVD-quality video takes up nearly 20MB a minute, so you have to seriously want it to devote the time to downloading it. But even with fewer people trading video files, their size alone causes them to take up a significant amount of bandwidth.

Pictures

Next come pictures—any type of digital images that people want to trade. As you'd imagine, many of these pictures are of celebrities, movie stars, and rock stars. But the overwhelming majority of them are pornographic. (Not that pornography is necessarily distinct from the other categories, as Pamela Anderson and Tommy Lee undoubtedly know.)

Software

After pictures comes software. Software has long been a target for digital pirates, mostly because it has been much easier to rip off copies of software than of most other business or consumer products.

Before CD-R and CD-RW drives became widely available, it was difficult and expensive for the consumer to make a bit-for-bit copy of a CD. (You could copy the entire CD to a hard drive and try to install it from there, but many programs were smart enough not to let this work—and the software wasn't nearly as portable once installed as it had been on the CD.) But it was easy to borrow a CD (or, in the old days, a floppy) from a friend or colleague, install it on one or more computers, and then return it.

Now it's even easier. Pirates use warez sites and P2P technologies to share illegal copies of software. Once a pirate has downloaded software, all they need is the serial number for it. As a result, one of the most frequent types of messages you'll see on hacker newsgroups is requests for serial numbers for operating systems and applications. (Because most hackers regard software piracy as lame, many of these messages get comprehensively flamed.)

Texts

Last in the amount of bandwidth consumer comes text. Piracy of text is least popular for a number of reasons:

- First, many people don't like to read a large amount on screen. Hell, many people don't like to read at all. But most of those who do like to read find the paper-based book or magazine the most convenient format for sustained reading.

- Second, most books are cheap compared to music, DVDs, and software.

- Third—and the killer—it's much harder to get text from a book into a file than to rip a CD track to MP3, rip a DVD track to a video file, or scan a picture. To get the text of a printed book, you need to scan all its pages and then perform optical character recognition (OCR) on them. This takes a long time, and few people find it worth the effort.

Why Do They Do It?

The short answer to this question is: Because they want the stuff, and because they can. For most pirates, the reasons are in that order; for a few, they're the other way around.

As you'll know if you've ever received a worthwhile freebie, it's great to get what you want without having to pay for it. P2P technologies have made it easy for people to exchange files with people they don't know.

Widespread piracy has been enabled by a variety of technologies:

- First, and most obviously, computers in the home and the dorm. (Some piracy goes on inside corporations, but these days, most administrators scan frequently for illegal files and suspicious activity on Internet connections.)

- Second, and equally obviously, the Internet has provided the connectivity needed to get the files from one computer to another.

- Third, the recent explosion of bandwidth has encouraged people to transfer more and larger files. Many people are still stuck with 56K modems, but the increasing availability of high-speed connections such as cable, DSLs, and satellite links has encouraged others to trade files like never before. However, bandwidth still remains a bottleneck on P2P file sharing, especially on video files.

- Fourth, MP3 and other compressed-audio formats (including WMA and to a much lesser extent TwinVQ) have reduced high-quality audio files to manageable sizes, both for storing in large numbers on computers and for transferring via the Internet. Video-compression formats are improving, making video files less cumbersome to transfer—though because of the amount of information they contain, video files remain dauntingly large for all but the fastest connections.

- Fifth, CD-R and CD-RW drives have made it easy to burn custom CDs, either for backup or to share with a friend.

- Sixth, affordable scanners and OCR have made it possible to digitize books and articles. Nobody wants to retype a whole book, but scanning it is a different matter. With a sheet-fed scanner and feeder, you can set 30 to 50 pages scanning and leave it for a while. Reading through the resulting OCR'ed text is still a labor of love, but there are people prepared to do it. For example, Project Gutenberg now has hundreds of texts available on the Internet.

When Do They Do It?

Basically, whenever they get the chance. All the pirate needs is a computer and an Internet connection, so they can commit piracy at any time they're online. And because most of the time involved in piracy is taken by downloading, the pirate can set a large number of downloads (or a number of large downloads) to run while away from their computer—for example, overnight—and return later (or the next day) to sample and enjoy the pirated material.

How Do They Justify It?

Some pirates couldn't care less about justifying their piracy. But others will trot out various justifications. This section examines those justifications. Some of them specific to particular file types (for example, music); others are more general.

Here's the short list:

- "There's no copyright notice on it."
- "Everyone does it."
- "It's just a couple of files here and there."
- "Well, it's okay to make a tape of a few tracks for a friend…"
- "I'm not charging for it, so it's okay."
- "CDs (or DVDs) are too expensive."
- "I'm promoting the artist by sharing their music."
- "It's fair use."
- "It's there for free on the Net."
- "It's freeware or shareware."
- "It's in the public domain."
- "It's copyleft."
- "It's not hurting anybody."

Let's look at these arguments in turn.

"There's No Copyright Notice on It"

There's no copyright notice on an item—so it's not copyrighted, right?

Wrong.

Almost every original work is copyrighted, even if no copyright notice appears on it. Since the Berne Convention, it's not necessary to include a copyright notice on a work, though it remains a good idea.

Unless you know for sure that a work is out of copyright and thus in the public domain, assume that it is copyrighted, and act accordingly.

"Everyone Does It"

At first sight, "everybody does it" seems a poor justification for piracy—but in the last couple of years, it has become increasingly true. Fueled by Napster and the P2P technologies it spawned, piracy has spread like gas gangrene on a half-treated wound.

Because so many people are now pirating material, there remains little or no moral stigma attached to it. In a way, it's like speeding: Everybody knows there are laws against it, but because everybody's doing it, nobody cares much unless someone offends particularly egregiously—the equivalent of barreling along a crowded freeway at 150 m.p.h. heaving tire-busters out of the window.

The main difference between piracy and speeding is that the penalties for piracy are far more severe, as you'll learn in the next chapter. But because—again, as with speeding—enforcement of the law tends to concentrate on the most blatant offenders, most people feel safe casually pirating copyrighted material. In fact, unless people are taking precautions, this feeling of safety is completely illusory.

"It's Just a Couple of Files Here and There"

The next justification is that the pirate doesn't make a habit of the piracy—they just download a couple of files here and there, and it really doesn't amount to much.

With some people, this is more or less true at the start. But like a couple of drinks or a couple of lines, the habit tends to grow. And while you get your social drinker and your social snorter, you don't really get your social pirate—except for those who socialize by hanging out online with other pirates, finding out which files they have to trade, and getting ever deeper into piracy. In extreme cases, piracy takes over the pirate's life, and they devote more and more time to acquiring and sharing as many files as they can—sometimes without troubling to listen to, watch, or look at the files.

Most pirates keep their piracy under control as a hobby or as a useful way of saving money—instead of buying CDs, they download MP3 files, and instead of buying DVDs, they download movies. It may seem reasonable, but it sure ain't legal.

"Well, It's Okay to Make a Tape of a Few Tracks for a Friend..."

The next justification that many pirates use is that it's okay to make a tape of a few tracks for a friend, so it's okay to shove a few MP3 files their way. Alternatively, you'll hear that it's okay to videotape a broadcast (or capture it by using a dedicated device such as a TiVo or Replay) and give it to a friend, so it's okay to share with them a few AVI files or scenes ripped from a DVD.

There are a couple of things going on here that really muddy the waters. We'll examine them in more detail in Chapter 2, "Crime and Punishment: Piracy and the Law," but here's a quick preview:

- First, under certain circumstances, it's legal to make a copy of a copyrighted work on another medium so that you can enjoy it more easily. For example, it's legal to make an MP3 file or a WMA file from a track on a CD so that you can listen to the track on a portable player. But it's not legal to give that MP3 file or WMA file to someone else—that's a violation of copyright.

- Second, certain consumer products have a levy built into their price that goes into a fund to pay copyright holders royalties for the rights a consumer *might* infringe by using the consumer product. For example, each time you buy a blank audio cassette, some of the purchase price goes towards paying royalties to artists and record companies, because you *might* use the cassette to tape a copy of a CD. The same kind of thing happens with blank video cassettes and recordable CDs designed for audio purposes (but not with recordable CDs designed for computer use).

Despite these two things, taping a few tracks for a friend is *not* legal: It's piracy. But the record companies have condoned this type of piracy for several reasons:

- First, the piracy promotes the artists and bands without the record company having to put in any effort or marketing money.

☠ Second, cassette-based piracy wasn't too harmful for the record companies and artists because the costs involved kept it small scale. A cassette worth having costs a buck or two, so no consumer is likely to rip off thousands of copies of a record or CD and sell the cassettes—and if anyone did bother selling a large number of pirated cassettes, they might well be caught.

☠ Third, the record companies (and artists) have been receiving some money for nothing from the levy on cassettes. Sweet.

Because the record companies have condoned cassette-based piracy, they weren't in a great position to counter Internet piracy when it surfaced. More on this later in the book.

"I'm Not Charging for It, So It's Okay"

The pirate may also tell you that because he or she is not charging for the files he or she is distributing, it's not a copyright violation.

This justification is a red herring. Distributing the files is the copyright violation; in the eyes of the law, it matters little whether the violator charges for the files or not. The only difference that charging for files or distributing them for free can make is in the amount of damages that may be awarded in a court settlement for a copyright infringement suit: The pirate selling files may well get hit with heavier damages than the pirate who's just giving files away. But (a) it's not worth betting on this, and (b) both pirates get punished.

There's one other difference that charging for the files might make. Most copyright infringements draw civil lawsuits. However, the U.S. Attorney may conduct a criminal investigation in cases of willful infringement for profit.

"CDs (or DVDs) Are Too Expensive"

This is one of the toughest arguments to counter—because nobody (apart from the record companies and the Recording Industry Association of America) can deny that CDs are much more expensive than they ought to be. From the consumer's point of view, it looks as though the CD was introduced to be a more expensive medium than the LP that it replaced as well as a medium that delivered better sound quality. And much the same is true of DVDs: Designed to replace videotapes and deliver higher quality (and, incidentally, provide effective copy-protection), they're also much more expensive than videotapes.

Still, as a justification for piracy, this holds no water. It's like complaining that Ferraris are too expensive. But nobody has the right to steal a Ferrari, and nobody has the right to steal the contents of a copyrighted work, be it on CD, DVD, paper, canvas, or whatever.

"I'm Promoting the Artist by Sharing Their Music"

If the pirate is ripping off audio, they'll often tell you that they're promoting the artist by distributing copies of their tracks. This may be true—but unless the artist or copyright holder has specifically granted permission to the person to distribute the track, or has granted blanket permission for distribution of that track, it's illegal. It doesn't matter whether the pirate benefits from distributing the track or not. It hardly even matters whether the artist or copyright holder benefits in some way—because copies of copyrighted material are being stolen, the artist or copyright holder will be assumed legally to be losing money.

Unfortunately, it's almost impossible to tell which tracks are being distributed with permission and which are being distributed without permission. The best way to get an idea of the legality (or otherwise) of an audio file is its provenance: If the file is available for download from a major music site, it's probably legal. For example, a RealAudio file available for download on the Columbia Music Web site is almost certainly legal, as is an MP3 file available for download on MP3.com. If the source of the file seems dubious, the file is probably illegal. For example, an MP3 file available for download on an FTP site that drew your attention by promising naked pictures of Ricky Martin would probably be illegal. And about 99 percent of the MP3 files available for download via P2P technologies such as Napster and audioGnome are illegal.

The only exception to this comes when an artist, band, or copyright holder gives blanket permission for certain tracks to be distributed freely. They may do this for specific tracks in a given format (for example, MP3) to promote their music, or for a certain category of tracks. For example, Metallica contributed greatly to its popularity by encouraging its fans to freely trade recordings of the band's live shows, much as the Grateful Dead had done in their time to help build perhaps the most devoted audience in rock history. However, when the Napster phenomenon broke and Metallica learned that MP3 files of its studio recordings were being shared at a phenomenal rate, it became one of the first bands to launch a legal challenge against Napster, Inc.

Other bands have accepted the MP3 and P2P phenomenon with more equanimity. Radiohead professed themselves delighted with the interest when MP3 files of their October 2000 album *Kid A* became available on the Internet before the album was released—and the album quickly became a bestseller on physical media as well. And in September 2000 the Smashing Pumpkins, galvanized by a contract dispute with their record company, chose to release *Machina II* in MP3 format and in a limited vinyl edition, scorning the CD format completely and encouraging their fans to share the MP3 files freely. But most artists, and almost all record companies, see MP3 and P2P as a threat rather than as an opportunity.

"It's Fair Use"

The next justification the average pirate will trot out is that what they're doing (ripping off copies of files) is "fair use." Some of them actually believe this. Others are just saying it. Both groups are wrong.

Briefly, fair use is a provision of copyright law that lets you reproduce part or all of a work for reasons of comment, criticism, parody, and so on. We'll examine fair use in more detail in Chapter 2. But for the moment, be assured that fair use does *not* allow anyone to violate copyright law left, right, and center—which is what most of the people who cite fair use are doing.

"It's There for Free on the Net"

As you'll know if you have a Web page or FTP site of your own, or you've visited a Web page or FTP site that you'd rather not have seen, the Internet has made it possible for anyone with access to a computer to publish just about any digital information almost instantly. And because, in the context of the Internet, publishing involves no more effort or expense than copying files to a Web server or FTP server, people can—and do—publish just about every type of information.

As a result, you'll find all kinds of digital information on the Internet that shouldn't be there: copyrighted software, copyrighted images, copyrighted texts, copyrighted music, and copyrighted video. The fact that copyrighted information is available on the Internet means nothing more than that someone else has violated copyright by making the file available for distribution. It's still illegal for you to download the file and to possess a copy of it. Similarly, if someone smashes open an ATM and leaves its innards hanging out, it's still illegal for you to help yourself to the money in it—even if it is apparently there for the taking.

"It's Freeware" *or* "It's Shareware"

More likely than the other justifications to be true, this justification still bears the closest of scrutiny. If the software in question really is freeware, then well and good. If the software is shareware and still within its evaluation period, then again, all is fine.

Most freeware programs and shareware programs use their readme file to make clear their status. If you don't find this information in the readme file, it may well appear during the installation routine or (if installation is a simple unzip operation) in a splash screen the first time you run the program. If you're still in doubt, run the Help ➤ About command or local equivalent and see how the software introduces itself.

Most freeware and shareware authors actively encourage users to distribute their programs so that they can find their audience. So it should be easy enough to tell if software you run into is freeware or shareware.

"It's (in the) Public Domain"

Next, you'll hear that the material being traded is "public domain" or "in the public domain." The public domain (which we'll examine in more detail in Chapter 2) comprises all works that are not (or are no longer) protected by copyright.

It's sometimes true that material is in the public domain, but usually it's not true. Generally speaking, most material worth having is *not* in the public domain. There are notable and worthy exceptions to this, but you can be more or less sure that anything you'd normally need to pay for is not in the public domain. For example, if you encounter a text file of the latest John Grisham novel on the Internet for free download, you can be pretty sure that it's not in the public domain. The same goes for music (tracks from the latest U2 CD, say) and video.

When material *is* in the public domain, you can use and distribute it frequently. For example, most of the e-texts distributed by Project Gutenberg are public domain. So you can download them (of course); distribute them directly to other people, by posting them on a Web site, or by sharing them via P2P technologies; or convert them to other formats.

Typically, a file is in the public domain for one of two reasons:

- First, because someone has chosen to put a work whose copyright they hold in the public domain. For example, someone may create a software application and put it in the public domain so that others can freely use it.

- Second, because the copyright has expired or been lost.

Many items in the public domain are clearly marked as such. If an item isn't marked as being in the public domain, the only way to find out whether it is public domain or not is to check the status of its copyright. The fact that a file is available on the Net *does not* mean that it's in the public domain—its availability may well mean nothing more than that someone else has violated copyright and ripped off a copy of it.

"It's Copyleft"

A pirate may tell you that software is copyleft. This might be true; equally, it might not.

Copyleft, a serious pun on copyright, is a licensing mechanism designed to encourage the spread and development of the software in question. Under a copyleft agreement, any distribution of the software must include its full source code. Anyone is free to modify or improve the software and distribute it further, provided that they make their modifications and improvements available to all subsequent users.

"It's Not Hurting Anybody"

If pushed, the pirate may claim that their piracy isn't hurting anybody—that because all they're doing is sharing and downloading copies of digital files, it's very different from stealing something physical, such as a CD or a DVD.

On the face of it, this argument has some appeal, because it's true that no physical object is involved. But because (from a legal point of view) creating a copy of a copyrighted work is assumed to cost the creator or copyright holder of the work the benefit that they should have derived from selling that copy of the work, this piracy is considered to harm the creator or copyright holder.

Most buyers of music find it hard to feel much sympathy for the record companies, who they believe have been fleecing the public with inflated CD prices since the late 1980s. (There's no intrinsic reason why a CD should be much more expensive than a vinyl LP, especially now that production costs for CDs have decreased. CDs are more expensive because they were designed to be more expensive.)

Likewise, few members of the public can dredge up much concern for the movie studios with their $100 million movie budgets and $25 million stars. If they lose the price of a few DVDs, many people feel, who's to care?

With software, the situation is even worse. Software has been widely stolen for many years for several reasons:

- First, software used to be really expensive—and much of it still is expensive. Many people either simply don't want to pay for the software, or they want to try it before they buy it. In the latter case, they often forget (or "forget") to pay for it when they find they like it.

- Second, it's easy to pirate software. In many cases, you can install an illegal copy of an application by borrowing a CD and a serial number from a friend or colleague for half an hour. Now that CD burners have become widespread, anyone can create a bit-for-bit copy of a CD in a quarter of an hour or so.

- Third, much if not most software piracy goes undetected. Barring the occasional raid or an upstanding or embittered employee ratting out the company to the Software & Information Industry Association (SIAA), it's relatively safe for businesses to pirate software, either deliberately or by sloppily installing more copies of operating systems or application suites than they have licenses for. And it's safer still for private computer users—there's almost nobody to check up on them.

- Fourth, some *detected* software piracy goes unpunished, especially in countries with less than a sterling regard for the laws of copyright. Here's a quick anecdote: In the early 1990s, Novell was reputed to have cornered 90 percent of the networking market in China—but it had sold only one copy of NetWare there. (The rumor went on to add that, curiously, piracy of Novell products in Hong Kong was minimal—curiously, that is, until it was revealed that the Novell distributor had Triad links.) In the late 1990s, Novell's share of the Chinese networking market dropped precipitously as the Chinese pirates gained enthusiasm for Windows NT Server instead.

Worse yet, some of the leading software companies have become so widely reviled that an impressively large community considers ripping off copies of their software to be an okay or even praiseworthy act. Microsoft is a particular target, because it is perceived to have been gouging customers with endless and marginally worthwhile "upgrades" to its operating systems and office suites.

Of course, it's not true that piracy doesn't hurt anybody. Artists such as musicians and authors live (or die) by the money or royalties they receive from the sale of their works. If this revenue stream dries up, it's unlikely that they'll be able to continue creating their works; they may be reduced to assembling Grande Meals and Big Macs for a living. Actors need their fees, exorbitant as some of them may be. And even publishers, movie studios, and (I hesitate to say this) record companies need to receive money for the education and entertainment provided by their better efforts.

Why Piracy Is Wrong

Didn't we go over this already? Piracy is wrong because it's stealing. The law says stealing is illegal (more on this in Chapter 2), and moral codes say that stealing is immoral.

Unfortunately for some of the bodies that would like to see piracy stamped out, though, there's plenty of precedent for piracy, as you saw from some of the justifications dissected earlier in this chapter. This precedent genuinely confuses some people, while others choose to exploit it to argue that piracy is reasonable, or at least acceptable in moderation.

What Effects Is Piracy Having?

At this writing, it's hard to see clearly what effects piracy is having on the markets for the pirated items and their producers. Much of the piracy is new, so its effects have yet to become apparent, and there's some evidence one way and the other. But it seems likely that different types of piracy are having different effects.

Let's look at it category by category.

Effects of Piracy on Music Sales

Music sales is where piracy, particularly in the form of Napster and post-Napster P2P technologies, seems to be having the most effect. This is easy to understand, because music is currently the most widely pirated item on the Net.

It's hard to get into the minds of the record companies (and I'm not sure I'd want to if I could; you never know what you might find in there alongside fond memories of decaying seventies progressive rock). But you have to assume that the record companies' principal objection to Napster and other P2P file-sharing technologies is that these threaten to cut into their revenue stream by killing CD sales. (No doubt the record companies care about copyright in the abstract as well, but on past form, money and survival must be much further up their interest tree.)

But have Napster and P2P actually cut into CD sales? On the face of things, this would hardly be a surprise. Strangely, the evidence so far points the other way—though the P2P phenomenon is new enough that the evidence is hardly conclusive. Still, it appears that P2P may have *increased* the number of CDs sold rather than decreasing it. That is, the number of CDs being sold has increased, and even people who use Napster and P2P profess themselves to be buying more CDs than they used to.

Of course, you could also look at the results another way: CD sales have increased over the period of time surveyed, and P2P may have had nothing to do with the increase. CD sales grew about 3 percent from 1998 to 1999, but most of this growth is attributable to people buying CDs instead of cassettes. (Sales of cassettes fell by 7 percent in the same period.)

Nobody could deny that there are a number of people (many of them students) who never buy CDs because they're able to download all the music they want for free. This number of people is almost certainly on the increase—the massive number of users of Napster and other P2P technologies alone suggests that, and you don't need to be cynical to believe that if people can get the same music for free as if they have to pay for it, some will choose the free option. But if these are the same people who used to tape (or rip, or copy, or merely borrow) their friends' CDs, and have never bought a CD in their life, they don't represent a loss for the record companies.

If the increase in CD sales *is* attributable to P2P, the reason is presumably that P2P spreads music to people who would otherwise not have heard it. These people then buy CDs for whatever reason: because they feel morally obliged to; because they want the ultimate in music quality; because they like to possess the physical CD; because they want to support the artist or band; or because they're so used to playing music from CD that they haven't yet made the transition to digital audio. In other words, people are using P2P as a sort of directed radio that enables them to find and listen to music they like rather than having radio feed them half-digested pap.

Then they buy the music on CD. But it's hard to believe that they'll continue to do so. As computers and Internet access become ever more widespread, it seems inevitable that CD sales will take a hit—especially when (or if) higher-quality audio formats than MP3 hit the mainstream.

Certainly the record companies seem to think so, because they've started to experiment with digital distribution of their music. At this writing, the experiments appear to be not only too little, too late, but also misconceived. For example, Sony has started selling individual tracks via download. This would be commendable, except that it has chosen to price them at $2.49 each—far too high, especially considering that selling the tracks entails no costs for physical media or distribution. If the tracks are more expensive to get via download than on physical media and if they're locked to the computer on which you download them, you'd be a fool to buy them unless you absolutely must have them as immediately as your bandwidth can manage.

In a more positive direction, some record companies (including Columbia Records) offer streaming RealAudio tracks that you can play on their Web sites. This lets consumers get to know the music without (in theory) exposing the record company or artist to losing too much music. I say "in theory" because anyone who's mastered a drag-and-drool interface will have little difficulty in saving a RealAudio track to disk and creating from it an MP3 file that they can distribute freely.

Effects of Piracy on the Movie Business

At this writing, it seems likely that digital piracy is having only a small effect on movies. The movie theater is the premier way of getting your brains blown out through your ears by thunderous THX effects, and it's likely to remain so until home projectors drop drastically in price and microwave popcorn improves heroically in quality.

That said, digital piracy appears to be starting to have a small effect on the video-rental business and the DVD-rental business. DVD rentals are gradually beginning to cut into video rentals as (a) more DVDs are released, (b) more rental businesses carry a decent stock of DVDs, and (c) more people buy DVD players (not necessarily in that order). But as the sharing of digital-video files becomes more common, digital piracy will start to have an increasing effect on video and DVD rentals.

Effects of Piracy on the Graphical Arts

It's hard to tell what effect digital piracy has had so far on the graphical arts. But it's likely to be small—at least, if you don't consider pornographic photographs a graphical art.

There's no question that some users are sharing graphical images via P2P technologies, much as they have been via the Web and newsgroups for many years.

However, many of these users are using the Internet to acquire images that they wouldn't purchase, so the effect on sales of the images is debatable.

Effects of Piracy on the Software Business

On software, however, digital piracy has had a major impact for a long time—and will continue to do so for the foreseeable future.

As mentioned earlier, software has long been a favorite for pirates because of its digital form and its high value. P2P technologies have made it easier to find and get pirated software, so they seem likely to increase the amount of pirated software being used. Furthermore, the number of computers in households continues to increase, as does the amount of software that a typical user uses (or at least wants to have). Greater bandwidth allows faster and more convenient downloading of large applications, and serial numbers can be shared instantly via media such as chat, newsgroups, and the Web.

Effects of Piracy on Publishing

To date, piracy seems to have had only a small effect on hard-copy publishing of books and magazines. You'll find copies of various texts online and being traded, of course, but few of them are in strong demand. Among the most popular titles are sci-fi favorites by authors such as William Gibson, Robert A. Heinlein, and Larry Niven.

Some of the hottest action is in computer books, because publishers have taken to distributing electronic versions of the books on CD with the hard-copy books. Copy-protection schemes of varying degrees of ingenuity notwithstanding, most of these electronic versions are relatively easy to pirate—much easier, anyway, than scanning and OCR-ing copies of the books, which tend to be several to many hundred pages long. And because the books command a higher price than your common-or-garden novel, there's a strong demand for electronic versions for free.

Many of the pirated versions of older computer books appear to have been derived from the HTML versions of books that some of the Macmillan imprints released on their Web sites in the late 1990s. Some of these HTML versions contained the final text of the book in question, but others were "beta-books"—works in progress—and contained mistakes that persist in the pirated versions.

The current decline in sales of hard-copy books is more attributable to other factors than to piracy. These factors include a sad decline in reading skills and a loss of interest in reading in the face of more immediately stimulating entertainments, such as TV, movies, and video games.

Up Next

In this chapter, you've learned who the pirates are, what they do, and why they do it. You've also learned how some pirates try to justify what they do, and why none of the justifications hold any water.

In the next chapter, you'll learn how the law regards piracy—and how it punishes it. Punishes… there's a pun in that…

Before that, though, here's the first of "A Pirate Speaks" sidebars I told you about in the introduction.

A Pirate Speaks: The Publisher Pirate

I'm a music publisher. I'm just as much of a publisher as Universal or EMI or Warner or any other publisher out there.

But the funny thing is, I'm sort of the "people's publisher." I've got a lot of old records—actually, a lot of old records, tapes, and CDs—and I have access to thousands more. There are a lot of people out there in the world who like bands that are 30 years old, or 40 years old, or even more. But those albums aren't being offered by music publishers anymore.

For example, there are innovative LPs from the 60s that have become incredible collectors' items now, and they're just not available; they're worth hundreds and hundreds of dollars. And the only way that anybody is going to be able to own something like that is to spend, like, $300 for Titus Groan's only album to hear *In the Hall of Bright Carvings*, one of the best psychedelic songs ever recorded.

Way I see it, it's real sad that those types of music aren't being offered by music publishers anymore. Any fool can see *why* the publishers don't offer them. The audience for these types of old albums and old CDs is probably pretty damn small. How many people really specialize in 60s psychedelia, for example, or blues from the late 50s? Most of these groups disbanded decades ago and a lot of these artists really aren't popular any more, and of course they wouldn't sell. But there are plenty of people out there who have a tremendous interest in that part of our popular culture, or that era, or that genre of music. We can't just let that music disappear because the publishers' bean counters can't justify the risk of putting it out on CDs.

So here's what I started doing. It began real small. I brought out my old turntable and I dug out some old LPs that were no longer in print from the 60s. I digitized a lot of them. I cleaned them up. I started publishing them on Napster. And after about a month, I had a *huge* following

A Pirate Speaks: The Publisher Pirate (*continued*)

of people, people who were complimenting me on putting these things on the Internet and thanking me for introducing them to these new artists.

It was amazing. I actually became pretty well known—in fact, I *am* well known on Napster just now. I won't tell you what my name is, but many people really look to see me publish, and I'll publish at least an album a week on the Internet. None of them are available through any commercial publishers out there. They're all out of print. They're all specialized. There's a lot of great Canadian music from the 60s and 70s, for example, that was never played in the U.S. People are only now discovering how much they missed. There's a lot of garage music— bands that cut one album that sold 500 copies and now are huge collectors' items. Things like *Sussex* by Bent Wind—probably the most expensive album you can buy in Canada. I digitized that and made it available. Now there are hundreds of people, maybe thousands—who knows how many people have downloaded it from other people—enjoying that music.

I would like it if the publishers could go out of their way and recognize that there's a sub-market, a subculture, and maybe offer this stuff from the original master tapes. These would be better in quality than what I can produce, of course. But they don't. It's not economically feasible, I guess, from their point of view. And that's fine.

Remember, I don't make any money on this—all I'm doing is sort of letting other people enjoy the things I enjoy. They don't *have* to take them. They don't have to *like* them. But I make them available. And it's amazing how many people really appreciate that.

A Pirate Speaks: The Publisher Pirate (*continued*)

With the Internet being what it is now, I'd like to see the recording companies open up their archives and publish this music themselves. People would pay for the music; I certainly would pay for it myself if they made all the old tapes available. Old soundtracks, live sessions, classics like *Glass Harp*, *Plastic Cloud*, *Lord of the Dark Skies* by Outskirts of Infinity, and *Having a Rave-Up* by the Yardbirds. Things like that.

Anyway, the point is that there are literally thousands of wonderful albums out there that aren't available to music listeners. And that's really not fair to the artists who made the albums or to the people who would enjoy the music. It's a waste. It's not right. So I make them available. I don't get paid for it. I just do it because I think it's the right thing to do. Am I a pirate? Was Robin Hood?

Chapter 2

Crime and Punishment: Piracy and the Law

This chapter discusses how piracy and the law relate to each other, what you can legally do (and why), what you can't (and why), and what the penalties are.

Given the massive use of P2P technologies, there's a huge amount of ignorance and confusion as to what you can and cannot legally do with P2P technologies. There's an even bigger amount of crime going on, and (at the moment) only a little punishment.

The truth is straightforward. Much of it is even logical (though unfortunately some of it isn't). You probably won't have any problem wrapping your brain around it—and it's much better to understand the legal issues before you start breaking the law left, right, and center.

At the beginning of the chapter, I'll lay out for you what's legal and what's not legal in the five categories of content that most pirates are interested in: audio, video, graphics, text, and software. This is an executive summary in case you're too busy or too lazy to read the rest of the chapter at the moment, and it explains neither why what's legal is legal nor why what ain't legal ain't.

After that, we'll get into the serious stuff. First, I'll briefly discuss intellectual property, because intellectual property is central to copyright law, and copyright law is central to the issues surrounding P2P. After that, I'll cover what copyright is, what it applies to, and how it works; what fair use and personal use cover; and what the public domain is. Copyright law covers much of what you need to know, but because technology has moved along since the main copyright laws were written, there are a number of exceptions that you need to know about.

I'll tell you what you can do and can't do with P2P, and what most people are currently getting away with that they shouldn't be. We'll also look at the specific legal issues that P2P technologies raise, including why Napster wasn't stomped into legal oblivion two seconds after it started—and why it may soon be shut down.

Along the way, I'll mention some of the key pieces of legislation that affect P2P file sharing—and the punishments that you can draw upon yourself by sharing files you don't have permission to share.

Before we get started, here's a quick disclaimer: This chapter provides information about the law (as it stands at this writing) in order to help you understand the issues involved with digital piracy and P2P technologies. This information is for educational purposes only and is not to be taken as legal advice. Not only do laws change nearly as rapidly as the price of oil, but many laws are less cut-and-dried than dependent on specific circumstances or interpretation. If you're in doubt about the legality of something, consult a lawyer you can trust.

What's Legal and What's Not

This section gives you the brief version of what's legal and what's not legal, without explaining why (or why not). It's for people who don't want (or can't be bothered) to read the whole chapter.

First, there's an ultra-summary. Then there's a section on general Internet stuff. After that, there's a section on each of the five main categories of content—audio, video, graphics, text, and software—and a section on the Web. The sections are a little repetitive in case you choose to read one without reading the others, but be sure to read the Ultra-Summary first.

Ultra-Summary

Here's the summary of the summary:

- You can create digital files from content in some media for your personal use. Yes, that's kinda vague, because the law is different for different types of content. But for example, if you buy an audio CD, you can legally create MP3 files from it for your personal use.

- If you hold the rights to content, or have been legally granted the right to distribute that content, you can distribute digital files containing it. Such distribution might take many forms, from posting the file on a Web site or an FTP site, sharing it via Napster or another P2P technology, or a physical medium such as a CD or a removable disk. For example, if you create an original image, you could post a digital version of the image on your Web site or distribute CDs containing copies of a digital file of the image.

- Unless you hold the rights to content, or you have been legally granted the right to distribute that content, you cannot legally distribute digital files containing it. Again, such distribution might involve a Web site, an FTP site, a P2P technology, or physical media. All means of distribution are illegal if you don't have permission. For example, I mentioned in the first bullet point that you can legally create MP3 files from audio CDs you buy, but you can't legally distribute those MP3 files unless you've been granted the right to do so.

- If you have legal copies of digital files of content whose copyright is held by other people, you can burn CDs or DVDs containing them for backup or for your own personal use.

- Unless you hold the copyright or the copyright holder has explicitly granted you permission to distribute it, you cannot sell digital files of any copyrighted material.

- If you have bought a legal copy of copyrighted material in a digital file, you can sell it to someone else in much the same way as you would a physical object. After the sale, you must not retain a copy of the file, so that you have transferred the digital file to the other person and not kept a copy yourself. For example, if you purchase an e-book and download it as a digital file, you can sell the digital file of the e-book to someone else just as you could a physical copy of the book. But once you've transferred the digital file to the purchaser, you must not retain a copy of the digital file.

Internet Stuff

Legally, you can do the following on the Internet:

> ☠ View a Web page in a Web browser.

> That you can view a Web page in a Web browser seems to go without saying, because what use is a Web page if nobody is allowed to view it? The problem is that any Web page can itself be a copyrighted work (many are) and can contain copyrighted works—and when you view a Web page, your computer is downloading a copy of that page and all its contents.

> ☠ Publish your own original material and copyrighted material to which you hold the rights on your Web site. This material could be anything: text, photos and graphics, software, digital audio, or digital video.

> ☠ Access any Internet site that doesn't require a password or to which you have a password.

> ☠ Download legal files from any Internet site that you can access without cracking.

Legally, you can *probably* do the following on the Web:

> ☠ Save Web pages to your hard drive so that you can access them at a different time or in a different place (for example, when you're not connected to the Internet).

Legally, you cannot do the following on the Web:

> ☠ Distribute digital files of copyrighted material unless you hold the copyright to that material or the copyright holder has explicitly granted you permission to distribute it. Such distribution might involve posting the files on your Web site or FTP site, on another Web site or FTP site, or making them available directly from your computer via a P2P technology.

Audio

Here's what you can legally do with audio:

- Listen to streaming audio from a Web site or an Internet radio station, even if the site or person streaming the audio is doing so illegally.

- Record audio from a medium you own (for example, a CD) to a different medium (for example, a cassette) so that you can listen to it at a different time or in a different place.

- Download a digital file that contains copyrighted material from a Web site or FTP site *provided that the copyright holder has granted the distributor permission to distribute it.*

- Download a digital file from a computer via P2P technology (for example, Napster, audioGnome, or gnutella) *provided that the copyright holder has granted the distributor permission to distribute it.*

- Create digital-audio files (for example, MP3 files) of tracks on CDs you own for your personal use.

- Distribute a digital-audio file to which you hold the copyright or for whose distribution the copyright holder has granted you permission.

- Download (or copy) MP3 files or other supported digital-audio files to portable audio devices (such as the Diamond Rio or the Creative Labs Nomad).

- Broadcast licensed audio across the Internet.

Here are some of the key things that you cannot legally do with audio:

- Download a digital-audio file that contains copyrighted material if the copyright holder has not granted the distributor permission to distribute it.

- Distribute a digital-audio file that contains copyrighted material if the copyright holder has not granted you permission to distribute it.

- Lend a friend a CD so that she can create digital-audio files from it.

- Borrow a CD from a friend and create digital-audio files from it.

☠ Upload digital-audio files from a portable audio player that supports music uploading (such as the I-JAM or the eGo) to another computer. (In this scenario, you're essentially using the portable player to copy the files from one computer to another.)

Video

Legally, you can do the following with video:

☠ Watch streaming video from a Web site or an Internet broadcast, even if the site or person streaming the video is doing so illegally.

☠ Download digital-video files that contain copyrighted material from a Web site or FTP site *provided that the copyright holder has granted the distributor permission to distribute it*.

☠ Download (or copy) video files to a portable device (such as a Pocket PC) for viewing at a different time or place.

☠ Copy digital-video files from a CD to your hard drive in order to watch them at a different time or in a different place.

☠ Distribute digital-video files that contain copyrighted material to which you hold the copyright or for whose distribution the copyright holder has granted you permission.

☠ Stream digital-video files that contain copyrighted material to which you hold the copyright or for whose distribution the copyright holder has granted you permission.

Legally, you *may* be able to do the following with video:

☠ Create digital-video files from movies on DVD for your personal use.

Legally, you cannot do the following (among other things) with video:

☠ Download a digital-video file that contains copyrighted material if the copyright holder has not granted the distributor permission to distribute it.

☠ Distribute a digital-video file that contains copyrighted material if the copyright holder has not granted you permission to distribute it.

☠ Lend a friend a DVD so that he can rip it to digital-video files.

☠ Borrow a DVD from a friend and create digital-video files from it.

Graphics

Legally, you can do the following with graphics:

- Download a copyrighted graphic from a Web site or FTP site provided that the copyright holder has granted the distributor permission to distribute it.

- Create digital files by scanning copyrighted images as long as these files are for your personal use.

Legally, you cannot do the following (among other things) with graphics:

- Download a copyrighted graphic unless the copyright holder has granted the distributor permission to distribute it.

- Distribute a copyrighted graphic unless the copyright holder has granted you the right to distribute it.

- Use a copyrighted graphic on your Web site unless the copyright holder has granted you the right to use it.

Text

Legally, you can *usually* do the following with copyrighted text:

- Photocopy portions of it for a purpose that qualifies as fair use. For example, you might need to photocopy several pages from a novel, or a couple of poems from an anthology of poetry, for a class you are teaching.

- Perform optical character recognition (OCR) on portions of text so that you can use or store it on computer. For example, you might OCR a couple of paragraphs out of an article so that you could keep it in a digital file.

- Include parts of the text of another work in your own writing for purposes of parody, comment, or criticism.

You saw the word "usually" in the first paragraph of this section. The reason it's there is that most of what you can legally do with text rests on the principle of fair use, which is notoriously vague (and which we'll examine later in this chapter).

Legally, you cannot do the following with text:

- Publish and distribute a text (for example, a book) whose copyright is held by someone else unless they've granted you the rights to do so.

Software

Legally, you can do the following with copyrighted software, including games:

- ☠ If the software is freeware, you can use and distribute it freely.

- ☠ If the software is shareware, you can use it freely during the agreed evaluation period. Beyond that, you are required to register the software. The copyright holders of shareware generally encourage you to distribute the shareware freely.

- ☠ If the software is copyleft, you can use it freely and distribute it provided that you include the full source code and make available to all subsequent users any modifications or improvements you make.

- ☠ Create a backup copy of the software.

Legally, you cannot do the following with copyrighted software:

- ☠ Lend a copy of software you own to someone else so that they can install it on their computer.

- ☠ Borrow a copy of software from someone else and install it on your computer.

- ☠ Copy the software (other than creating a backup of it) unless the copyright holder has granted you the right to do so.

- ☠ Distribute the software unless the copyright holder has granted you the right to do so.

Intellectual Property

Intellectual property is the cornerstone on which the system and concepts of copyright are based, so I'll discuss it briefly here.

Intellectual property is sometimes abbreviated to IP, but because that abbreviation is more widely used to denote "Internet Protocol," I won't use it here. Given that both abbreviations can be used in relation to computers and digital audio, it can become confusing. (Typically, "IP concerns" would refer to intellectual property, while "IP configuration" would refer to the Internet Protocol—but "IP security" might refer to either.)

Physical property is easy to understand because most everybody owns enough of it to want to object violently when some of it's taken away. Most moral codes and their related legal structures classify the removal of property belonging to someone else as stealing and say it's a bad thing.

By its nature, intellectual property is much more slippery, as it deals mostly with nonphysical objects. If Dick has a really nice Stratocaster, and Jane takes it away from him against his will, he won't have it any more. That's stealing, plain enough. But a work such as a poem, a song, or a novel doesn't have a fixed physical format and can easily be copied and distributed. Intellectual property says that such art has a value and that the creator has the sole right to make and distribute copies for it, so that the creator can gain from creating the work in the first place. (In many cases, the creator assigns the right to make and distribute the copies to a third party, such as a publisher for a book or a record company for a song.) So if Jane writes the ultimate doom-rock dirge, and Dick records a version without her permission and makes it a hit, Dick has broken the law, and Jane can sue him for money putatively lost. (In practice, Jane probably won't sue Dick if he pays her enough money.) And if Dick writes a mega-selling novel, it's illegal for Jane to publish and distribute an edition of it without getting the rights to do so—which usually involves paying Dick for the privilege.

Intellectual property law covers several different areas, including copyright law, patent law, trademark law, and trade secret law. For our purposes, copyright law is the important one.

Copyright

Most of the legalities surrounding Internet piracy and P2P technologies hinge on copyright, so it's vital to know the basics of copyright law. Copyright essentially works in the same way the world around because of various international copyright treaties including the Berne Convention (to which almost all industrialized nations subscribe) and the General Agreement on Tariffs and Trade (GATT for short). What I describe here is the U.S. implementation of copyright. If you're in a different country, things may work a bit differently.

The basic idea behind copyright is straightforward, but the application of the idea is complex. In this section, I'll probably be guilty of oversimplification in the cause of getting the message across. So take this information as a starting point rather than gospel.

As defined in the Copyright Act of 1976, copyright extends legal protections to the copyright holder of fixed forms of original expression in many forms including literary, dramatic, and musical works; sound recordings; audiovisual works (such as movies); performance expression (such as pantomimes and choreography); architectural works (such as buildings); and graphic, pictorial, and sculptural works. These works are technically referred to as "works of authorship;" for concision, I'll stick to "works" here.

That probably seems quite a comprehensive list, but there are a number of things that are not copyrightable:

- Ideas are not copyrightable—though the expression of an idea is.

- Facts are not copyrightable, because the information is not expression. For example, you couldn't copyright the fact that John Lennon was shot in 1980. But you could copyright the poem "John Lennon was shot today. Tragedy? I was surprised." (Actually, *you* can't copyright that poem, because *I* hold the copyright to it. But you get the idea.)

- Works that consist entirely of common information and that do not contain any original authorship are not copyrightable. For example, a standard calendar is not copyrightable. But if somebody compiles the common information in such a way that the work itself is an expression, it may be copyrightable. Likewise, a compilation may earn copyright protection due to the hard work or the (virtual) "sweat of the creator's brow" invested in making the compilation.

- Links and URLs are not copyrightable, because they're like facts.

- Names and titles are not copyrightable—though you can trademark distinctive names and titles if you get to them before anybody else does.

- Systems and procedures are not copyrightable, though the expression of a system or procedure may be. For example, you couldn't claim copyright on the ingredients in a recipe, though you could claim copyright on the expression of the recipe or its instructions. (Guess this is why the Coca-Cola Company has been keeping its Coke recipe so secret for so long.)

- Short phrases are not copyrightable, although, again, you can trademark them if they're distinctive and haven't been trademarked yet. Just do it® carefully.

As soon as you create an original work and "fix" it in a tangible format, you hold the copyright on that work. For example, if you write a poem (however short, however bad—see the example in the second bullet point above), compose a melody (however short, however bad—as long as it's distinct enough from other melodies to be considered original), or draw a picture of a miniature Stonehenge (however crude) on a napkin, you have a copyrighted work. You don't need to publish the work for it to be copyrighted.

It's that simple—but there are several key points:

☠ First, the work needs to be original. If you write down a poem that somebody else has already written down, you're copying a copyrighted work, and you're infringing the copyright. Similarly, if you compose a musical piece that consists entirely of sections lifted from other people's copyrighted works, chances are you're infringing the copyright. (There are some exceptions, such as fair use—which I'll discuss in a minute or two—and parody.)

☠ Second, the work needs to be "fixed" in a tangible format. What constitutes a tangible format is vague, but the work essentially needs to be detectable to the appropriate sense. For example, you could draw a logo on your computer and store it there or record a song onto a cassette, and each would be a copyrighted work. The work doesn't have to be stored on paper or in a visual medium. The main point is that you can't create an original work only in your head, because nobody else will be able to detect that it exists. So if you compose a poem, you need to write it down, though the medium doesn't matter—clay tablets, papyrus, lead type, and bits-'n'-bytes are all fine. Note especially that speech is not fixed—and therefore not protected by copyright—unless and until you record it.

☠ Third, you don't even have to include a copyright notice on your work, though it's a good idea to do so. Because the copyright symbol (©) is displayed prominently on most published copyrighted works (such as this book), many people have gotten the idea that you need to include a copyright notice such as "Copyright © 2001 Jane Doe. All rights reserved" in order to claim copyright. You don't—the notice is just a formality identifying the copyright holder—but it's certainly a good idea to include a copyright notice.

Duration of Copyright

So you've authored a copyrighted work. But how long does your copyright last?

Briefly—a long time. Unless you achieve reincarnation, it outlasts you by a good way. But before we get into the specifics, a little history. (Don't worry; it's relevant.) Before 1978, copyright used to last for a first term of 28 years from the date that it was secured. *Secured* meant either that the work was published or that the work was registered in unpublished form. The copyright holder could renew the copyright during the 28th year of the first term, which gave them a second term of another 28 years. But if the copyright holder failed to renew the copyright during that year, it expired, and the work entered the public domain.

The Sonny Bono Copyright Term Extension Act (yes, yes—Cher, death on skis—*that* Sonny Bono), which was signed into law on October 27, 1998, extended copyright terms, making them as follows:

- ☠ If the work was created before 1978 and was still under copyright (original or renewed) in October 1998, the copyright term is 95 years from the date that copyright was initially registered.

- ☠ If the work was created after January 1, 1978, the copyright term lasts for the life of the author (or the last surviving author, for a joint work) plus 70 years. If the work is anonymous or pseudonymous or a work for hire, the copyright term is the shorter of 120 years from the year of creation or 95 years from the year of first publication.

- ☠ If the work was created before 1978 but not published or registered by then, the copyright term lasts for the life of the author plus 70 years, and at least till the end of 2002. If the work is published before the end of 2002, the copyright term lasts at least until the end of 2047.

The Copyright Notice

I gave you an example of a copyright notice a moment ago: "Copyright © 2001 Jane Doe. All rights reserved." This example is fine, but it's partially redundant. You can use either the word "Copyright" or the © copyright symbol, but you may want to use both in cases where the symbol may not be correctly displayed. (For example, some Web browsers do not render the © character correctly, so it's best to spell out "Copyright.")

The copyright statement must include the year of publication. In many cases, you'll do well to include the full date (month, day, year) on the work in case your copyright is challenged by someone else claiming to have created the work before you.

The copyright notice must include the name of the owner of the copyright. In many cases, the owner of the copyright will not be the author or creator of the work. For example, if you create a work for your employer as part of your employment, the employer will usually hold the copyright on it. On the other hand, if you write that novel you've always felt is in you, you'll hold the copyright on it.

In order to get copyright protection in Bolivia and Honduras, you need to include the reservation-of-rights phrase specified by the Buenos Aires Convention (*All rights reserved*) in the copyright notice. If you don't care about those two countries, you can skip the phrase.

Registering the Copyright

As I mentioned, simply creating an original work in a tangible form gets you the copyright for the work: You don't need to register the copyright in order to get it. But if you want to be able to sue anybody who infringes on your copyrighted work, or if you want to be able to get statutory damages in the event of an infringement, you must register the copyright with the Copyright Office within three months of the date you first published the work. If you don't register the work, you can only collect actual damages, which may be minimal or nominal (and these days, nominal is a kissing cousin of nothing).

> Another reason why it can be hard (or impossible) to collect actual damages is the difficulty in proving that an infringement incurred actual damages. It's next to impossible to prove valuation of an intangible asset that hasn't reached the market. Proving actual damages might eat up your entire legal budget, and the return might be next to nothing.

Registering a copyright involves completing an application form and sending it with a non-refundable filing fee of $30 and a non-returnable copy of the work to the U.S. Copyright Office. Copyright registration is effective on the day your work arrives, and eventually you get a certificate of registration. (At this writing, the Copyright Office mentions eight months as an approximate timeframe, so you'd be ill advised to hold your breath.) Use a registered delivery service so that you know when your work arrived at the Copyright Office.

Word to the Wise: You Can't Register Copyright by Mailing Yourself a Copy of the Work

There's a myth circulating in popular culture and around the western spiral arm of the Internet that you can copyright a work by mailing a copy of it to yourself via registered mail.

Quite simply, this isn't true.

A copy sent via registered mail *may* help prove the date of the work's creation (if the envelope is still sealed with its original seal), but will do nothing to entitle the copyright holder to the legal protections accorded under U.S. copyright law and the official copyright-registration system.

About the only time you may benefit from mailing a copy of a work to yourself is if you have a sudden premonition that your house is about to burn down, and the premonition comes true before the mail arrives. But even if you're psychic (and you like receiving packages containing copyrighted works), you'd do better to use a safe-deposit box at an institution you trust.

The Five Exclusive Rights

Once you're the proud owner of a copyright, you have these five exclusive rights to the copyrighted work:

Reproduction Right   You have the right to duplicate, copy, imitate, or transcribe the work. For example, if you write a novel, you can make copies of the manuscript.

Distribution Right   You have the right to distribute copies of the work to the public. This includes selling copies of the work, renting or leasing them, or lending them. For example, you might choose to distribute copies of your killer music tracks. Alternatively, you might choose to allow a third party to distribute them for you.

Modification Right *or* Derivative Works Right   You have the right to create new works derived from (based on) the copyrighted work. For example, if you wrote a best-selling play, you might create a screenplay based on it. This would be a derivative work and would create its own copyright.

Public Performance Right   You have the right to perform the work in public or transmit the work to the public. For example, if you make a movie or video, you might want to exercise your public performance right by showing it in public in its normal order. (Showing a work out of its normal order is governed by the public display right, discussed next.). The public performance right does not apply to recorded audio.

Public Display Right   You have the right to transmit the work to the public or show a copy of the work in a public place. For movies and audio-visual works, the public display right covers showing the work out of its normal order.

Some visual works of authorship have "moral rights" as well as the five rights detailed above. Moral rights ensure that anyone who wants to modify the work or use the creator's name in connection with it needs to get the creator's permission.

Granting Rights to Someone Else

Once you've created that original work and claimed the copyright to it (perhaps explicitly, perhaps not), you've got a bunch of rights. But if you want to have somebody else publish the work, you'll typically need to grant them the rights to do so.

Which right or rights you grant depends on the relationship between you as the creator of the original work and your publisher. In some cases, the creator may grant a full suite of rights to the publisher, including the reproduction right, the distribution right, and the derivative works right. In other cases, the creator may limit the grant of rights—for example, the creator might choose to grant only the distribution right to another party. Either way, the copyright rights remain in effect, although the holder of the rights may have changed.

Rights can be sold, leased, or granted using a variety of legal instruments, such as a legally binding written contract, a will, or a trust document. Rights can also be granted due to the relationship between the creator of the work and the copyright holder—for example, when an employee creates a copyrighted work for their employer, or when a worker on a work-for-hire contract creates a copyrighted work for a client. Also, a copyright holder can record the legal transfer of exclusive ownership of a copyright by filing a form with the Copyright Office.

Fair Use

The next concept you need to understand is *fair use*. For practical purposes, you'll need to know about fair use mostly if you sample or parody works, if you criticize works, or if you're involved in education. But because a lot of people use the term wrongly to justify assorted law-twistings at the hands of digital pirates, you need to know approximately what it means, even if you're just interested in downloading music and playing it to amuse you and yours.

Fair use is a provision in the Copyright Act that essentially lets you use a portion of a copyrighted work "for purposes such as criticism, comment, news reporting, teaching (including multiple copies for classroom use), scholarship, or research" without infringing copyright.

Four factors are taken into account in determining what does or does not constitute fair use:

1. The "purpose and character" of the use: commercial, educational, reporting, scientific, and so on. Using a portion of a copyrighted work in a commercial work isn't wrong, but usually works that are created for nonprofit purposes are more likely to qualify for fair use.

2. The type of the copyrighted work. Some works are deemed more worthy of copyright protection than others. Very generally speaking, original creative works (such as songs, movies, novels, or pictures) are more tightly protected than factual works (such as newspaper articles or histories).

3. The amount of the copyrighted work used in relation to the whole work. Essentially, the amount of the copyrighted work used shouldn't be more than is necessary for the purpose of copying. That doesn't mean that there's a set maximum percentage of a work that you can use: It might well be fair use to include the whole of a haiku in an essay on Japanese poetry, where it might not be fair use to include a couple of paragraphs of *Finnegan's Wake* in an article on Joyce. (In one classic fair-use case in 1977, the Supreme Court

found that The Nation's use of between 300 and 400 words' worth of excerpts from President Gerald Ford's forthcoming memoirs did not constitute fair use because of the importance of the words taken and the likely effect on the market for the book.)

4. The effect that the use will have on the value of the copyrighted work or its potential market. For example, if you use a substantial, critical portion of a copyrighted work in such a way that nobody will be interested in that work (because of yours), it probably won't be regarded as fair use. The value and potential market for the copyrighted work include its derivative works—works derived from it.

That probably seems pretty vague. Fair use is certainly an extremely gray area of the law, and various lawsuits have attempted to push the boundaries of fair use this way and that. But you can be pretty sure that stealing copyrighted material is never going to be considered fair use, so fair use doesn't allow the wide-scale piracy that often cites it.

Personal Use

Fair use, discussed in the previous section, is a key component of the Copyright Act. *Personal use,* a provision of the Audio Home Recording Act (AHRA) of 1992, is completely different and lets users of digital audio recording devices make copies of copyrighted works on other media. For example, if you buy a Korn CD, you can record it onto a cassette so that you can listen to it on your Walkman. As the term's name implies, that copy is for your personal use. If you give the cassette to a friend so that they can get the full Korn experience, that's illegal.

So far, so simple. But there's a twist: You'll notice that I said "digital audio recording devices" in the previous paragraph. Computers don't qualify as digital audio recording devices (although they can record audio digitally) but rather as "multipurpose devices." This means that, technically, audio copies you make on computers are not covered by the AHRA and personal use. However, most authorities seem to agree that making digital-audio files of copies of music you own for your personal use *is* legal. For example, you can make MP3 files from that Korn CD as long as they're for your personal use. You're not allowed to give those MP3 files to a friend.

First Sale Doctrine

Just about the only exception to the law on distributing files without the copyright owner's explicit written permission comes when you're selling a file that you've purchased legally. (For example, sites such as EMusic.com sell individual tracks in MP3 format with the artist's or record company's blessing, because they get royalties from the transaction.) Under the First Sale Doctrine laid out in the Copyright Act, you can sell (or give) your copy of an audio recording to someone else in much the same way that you could sell them a (legal) CD or other physical object.

The key to this provision is that when you've transferred your copy of the file to the other person, you have to get rid of your own copy. Otherwise, you've simply copied it, and either you or the recipient has an illegal copy. Similarly, you can't legally copy a CD or DVD and then sell somebody else the original.

As you'll readily see, there are two problems with this:

- ☠ First, enforcement. Until some monstrous and effective system for maintaining and tracking electronic copies is implemented, nobody's going to be able to tell whether you've really deleted your copy.

- ☠ Second, some of the current mechanisms for protecting copyright, such as Sony's SDMI-compliant OpenMG software, locks a legal audio file to a particular computer, preventing you from exercising your rights under the First Sale Doctrine. (You can sell someone your copy of the digital-audio file, but it won't work on any computer other than your own.) It's possible to argue that consumers might be justified in using hardware or software tools to circumvent such locking in order to preserve their rights under the First Sale Doctrine. It'll be interesting to see what happens when someone tries arguing that in court. SDMI is discussed in the sidebar on page 46.

Viewing a Web Page

As mentioned earlier, even the apparently simple act of viewing a Web page brings up questions of copyright, because you can't view a Web page without copying it to your computer. Your Web browser requests the page from the Web server, which transfers to it a copy of each file that makes up the page. At this point the files are held in RAM rather than being saved to your hard drive.

Tech moment: If your computer is running out of RAM, some or all of the files that make up the Web page may be saved to your hard drive in your computer's swap file. The swap file acts as extra RAM, and you can't retrieve files from it in the same way that you retrieve them from regular storage on your hard drive. And (in theory at least), the contents of your swap file are cleared when you shut down the operating system. However, some Web browsers (such as Internet Explorer) automatically save (to disk) temporary copies of Web material they've downloaded so that you can access those items more quickly the next time you go to load the page (a process called *caching*). Unlike the material in the swap file, the material in your browser's temporary files is directly accessible from the user interface and is not automatically deleted by the browser. A plausible argument could probably be made that these temporary files constitute unauthorized copying and a violation of copyright.

Depending on which browser you're using, the Web page may look a little different than it did in its creator's browser, but the underlying design will be the same, as will the contents. The design of the Web page may well be a copyrighted work, and at least some of the contents are likely to be copyrighted works.

The National Information Infrastructure (NII) has proposed that the act of downloading a Web page be considered copying. Most people (outside a few lawyers who've never seen the Web and don't understand how it works) consider this a stupid and unworkable suggestion that complicates matters unnecessarily. But most people agree that once you actively save the Web page to your hard drive (for example, by using the Save As command in your Web browser), you *have* copied the page. The question then arises of whether you have the right to perform that copying operation without explicit permission or whether the copying is acceptable under fair use.

Permission and Requests for Use

Once you have established that a work is still in copyright and that your usage of it would violate copyright, you need to get permission before you can legally use it. This permission comes from the copyright holder, who may or may not be the author of the work. You may or may not have to pay for using the work. Often, whether you have to pay depends on what you're hoping to do with the work.

Identifying the copyright holder may be trivial or tricky. If the work contains a copyright notice, it should identify the copyright holder. For example, in the front of this book (on a page known as the copyright page), you'll find a copyright notice that says "Copyright © 2001 Sybex Inc." This tells you that Sybex is the copyright holder for this book (rather than I, the author), so you would contact Sybex in order to get permission to reuse parts of it.

Depending on what you were planning to do with the book, Sybex might well grant you permission. For example, if you wanted to print an extract of the book in a magazine that Sybex thought would reflect well on the book or lead to sales of more copies, Sybex would probably give you permission. If you planned to make 1000 photocopies of the entire book and give them away for free to the rich, however, Sybex probably wouldn't give you permission unless you paid them an obscene amount of money.

You'll find much the same happens with copyrighted audio and visual works. For example, if you want to perform (in public) a version of a song by someone else, you'll need to get permission. The copyright holder may well give you that permission, as your performance would benefit the copyright holder. On the other hand, if you want to distribute free copies of the work as MP3 files, the copyright holder is unlikely to be as enthusiastic.

Normally, you'll want to get the permission in written and signed form. This usually means a letter or a fax. When digital signatures become binding, accepted, and widely used, e-mail will also be satisfactory; in the meantime, without a signature, it's not such a great way of getting permission. Legally, a telephone request is sufficient to grant permission, but you'd do well to note the date, time, and details of the person who granted the permission to you.

The Copyright Clearance Center (abbreviated to CCC, and found at www.copyright.com) acts as a central point on behalf of many publishers and authors. On their Web site, you'll find a sample letter for requesting permission.

Secure Digital Music Initiative (SDMI): Salvation through Technology?

The Secure Digital Music Initiative (SDMI for short; `www.sdmi.org`) neatly illustrates the problems involved with using technology to implement parts of the law.

SDMI is a forum of more than 180 companies and organizations interested in developing "a voluntary, open framework for playing, storing, and distributing digital music in a protected form." The companies and organizations involved come from a variety of industries and include the following:

- The recording industry, including the RIAA and Sony Music
- Agencies, including the powerful Harry Fox Agency
- Distributors and retailers, including Broadcast Music, Inc. (BMI)
- Consumer electronics companies, including Casio, Sony Electronics, JVC, Matsushita, and Motorola
- Information technology companies, including Microsoft and Sun Microsystems
- Computer hardware manufacturers, including Compaq and Toshiba
- MP3 hardware and software companies, including MusicMatch, Audio Explosion/Mjuice, i2Go.com, Liquid Audio, and Napster

All in all, it's an impressive group of heavyweights and wannabe heavyweights.

SDMI aims to create a musical framework that will please everybody by giving customers "convenient accessibility to quality digital music" while allowing artists to protect their copyrighted works against piracy, which would let the recording industry and information technology companies make money from selling music. The good news for consumers is that

Secure Digital Music Initiative (SDMI): Salvation through Technology? (*continued*)

SDMI recognizes that some people will want to distribute music in insecure formats, and the standards (specifications) it creates are designed to allow end users to play both secure and insecure music. So (at least in theory), you'll be able to play your utterly insecure MP3 files on SDMI-compliant devices.

To some extent, this has been borne out in the first SDMI-compliant devices that meet SDMI's first specification, which describes portable digital-audio devices. The Sony VAIO Music Clip and the Sony Memory Stick Walkman are players that comply with this specification, and they work with both existing MP3 files (by converting them in a clumsy procedure to secure files) and with already secure files.

Unfortunately, Sony's SDMI-compliant software for ripping, encoding, and managing your music is truly execrable, making for a miserable user experience, giving a bad impression of the SDMI standard to the public, and setting a bad example for other implementers. Because this software locks tracks that you purchase and download to the computer onto which you download them, and because it does not let you restore your tracks from backup (for example, after a crash), it violates both the First Sale Doctrine and the basic tenets of common sense.

Time-Shifting and Place-Shifting

An important exception to the rule of one's needing to get permission to make a copy of a copyrighted work comes in the concepts of time-shifting and place-shifting.

Time-shifting means using a recorder to enable you to watch or listen to a broadcast at a later time than it was transmitted. For example, if you record a program using a VCR or a device such as TiVo so that you can watch it later, you've time-shifted it. Nothing to it. In the Betamax Decision (which I'll discuss later in the chapter), the Supreme Court found that "even the unauthorized home time-shifting of respondents' programs is legitimate fair use."

Place-shifting (also called *space-shifting* by some people, primarily because the term sounds cool) means using technology to enable you to watch or listen to a work (broadcast or static) in a different place from the medium in which you received it. That's a mouthful because of all the possibilities involved. For example, if you record MP3 files of the tracks from an LP so that you can load the files on your Rio or Nomad and go jogging with them, you've place-shifted them. (You couldn't have taken your gramophone out jogging with you. Well, not realistically.) If you tape a radio show so that you can listen to it later in the car, you've time-shifted it *and* place-shifted it.

Time-shifting and place-shifting are legal as long as they involve making a copy of a copyrighted work for personal purposes rather than in order to distribute it to other people.

TiVo and similar technologies threaten to make time-shifting so appealing, so easy, and so convenient that nobody will need to watch ads on TV any more unless they actively want to. While blissful for most TV viewers, this quasi-utopian development of ad-free TV would take a severe toll on the broadcasting corporations and TV companies. We'll visit this possibility in more depth in Chapter 9, "The Future of Piracy, Digital Content, and P2P."

Royalties on Products Used to Infringe Copyright

Another piece in the jigsaw of what you can and cannot legally do takes the form of blanket royalties imposed on products that can be used, or are likely to be used, to infringe copyright. For example, when you buy a new video recorder, a blank video tape, an audio recorder, a blank audio tape, a DAT recorder, or a blank DAT, the cost includes a royalty.

Depending on how you look at these royalties, they're either a good if somewhat unfair idea or completely despicable. The former view is perhaps more tenable: It's hard to deny that many users of these products do use them to record copyrighted material, so it makes sense to have an arrangement that allows people to do the recording without being prosecuted and to have an easy mechanism by which they pay for it. Those holding the latter view get all steamed up about the presumption of guilt that the royalties impose. For example, if you buy a blank DAT to record your children's screams (or your parents'), you're not going to infringe copyright. So you shouldn't have to pay the royalty tax on that DAT. But there's no way to distinguish between recorders and media that will be used to infringe copyright and those that won't.

When the royalties were first imposed on these products, it drew some public notice and media outrage. But by now, most people have forgotten about the royalties, which are modest enough to be hidden in the cost of the product.

One exception to the cost of the product is audio CD-Rs—those sold specifically for audio purposes as opposed to for computer purposes. As you'll know if you've made the mistake of buying these audio CD-Rs by mistake, they're far more expensive than regular CD-Rs. Part of the reason is that the audio CD-Rs bear a royalty, but the much bigger part of the reason is that the manufacturers have no objections to boatloads of cash. General-purpose CD-Rs attract no royalty, and the market is much more competitive. (Some audio-only CD recorders are designed to require special discs and will not work with regular CD-Rs. It's hard to recommend buying such recorders, because if you do, you'll be stuck buying the overpriced media.)

File Formats Are Legal

In all the confusion about what you can and can't legally do with copyrighted material, computers, and the Internet, one bizarre canard sometimes surfaces: Some file formats are illegal.

This is nonsense.

No file format is illegal. It's the content that matters. For example, there's nothing legal or illegal about the MP3 file format. Anybody can create an MP3 file, and anybody can use one. But if the content of a particular MP3 file is an unauthorized copy of a copyrighted work, that MP3 file is illegal. Similarly, there's nothing legal or illegal about a text document, but its contents can contain material that infringes copyright on a copyrighted work.

It's hard to see where this canard flew in from. At one point, the recording industry was talking of making MP3 "illegal" somehow (it wasn't clear how), but the MP3 file format is unquestionably legal. There's been confusion over the provisions in the

Digital Millennium Copyright Act that make it illegal to circumvent anti-piracy measures such as those on DVDs, but it's certainly legal to have files in the VOB format that's used on DVDs.

Public Domain

As you saw in Chapter 1, the public domain contains all works that are not protected by copyright. If a work is in the public domain, you're free to use or distribute it without needing to get any permission.

NOTE One way to find out whether a work is in the public domain is to search the records of the U.S. Copyright Office. You can either search the records in person for free or have the Copyright Office search for you for a cool $65 per hour.

Works in the public domain typically fall into five categories:

☠ Works whose copyright has been granted to the public domain

☠ Works that are not copyrightable

☠ Works whose copyright has been lost

☠ Works whose copyright has expired

☠ U.S. Government documents

The following sections examine each category in turn.

WARNING You can create a new copyright by making a new work that uses a work in the public domain but that adds information or value to it. For example, you can create a new copyright by publishing a new edition of a book that's in the public domain and adding notes, commentary, and introduction, and so on. Likewise, a movie made from a Shakespeare play that's in the public domain will have its own copyright. So when dealing with a work that's you believe to be in the public domain, you need to be careful not to infringe copyright of new material added to the public domain work.

Works Granted to the Public Domain

Most creators choose to assert copyright to their works so that they can derive benefit from them (for example, by selling the works or copies of the works). However, some creators choose to forego copyright on their works and grant them to the public domain so that others can enjoy them freely. You'll run across such works in most areas of copyrightable human endeavor, from digital art to software to pornographic stories.

Works That Are Not Copyrightable

As you saw earlier in this chapter, various items are not copyrightable because of their nature. These items include ideas, facts, links and URLs, names and titles, and short phrases. All of these are in the public domain.

Works Whose Copyright Has Been Lost

Also in the public domain are works whose copyright has been lost. Any work that was published before January 1, 1978 and that did not contain a valid copyright notice has been deemed to have lost copyright protection and to be in the public domain.

Works Whose Copyright Has Expired

Any work for which the statutory copyright period has expired is in the public domain. As you saw earlier, any work published before 1978 got a first term of 28 years of copyright, and the copyright holder had to renew the copyright in the last year of the 28. If they forgot to renew it, the copyright expired at the end of the term, and the work entered the public domain.

Never assume that a work must be in the public domain because it was created many years ago. If the copyright holder sees the work as valuable, they may well have renewed the copyright. For example, many people assume that the song "Happy Birthday" (you know: "Happy birthday to you," and so on) is in the public domain because it seems to have been around for ever, everybody knows it, and nobody knows who wrote it (so they assume it must be anonymous). In fact, "Happy Birthday" is still firmly copyrighted (until 2021) and reportedly pulls in around $1 million a year for its current copyright holders.

U.S. Government Publications

U.S. Government publications under the authorship of the Federal Government are not copyrighted and so are in the public domain. This means that you can download a U.S. Government document and distribute it to your heart's content. You can also enhance a U.S. Government document by adding to it annotations, explanations, formatting, and so on, and then claim copyright over the work.

Acts of the Apostates

The Copyright Act of 1976 laid out the law on copyright, including much of what we've discussed in the previous sections. But changes in technology since then have required a number of changes to, additions to, and clarifications of copyright matters.

This section discusses four decisions and pieces of legislation relevant to the creation and distribution of files containing copyrighted content:

- The Betamax Decision of 1984
- The Audio Home Recording Act (AHRA) of 1992
- The No Electronic Theft Act (NET Act) of 1997
- The Digital Millennium Copyright Act (DMCA) of 1998

If you've read the section titled "What's Legal and What's Not" earlier in this chapter and are clear on what you can and cannot legally do with P2P, you don't *need* to read this section right away. I'd be the first to admit that some of the material in this section is a little dry—but hey, it's law, so what do you expect? I'll go easy on the direct quotes from legislation except when they're helpful.

Betamax Decision, 1984

The Betamax Decision of January 17, 1984 provides a little background to the current use of P2P technologies. This decision established that home taping of broadcasts for personal use was legal.

You'll recall that Betamax was Sony Corporation's favored video-cassette technology. Introduced in November 1975, Betamax competed with VHS for the video-cassette recorder (VCR) market. Despite offering better technology and picture quality,

Betamax ended up losing the battle for market share to VHS, in part because VHS was adopted by the pornography industry, which drove a substantial portion of sales.

Anyway, in the 1970s, the VCR appeared to threaten the movie industry. (As everyone knows now with hindsight, the VCR turned out to be enormously beneficial to the movie industry.) In November 1976, Universal City Studios sued Sony Corporation for contributory copyright infringement, claiming that home taping of programs broadcast over the air was illegal.

The battle went back and forth. Sony Corporation won at trial. Then in 1981, the U.S. Court of Appeals for the Ninth Circuit reversed the verdict, deciding that home time-shift recording was copyright infringement and that Sony Corporation was a contributory infringer.

The Supreme Court took one crack at the case in January 1983 but didn't reach a decision, had a second crack in October 1983, and reversed the Ninth Circuit's verdict in January 1984 by a single vote. The Supremes seem to have gotten well into the issues, considering that the law should go easy on invading people's privacy by trying to control what they do in their homes; that it wouldn't be a great idea to suddenly tell the millions of VCR users that they had been breaking the law; that the VCR was a useful product; and that the copyright holders who were complaining about the VCR appeared not yet to have suffered any harm.

Audio Home Recording Act, 1992

Signed by President George Bush on October 28, 1992 and put into effect immediately, the Audio Home Recording Act (AHRA) went a long way to clarifying the rights and wrongs of home recording. The AHRA was created for the technologies current and forthcoming at that time, which included digital audio recording methods such as digital audiotape (DAT). Because at that time MP3 and other compressed audio formats hadn't been invented, they were not covered by the AHRA.

You can find the full text of the AHRA on the Home Recording Rights Coalition Web site at www.hrrc.org/html/ahra.html, among other places.

Put crudely, the AHRA compromised between the widely differing demands of the music industry, the consumer electronics industry, and consumers. The music industry wanted to protect the rights it held to its music while at the same time selling more copies of it. The consumer electronics industry wanted to sell consumers new technologies for recording and playing audio. And consumers wanted to be able to use those technologies freely to enjoy music.

For consumers, the good news in the AHRA is that no lawsuit alleging copyright infringement can be brought against them for noncommercial copying of prerecorded music using digital audio recording devices or analog audio recording devices. In other words, you can't be sued for taping prerecorded CDs, records, or cassettes. Here's the relevant section of the AHRA:

> No action may be brought under this title alleging infringement of copyright based on the manufacture, importation, or distribution of a digital audio recording device, a digital audio recording medium, an analog recording device, or an analog recording medium, or based on the noncommercial use by a consumer of such a device or medium for making digital musical recordings or analog musical recordings.

As you can see, the legal position is a little poky: It's not exactly legal to do such recording, but you can't be sued for it. Most people figure that's good enough.

The bad news for consumers is that the AHRA applies to analog recording devices (such as cassette recorders) and "digital audio recording devices." A digital audio recording device is a device "the digital recording function of which is designed or marketed for the primary purpose of, and that is capable of, making a digital audio copied recording for private use." Given this definition, it's perhaps not surprising that the AHRA does not apply to personal computers. But because computers now figure prominently in home recording, it's certainly disappointing.

These digital audio recording devices must include a serial copy control system that allows the user to create first-generation digital copies of prerecorded audio works but prevents the user from creating subsequent-generation (serial) digital copies. For example, a MiniDisc recorder lets you create a first-generation digital copy of a track by recording it from a CD, but you cannot then create subsequent digital copies from that track. (You could create an analog copy by playing the track from the MiniDisc recorder's analog output into another recording device, such as a cassette player, but you would end up with a lower-fidelity copy.)

The AHRA specifies that digital audio recording devices must include either the Serial Copy Management System (SCMS), a system that performs equivalently to

SCMS, or another serial copy control system certified by the U.S. Secretary of Commerce. In practice, this usually means SCMS itself, which you'll find incorporated in DAT, MiniDisc, and DCC recorders sold on the U.S. market. (In case you blinked, DCC—digital compact cassette—was a Philips competitor for DAT. It didn't take off, and Philips killed it in 1996.)

So the consumers get to use the new technologies, and the manufacturers get to sell the consumers the devices. What's in the AHRA for the music industry? Some of those enticing royalty payments you learned about earlier; royalty payments on all digital audio recording devices and all digital audio recording media sold in the U.S. Royalties on the devices are $1 to $8, based on 2 percent of the wholesale price but with a floor and a ceiling, and royalties on the media are 3 percent of the wholesale price. Two-thirds of the royalties go into a Sound Recordings Fund that's split among featured artists, non-featured artists and backup musicians, and record companies. The remaining one-third goes into a Music Works Fund that's divided equally between songwriters and music publishers.

No Electronic Theft Act (NET Act), 1997

Passed into law on December 16, 1997, the No Electronic Theft Act (NET Act for short—a nice acronym) is a must-know for anyone sharing files over the Internet. The NET Act amends U.S. copyright law "to provide greater copyright protection by amending criminal copyright infringement provisions" and for other purposes. Briefly, the NET Act changes copyright law "to define 'financial gain' to include the receipt of anything of value, including the receipt of other copyrighted works."

So under the NET Act, you're considered to have gained financially if you trade any files that contain copyrighted material. For example, if you make available one copyrighted file that you don't have the right to distribute and receive one illegal file in return, you're considered to have gained financially. So you can see that many (if not most) people who are sharing files via P2P technologies are committing a crime.

The NET Act sets up a vicious penalty structure for those ill advised enough to willfully infringe copyright either "for purposes of commercial advantage or private financial gain" or "by reproducing or distributing, including by electronic means, during any 180-day period, one or more copies of one or more copyrighted works with a total retail value of more than $1,000."

Here's the penalty structure:

- ☠ Up to three years' imprisonment and fines for a first offense involving the reproduction or distribution of 10 or more copies of one or more copyrighted works with a total retail value of $2,500 or more.

- ☠ Up to six years' imprisonment and a fine for a second or subsequent offense involving the reproduction or distribution of 10 or more copies of one or more copyrighted works with a total retail value of $2,500 or more.

- ☠ Up to one year's imprisonment and a fine for reproducing or distributing copies of one or more copyrighted works with a total retail value of more than $1,000.

Rough, huh? The only good news for P2P users is that the NET Act "provides that evidence of reproduction or distribution of a copyrighted work, by itself, shall not be sufficient to establish willful infringement." In other words, your having reproduced a copyrighted work, or distributed a copy of it, doesn't necessarily establish you as a guilty sinner. (You could have done it all ignorant, like.)

You may also be seeing a glimmer of hope if you're looking at that phrase "total retail value of more than $1,000." No audio track or DVD scene is worth that much, right, because most CDs cost $15 or less and most DVDs $25 or less?

Wrong. The courts get to set the value of materials whose copyright has been infringed. A court could well decide that because you've made that file available to the-deity-knows-how-many people via the Internet, it's worth much more than $1,000—and then you're caught in the NET.

In August 1999, a student from the University of Oregon became the first person to be prosecuted under the NET Act. Jeffrey Gerard Levy pled guilty to making available more than $5,000 worth of copyrighted material on his Web site. Levy could have received a full house of three years in prison and a $250,000 fine. He got off relatively lightly with two years' probation, limitations on his access to the Internet, and periodic drug testing. (The drug testing was incidental—Levy was found to have gotten spliffed after being busted. If your system's dope-free, you probably won't get periodic drug testing under the NET Act.)

One of the reasons that Levy got probation and periodic probing rather than the slammer and a severe crimp in his financial future was that the FBI and D.A. didn't closely assess the amount of material he had pirated. Levy had about 1000 MP3 files, most of which were pirated, together with movie clips and software including Adobe

Photoshop (which retails for several hundred dollars). But the D.A. and Levy agreed to a value of more than $5,000.

Federal sentencing guidelines recommend that the length of the sentence depend on the value of the material whose copyright was infringed. So you can be hanged twice as high for a sheep as for a lamb, and higher still for a whole flock of infringements.

Digital Millennium Copyright Act (DMCA), 1998

Signed into law on October 28, 1998, the Digital Millennium Copyright Act (DMCA) implemented several major changes to U.S. copyright law to make it more appropriate to and effective for the Internet age.

You'll sometimes hear the DMCA called "WIPO," "WIPO Copyright Implementing Legislation," or even "WIPO Copyright and Performances and Phonograms Treaties Implementation Act of 1998." WIPO (www.wipo.org) is the World Intellectual Property Organization, the international body under whose auspices the DMCA was drafted.

The DMCA's Five Titles

The DMCA has five titles, three of which are of interest to those using P2P technologies:

- ☠ Title I changes U.S. copyright law so that it complies with the WIPO Copyright Treaty and the WIPO Performances and Phonograms Treaty of December 1996. These treaties detail "obligations concerning technological measures" that provide "legal remedies against the circumvention of effective technological measures" used to protect copyrighted works. In other words, if someone applies a fancy copy-protection scheme to a work, it's a crime to crack it.

- ☠ Title II limits the liability of an online service provider (OSP) for copyright infringement. One of the definitions of an OSP is as "a provider of online services or network access, or the operator of facilities therefor," which has allowed a number of companies that would not generally be understood to be providers of online services to claim the protection of Title II. More on this near the end of the chapter.

☠ Title IV contains assorted amendments to the Copyright Act. Of greatest interest here is the extension of the exemption for ephemeral recordings, which gives digital broadcasts the same privileges that analog broadcasts have, and the provision of a statutory license for Internet broadcasting.

Title III (which provides exemptions from infringement for independent service organizations that need to turn a computer on in order to service it) and Title V (which provides new protection for original boat hull designs—yes, you read that right) are of little interest to those using P2P technologies.

Illegal to Circumvent Copyright Protection Technologies

Title I is pretty tough. It's illegal to "circumvent a technological measure that effectively controls access to a work protected under this title." This prohibition didn't take effect immediately when the DMCA was passed. Instead, there was a two-year period during which the Librarian of Congress was to review the prohibition and see if any exceptions were needed. But this two-year grace period is now up.

However, the consumer's freedom to hack and crack protected works is not totally lost yet. The DMCA provides a (relatively) explicit exception to the prohibition on circumventing technological measures in order to make the work usable or interoperable. Here's the relevant section of the DMCA:

> Notwithstanding the provisions of subsections (a)(2) and (b), a person may develop and employ technological means to circumvent a technological measure, or to circumvent protection afforded by a technological measure, in order to enable the identification and analysis under paragraph (1), or for the purpose of enabling interoperability of an independently created computer program with other programs, if such means are necessary to achieve such interoperability, to the extent that doing so does not constitute infringement under this title.

So while it's illegal to crack a copy protection scheme designed to protect a work, and it's illegal to "manufacture, import, offer to the public, provide, or otherwise traffic in any technology, product, service, device, component, or part thereof" designed to circumvent technological protection on a work, it may sometimes be necessary for the consumer to break that protection in order to enjoy the work or make it interoperable. One example of this is DeCSS, which I'll discuss in a couple of minutes' time.

The DMCA also has a loophole by which security experts can reverse engineer copyright protection so that they can test the security of the products or make software or hardware that works with the copyright protection technology. But as you'd imagine, few people will be able to slip through this loophole.

The DMCA sets vicious penalties for breaking the copy protection on copyrighted works. If you violate the provisions "willfully and for purposes of commercial advantage or private financial gain," you can be fined up to $500,000 and imprisoned for up to five years, or both, for a first offense. For a second offense, you're facing fines of up to $1 million and 10 years in jail. When you remember that "private financial gain" can involve nothing more than receiving one illegal file and distributing one illegal file, the DMCA looks very unfriendly.

Safe Harbors for Online Service Providers

For OSPs (online service providers), the DMCA provides just what the average pirate longs for—safe harbors. These harbors are safe from prosecution rather than naval frigates, but none the less welcome for that.

If an OSP is merely passing along material, rather than supplying it or altering it, the OSP is not liable for infringement of copyright. Here's some of the relevant passage:

> A service provider shall not be liable… for infringement of copyright by reason of the provider's transmitting, routing, or providing connections for, material through a system or network controlled or operated by or for the service provider, or by reason of the intermediate and transient storage of that material in the course of such transmitting, routing, or providing connections…

…provided several things, of which these are the main ones:

- Someone other than the service provider initiated the transmission (etc.) of the material.

- The transmission (etc.) is carried out automatically, without the service provider having selected the material.

- "The service provider does not select the recipients of the material except as an automatic response to the request of another person."

- The service provider doesn't keep a copy of the material other than a temporary copy necessary to transmit it. (For example, the service provider can cache the material temporarily in order to transmit it.)

- The service provider doesn't modify the contents when it transmits them.

I've given you these provisions at some length, because we'll revisit them at the end of the chapter when we talk about the legality (or otherwise) of Napster.

Likewise, the OSP is protected by the DMCA from being liable for copyright infringement because of infringing files that users have stored on their servers as long as the OSP doesn't know that the infringing files are there and that the OSP "responds expeditiously to remove, or disable access to, the material that is claimed to be infringing." So if you store an illegal file on your OSP's servers (for example, if you receive an illegal MP3 file via e-mail) without the OSP's knowing, the OSP's not liable. If someone tells them the file is there, they have to respond expeditiously to remove it. In practice, they'll probably expeditiously remove you as well.

Ephemeral Recordings

Title IV's provision for a statutory license and ephemeral recordings go a long way toward making Webcasting (Internet broadcasting) easy and legal. We'll discuss the legal issues involved in Webcasting later in this chapter.

DeCSS

The year 2000 saw a great deal of excitement in videophile and movie-industry quarters about DeCSS, a utility created to crack the Content Scrambling System (CSS) security used to protect the contents of DVDs from copying. CSS encrypts the data on DVDs so that users cannot read the contents of the DVD without a decryption key or, more importantly, copy the files from the DVD to a hard disk or other storage. Every hardware DVD player and every software DVD player includes an encryption key. The players are licensed by the DVD-Copy Control Association (DVD-CCA).

The problem was that no software DVD player was available for Linux. This meant that to anyone running Linux, a DVD was even less useful than an AOL CD (though infinitely more expensive).

Norwegian hackers in the LiVid (Linux Video group) were able to create DeCSS by lawful reverse engineering when they discovered unencrypted code left in a software DVD player. DeCSS makes DVD contents readable by copying the encrypted files from the DVD to unencrypted files on the hard drive. The immediate effect of DeCSS was to make it possible to play DVDs on Linux boxes. A knock-on effect was to enable people to create DVD players without DVD-CCA authorization.

Word to the Wise: Where Does the First Amendment Come into This?

At this point, you may be asking where the First Amendment comes into play. After all, doesn't it hold free speech to be a right? And if so, what does that mean?

Here's what the First Amendment says:

> Congress shall make no law respecting an establishment of religion, or prohibiting the free exercise thereof; or abridging the freedom of speech, or of the press; or the right of the people peaceably to assemble, and to petition the government for a redress of grievances.

(Okay, so you should have known that by heart. Give yourself a pat on the back if you did. If not, take a minute to memorize it.)

For our purposes here, the key part of that is the "freedom of speech, or of the press" part. This part is generally understood to guarantee individuals the right to express themselves freely without the government interfering. (The "or of the press" phrase means that the individual may express themselves by publishing or disseminating their opinions. It doesn't mean that members of the press have a special set of rights that Joe and Jane Sixpack don't have.)

As you probably know, freedom of speech isn't exactly absolute. The Supreme Court (which gets to interpret how to apply the United States Constitution to the tricky business of real life) has made it clear that the government may prohibit speech that's likely to cause trouble. The canonical example of shouting "Fire" in a crowded theater has perhaps been superseded these days by speech inciting violence or racial hatred. (After all, who goes to the theater anymore?)

Most people accept that. But when you put the First Amendment in the same room as copyright law, you notice that they don't get on all that well. The problem is that the First Amendment is extremely sweeping

Word to the Wise: Where Does the First Amendment Come into This? (*continued*)

in what it says and (hardly surprisingly) was not written with modern technology in mind. Given that the Copyright Act definitely limits the freedom of speech and the freedom of the press for material that is protected by copyright, people can (and do) argue that the Copyright Act is unconstitutional. "Congress shall make no law... abridging the freedom of speech," etc.—but Congress passed the Copyright Act, which does just that.

(You'll recall that there are similar problems with the Second Amendment, with some people interpreting the right to bear arms as giving them the right to stack up assault weaponry or assemble ICBMs in their backyards. Sheesh! What was Congress thinking when it ratified those SALT Treaties, anyway, and when it banned the sales of bazookas to fine, upstanding citizens?)

Most people who don't permanently keep an eye on the horizon watching for incoming black helicopters from FEMA take the view that the Copyright Act is intended to provide a balance between certain forms of expression (which are protected by copyright) and underlying ideas (which are not protected by copyright). In other words, Congress passed the Copyright Act to protect property rights in expression guaranteed by the First Amendment, but within the generally accepted parameters of intellectual property. Some copyright experts take the view that, because it grants what can be viewed as limited monopolies to the creators of works, copyright law actually *encourages* free speech. These people reason that if the works could legally be ripped off left, right, and center, their creators would have little motive to create the works. I don't entirely buy this argument—it smacks of retrofitting reasons to events—but it has a certain appealing neatness in its reconciliation of the apparently irreparably divorced.

Word to the Wise: Where Does the First Amendment Come into This? (*continued*)

Copyright law has so far stood the test of time. In several challenges, the Supreme Court has held that copyright law can be used to prevent the unauthorized use of another person's copyrighted material and that this does not violate the First Amendment.

So while the First Amendment guarantees freedom of expression, it doesn't give you the right to infringe copyright. Likewise, you don't have the right to "express" yourself freely by looting a department store or by shooting somebody; these acts could be argued to be forms of self-expression, but there are laws that specifically prohibit them.

I mentioned a moment ago that not all speech is protected under the First Amendment. Apart from dangerous speech likely to affect public safety or peace, commercial speech (such as advertising claims and commercial circulars) are not protected. But apart from that, pretty much all speech is protected.

Protected, that is, until the DMCA comes along and shoots holes in the rigging of the First Amendment. Under the DMCA, you'll remember, it's illegal to crack or circumvent copyright protection without authorization from the copyright holder. That seems okay at first—but it means the DMCA prohibits expression in the form of code-cracking code. If you're a programmer, you can't legally express yourself by writing code that circumvents a copyright-protection technology. Ouch.

I'm not a legal expert, but there seems to be little precedent for this infringement of the First Amendment by the DMCA. You can see why the corporations want the DMCA's protections of their copyrighted material. But the anti-circumvention provisions of the DMCA threaten free speech—and this is why the EFF is representing Goldstein over DeCSS and why the DeCSS case may result in a challenge to the constitutionality of the DMCA.

As you might imagine, the DVD-CCA and the movie industry didn't see unauthorized DVD players as a good thing and decided to do something about DeCSS. The MPAA's Norwegian lawyer filed a complaint against two of the authors of the DeCSS code, Jon Johansen and his father, Per Johansen, for publishing the DeCSS code. The case is currently pending, with the two Johansens facing a sentence of two to three years in prison if found guilty.

In August 2000, the Motion Picture Association of America (MPAA) sued Emmanuel Goldstein (also known as Eric Corley), the editor of the 2600 Magazine Web site, for posting the source code to DeCSS on the site, accusing him of trafficking in a technology designed to circumvent protection without authorization from the copyright holder (remember Title 1 of the DMCA?). Corley had posted the code in a report about the DVD-CCA's attempt to crack down on DeCSS.

Because the movie studios have admitted that DeCSS had not led to a single instance of piracy, it appears that the motivation for the case is to maintain a monopoly on the DVD player market. In other words, the MPAA seems to be maintaining that consumers aren't to be allowed to watch DVD content unless they buy a player authorized by the DVD-CCA. This wouldn't be great for the DVD market, and it would set a wretched precedent for other technologies that use encryption in the future.

Beyond DeCSS, the case raises an interesting question of freedom of expression. If computer code—a form of expression—is ruled not to be worthy of First Amendment protection, there could ultimately be no freedom of expression on the Internet. The Electronic Frontier Foundation (EFF) is representing Goldstein in the case, which may end up challenging the constitutionality of the DMCA.

Someone's Looking at You

Given the penalties involved, it doesn't make much sense to be caught violating copyright. But how likely are you to be caught? You may think the feds are unlikely to come busting in your door to search your computer for the occasional MP3 file or pirated software application. You'd probably be right—but you may learn only too late that other people have been watching your actions.

Apart from copyright holders interested in policing their copyrights, bodies interested in prosecuting copyright violations include the following:

☠ The Federal Bureau of Investigation (FBI) investigates copyright violations (together with just about any other federal crime you might care to name).

- Most non–open source software companies do as much as they can to fight widespread piracy of their software while recognizing that small-scale piracy can help bring their products to a wider user base.

- The Business Software Alliance (BSA; `www.bsa.org`) is an international body that promotes the legitimate use of software and fights software piracy.

- The Software & Information Industry Association (SIAA; `www.spa.org`) is a trade association of software publishers and digital content producers in Europe. The SIAA was formed in January 1999 by a merger of the Software Publishers Association (SPA; occasionally mis-referred to as the Software Piracy Association, not to their amusement) and the Information Industry Association (IIA).

- The record companies tend to work vigorously to preserve their copyright. Most vigilant are the Big Five record companies (Sony, Universal, Warner, EMI, and Bertelsmann) and the Recording Industry Association of America (see the next bullet item).

- The Recording Industry Association of America (RIAA; `www.riaa.com`) is active in trying to reduce copyright infringements of the companies and artists it represents. Among other activities (such as suing MP3.com and Napster, Inc., trying to ban the Diamond Rio, and searching for copyright infringements of music on the Internet), the RIAA runs a "soundbyting" program with chosen universities designed to educate students about the legalities of reproducing and distributing music on the Internet.

- Organizations including the National Academy of Recording Arts & Sciences, the Music Publishers Association (MPA), the National Academy of Songwriters, and the Nashville Songwriters Association work to protect copyright for creators and publishers of music.

- The movie studios are very unenthusiastic about piracy of movies, DVDs, and videocassettes.

- The Motion Picture Association of America (MPAA; `www.mpaa.org`) and its international counterpart, the Motion Picture Association (MPA; also `www.mpaa.org`—*not* `www.mpa.org`, which is the Music Publishers' Association, also abbreviated to MPA), act as the voice of the American motion picture industry, home video industry, and television industry. Recent MPAA activities include trying to ban the distribution of the source code for DeCSS.

Beyond these people and organizations interested in prosecuting copyright violations, most companies and organizations are interested in avoiding copyright violations by their employees and members. Network administrators at most companies scan their networks and servers (and sometimes local hard drives) regularly for illegal and inappropriate files and activities. Some of the more exciting cases make the headlines, such as when a company fires a number of people for misuse of their systems, but most cases involve internal disciplinary measures (reprimand, demotion, 30 lashes with the HR cat-o'-nine-tails, that kind of thing) and don't get broadcast outside the company.

Colleges and universities also typically watch for gross piracy in their accounts, especially because P2P file-sharing is huge among students. Again, many violations are dealt with quietly, but some pop out into public view. One example came in October 1999, when Carnegie Mellon University in Pittsburgh, PA, after being threatened with legal action by the RIAA, conducted an unannounced and random search of 250 student files. As a result, it disciplined 71 students for illegal use of MP3 files. The discipline wasn't too severe—the university cancelled the students' Internet connections and made them attend a forum on copyright law before they could go online again.

If you're feeling cynical, you might draw a parallel between the copyright laws and the speeding laws. The highway patrol tends to tolerate most people cruising a few miles per hour above the speed limit, only pulling over vehicles that blow past them at grossly illegal speeds, weave, or whose drivers flip them the bird. They're also only looking at a tiny minority of cars on the road at any given time. Similarly, the forces of the law currently seldom bother swinging the heavy hammer of copyright infringement law at relatively discreet individuals. In practical terms, the copyright police expend most of their effort on the gross violators—for example, shutting down as soon as they can those pirate MP3 sites that they find.

How to Know If a File Is Legal

Given that it's illegal to download or to have illegal copies of digital files, you may well be asking at this point how you can tell whether a digital file is legal or not.

Sad to say, there's no clear-cut way of telling whether a digital file is legal or not unless you know because you've created it yourself. Typically, you can't tell the copyright status of the work from the file that contains all or part of it.

Generally and non-legally speaking, the more closed file formats give their contents a better chance of being legal than the more open formats. A *closed* file format is one that's difficult for the average consumer to make, while an *open* file format is one to which consumers have free access. For example, the a2b audio file format is closed, in that the technology for creating a2b files isn't available to the end user. As a result, it's more likely that any a2b files you run into are legal. By contrast, the MP3 file format is wide open: Anyone can create an MP3 file by using universally available software.

So MP3 files are likely to be illegal—but you'll also find a large number of legal and authorized MP3 files online. You'll need to use your judgment as to whether a file is legal or not. If it's an MP3 file posted on a big-name public site, such as EMusic.com, Riffage.com, or MP3.com, you're pretty safe to assume that it's a legal copy. Likewise, if the file is posted on a known record company's site or on the band's own official site, it should be legit. And in the rare cases in which the band has a publicly stated policy of encouraging bootleg tapes and audio files of their live performances (as the Grateful Dead did, and as Metallica used to do), you probably don't need to worry. (The apparent contrast between Metallica's encouragement of live bootlegs and its legal assault on Napster for unauthorized trading of its studio recordings confused and dismayed many long-time Metallica fans.)

Anywhere else, you need to be on your guard. Any digital-audio files of music by big-name artists posted on personal Web sites should be regarded as highly suspect, as should video clips from popular movies posted just about anywhere. Beware of files posted on anything that identifies itself as an MP3z site or a warez site. (*Warez* is a term for pirated software, and *MP3z* is used to mean illegal MP3 files.)

MP3 files have a copyright bit that, in theory, is used to indicate whether the track is copyrighted or not. The idea is that you can set the bit to indicate that it's illegal to copy the track. The problem is that because many programs let the user change the setting of the copyright bit, it's essentially useless in the real world.

The Law and Internet Broadcasting

As you saw earlier in this chapter, most commentators reckon you can legally rip tracks from prerecorded CDs and encode MP3 files of them for personal use the way you can legally tape records or CDs on cassettes. (Some commentators disagree—typically, those with money to lose from your ripping and encoding the CDs.) Anyway, as long as you keep the resulting MP3 files to yourself, who's to know you've made them?

When you're distributing music, things tend to be a little more clear cut. To distribute digital copies of any music, you need the rights to do so. If you created the music yourself and you haven't assigned the rights to anyone, you're most likely in the clear. If you created the music with other people, you need their permission to distribute it. And if you're signed to a record company, chances are that you'll need their consent to distribute any music on your own—even if you made the music yourself in your own studio without the record company being involved in the slightest.

Bottom line: Before you distribute *any* MP3 files, make sure you have the rights to distribute them. Even if you're drawn to the law, intellectual property's an area you really don't want to go spelunking in unless you have time and money to burn.

If you're an artist and are thinking of signing with a record company, make sure that you retain the rights to distribute your music over the Internet. As a promotional tool for artists, MP3 is invaluable—but as we've seen, the record companies are, for the most part, still scared of how it could chew up their profit margins.

Here, "distributing" means sending people music files or providing music files for download. If you're broadcasting music (or other audio), the rules are different, and somewhat more in your favor. Basically, you can broadcast, but you're probably going to have to pay for the privilege. Read on.

If you're going to broadcast, you probably want to apply for a statutory license under which to operate. Statutory means that the license is provided by the law rather than granted by the copyright holders in question. At this writing, you need to file an Initial Notice and $20 with the Copyright Office at the Library of Congress. You'll find a suggested Initial Notice at the Library of Congress Web site (www.loc.gov/copyright/licensing/format.html). There isn't a set royalty rate for the statutory license, which means that you either need to negotiate with the RIAA directly or accept a rate that will be set by an arbitration panel "by early 2001." Check the RIAA site (www.riaa.com) for the latest information.

The alternative to getting a statutory license is to enter into licensing agreements with individual artists or record companies for the rights to broadcast their music. Unless your station's going to stick to promoting only a few artists, or perhaps just one record label, these licensing agreements will prove such a pain in the seat that you'll run screaming to the RIAA and its cohorts.

> If you're going to get heavy into webcasting, you ought to read the U.S. Copyright Office Summary of the DMCA. You'll find this at lcweb.loc .gov/copyright/legislation/dmca.pdf.

As you saw earlier in this chapter, the DMCA makes provisions for webcasting. Here are the key points from the webcaster's point of view:

- Your ISP isn't responsible for any copyright infringements that you perpetrate using their services—provided they're ready to give your contact information to copyright holders who demand it, and provided that they actively try to prevent you from offending again. Statistics are hard to come by, but anecdotal evidence suggests that many ISPs will not only give an accused subscriber's details to the first copyright holder who complains but will also terminate their Internet connection.

- You're allowed to make an *ephemeral recording* of music. An ephemeral recording is a copy of a recording "to facilitate performance"—for example, an MP3 file that you've created so that you don't need to use the CD. For the MP3 file to qualify as an ephemeral recording, it must be the only copy that you have of the recording, you must be the only person using that copy, you must destroy the copy within six months unless you're keeping it as an archive, and you can only transmit the copy "in the webcaster's local service area." The local service area requirement makes no sense, since everyone on the Internet can receive your broadcast. But the other three requirements are easy enough to comply with.

- You're allowed to webcast sound recordings on the Internet, and you're obliged to identify the track, artist, and album, but you can't announce the details of your playlist in advance. This is to prevent you from telling people that you'll be playing a particular track at a given time, because that makes what you're doing too close to providing a digital jukebox for it to be considered a bona fide webcast.

Webcasting software such as SHOUTcast and icecast can automatically broadcast artist and track information for you, so you don't need to announce tracks verbally to comply with the identification requirement.

☠ You have to take "steps" not to "induce copying," and you're not supposed to transmit bootlegs.

☠ There are a number of restrictions on what you can and can't play. For example, you can't play more than three tracks from any given album in a three-hour period, and you can't play more than two tracks from any given album consecutively. And if that's not enough, you can't play more than four tracks by any given artist or from any given box set within three hours, and you can't play more than three tracks by any given artist or from any given box set consecutively.

☠ If you loop a program, the loop must be more than three hours long. For a program to differ from another program, you need to make it substantially different—swapping out a couple of songs won't do the trick.

If you don't get a statutory license, you'll need to get licenses from licensing agencies such as the following:

ASCAP   The American Society of Composers, Authors, and Publishers (www.ascap.com) bills itself as "since 1914 the leader in music licensing" and licenses the rights to "millions of songs created or owned by more than 80,000 of America's and hundreds of thousands of the world's best songwriters, composers, lyricists and publishers." ASCAP's lowest fee is $250 a year.

BMI   Broadcast Music, Inc. (www.bmi.com) claims to represent the public performance copyright interest of more than a quarter-million songwriters, composers, and music publishers, giving it a repertoire of more than three million musical works. BMI's fees for webcasting are $250 annually for a site with revenues up to $12,000; $375 annually for a site with revenues up to $18,500; and

$500 annually for a site with revenues up to $25,000. (Someone should introduce BMI to the concept of buying in bulk and saving.) If your site pulls in more than $25,000 a year, you're looking at paying BMI a percentage: either 1.75 percent of total site revenues or 2.5 percent of music area revenues. (If your site makes this much money, get your bean-crunchers to work out which option is better for you.)

SESAC   SESAC, Inc. (`www.sesac.com`) describes itself modestly as the "second oldest and most innovative performing rights organization in the U.S." Innovation aside, SESAC seems to me to license the rights to fewer interesting artists than ASCAP and BMI. SESAC's lowest fee is $50 per six-month period.

The Battle of Napster

To round off the chapter, I'll briefly discuss the legal issues involved with Napster, because they nicely illustrate some of the points raised earlier in this chapter—and some of the legal uncertainties over P2P file sharing.

As you're no doubt aware by now, Napster pioneered P2P file sharing over the Internet. Shawn Fanning, a music and MP3 fan, dreamed up the Napster software and technology in order to provide an easy way for users to share MP3 files with each other.

In case you haven't seen (or didn't see) Napster in its original incarnation, here's the brief version of how it works (or worked). Each Napster user with files to share designates one or more shared folders on their computer and logs into a Napster server. (At this writing, there are many Napster servers, with a central server dynamically assigning each user who logs into the system to one of the available servers. Napster, Inc. has announced plans to link all the servers together into one huge community at some unspecified date, but the service itself may change out of all recognition instead.) The user can then access any of the MP3 files that any of the other users logged into that server are sharing—and those other users can access the files that our protagonist is sharing. Once someone finds an MP3 file they're interested in, they can download it.

From the user's point of view, Napster is wonderful. With a bit of patience, you can find and download the music you want. You can investigate any other type of music that catches your fancy. And you can promote your own files worldwide—all for the price of your regular Internet connection. So it's not surprising that Napster use grew more rapidly than mold on agar—from a few thousand users in 1999 to more than 50 million by February 2001.

Also not surprising (given how few music files most people can legally share) is the huge number of illegal files traded via Napster. Even less surprising is the reaction of most artists and of the music industry, who saw their livelihood (or at least their profits) disappearing down the plughole of the Internet like dirty bathwater.

In May 2000, Metallica delivered Napster, Inc. a list of a third of a million names of Napster users who were offering MP3 files of copyrighted Metallica tracks (an estimated average of five tracks apiece) and forced Napster to remove these users from its system. This number is impressively large, especially given that the names were gathered over a two-day period at the end of April 2000, but they were probably substantially inflated by a bizarre design choice in Napster that shared the user's download directory as well as their chosen upload directories. So if you downloaded a Metallica track, Napster made you share it automatically without your choosing to do so. (I call this a bizarre design choice because it virtually guarantees that many Napster users will share files illegally. Beta 5 of Napster 2 made this appear to be a bug, but Beta 6 made clear that it was a deliberate design choice—designed, presumably, to expand the Napster community.) Many of these users, on finding themselves blocked from using Napster, uninstalled the software and reinstalled it, giving themselves a new screen name to change their identity.

The RIAA then sued Napster, Inc. on behalf of the record industry, claiming Napster, Inc. was a contributory copyright infringer because the company's service and software contributed to copyright infringement. The RIAA's position is that virtually all Napster users directly infringe copyright by downloading and uploading unauthorized MP3 files of copyrighted material. But since the RIAA could not effectively sue many million Napster users, it chose to target Napster, Inc. instead. The charge of contributory copyright infringement argues that Napster, Inc. has actual knowledge that Napster users are trading illegal MP3 files and that Napster, Inc. contributes to the infringement because the Napster software makes it possible. There's also a charge of vicarious infringement that argues that Napster, Inc. can monitor and control user activities (for example, by kicking users off the system) and that Napster, Inc. has benefited financially from users' copyright infringements (in that its stock valuation is poking new holes in the ionosphere).

On Wednesday, July 26, 2000, Judge Marilyn Patel bought the RIAA's arguments and ordered Napster shut down that Friday, July 28. Napster use immediately soared as Napster users frantically tried to download everything of interest to them before Napster closed. But Napster, Inc. won an eleventh-hour stay of execution pending appeal and remained open—and the number of users has increased dramatically every week since. During the appeal procedure in October 2000, Napster, Inc. secured an agreement with Bertelsmann to develop Napster into a secure, subscription-based service for sharing music legally. At this writing, Napster, Inc. is negotiating with the RIAA and the other four of the Big Five to put similar arrangements in place.

On February 12, 2001, the Ninth U.S. Circuit Court of Appeals issued a ruling upholding most of the aspects of the July 2000 injunction against Napster, Inc. The appeals court found that this injunction was "over-broad" and ordered Judge Patel to write a narrower injunction that would force Napster, Inc. to prevent users from sharing material that the record companies had specifically notified Napster, Inc. was copyrighted. Napster, Inc. announced its intention to appeal the ruling, noting that the appeals court "ruled on the basis of what it recognized was an incomplete record before it.

But why wasn't Napster shut down straightaway? With so many MP3 files of copyrighted music being shared without permission, it's hard to deny that the software and service was being used for infringement of copyright on a massive scale.

Napster's position is that they're just making the software available—which is true, although Napster's Web site early on advertised the software as enabling the user to find just about any music they wanted and download it for free. Napster's license agreement makes the user acknowledge that they understand that it's illegal to distribute MP3 files without permission, and each time a user logs into a Napster server at the start of an Napster session, they see a message warning them about illegal MP3 files.

These are the arguments for Napster being legal:

- First, Napster doesn't control any of the music that is being shared. The music doesn't even pass through Napster's Internet site; the Napster server builds and maintains a database of the users currently logged in and the tracks that they're making available, but the MP3 files are stored on the individual user's hard drive. When another user requests to download a track, it's transferred directly from user to user. However, in May 2000, a court ruled that Napster cannot claim to be an ISP to protect itself from lawsuits. (You'll remember from the DMCA that ISPs—OSPs in the DMCA's nomenclature—are not responsible for the content they carry unless they select, control, or modify it.)

☠ Second, the plaintiff needs to prove that Napster is inducing illegal activity—not just that it's possible to use Napster to perform illegal activity. As I mentioned a moment ago, Napster's Web site once appeared to be encouraging if not inducing illegal activity, though that's no longer the case.

☠ Third, some law experts say that the plaintiffs have to prove that the Napster software is used almost exclusively for performing illegal activity. Because there's no question that some of the MP3 files that are being distributed via Napster are being distributed legally, that might be very hard to prove.

On the other side, some lawyers argue that because Napster, Inc. knows that some of its users are using Napster to infringe copyright, the company should be held responsible for their misconduct. This argument may be tough to make stick because of the wider implications it could have. With fair logic, you could say that car manufacturers know that some drivers use their vehicles to commit crimes, so the manufacturers should be held responsible. Clearly this would be absurd. But consider the recent lawsuits against gun manufacturers such as Smith & Wesson because some of the guns they made and sold (legally) were used to commit crimes.

Another argument in favor of Napster was that the uploading and downloading of MP3 files was private use. Judge Patel didn't buy that, as you can see from this excerpt from an expansion on her original decision:

Given the vast scale of Napster use among anonymous individuals, the court finds that downloading and uploading MP3 music files with the assistance of Napster are not private uses.…Moreover, the fact that Napster users get for free something they would ordinarily have to buy suggests that they reap economic advantages from Napster use.

In early and mid 2000, a number of universities banned Napster, some because of intellectual-property concerns (including three that were named in Metallica's lawsuit against Napster), but more of them because of the massive amount of bandwidth that Napster users consume. In response, Napster, Inc. began working on adding features that allow administrators to allocate bandwidth effectively to reduce such problems.

And students at some universities registered enough discontent to make their universities un-ban Napster.

At this writing, it seems unlikely that Napster will survive in its current form. But whether Napster is closed down or mutates into a subscription service, other P2P file-sharing technologies stand ready to take its place. Some of these are designed specifically to resist being closed down from a central point and make no bones about copyright infringement. Chapter 7, "Post-Napster Technologies," discusses these P2P technologies.

The First Amendment surfaces in the Napster case too. In an Amicus brief to the U.S. District Court Northern District of California, the American Civil Liberties Union (ACLU) argued that the July 2000 injunction shutting down Napster was too broad because, by requiring Napster "to limit the use of its software to those users who can prove that the files they wish to exchange do not infringe plaintiffs' copyrights," it suppressed more speech than was necessary to protect the plaintiffs' legitimate copyright interests. The brief also argued that the injunction threatened the architecture of the Internet because it "could force intermediary hosts of file-sharing programs to be choke points for reviewing the speech of every individual before it could be sent to its intended audience."

Up Next

In this chapter, you've learned what intellectual property and copyright mean and what their implications are for P2P file sharing. You now know what fair use and personal use let you do (and what they don't), what the public domain is, and how to go about getting permission from the copyright holder to use a copyrighted work. You've learned that the penalties for copyright infringement can be severe, and you've poked a finger into some of the legislation that says what constitutes piracy.

In the next chapter, I'll lead you through the basic tools that pirates use—and that you'll need to perform legal file-sharing operations on the Internet.

A Pirate Speaks: The Unabashed Pirate

I've stolen thousands of programs—*thousands*—over the course of the years. Everything from games to utilities to operating systems. Antivirus programs. Office suites. You name it, I've stolen it.

It's so easy to get the programs. I've got them off of warez sites, I've got them off of friends, I've got them off of the Internet, from being in chat rooms and asking where I can go get this stuff. People have even e-mailed me programs.

People ask me, why do I steal all this stuff, why do I need all this software? Thing is, I like to take a look at everything. I like software. I like to see what's going on, where things are going. I don't have an unlimited hard drive here—it fills up. So I eventually delete most of the software I steal. Sometimes I make CDs of the software; sometimes I don't.

The interesting thing is, when I find programs that I like, I actually buy them. I've stolen Windows before—but now my copy of Windows is perfectly legitimate. It came on my latest machine. I've stolen Office before—but now it comes on my machine and I know how to use it. As it turns out, pretty much everything that I like, I eventually buy. I've even bought a copy of Corel Linux, and you don't even have to pirate that because you can download it for free.

But I pirate it all first. I take a look at everything. I like evaluating the different word processors, the different ways they do things. I like playing different types of games and seeing which ones appeal to me. But what happens is, even though I've stolen thousands and thousands of pieces of software, in the end I buy the things that I use a lot and the things that I like.

Is this a rationalization? Well, I'm not one of those people who say all software needs to be free. There are people out there like that—I'm not one of them. I do believe that most software is too expensive. I also believe that there's a lot of junk out there. I believe that 90 percent of

A Pirate Speaks: The Unabashed Pirate (*continued*)

the software out there is junk. I don't see that it's wrong for me to evaluate it and decide whether I want to buy it or not. I take a look at it, and just because the box says it has a license on it, and if I open that little flap, I'm *committed* to *buying* it—I don't think that's reasonable. If I open a box or if I look at a program and it doesn't do what I want it to, and it's clunky and not very useful, why should I buy that? Why should I have to buy something like that?

I try *everything* before I actually buy it. And I don't feel that there's a problem in that. I only eventually buy the things that are good, the things that I feel are useful, the things that are constructed well, that don't have bugs. The only way that you can find that out is by trying it all. And I do. I try it all. I admit it.

I may copy things off onto CD and put them off to the side, but that's only because I may find a need for them later—and if I do, I'll evaluate them again later. And if I decide that it's one of the programs that I'll be using in my profession or during the course of my work, I'll end up buying it. A legitimate copy will find its way onto my machine. And that's just the way it is.

I look at piracy as not piracy at all, because all software should be tested and evaluated by the people who will be using it. Why should I commit to a product just because Microsoft made it, or just because it's endorsed by Apple? I need to try it before that. And you know what, if I buy a box and open it up and then try to send it back, it's almost impossible: They just think I copied it and am sending it back.

I find this is the only way to evaluate software. That's why I do it. I try everything. And if the software companies don't like it, that's tough for them.

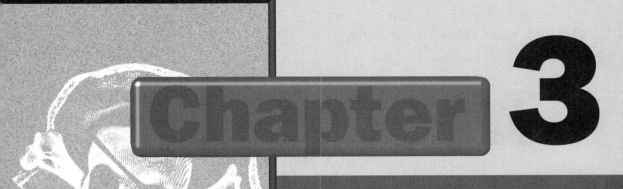

Chapter 3

The Pirate's Basic Tools

Featuring

- Computer
- Operating system
- Antivirus software
- Internet connection
- Storage
- CD burner
- A well-developed sense of paranoia

Much as any effective pirate of yore needed a fast ship, a gang of swarthy ruffians, barrels of rum and biscuit, and the occasional lime, the effective pirate of today needs some basic equipment. Here's the list:

- ☠ A computer of some description or other
- ☠ An operating system to make the computer useful
- ☠ An Internet connection for contacting other pirates and uploading and downloading files
- ☠ Antivirus software to make sure downloaded files contain nothing lethal
- ☠ Plenty of storage—typically, hard-disk space—on which to store the spoils
- ☠ A CD burner (or DVD burner) with which to create back-ups or archives
- ☠ A well-developed sense of paranoia (or "security," if you must)

If you're going to find, get, and enjoy legal files on the Internet, you'll need the same equipment. This chapter discusses these requirements, putting emphasis where emphasis is due and skating lightly over what you're bound to know already.

Computer

The first thing you need is a computer. Chances are, if you're reading this book, you have one already, and we needn't get bogged down here. Basically, any new, recent, or semi-recent computer is fine, depending on what you're trying to do with it. PC, Mac, or Linux box—all are fine, provided that you don't need any esoteric software that's available only for another platform.

Sharing files doesn't take a great amount of horsepower, so you can get by with an ancient (by 2001 standards) processor, such as a Pentium-MMX 233, a slow K6, or a slow G3 PowerPC (say, 233MHz). More important are the Internet connection (discussed later in this chapter) and plenty of storage space (also discussed later in this chapter).

To enjoy audio (for example, MP3 files), you need a workable sound card. To create MP3 files from audio CDs, you need a CD-ROM drive or DVD drive. Some MP3 rippers and encoders require a sound card, but the better ones do not. That said, to listen to the files you rip and encode, you'll need a sound card unless you have USB speakers or headphones.

To enjoy video, you need a video card capable of speed and resolution sufficient to satisfy your eyes. This video card doesn't have to be the latest model with 64MB of RAM; most people can get by with something far more modest. You'll also need software capable of playing DVD files (or files ripped from DVD) and AVI files. This software is easy to come by, especially if you buy a DVD drive.

Storage

Perhaps the most important component of your computer is plenty of storage for all the files you download. Even if you confine yourself strictly to legal files, you'll need plenty of space.

These days, you can't be too rich, Courteney Cox Arquette and Cameron Diaz can't be too thin, and your computer can't have too much storage. (Okay, Cox Arquette and Diaz *are* too thin for most people, but that's their business.) In bulk, audio files need large amounts of storage space, and video files need huge amounts.

As usual, the storage can be either on hard drives or on removable media. Hard drives should be your primary storage for any files you want to have at hand. Hard drives typically provide the least expensive means of mass storage apart from backup tapes (which are inconvenient to access), and with capacious hard drives available at very affordable prices, you can pack a huge amount of storage into a desktop computer without breaking the bank.

If you're planning a new computer or a serious refit of your existing computer, your first decision should be what kind of drives you'll use in it: EIDE or SCSI? Usually this question comes down to cost and performance, though there's an element of capacity as well:

Cost   Money talks and storage walks. Decide whether you want to pay the extra for a SCSI controller: It'll give you extra flexibility for your computer, because you can attach more drives and devices to a SCSI bus than to an EIDE bus, but it'll cost you substantially more than a standard EIDE setup. SCSI drives will typically set you back a bit more than EIDE drives as well, but you'll be able to build more storage capacity. You can put up to four EIDE devices in most modern PCs; most people will go for two or three hard drives and one CD-ROM drive, CD-R drive, CD-RW drive, or DVD drive, depending on their needs.

Performance   If you're planning to do a lot of multitasking, or to use your machine as a server, SCSI may suit you better than EIDE, because a SCSI disk can respond more quickly than an EIDE disk to multiple requests. Under conventional stimulation, though, EIDE disks are more than fast enough, so don't feel that you have to pay the extra for SCSI.

Hard drives keep growing in size, roughly doubling year by year, but if you have a truly impressive collection of audio and video files, you'll be looking at using multiple drives. Under Windows, each drive appears as a separate letter, so each time you go to access a file, you need to remember (or work out) which drive it's on. Under other operating systems, you may be able to span the drives, so that the disks containing your files appear as just one drive. (If you're using a network, your network administrator almost certainly does this with your major network drives, which you probably call the F: drive or the U: drive.)

Whether you decide to go SCSI or EIDE, don't fill your computer to capacity with drives at this point. Leave yourself some room for expansion with a bigger drive or two next year. At this writing, 80GB drives are affordable, and 100+GB drives will undoubtedly become common in mid 2001. A couple of large drives will give you a good amount of storage space to get started, and you'll be able to add a 250GB drive next year and a one-terabyte (1TB) drive the year after that and…you get the idea.

If you can't add any more hard drives to your computer (for example, if it's already stuffed to the gills with drives, or if you have a laptop), consider attaching one or more external hard drives via the parallel port, a USB port, a FireWire port, via SCSI, or via a PC card. External hard drives tend to be slower and more expensive than regular hard drives, but they're portable and effective. They're also good if you need to move your storage from one computer to another. Generally speaking, you should avoid parallel port and USB 1.0 connections—you probably won't be happy with the speed (if that's the word) that they deliver. Stick to USB 2.0, FireWire, or SCSI for cable-connected external drives.

FireWire, as you probably know, is the most widespread snappy name for the IEEE 1394 high-performance serial bus. Sony, determined to continue its assaults on the English language, calls it i.LINK instead.

Storing Stuff on Online Drives

One storage option that you may want to use from time to time is an online drive service such as FreeDrive or Visto. FreeDrive (www .freedrive.com) provides 50MB of space free; Visto (www.visto.com) provides 15MB of space for free for personal use and 25MB for each group that you create. (You can also pay FreeDrive or Visto for more space.) If you're a member of Yahoo!, you can store 10MB for free by using its Briefcase feature.

Given that the space is either limited or expensive and that you'll be uploading and downloading files via the Internet, online drives are primarily useful for keeping backups of vital files or for transferring files from one computer to another. As you'll see later in the book, pirates favor online drives for sharing files with each other without needing both parties to be online at the same time. But unless you have a blazingly fast Internet connection, you won't want to try to store a large collection of digital-audio files on an online drive—it'll be too awkward, and your access speeds will be too slow.

One online drive service that offers a huge amount of space is myplay, inc. (www.myplay.com), which gives you 3GB to use. The catch is that they try to grab a bunch of rights for anything original you upload. More on this later in the book.

For portable storage, consider removable media such as Zip drives (either the 100MB Zip Classic or the 250MB Zip 250), Jaz drives (either the 1GB original Jaz or the Jaz 2GB), or the Orb from Castlewood Technologies (2.2GB). These all come in internal and external versions. You'll get the best performance from SCSI connection and the worst performance from parallel port connections. You may also want to consider floppy-drive replacements such as the SuperDisk and LS-120. Forget about floppy disks—they're too small to provide serious storage anymore. By way of example, a floppy disk holds less than a minute and a half's worth of MP3 data encoded at the popular 128kpbs rate, or a few seconds of rather disappointing video.

If you have a CD-R or CD-RW drive, you can burn CDs for storage, transfer, or backup. CD-R and CD-RW media hold 650MB each (or 700MB for extended-capacity CDs), so you can fit a good amount of compressed digital audio on to them—more than 10 hours of MP3 data encoded at 128kbps. The next section discusses how to choose a CD-R or CD-RW drive.

For higher capacity, consider a DVD-RAM drive. Each side of a DVD-RAM disk holds 2.3GB, and you can get either single-sided disks or more expensive double-sided ones. At this writing, DVD-RAM is far more expensive than CD-R or CD-RW as a storage medium, but if you need and can afford the capacity, it's a good alternative.

CD Recorder or CD Rewriter

A CD recorder or CD rewriter is a vital tool for the P2P user. Not only are recordable CDs one of the best ways of backing up your critical files, but they also make it easy to share files with other people. Better yet, you can burn audio CDs from digital-audio files that you download and play them in almost any conventional CD player.

If you don't have a CD recorder or CD rewriter but want to get one, this section explains what you need to know.

For general discussion (for example, of speeds), I'll use the term *CD recorder* to encompass both CD recorders that write only once and CD rewriters.

Get a Fast Recorder

First off, you'll probably want to get one of the fastest CD recorders you can afford. This doesn't necessarily mean the fastest CD recorder available to you, as there are several considerations that you need to keep in mind when choosing your CD recorder.

CD recorder speed is measured by the same rating system as regular old read-only CD drives: 1X, 2X, 4X, and so on. Each X represents 150kbps (the nominal read rate of the first CD drives), so a 4X drive chugs through 600kbps, an 8X drive handles 1200kbps (1.2Mbps), and a 12X drive manages 1800kbps (1.8Mbps).

At this writing, CD recorders that write at 16X are just starting to appear on the market, while 12X recorders are widely available. Writing full bore, a 12X drive can fill a whole CD in 6 minutes or so. (The speed will vary a bit depending on your system—if your other components are lame, chances are the CD recorder will have to scale back its speed so as not to choke them.) 12X writers are generally much more expensive than slower drives, with external models costing as much as $400 or $500.

6X and 8X CD recorders are much more affordable, with many available between $150 and $350. 4X CD recorders tend to be cheaper still, but with prices on the 6X and 8X recorders dropping, you may want to forgo a 4X recorder unless either your primary interest is an incredible bargain or you need a parallel or USB connection. (USB cannot reliably handle transfer speeds of faster than 4X.)

That said, you shouldn't need to put yourself into bankruptcy and buy a 12X or 16X drive unless you're burning many CDs or your time is very precious. A 2X drive takes 36 minutes to write a CD, which is far too slow for most people. The 18 minutes that a 4X drive takes is likewise too long for some people; but the difference between the 12 minutes that a 6X drive takes and the 9 minutes that an 8X drive takes is almost negligible, unless you'll be holding your breath watching the CD being burned. Still, it'll be great when some friendly hardware manufacturer comes out with a 96X drive that can spit out a smoking new CD within 30 seconds of your having set it a-burning.

CD recorders almost invariably read data at a faster rate than they write it. Some CD recorders now read up to 32X, making them almost as fast as a dedicated CD drive. Even so, unless you're out of drive bays or ports, look to add a CD recorder to your computer rather than replace your existing CD drive with a CD recorder. That way, you'll be able to duplicate a CD (assuming that you have the right to do so) or install Quake at the same time you're enjoying the cannons in Tchaikovsky's "1812 Overture."

Check out the range of CD recorders at your local computer superstore or online paradise, and choose a recorder that satisfies both your budget and your temperament.

Internal or External?

Generally speaking, an internal drive will cost you less than an external drive, but you'll need to have a drive bay free in your computer. An external drive will usually cost more, will occupy space on your desk, and will need its own power supply. In addition, most external drives are much noisier than internal drives because they contain their own fans. But if your main computer is a notebook, or if you want to be able to move the drive from computer to computer without undue effort, you'll need an external drive.

Most external drives include a cable (SCSI, parallel, USB, or FireWire) for connecting to your computer—but many external drives don't include an audio cable for connecting their audio output jacks to your sound card's input jacks, which you'll need to do if you want to get analog audio out of the drive. Before you go shopping for an external drive, determine what type of connection you'll need at the PC end (typically a ⅛-inch miniplug, but sometimes two RCA jacks). Then check the connection on the CD drive, find out whether the package includes the cable, and buy a cable if necessary.

EIDE drives are all internal. SCSI drives can be internal or external. Because the parallel port, the USB ports, and any FireWire ports are external connections, almost all of these drives are external only. (You can find internal FireWire CD-R drives if you look hard enough.)

EIDE, SCSI, Parallel Port, USB, or FireWire?

The next question is: How will you connect the drive to your computer? If you have a SCSI card in your computer, you'll probably want to get a SCSI CD recorder, because it will typically perform better *and* put much less burden on the processor than an EIDE CD recorder will.

There's one restriction you must know if you need to copy CDs: Most SCSI CD recorders will copy CDs directly only from other SCSI drives, not from EIDE drives. If you have a SCSI CD recorder and an EIDE CD drive, you'll need to copy the CD to the hard disk and then burn it to CD from there.

SCSI drives cost a bit more than EIDE drives of the same speed, but if your computer's already got SCSI, the extra cost is probably worth it. If you don't have a SCSI card, remember to factor in the cost of the card in your cost analysis. Some SCSI CD recorders come with a bundled SCSI card, but most don't, so in most cases you'll have to budget for the card as well. (Check the specifications or the box to make sure you know what you're getting.) If you don't have SCSI, but you want the best, bite the bullet and cough up the cash for a good SCSI card and SCSI CD recorder.

If you don't want to pay for SCSI but you want an internal drive, or if your CD player is EIDE and you want to do a lot of CD-to-CD duplicating, EIDE is the way to go. Before you buy, make sure that you have an EIDE connector available on your computer. If it's already chock-full of drives (most modern machines can take four EIDE devices), you won't be able to add another without sacrificing an existing one.

If you're looking at an external non-SCSI drive, your current choices are a parallel port drive, a USB drive, or a FireWire drive. The performance of parallel-port drives is miserable because the transfer speed of the parallel port is far less than that of EIDE or SCSI. But they're compatible with most computers ever built, and they get the job done—eventually. USB is much more promising, provided your computer has USB ports and your operating system supports USB. (If your desktop computer doesn't have USB ports, you can add them via an internal adapter or a PC card.) USB delivers better speed and (in theory) the convenience of being hot-pluggable.

TIP Though slow, a parallel port CD drive can have an additional benefit: If you have a computer without a built-in CD drive, such as a subnotebook, you can use a parallel port CD drive to install an operating system, or to reload it after a fatal crash. Usually, you'll need to install a driver to access the CD drive, but you can install the driver after booting from a Windows 95 or Windows 98 boot diskette—or from DOS, if you still have a copy.

Barreling down the shoulder of the hardware turnpike are FireWire CD recorders, which promise greater speed than USB drives and greater convenience than external SCSI drives. Consider a FireWire CD recorder only if you have a FireWire-capable computer or if you have another compelling reason to add FireWire to your current computer. (For example, you might be feeling a burning need to start editing digital video.)

At this writing, built-in FireWire ports are more or less confined to Macs and Sony computers, meaning that FireWire drives have a select and largely enthusiastic clientele. You can add FireWire to an existing computer via a PCI card (about $100) or a PC Card (about $150), but for most people the expense doesn't justify the relatively meager benefits. As more FireWire peripherals are introduced, though, this will change, so keep an eye on the market if you're interested.

CD-R or CD-RW?

Next, decide whether you want just a CD-recordable drive (CD-R) or a read/write drive (CD-RW). Burning a CD-R disc is essentially a one-time process: Once the data is written to the CD, you can't remove it or change it, although you can read it as many times as you want. (However, see the sidebar on packet writing.) With a CD-RW drive, on the other hand, you can write to the disc multiple times, erasing and changing the data as you see fit. (If you'd like the acronyms, CD-R discs are *Write Once, Read Multiple* media—*WORM* for short—while CD-RW discs are *Write And Read Multiple* or *WARM* media.)

Needless to say, CD-RW drives are more expensive than CD-R drives, although the gap is shrinking. CD-RW prices have dropped dramatically over the past year or so, and they now cost only a little more than CD-R drives. However, CD-RW blanks are two to three times as expensive as CD-R blanks, which you can get for less than a buck if you buy in bulk and maybe send in coupons.

For most people, the price difference on the drives is negligible, and the benefits of a CD-RW drive over a CD-ROM drive are huge. CD-RW drives can write both CD-RW discs and CD-ROM discs, making them a good investment.

Because CD-RW discs use a different technology than regular CD-ROMs, they're not as compatible with all CD-ROM drives. If you want to share a CD with someone else, a CD-R disc is a better bet than a CD-RW disc. Likewise, only the most recent audio players can play CD-RW discs, whereas most audio players can play only prerecorded CDs and CD-R discs.

Packet Writing: Flexibility for CD-R

Early recorders and CD-R software let you write only once to a disc, making for something of an exciting operation. You would line up all the files you wanted to write to the CD, double-check that they would (in theory) fit, and set the CD burning. You would then be very careful not to interrupt it before it finished...and if you were lucky, the CD would be written correctly. All too often, though, something would go wrong in the course of the burn, and you'd be left with another toasted coaster to add to your collection of AOL beer-mats.

If your recorder and operating system support *packet-writing software*, you can treat a CD-R disc more or less like a giant (and rather shiny) floppy or removable disk—with a couple of differences:

- You can write only once to any given sector of the disk, so you can't reclaim any space by deleting files that you've already written to the CD—the files will be deleted, but the space they occupied will be used.

- Each session that you write also costs you some space on the disc in overhead.

For all but the most demanding uses, these limitations aren't too serious—with 650MB to burn (yes, pun intended) on each CD, you can usually afford to squander a dozen megabytes here and there.

CD-R and CD-RW Media

If you've looked at CD-R or CD-RW discs, you'll know that most of them look very different from prerecorded audio or data CDs (*pressed* CDs). Depending on their make and type, CD-R and CD-RW discs may have a gold, green, or bluish coating on their data side. Typically, this is a polycarbonate substrate over a reflective layer of 24-carat gold (real gold, but real thin) or a silver-colored alloy.

Information is transferred to CD-R and CD-RW discs by a different process than for pressed CDs. While pressed CDs are pressed in a mold from a master CD, CD recorders and CD rewriters use a laser to burn the information onto the CD-R or CD-RW media. Pressed CDs use physically raised areas called *lands* and lowered areas called *pits* to store the encoded data. Recordable CDs have a dye layer in which the laser burns marks that have the same reflective properties as the lands and pits.

Not only do CD-R and CD-RW discs look different than pressed CDs, but they're also less robust. You can damage them more easily with extreme heat and moderate cold, by scratching or gouging them, or by leaving them in direct sunlight. The data is actually stored closer to the label side of the CD than to the business side, so if you're compelled to scratch one side of the CD, go for the business side over the label side.

When buying CD-R and CD-RW discs, you need to balance economy with quality. Beware of cheapo discs, because they may give you skips and errors—or even lose your precious music or data. If you can, buy a few discs for testing before you drop the dough for a bargain bucket-full.

One way to save some money is to buy CD-R and CD-RW discs without jewel cases. This makes for a good discount, as the jewel cases are relatively expensive to manufacture and bulky to package (and easy to break, as you no doubt know from personal experience). The discs are typically sold on a spindle, which makes for handy storage until you use them—after which you'll have to find safe storage for them on your own. (One possibility is a CD wallet, which can be especially handy if you need to take your CDs with you when you travel. If you buy one, make sure it has soft pockets that won't scratch the CDs as you insert them, and sweep out travel grit frequently.)

Some manufacturers try to sell you special CDs that are supposed to deliver better results at higher writing speeds than less worthy media. Don't take the virtues of these überCDs as gospel. On the one hand, you want your dangerously expensive CD recorder to record as fast as possible. But on the other hand, chances are that you're paying enough for regular media anyway. You may want to spend extra on CD-RW discs if you find those higher quality discs appear to deliver on the performance claim, but you're unlikely to want to spend extra on CD-R discs unless your time is mighty precious.

Operating System

Next, you need an operating system to make the hardware useful as a computer rather than as a dead weight. As with the computer hardware, which operating system you use is important only in so far as it provides the functionality you need.

Obviously, if you're interested in snappy audio and video playback, an outmoded and character-based operating system such as DOS will be of little interest. But provided the OS has a graphical interface and all the bells and whistles that a modern user expects and needs, which OS is a matter of practicality and personal preference. Windows, MacOS, and Linux pick up most of the market between them, and each has a good variety of P2P clients. Solaris and other flavors of Unix may offer compelling features for those already familiar with them. OS/2 would be a strange choice, given that it's well on its way to Davy Jones' locker, but some might find it viable for their needs.

Antivirus Software

Much more important than the operating system is an antivirus software package designed for that operating system. Both piracy and the legitimate use of the Internet and P2P technologies expose your computer to viruses of all kinds, some spread through ignorance by the infected and infectious and some spread out of malice by would-be infectors.

It *is* possible to keep your computer safe by practicing safe computing and always imagining you're wearing a condom, but if you use the Internet aggressively, your chances of not picking up something in the long run are slim. No sane pirate risks the safety of their computer by shunning the protection that antivirus software can offer, and you shouldn't either.

Which antivirus software you get depends on your operating system, your needs, and your pocket book. Bear these two things in mind:

- First, you'll probably have to pay for your antivirus software. You may be able to get by for a month or two with a trial version, but most trial versions are such determined nag-ware that you'll eventually need to upgrade.

- Second, because they dig so deeply into your operating system, antivirus packages can be difficult to uninstall. It's best not to mess with multiple antivirus packages if possible: Try to choose the antivirus package that best suits your needs and stick with it. If you do need to switch to another package, uninstall the first before installing the second. Antivirus packages are quite capable of disagreeing with each other, and the disagreements can be messy.

Most antivirus packages offer you the choice of continuous scanning of all the files you run (directly and indirectly), access (ditto), and download (likewise). Continuous scanning offers you the most protection from viruses and other nasties, and in most cases it's worth using. Turn continuous scanning off only if it slows your computer down too much (it requires constant horsepower to keep an eye on things, so your computer *will* run more slowly) or if it causes software conflicts.

If your computer is fast enough, you may be able to let the antivirus software perform scans in the background without its slowing down your work appreciably. Otherwise, schedule regular scans for times when your computer will be running (and not suspended) but not in use—for example, 3 A.M. each day.

Update your antivirus software and its virus-definition files regularly. Most packages include a facility to automatically check for updates; in most, this facility is set to run by default and to nag you to upgrade the package whenever anything new is available. This nagging is tedious but necessary, and I recommend you submit to its tender ministrations. Most experts agree that it beats being keelhauled by a virus.

Internet Connection

The next thing you need is as fast an Internet connection as you can get and can afford.

I realize I'm probably preaching to the choir on this topic, but this section provides a brief summary of the options you should be considering if your current Internet connection is a 98-pound weakling. In case you stop reading at the type of connection that seems most suitable to you, I'll start by mentioning security briefly.

Security

Some Internet connections are less secure than others—but these days, whichever kind of Internet connection you have, you should consider securing it with a firewall.

(A *firewall* is a barrier through which all Internet traffic—inbound and outbound—must pass. The firewall scrutinizes the data and denies passage to anything it doesn't like.) For a hardware firewall, evaluate products such as the Linksys Instant Broadband EtherFast Cable/DSL Router (less than $200) or the UMAX UGate series (which range from $180 to $350). For a software firewall, consider products such as BlackICE Defender from Network ICE ($39.95; `www.networkice.com`) or Zone Alarm from Zone Labs ($19.95; `www.zonealarm.com`).

Fiber

The fastest affordable Internet connection available in the U.S. is optical fiber, which can deliver speeds of around 100Mbps—the same speed as the Fast Ethernet networks used in many companies and on many campuses. This bandwidth is typically shared, so you usually won't be able to download at the full 10+MB per second it offers, but you'll find it plenty fast enough.

If you can get fiber, go for it. Unfortunately, the chances of your being able to get it are minimal at this writing. Some new housing communities in high-tech areas (such as Silicon Valley) are being built with fiber to the home, and some apartment buildings in major cities are being refitted with fiber. But if you live anywhere else, you're apt to be straight out of luck.

As you'd expect, fiber tends to be more expensive than other technologies, but when it's run to the home (rather than to a business), it's usually more or less affordable. You may need to cut back on your daily double latte in order to make the monthly payments, but almost certainly you'll find the sacrifice worthwhile.

Most people shudder at the thought of living in Singapore, but if you want to live in a place in which most dwellings offer fiber Internet connections capable of sustained sizzling speeds, it's the place to be. If you decide to move, be sure not to chew gum or spit on the sidewalk.

Cable Modem

If cable modem access is available where you live, go for it. After fiber, cable provides the fastest affordable residential access—up to several megabits (millions of bits) per second.

Cable has three main drawbacks:

☠ First, the bandwidth is shared with your neighbors, so if everyone gets online at the same time, the speed drops. Ask the cable company what the network's capacity is, among how many people share that capacity, and what the minimum bandwidth they guarantee you is. (They may not guarantee any minimum bandwidth.) If you find the speed dropping to unacceptable levels, lobby the cable company vociferously to add bandwidth to your loop. Get your neighbors to lobby too if you can pry them away from their computers.

☠ Second, many cable companies implement an *upload speed cap*, which limits the amount of data you can upload per second, typically to prevent you from running a Web server or FTP server. If you're neither going to be running a server nor sharing many files via P2P technologies, this shouldn't be a problem, but make sure that you know what the company's policy is before you sign up.

☠ Third, because the wire is shared, your computer is essentially networked with your neighborhood, so it's vital that you use a firewall to secure it. Also, be sure to turn off file-sharing on any computer that's connected to the Internet via a cable modem.

Digital Subscriber Line (DSL)

If digital subscriber line (DSL) connectivity is available and affordable where you live, get it. DSL typically offers between 384kbps and 1.5Mbps downstream (to the consumer) and slower upstream (to the ISP) speeds. At this writing, the Baby Bells are vying with the cable companies for high-speed customers, so the cost of DSL is reasonable—from $35 to $50 per month for good service, including an account with their ISP.

Because DSL is always on, your computer is continuously connected to the Internet, so there's a threat of your computer being attacked across the wire. With DSL, the threat is significantly lower than with cable (because the wire isn't shared in most U.S. implementations), but you'll still need a firewall.

Unlike with cable, you're not on the same local network as your neighbors, so the bandwidth isn't shared, and you should be able to get the minimum guaranteed rate (sometimes referred to as the *committed information rate* or *CIR*) any time of the day or night.

The main disadvantage of DSL is that it works only within a relatively short distance from the telephone company's central office, which means in effect that it's confined to urban locations. Some non-telco DSL providers are more aggressive with the distance than the telcos, but you'll typically have to pay more, and you'll get a lower-speed connection. If you live out in the sticks, you're almost certainly beyond the range of DSL.

Integrated Services Digital Network (ISDN)

If you can't get cable or a DSL, your next choice should be ISDN (Integrated Services Digital Network). An ISDN is a digital line that's not as fast as a DSL but is more widely available, especially for people outside major metropolitan areas. ISDN's *basic rate interface (BRI)* provides two *bearer channels* that deliver 64kbps each, plus a 16kbps signaling channel, so it delivers decent speeds when both bearer channels are open. The signaling channel is more formally called a *data channel*, and you'll sometimes hear BRI referred to as *2B+D*—two bearer channels plus one data channel.

Check the prices before you order ISDN: It's traditionally been a business service, and it can be expensive, with most companies levying per-minute charges for each channel.

The good news about ISDN (apart from its wide availability) is that most implementations are symmetrical, so you get the same speed upstream as downstream.

Satellite Solutions

If you're too rural to get ISDN, or if ISDN is too slow for you, consider one of the satellite solutions available, such as DirecPC. These solutions typically offer speeds of around 400kbps downstream, so they can be good if you need to download large chunks of data (such as audio or video files).

Most current satellite solutions have one major drawback: The satellite provides only downlink capabilities, so you have to use your phone line to send data to your ISP to tell them which information to deliver by satellite. But given that your only alternative is likely to be a modem connection, you may find this flaw quite sufferable. DirecPC currently offers plans starting at $19.99 a month for a truly miserable number of hours. Make sure that the plan you choose provides enough hours each month so that you don't start incurring expensive extra hours every month on your normal level of usage.

Here's another thing to watch for: Some satellite services have a *fair access policy* (FAP) by which they reserve the right to throttle back your download speed if you continuously run it full bore—in other words, you can have your 400kbps (or whatever speed the provider offers), but you can't have it all the time. This can put a serious crimp into your ability to download a massive amount of audio or video every day via a satellite hookup. So read your signup agreement carefully for details of the fair access policy, and be especially wary of clauses that allow the service provider to modify the terms of the contract without your explicit consent.

Another alternative that may be coming to a satellite near you in the not-too-distant future is a *two-way* satellite connection. It's available now in very restricted areas and is expensive, but like all things computer, the cost will drop in the future. Make yourself aware of all relevant restrictions and access policies before you buy.

Maximizing Your Modem Connection

If you're stuck with modem access, here are four things worth trying to make the most of it:

- ☠ First, try to get 56K modem access—the fastest possible. As you probably know, 56K modems are limited by the FCC to downloading at a little over 53kbps and by line limitations to uploading at 33.6kbps. Still, you want every kilobit you can get your hands on.

- ☠ Second, consider getting a *dual-line modem* that bonds together two conventional modems (on two separate phone lines) to increase your speed. You need an ISP that supports modem bonding for this to succeed—and two phone lines, of course. (You'll also hear dual-line modems referred to as *shotgun modems,* after the hunting shotguns with two barrels side by side used in the days before the shotgun became a weapon of urban combat and pacification.) Alternatively, if your operating system and your ISP support multilink, get a second modem and phone line, activate multilink, and use both modems at once. (Windows 98, Windows Me, and Windows 2000 all support multilink.)

☠ Whatever speed modem you have, make sure you're getting maximum performance out of it. Use a utility such as TweakDUN (DUN is the acronym for *dial-up networking*) or MTU Speed Pro (MTU is the abbreviation for *maximum transfer unit*). Both TweakDUN and MTU Speed Pro tune your TCP/IP settings to make sure that your connection is as efficient as possible. TweakDUN and MTU Speed are shareware and are available from many shareware archives. They're not infallible, but they're worth a try.

If you are (still) using Windows 95, you should definitely give one of these utilities a whirl, because the TCP/IP settings in Windows 95 were set to be less than optimal. This problem has been fixed in later versions of Windows, but depending on your connection, you may still need to tweak some parameters.

☠ If your connection is less speedy than you'd like, get a download-scheduling utility such as GetRight from Headlight Software (`www.getright.com`) or AutoFTP from PrimaSoft (`www.primasoft.com`) that will let you line up your downloads to perform at a time when you don't need to do other things on your computer. For example, you can arrange to download a hundred megabytes of music at an antisocial hour in the early morning, when your corner of the Internet is likely to be less busy.

E-mail Account

You're barely alive without an e-mail address these days, so it should hardly be surprising that every pirate needs one. Actually, every pirate needs several e-mail addresses, with at least one or two devoted to piratical activities.

Because the pirate needs to expose an e-mail address to anyone they want to let contact them via e-mail, chances are good that sooner or later they'll share an e-mail address with some people they never want to hear from again. To prevent themselves hearing from such people again, the pirate can use spam filters (available with most decent e-mail applications), but before too long, they'll probably abandon the burned e-mail address and start using another. This is easy enough to do—but it means that they'd be insane to use their main e-mail address for any piratical correspondence.

With the number of weird people on the Net, you'll probably find yourself needing to close down e-mail addresses and create new ones—even if you stay firmly on the right side of the law.

Online e-mail services such as HotMail (`www.hotmail.com`), HushMail (`www.hushmail.com`), Yahoo! Mail (`mail.yahoo.com`), and their assorted brethren are your friends. With these services, you can easily create e-mail accounts as you need them—and unless your conscience makes a coward of you, you don't need to give them any real information. The terms and conditions of most of these services make you agree not to use them for illegal purposes—but should you feel compelled to flout such a commitment, you'd be far from the first. And when the e-mail address gets too public, or gets burned, you can abandon it and create another at a moment's notice.

HushMail is a particular favorite, as it gives you the option of creating an account with an automatically generated address name without your needing to supply any personal information. It also lets you send encrypted e-mail to other HushMail users, thus helping you prevent people from eavesdropping on your communications.

If you're working in newsgroups, you'll typically want to add some nonsense to the e-mail address you expose to prevent your address from being harvested by spammers but allow sentient humans to establish the real e-mail address with a minimal application of sentience. For example, if your e-mail address is `peterpiper@pacbell.net`, you might post with an address of `peterpiper@nospam.pacbell.net` and add a note saying "remove nospam from the address when replying." This is enough to defeat most bots, though nospam is getting long in the tooth at this writing—so you might want to try a custom addition to your address.

Passwords

To keep their computers, e-mail accounts, and P2P accounts secure, pirates need unbreakable passwords. To protect yourself, you'll need unbreakable passwords too.

These are the golden rules of creating passwords:

- Create a password of an appropriate length. Many ISPs and services will let you create passwords of any length between 6 characters and 15 characters. Treat 6 characters as the absolute minimum. Aim for a password of at least 8 characters, and more like 12 if you're feeling insecure. Passwords of 5 characters or fewer are relatively easy to crack by brute force; passwords of 6 characters are much harder; and longer passwords are much harder yet. If you're allowed to create a password of any length, be sensible and limit the password to a length that you can remember and type without undue stumbling.

No password is totally secure. Any password can be broken by an attacker who has sufficient time, determination, and computer operations. But most crackers will not be prepared to spend more than a few minutes (or, at the most, hours) on any given password, and will swiftly move on to other pastures that should prove greener. So your goal is to keep your passwords secure against random attackers, not against the NSA. If the NSA is on your case, you'll have much worse things to worry about than whether your passwords are strong enough. (Hint: Start by dismantling your computer and physically destroying the hard disks. As Monica Lewinsky found out, formatted-over hard disks can still be read by experts.)

- Never use a real word in any language for a password. Real words can be broken easily by a dictionary attack: The attacker runs a script that tries to match each word in a specified dictionary with your password until it gets a hit. The dictionary can be in any language or a mixture of languages, and will usually contain all popular passwords in all major languages at its beginning.

- Instead, use symbols (@, $, %, ^, !, &, and so on) as substitute characters in a word or phrase, or reduce a phrase or sentence to its initial letters or key letters. Mix letters and numbers. Use uppercase and lowercase creatively. Alternatively, open a text editor, close your eyes, and whale randomly at the keyboard for a few seconds, making sure to hit the Shift key at intervals. Then pick a particularly cryptic part of the result to use as a password.

- ☠ Never use any example password that you see, no matter how compelling it may seem. For example, books on security provide example passwords. These may look wonderfully cryptic, but you should assume that they're all known to crackers and included in cracking dictionaries.

- ☠ Never use any option that offers to save a password for you. For example, Windows offers to store your dial-up passwords so that you can access your dial-up accounts more easily. These passwords not only let unauthorized users of your computer access your dial-up accounts effortlessly, but also can be cracked easily by commonly available programs.

- ☠ Use a different password for each account. That way, if one password is compromised, the others will still be secure. (Yes, of course it's difficult. If security were effortless, nobody in the world would have a problem with it.)

- ☠ Change your passwords frequently, even if you have no reason to suspect that they've been compromised.

- ☠ As soon as you suspect that a password may have been compromised, change it. Also change any associated passwords.

- ☠ Never repeat a password you've used in the past. Create an entirely new password each time you change a password.

- ☠ Memorize your passwords. Never write them down. If you write a password down, you've compromised it. If you must write a password down, keep it in the safest of places. If that place is virtual rather than physical, protect your password stash with another password—a good one.

- ☠ Never tell anybody any of your passwords—not even the ones you've stopped using. (They might be able to use these passwords to guess at your newer passwords.)

- ☠ Don't let yourself be social-engineered. *Social engineering* is the art of extracting passwords from the unsuspecting by posing as someone in authority—for example, as a system administrator or a troubleshooter for your ISP. No ISP and no system administrator should need to be given your password over the phone or in person.

Sad but true: Between 90 and 95 percent of all passwords are the same 100 words. Crackers try these popular passwords first because they work so often. Don't let yourself be numbered among these foolish users.

If you can follow the simple advice in the list above, you'll be ahead of 99 percent of the computer-using population—and measurably more secure than any of them.

Paranoia

I expect you know what I'm going to say here, and indeed I can't resist it: *You need to be paranoid, because they are out to get you.*

Digital pirates need to be especially paranoid, because the law is out to get them. As you saw in Chapter 2, "Crime and Punishment: Piracy and the Law," the penalties for piracy can be severe—though not as severe as when piracy meant high treason and hanging. But felony convictions, hefty fines, and imprisonment are enough to quail most modern mortals' hearts.

Before you go online, and even if you never intend to perform any activities approaching the piratical, you need to have an understanding of basic computer and Internet security issues. Briefly, anyone accessing the Internet needs to be aware that any file they download may harbor a virus or a macro virus that could perform any of a number of unpleasant actions on their computer. Web pages can contain malicious scripts or ActiveX controls that can damage your computer or wipe out your hard drive.

In this book, we won't get into details of the many threats to your computer. (If you don't know the basics of what's threatening your digital existence, grab a copy of *PC Confidential*, also published by Sybex.) But here are some basic precautions that you should take:

- Run antivirus software all the time if possible. If all the time isn't possible, quarantine the files you download and run them past your antivirus software before you try to do anything with them.

- Remember that file extensions in Windows do not necessarily reflect the contents of the file. Anybody can give an executable (EXE) file an apparently harmless extension, such as ZIP, JPG, AVI, or MP3. When you double-click the file to open it in the application the extension appears to indicate, the executable will run. It's safer to open the files directly from the associated application—but it's safer still to use your antivirus software to root out masked marauders before trying to open them.

☠ Treat all unsolicited files with the utmost suspicion. Your favorite deity may be on your side and you may receive unexpected files containing invaluable treasures, but that doesn't happen to most people. You're far more likely to be sent an infected document or a disguised executable file than a delightful treat—even if it is your birthday today.

☠ Beware of macro viruses. Any word-processing document (for example, a Word document), spreadsheet (for example, a 1-2-3 spreadsheet), presentation, or other complex file can contain a macro virus that can rampage all over your computer before you can do anything about it.

☠ Be sensible in your surfing. If a Web site or FTP site promises something unlikely to be true, there's almost certainly a catch. In particular, beware of sites that offer nude or sex pictures of non-porn celebrities. At best, you'll get a disappointing shot of a celebrity look-alike or some crudely assembled montage of the celebrity's face on a performer's body. At worst, or at the same time, you'll get an endless procession of browser windows designed to distract you while a script is run to find anything interesting on your computer—passwords, credit-card numbers, financial information, say—or install a malicious ActiveX control or script.

Up Next

This chapter has discussed the basic hardware and connectivity tools that pirates need—and that most legitimate users of P2P technologies need as well: a computer, a suitable operating system, and the fastest Internet connection they can get their hands on. It has also discussed how to protect yourself by using antivirus software, choosing effective passwords, using Web-based e-mail accounts, and maintaining a healthy sense of paranoia.

It's time to get into the realities of piracy. The next chapter covers the early days of piracy, in which pirates used crude tools such as e-mail and newsgroups to transfer files. Don't worry that these tools are out of date—they're still effective today, and you'll almost certainly need to use them from time to time. Turn the page.

A Pirate Speaks: The College Kid Pirate

Hey, I go to college, you know. When you take my tuition and my room and board and my books and my beer money all into account, I'm running at –$100 a month. On a good month.

Music's a big part of my life. Same goes for all the kids in the dorm here. The Internet allows us to do the things that our parents did with tape, only with less hassle. Everybody in the old days used to tape their albums on cassettes and pass them around. Nowadays the technology's just different. Nowadays people have CDs. They rip those CDs, burn their own CDs, pass those around, and put them on each other's computer. Everybody has a computer nowadays. So I've got a bunch of MP3 files on my hard drive and I listen to them while I do work. I've got a little player, a Rio, that I'll use while I go out and exercise or I'm walking around campus. I guess I just don't have the money to buy CDs. That's just the way college life is.

All the music is, like, *available*. We've got Internet connections through the university. I can download pretty much everything I want. It's just there. And if I don't download it, well, somebody else has downloaded it and then I just get the files from them. Burning a CD costs less than a buying a rubber nowadays, so it's within my means.

I realize that the artists aren't getting the money they should from me, but you know what? From what I see on MTV and E!, they're doing okay, and I'm not. So maybe after I graduate and get a good job, then I'll stop doing this. But in the meantime, hey, who am I really hurting? The artists are still making their money from the majority of people, and I get to listen to music I like. I'm not downloading albums and creating a huge album library of stolen material. I download the songs that I like, the pop songs that are out now, and some older classic tunes that I like. I'm constantly adding and deleting songs, and moving things around.

A Pirate Speaks: The College Kid Pirate (*continued*)

To tell you the honest-to-God truth, I don't see that I'm hurting anybody. It's just like taping a song from the radio and putting it on a cassette. I mean, how is it different from that? My parents did that, and their parents before them did that. I don't see why that's a big deal. I don't see why people should be making a big fuss about it. My room isn't filled with, you know, 2000 CDs of stolen material. I've got a couple hundred MP3s on my computer and, you know, a couple of CDs of stuff that I've burned that I like a lot and that I put on my Rio.

So what's the big deal? People want to call me a pirate, fine. But as far as I see it, I'm not doing anything that's any different from any other college kid any time in the last 30 years.

Chapter 4

The Early Days of Piracy

This chapter discusses the tools and techniques pirates used to exchange files in the early days of piracy: e-mail, newsgroups, FTP sites, dial-up connections and direct connections, and some physical media.

If these tools were what pirates used in the early days, why discuss them here? Not just for the historical context, fascinating though that may be. Most of these tools and techniques are still relevant today. In many cases, there are now easier alternatives that you'll want to try first. But when these fail, chances are that you'll need to fall back on the tools discussed in this chapter.

One tool that this chapter *doesn't* discuss is the BBS—bulletin-board system. In the 1980s and early 1990s, BBSes were widely used, widely useful, and very influential, providing virtual communities and access to information and software. With the growth of the Internet, and in particular the Web, in the mid to late 1990s, BBSes suffered a near-terminal decline. Now at the dawn of the 21st century, some BBSes are still operational, but the Internet has sidelined (or absorbed) the vast majority of them.

Transferring Files via E-mail

One of the most basic ways of transferring files from one person to another is via e-mail: Attach the file or files to a message and send the message on its way. In most e-mail software, the process of attaching the file is trivial, so I won't discuss it here.

The first advantage of transferring files via e-mail is that you can get them directly to your intended recipient or recipients (barring e-mail screw-ups). The second advantage is that the two (or more) of you don't have to be online at the same time;

each recipient can receive the message and its attached file any time after the sender has sent it (and it has been transferred from mail server to mail server). The third advantage is that sharing files via e-mail is relatively discreet: When you're sending files, you have to know the e-mail addresses of the recipients, so you know who the recipients are. (I know this is obvious—but contrast P2P file-sharing technologies, in which each user shares files in a public forum full of people they don't know.) So you control the distribution of the files. And if you choose, you can also encrypt the files you send so that no snooper can see what they contain.

There are two disadvantages to transferring files via e-mail. First, most ISPs block files larger than a certain size as e-mail attachments because they play havoc with their servers. This means that the sender has to chop up large files into a number of smaller ones in order to get them through the filter of the mail server, and the recipient needs to put the files back together again in the right order.

Vulnerability Factor: Transferring Files via E-mail

Transferring files via e-mail has a low vulnerability rating compared to most other ways of transferring files. You know the recipients—by e-mail address if not by anything else—so unless you're dragging your knuckles on the ground, you should be able to make sure you're not sharing files directly with the RIAA or the FBI.

Unless you send files massive enough or massed enough to choke your ISP's mail server, you're unlikely to draw unwelcome attention from your ISP. And unless one of the recipients rats you out, you shouldn't get any unwanted attention from the other end either.

Needless to say, your ISP can monitor your behavior bit by bit as usual, and any agency with sufficient authority can tap into your data stream at your ISP and see what you're doing. To protect yourself, you may want to encrypt your messages and the files you send by using PGP or a similar tool.

Second, most e-mail packages don't give the recipient warning before trying to download attachments. So when you check your e-mail, you can find yourself downloading a giant attachment and tying up your Internet connection at an inconvenient time. Some e-mail packages offer options for leaving messages of more than a specified size on the server rather than downloading them immediately. (For example, Eudora offers an option named Skip Messages over NN K in Size.) By turning such an option on and specifying a size larger than the largest message you expect to receive but smaller than an attachment that will choke your Internet connection, you can preserve your mail stream and your sanity.

In order to get large files through a mail server without its barfing on them, you may need to chop the files up into pieces. You'll find many shareware and freeware tools on the Net for breaking files into pieces and then reassembling them. Chances are your tool of choice for making ZIP files can do the job. Test the tool with a few files you don't care about before you entrust any vital file to it. If the reassembly operation doesn't go perfectly, or if any of the pieces of the file are missing or have a bit or two flipped, the resulting file won't be worth much.

Transferring Files via Newsgroups

Another old-style but still effective method of transferring files from one user to another is newsgroups. If you've used the Internet a bit, you're probably familiar with newsgroups and can skip the brief introduction in the next subsection. If you're not familiar with newsgroups, read on.

What Are Newsgroups?

Internet newsgroups are a very loose agglomeration of discussion areas based on the Network News Transport Protocol (NNTP to its friends). The collection of publicly accessible newsgroups is called USENET. A newsgroup consists of the messages (and sometimes attachments) that people post to the list. These messages, often referred to as *posts*, are available to anyone who chooses to take part in the group.

Internet newsgroups encompass most every topic under the sun. In the olden days of the early 1990s, newsgroups were divided up into a relatively formalized informal structure based around a dozen or so hierarchies of newsgroups with names such as `alt` (alternative topics), `biz` (business topics), `comp` (computer topics), and assorted others, with many groups in subgroups under each hierarchy. Nowadays, in concert with the near-anarchy of the Web, newsgroups are often named capriciously, so the best way to find a newsgroup covering topics you're interested in is to search for keywords (or get a recommendation from a friend).

Before you get involved with newsgroups, keep the following in mind:

☠ First, USENET newsgroups are public. In most cases, anyone who can get online can post to them. You're likely to meet a wide variety of people in them. Some of the people post offensive messages and attachments. There's not much you can do about this except not read the messages, not view the attachments, or not visit those newsgroups.

In addition to public, free-for-all newsgroups, there are also members-only newsgroups that you may be lucky enough to be invited to join. If so, behave yourself.

☠ Second, much of the information you find in newsgroups is incomplete, inaccurate, wrong, lies, disinformation, or even advertising. I doubt you believe everything you read on the Web; you'd be wise to apply an even greater standard of disbelief to newsgroups. If you're just looking for files, truth or lies might seem not to matter—but keep in mind that any files you download could be something other than they claim to be. For example, a hot video clip might turn out to be a virus or Trojan horse (or it might simply be infected with one or the other). An MP3 file might turn out to be a disk destroyer.

☠ Third, newsgroups tend to get archived. (For an example of an archive, point your Web browser at Deja.com, `http://www.deja.com`, where you can search through a truly frightening number of postings recent and ancient.) This archiving means that every throwaway posting has a good chance of remaining available more or less forever—or at least long enough to severely embarrass the poster. Before you dash off an inflammatory post or attach a few illegal files, remember that the result may stick around to haunt you for years.

☠ Fourth, spammers use *bots* (robot programs) to harvest e-mail addresses from newsgroups, both for direct use and for selling to other people. (Perhaps you've already received spam offering you *2 million valid e-mail addresses for only $29.99*? Right—many of those e-mail addresses will have been harvested from newsgroups.) This harvesting means that if you expose your real e-mail address, you're likely to get spam almost immediately from the current crop of spammers. As discussed in Chapter 3, "The Pirate's Basic Tools," you'll want either to doctor your e-mail address to defeat the bots (for example, by adding rubbish such as `nospam` or `removethis` to it) or to use an e-mail address that you don't mind abandoning when it draws flak.

☠ Fifth, many of the more specialized newsgroups tend to attract an expert audience that doesn't tolerate off-topic or ill-considered questions well. Before posting, be sure to read the frequently asked questions list (the FAQ) for the newsgroup, and check through its archives to make sure that the topic of your posting (a) is on topic for the newsgroup, and (b) hasn't been answered five times already in the last three months.

Advantages and Disadvantages of Transferring Files via Newsgroups

These are the advantages of transferring files via newsgroups:

☠ First, newsgroups offer an efficient one-to-many distribution system: One person posts a message or attachment, and the rest of the world can read it or download it.

☠ Second, newsgroups are asynchronous: The poster and the downloader don't need to be online at the same time. If a file is listed in your newsreader, it will most likely be available for long enough for you to download it. By contrast, with Napster and other P2P technologies, files become unavailable the moment the user providing them goes offline—which they can do at any moment.

☠ Third, newsgroups are (usually) public. You can share information and files with people whom you don't know (and who don't know you), and you can receive information and files from people you don't know.

☠ Fourth, newsgroups are categorized (albeit loosely) and are searchable and browseable. So if you're interested in a particular type of file, you can probably find a suitable newsgroup to look in. For example, if you're interested in 1980s music, you'll be able to search for specific tracks or bands. You'll also be able to browse assorted music from that decade.

These are the disadvantages of transferring files via newsgroups:

☠ First, you don't know where the files are going. If the files are ones you can legally distribute, this may not concern you, but it makes newsgroups a poor choice for spreading files illegally.

☠ Second, your misdemeanors (or felonies) will be archived. So posting a file illegally today could come back to haunt you in a few years' time. (You can protect yourself to an extent by adding to your posts the "X-no-archive: yes" header, flag to indicate that the message is not to be archived. However, the archiving software may or may not pay attention to the flag.)

☠ Third, you need to protect yourself against bots, spam, and other unwelcome attentions.

Less of a disadvantage, but more than relevant, is the fact that at this writing, newsgroups are declining as a method of transferring files. There are several reasons for this:

☠ First, newsgroups are a little more difficult and far more laborious to use than P2P technologies such as Napster and audioGnome.

☠ Second, depending on what you're looking for, the selection of files on newsgroups can be poor. Where the selection is poor, it tends to get poorer in a vicious circle as more and more users transfer their attention to P2P technologies instead.

☠ Third, newsgroups are traditionally a noisy place, with lots of spam, cluelessness, and flaming, so hanging around them looking for files can be more of a chore than a pleasure.

☠ Fourth, many of the files that you'll find in newsgroups are illegal copies of copyrighted material.

That said, you can still find a good amount of interesting material posted to newsgroups. Current versions of the three main browsers—Netscape, Microsoft Internet Explorer, and Opera from Opera Software—each provides a full-featured newsreader application, so chances are you already have one available to you. If not, consider getting a specialized newsreader, such as Forté's Free Agent (`www.forteinc.com`).

Posting Files to Newsgroups

Posting files to newsgroups could hardly be simpler: All you do is create a post to the appropriate newsgroup, then issue an Attach command (or local equivalent), specify the file you want to attach, and send it on its way. Figure 4.1 shows an example of using Netscape on Linux to post an MP3 file to a newsgroup.

Figure 4.1

Posting an MP3 file to a newsgroup

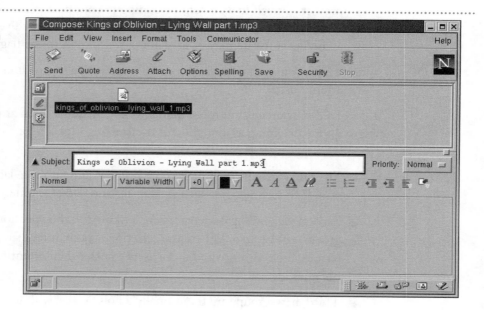

Finding Files on Newsgroups

Finding files on newsgroups is also straightforward, though it takes more work than most P2P technologies.

Here's an example of finding MP3 files via newsgroups. For variety, I'll use Internet Explorer's Outlook Express newsreader on Windows, but you can follow similar techniques with the other newsreaders.

1. Start your newsreader.

2. Display the Newsgroup Subscriptions dialog box by clicking the Newsgroups button or by choosing Tools ➤ Newsgroups.

3. Enter **mp3** in the Display Newsgroups Which Contain text box in Internet Explorer.

4. Select the Also Search Descriptions check box to have Outlook Express search the descriptions of the newsgroups as well as the names. Figure 4.2 shows the current selection of newsgroups devoted to MP3 files.

Figure 4.2

Search for MP3 to find the newsgroups devoted to MP3 files.

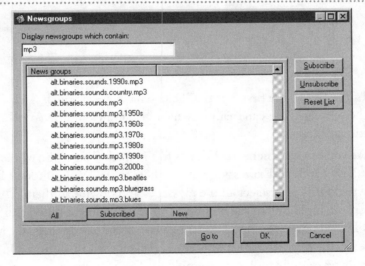

5. To subscribe to a newsgroup, double-click its name, or select it and click the Subscribe button. But first you'll probably want to examine it by selecting it and clicking the Go To button. If you find it useful, then subscribe to it.

When you visit one of the newsgroups, you'll find all sorts of files, as you see in Figure 4.3, which shows the `alt.binaries.sounds.mp3.1980s` newsgroup. Odds are that all these files are illegal—but if you search the right places, you'll be able to turn up legal files as well.

Figure 4.3
Many of the MP3 files that you'll find in newsgroups are illegal.

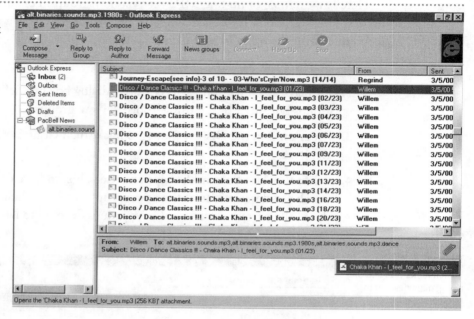

In the figure, the first part of Chaka Khan's classic track "I Feel for You" is attached to the message. You can easily download it by clicking the Attachment button in Outlook Express.

As you can see, there are 23 parts to the track. To get the whole thing, you would first have Outlook Express download all 23 parts. With Outlook Express, the easiest way to do this is to select all the messages and download them. Once the download is complete, highlight all the messages, right-click one of them, and select Combine and Decode from the context menu. Make sure that the message parts are in the right order in the dialog box that appears, and click the OK button. Outlook Express then uses its reassembly tool to reassemble the file from its component parts.

In the Outlook Express dialog box that appears, right-click on the filename listed in the Attach field to save it to your hard disk. Choose the location provided or use the Browse button and the resulting dialog box to browse to another location. Then click the Save button.

Alternatively, when you have a file that has been encoded and received as multiple parts and stored on your hard disk, you can use a slicer/rejoiner program to perform the combine and decode operation. Remember to make sure all the parts for the file you want are available before you start the download process—otherwise, you're wasting your time and bandwidth.

Vulnerability Factor: Transferring Files via Newsgroups

When you post files to newsgroups, your vulnerability is high. As mentioned earlier, messages and files posted to newsgroups remain in the newsgroups for a while (how long depends on the people running the newsgroups) and may be archived. Even if you don't use your real e-mail address for posting, or if you use a real address that you don't mind burning in due course, your ISP will be able to tie your ISP account to the files you have posted.

You're much less vulnerable when you download files posted to a newsgroup. As usual, your ISP can track your every virtual breath if they so choose, but they probably have better things to do than watch every byte that an individual user downloads. Unless, of course, some agency has leaned on your ISP to monitor a particular user....

FTP Sites

FTP sites have played a vital role in the spread of piracy. The file transfer protocol (FTP) has been a mainstay of the Internet pretty much since its inception. FTP sites have been around for a long time, but they're still popular today because of their simplicity and speed.

If you're a purist, you'll want to use a dedicated FTP client to access FTP sites. If you're a normal person, you'll probably be content to use the less-capable FTP client built into your Web browser for browsing FTP sites and downloading files from them. Figure 4.4 shows Netscape accessing the SunSITE Northern Europe FTP site. As you can see, the effect isn't pretty, but you can easily see what's available. To download a file, simply drill down to it and click (or double-click) its listing.

Figure 4.4

You can use a browser such as Netscape to access FTP sites.

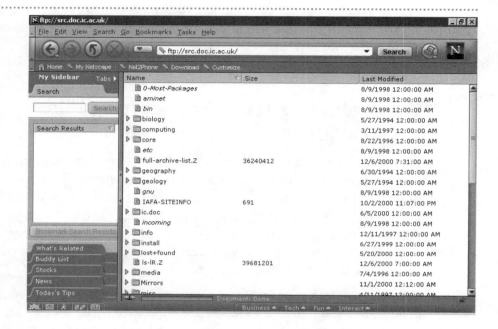

Vulnerablity Factor: Transferring Files via FTP Sites

When you're transferring files via FTP sites, you need to manage the amount of information your computer gives out.

As you know from the bucketful of cookies on your computer, Web browsers are relatively chatty. They make available to Web sites some information in the first place, including the e-mail address you've given them and your IP address. They store information from Web sites when requested (unless you've turned off cookies). And when a Web site asks for the information it (or one of its associated sites) has stored in a cookie, the Web browser surrenders it happily.

To minimize the amount of information given out when you access an FTP site, you'll do better to use a dedicated FTP client than a Web browser. All the same, each FTP transfer will be logged by the FTP site,

Vulnerablity Factor: Transferring Files via FTP Sites (*continued*)

which will probably store the username and password you've supplied and the IP address you're using. For anonymous FTP, the username isn't tied to you, and the password won't be unless you let your FTP client submit your real e-mail address as the password. (Hint: Don't.) The IP address can be tied to you as usual—and of course your ISP can track all your online movements should they be provoked into so doing.

Figure 4.5 shows Internet Explorer on the Mac accessing the same FTP site. It looks a bit different than the Netscape view, but it works in the same way.

Figure 4.5

Internet Explorer for the Mac accessing the same FTP site as in Figure 4.4

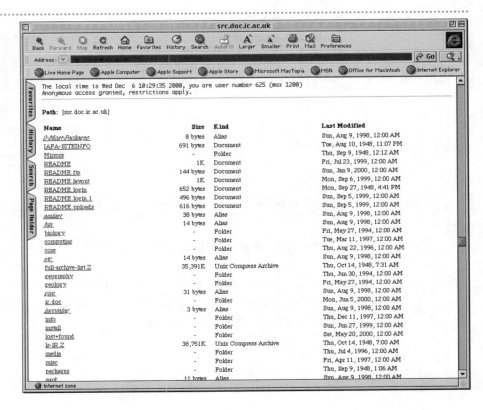

For uploading files (should you have files you can legally distribute), you may be able to get by with your Web browser, but a dedicated FTP client will give you more flexibility.

Windows and Linux come with FTP capabilities built in. The Windows FTP client is command-line only, so you'll need to be familiar with commands such as `ls` (to list the contents of the current directory), `lcd` (to display or set the local current directory), `get` and `mget` (to download files), and `put` and `mput` (to upload files). If you're comfortable with the command line, you'll find the Windows FTP client effective and fast. If not, consider getting a graphical FTP client, such as CuteFTP from GlobalSCAPE (www.globalscape.com or www.cuteftp.com). Figure 4.6 shows CuteFTP accessing the SunSITE Northern Europe FTP site.

Figure 4.6

If you don't like the Windows command-line client, get a graphical client such as CuteFTP.

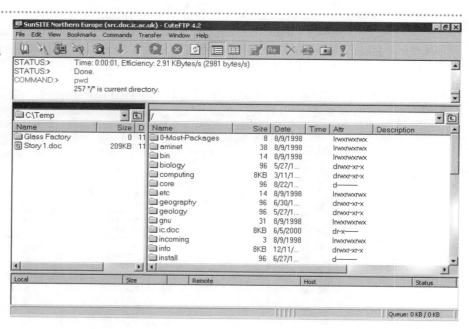

Needless to say, Linux comes with a command-line FTP client, but most distributions of Linux include one or more graphical FTP clients as well. For example, Red Hat includes the gFTP client shown in Figure 4.7.

Figure 4.7

Most distributions of Linux come with a graphical FTP client, such as gFTP, which ships with Red Hat.

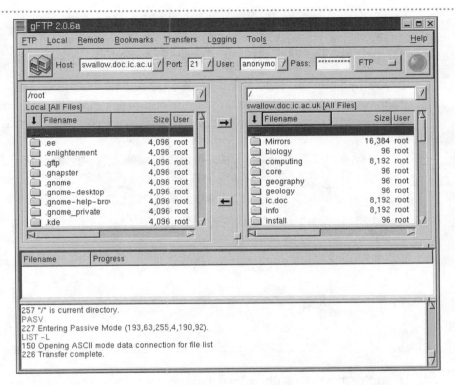

On the Mac, Internet Explorer and Netscape Navigator have FTP clients built in. If you're looking for a dedicated client, consider Anarchie, Fetch, or one of their competitors.

Beware Ratio Sites

Beware any *ratio site*—a site that lets you download files only after you've uploaded some files to the site. Ratio sites get their name because they typically allow you to download at some ratio to what you upload. For example, a ratio site might allow you to download 3MB for every 1MB you upload.

Beware Ratio Sites (*continued*)

If you're using an FTP client such as CuteFTP, you may see a message such as the one shown in the Login Messages dialog box below (which is demanding music with menace), when you run into a ratio site.

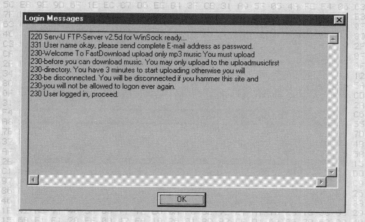

If you're trying to download from a Web browser, you may see messages such as the one shown below in Internet Explorer, saying that "the server returned extended information." This doesn't necessarily mean that the site is demanding an upload, but when you're trying to access an MP3 FTP site, it's very likely.

Beware Ratio Sites (*continued*)

Netscape gives a different message when it runs into this problem, as shown in the message box below. The message is perhaps a little misleading in that we know the file is there—we're just not allowed to get at it.

If you have music that you can legally distribute, feel free to go ahead and upload some. But keep in mind that because most people do not have music that they can legally distribute, these sites are pushing many people into uploading music illegally so that they can download music—which too might be illegal.

Direct Dial-Up Connections and Direct Connections

Back in the 1980s, before local area networks became ubiquitous, the Internet became widespread, and removable media gained useful capacity, pirates used dial-up connections and direct connections to transfer files from one computer to another.

Direct Dial-Up Connections

In the old style of dial-up connections, pirates would direct modem connections to connect two computers. Instead of each computer connecting to an ISP, and the computers finding each other via the Internet and the wonders of TCP/IP, one computer would dial the other computer's modem-line number, and the other computer would receive the call.

The advantages of such direct dial-up connections are that they're simple and secure. Assuming both computers have working modems and basic communications software, the connection is no harder to set up than a regular voice call. And if you know you can trust the person at the other end, the connection is secure. Short of the feds' tapping your phone lines, nobody can tell what you're doing on the connection—there's no ISP to monitor you.

The main disadvantages of such connections are the cost (which can be high) and the speed (which is almost guaranteed to be low). Because the call is essentially a regular circuit-switched call across the public telephone network rather than a packet-switched call across the Internet, you pay conventional phone charges for the call. So if the call is long distance, you pay regular long-distance charges. And because the speed of the connection is limited by the slower of the two modems used (and by any inadequacies of the phone lines), 33.6K is as good as it gets. (You'll recall that 56K modems require special equipment at one end—usually the ISP's end—in order to deliver better than 33.6K downstream, and they're limited to 33.6K upstream.)

Direct Connections

In any case, direct dial-up connections saw their heyday long before the 56K modem was a twinkle in the eye of any but the most optimistic telecom engineer. In the early 1990s, a 14.4K modem was hot technology, and most connections were between 2400bps and 9600bps. As you can imagine, transferring files of any size at those speeds took a while.

If you could get the computers within spitting distance of each other, you could speed things up a lot by linking the computers with cables. If you had network cards and cables, obviously, you had it made (and you could get up to llama world record spitting distances). But if you didn't have network cards and cables, a variety of other options stood ready, including null modem connections, serial port connections, and parallel port connections.

Briefly, a null-modem cable (also known as an *asynchronous modem eliminator* or AME) is a modified serial cable that lets computers communicate as if through a modem, using standard communications packages. A serial-port connection typically uses a serial-port-to-serial-port connection. Likewise, a parallel-port connection typically uses a parallel-port-to-parallel-port connection. Serial-port connections and parallel-port connections usually need software specially designed for the purpose, such as the Direct Cable Connection built into Windows 9*x*.

Demise of Direct Dial-Up and Direct Connections

Nowadays, almost all sharing is done either via local area networks (LANs), via the Internet, or via the more capacious of the physical media discussed in the next section and the next chapter. As a result, these dial-up connections and direct connections have largely fallen out of fashion. Direct connections between computers are still useful for backing up files when the computers do not have network connections, but that's about it.

Physical Media

In the 1980s and early 1990s, when communications were poor, bandwidth was minimal, and files were (in general) smaller, physical media played an important role in digital piracy. The floppy disk could take only a modest amount of information, but removable disks such as Syquest, Zip, and (later) Jaz and Orb held a serious amount.

These days, physical media have largely been relegated to a secondary role by the Internet and the long-awaited advent of bandwidth. The exception is recordable CDs, which I'll discuss in the next chapter.

Vulnerability Factor: Transferring Files via Physical Media

On the face of it, transferring files via physical media would appear to be one of the safer forms of piracy. If the pirate gives, say, a CD-R containing illegal copies of MP3 files to someone else, the only way it can be linked back to the pirate is if they've left fingerprints on the CD or case, right?

Vulnerability Factor: Transferring Files via Physical Media (*continued*)

Well, not exactly. Some CD-recording software includes its details on each disk it burns. Its details may include the name of the application, the serial number, and the username—plenty to tie the CD to the pirate. But as long as the pirate gives the CD to someone they know, they're pretty safe.

More dangerous for the pirate is watermarking. For example, some MP3-encoding applications watermark each track that they encode. This watermark can include information such as the user's name (real or imagined), Windows or other OS serial number, and computer serial numbers such as a Pentium-III serial number or the MAC address of the computer's network card (if the computer has one). Such watermarks can tie files to a particular pirate forever—so if the recipient of the CD then shares the files across the Internet, the original pirate appears to be the guilty party. Not good.

Up Next

This chapter has discussed the key tools used by the digital pirates in the early days—tools such as e-mail, newsgroups, FTP, dial-up connections and direct connections, and physical media.

The next chapter discusses how the pirate community grew in the mid to late 1990s through Web sites, company and college networks, IRC and ICQ, and record-able CDs. The tools and techniques discussed in the next chapter, like most of those discussed in this chapter, are still widely used today, so belay that temptation to skip ahead to the chapters on P2P technologies unless your chromosomes are savagely impatient.

A Pirate Speaks: The High-School Pirate

I'm in high school, so basically, I don't have any money at all. But I've got an old computer that works okay. I spend a lot of time playing with it—especially in the winter, when there's nothing happening around here and it's too cold to do stuff outside.

So I have to get programs any way I can. I trade games with my friends when they get something worth playing, or when I do. Last month I got MechWarrior 4, so we all played that for a couple of weeks. And we download stuff and share it with each other all the time.

Computing's fun, and I'll try out any software I can get. I've got Windows and Linux on my machine, dual-boot, and I've looked at most of the big stuff that's out there—Office, WordPerfect Suite, Star Office, Photoshop, Frame, all the popular stuff. I'm starting to learn some programming now with a couple of books I've downloaded. The books are a bit old, but most of the stuff in them still works if you keep messing with it. I've written some scripts for Office, and I'm playing with Visual Basic and C++. I guess you could call it part of my education. It's probably gonna be more useful than what I'm learning at school, anyway.

Like I said, I don't have any money, so I can't buy any software. That's why I download it or copy what my friends have. Most of it I'm not really, like, *using* anyway. I'm just playing with it so that I know how it works and I'll be able to use it to get some okay job when I get out of school.

You know, I'll buy a game now and then if I've got to have it the moment it's out. Usually I get my parents to buy it for me as an early present for Christmas or my birthday or whatever. They'll do that 'cause it's easy. But you know what? If you wait a few days—a couple of weeks at the most—you'll find somebody's Wrapstered a copy of the game and posted it online. Sometimes it's a big download, but I don't care if it takes all night. I've got plenty of time. And most games, you play them for a week or two, and that's it, you're done, they're finished. You don't want to play them again. I mean, my buddies and I still play Quake now and then for the action, but most of the time, we just want the new stuff.

A Pirate Speaks: The High-School Pirate (*continued*)

So I'm a pirate, am I? If that just means I get copies of software without paying for it, then sure, I'm a pirate. But it's no big deal. Like, it's only software. I don't even *keep* most of the things I look at. My hard disk's not big enough to keep a couple of hundred old games, and most of them aren't worth burning to CD.

I mean, what are they gonna do to me—put me in jail for downloading stuff that's freely available on the Net? Get real!

Chapter 5

The Pirate Community Grows

Featuring

- Pirate Web sites
- Company networks and college networks
- Removable disks
- Recordable CDs
- Other physical media
- Online drives

The previous chapter discussed the early days of digital piracy: piracy via e-mail, newsgroups, and some physical media. This chapter discusses how the pirate community grew in the early, mid, and almost-late 1990s.

Like the previous chapter, this isn't just history. Most of the tools and techniques discussed in this chapter are still useful today, both to pirates and to users who want to stay on the right side of the law. (A few of the hardware tools I'll mention are either dead or pensioned off nowadays, but I'll discuss them because they're important to give you the context.) That said, if you want to learn about the latest and greatest technologies used by pirates, turn ahead one, two, or three chapters.

Still with me? Okay, good. We'll start with a quick discussion of Web sites. I'll keep it short because you look as though you know what a Web site is and how you might take a look at it.

Pirate Web Sites

Web sites can be a prime source of files for pirates and a prime method of distribution. Web sites are easy for pirates to create and even easier for other pirates to access. They're also easy to host, either on the pirate's own server, on a rented server, or on a borrowed server.

How Pirates Host Their Sites

In the old days, many pirate servers were hosted in the Eastern Bloc, in countries whose law-and-order divisions took a robust "die, capitalist scum" view of other people's intellectual property. (You'll recall that most of these countries were pretty hot on protecting their own intellectual property—business processes, technology, that kind of thing—and state secrets.) Estonia was particularly big. Finland (okay, it's not in the Eastern Bloc, but it touches it) has also been big historically and has been a haven for anonymous remailers.

The Eastern Bloc servers used to stay up for days, weeks, or even months, so it made sense to advertise them through newsgroups: Provided that the post wasn't horribly out of date, the pirate stood a good chance of finding the server at the same IP address (or URL). But these days, things have improved (from the intellectual-property point of view) in the countries that used to be in the Bloc, so pirates have had to turn to other hosts.

Thanks to the strictures of the DMCA (discussed in Chapter 2, "Crime and Punishment: Piracy and the Law"), most ISPs are extremely, ah, *sensitive* to copyrighted material being discovered on their servers. Most of them, on being advised that a user has posted illegal files of copyrighted material, will drop the user's account like a live scorpion. The user can complain afterwards, of course, but the onus will be on them to prove their innocence before the ISP will restore their account.

So pirates now host an increasing number of sites surreptitiously on other people's servers when those other people aren't looking. Typically, what happens is this. A pirate discovers an insecure server with a decent-speed connection, builds some folders, and uploads material to them. Then the pirate advertises the material, usually by announcements in IRC (Internet Relay Chat) channels or on link sites. Other pirates, alerted by the announcements, jump on the server to download the warez. Before long, the server either crashes under the load or the administrators notice the server is getting an impressive number of hits, figure out that something is horribly amiss, and take it offline. So as you can imagine, these servers appear and disappear quickly, which is why they're normally advertised on IRC rather than on newsgroups.

The other main tactic that pirates use for Web sites is to protect them so as to admit only trusted people. One way to protect a site is to issue each trusted user a password, or a username and password. But unless the group is very small or each member is very well known, users can share their usernames and passwords and let other people in.

A more effective means of security is to limit access to secure IP addresses. This was the technique used by a group called Pirates with Attitude, which ran a software piracy ring on a Web site called Sentinel. Pirates with Attitude would require users to upload software before they could download anything, thus establishing their bona fides (so to speak), putting each user firmly on the wrong side of the law, and increasing their pool of software. Combine this legal two-step with determined monitoring of IP addresses, and the pirates can keep out most unwelcome visitors.

Vulnerability Factor: Getting Files from Web Sites

As you'll know from even the most cursory reading of newspaper headlines, the Web can be a dangerous place to hang out. Given the huge number of people online, it's not surprising that there are a large number of malcontents who seek to use the Web to harass and inconvenience other people.

Unfortunately, the power of the Web programming languages and tools that gives Web sites their flexibility also lets malcontents design aggressive and hostile Web sites. So quite apart from the viruses, worms, Trojan horses, and other types of malware that most people now know they must watch out for, anyone who accesses the Web needs to beware dangerous Web sites.

Between them, HTML, cookies, JavaScript, and ActiveX controls can take an extremely wide range of actions. Hit the wrong Web site, and it can start pulling information from your computer (let's say your name, address, passwords, bank details, and credit-card numbers for a start), using your computer to run denial-of-service attacks or send out harassing e-mail or spam, or simply formatting your hard drive for entertainment (theirs, not yours).

While you *can* disable cookies, JavaScript, and ActiveX controls, doing so is apt to disable above-board Web sites that rely on them to perform above-board actions. For example, if you disable JavaScript, you won't be able to buy a book on Amazon.com, which kinda negates the point of the exercise.

So before you visit any pirate sites or warez sites, you need to secure your computer as much as possible. (Actually, you should do this before you visit *any* Web sites at all, because you never know when you're going to run into a bad one.) The only reason for *not* securing your computer is if you are trying to demonstrate the capabilities of Web pages and malware. Should you choose to do this—and you won't find it hard—use a computer or virtual machine that does not contain any information

Vulnerability Factor: Getting Files from Web Sites (*continued*)

you value (so that you can reformat the hard drive and start over without losing anything) and that is isolated from any other computers you have (in other words, not connected to any other computer). For most people, the least expensive way of getting another computer is to use VMWare (on Windows 2000, Windows NT, or Linux) or VirtualPC (on the Mac) to create a virtual machine.

Use firewall software or hardware (or both) to secure your computer. Entire books have been written on firewalls (for example, Matthew Strebe's excellent *Firewalls 24seven*), so I won't get into detail here. But two popular personal software firewalls are BlackICE Defender from Network ICE Corporation (www.networkice.com) and Zone Alarm from Zone Labs (www.zonelabs.com). Zone Alarm is free to home users and nonprofit corporations. Hardware firewalls invariably cost money—usually between $100 and $200 for a personal firewall that's worth having—and form a good primary line of defense. However, most people who buy hardware firewalls also use software firewalls to make doubly sure of not receiving any jabs in the electronic kidneys.

Once you've installed and configured your firewall (or firewalls), you *must* make sure it's working before you put any trust in it. To find out what information your computer is giving out, point your Web browser towards the Gibson Research Corporation Web site (grc.com) and run the free ShieldsUP! and LeakTest utilities.

Beware download-management software such as RealDownload (from RealNetworks), Download Demon (part of NetZip), and Smart Download (part of Netscape/AOL). For each file you download, these utilities pass the full URL and a unique ID tag identifying your computer to the publisher of the program, giving them a full history of all the files you download. SmartDownload even includes your IP address, which pinpoints your presence on the Internet.

Finding Pirate Sites

So there are all these pirate sites out there—sites with warez, sites with crackz, sites with mp3z (or muzik), sites with cartoonz, sites with flikz, sites with gamez, sites with porn, and sites with all of the above. How do the pirates find them?

Easily enough.

In the old days (we're talking the 1990s here), pirates used to use newsgroups such as those in the `alt.2600` hierarchy and `alt.binaries.mac.applications` to hang out, to meet people, to share information, and to transfer files. They still do, to some extent, but much less than they used to. These days, the `alt.2600` groups are still going, but an unfortunate number of them have degenerated into a mishmash of conspiracy theories (JFK, black helicopters, etc.), ads ("REAL FREE CASH," "FREE DVD," "$$$$$ LEGAL MONEY $$$$$"), porn ads (you supply the text here), and flaming (likewise). Every now and then some loser pops up and requests a product key for commercial software, upon which a group of serious hackers and old-timers rises from the depths and *disdains* them loudly into going elsewhere. (I'm exaggerating a bit here. You'll find some product keys in `alt.2600.codez` and some cracks in `alt.2600.cracks`. You'll also find directions to link sites that will direct you to pirate sites and warez sites. Because these sites are only providing links rather than providing illegal materials, they tend not to get shut down as quickly as the pirate sites and warez sites themselves.) But the fact is, these newsgroups aren't as influential as they used to be.

At this writing, `alt.binaries.mac.applications` is in much better shape—flame-free and with interesting material being posted—than most of the `alt.2600` groups. Even so, this newsgroup is seeing much less activity than it used to.

One source of information is Web sites themselves. Pirate link sites maintain a veneer of legality by presenting pages of links to pirate sites (updated as frequently as possible) but not hosting any illegal content themselves. These sites, too, change at high speed—at least, compared with the glacial pace of hard-copy book publishing. One example was CracksAndWarez.com (`www.cracksandwarez.com`—where else?), which was influential for a while in 2000 before becoming (at this writing) a minefield of disappeared pages and missing links. You might take a peek to see if it's still going.

These days, most pirates seeking information on pirate sites, software, and so on have switched their focus to IRC, because there everything happens much faster, and they can learn of interesting Web sites before they get shut down. If you investigate EFNet, you'll find that some of its thousands of channels are devoted to ads for illegal materials and requests for specific materials. For example, at this writing, the `#exceed` channel is notorious for being the place to find high-ticket software.

Vulnerability Factor: Understanding the Dangers of Pirate Sites

Pirate sites offer more than enough to pull in the unwary Internet user: high-value software packages, images of stars (clad or otherwise), hot MP3s, video files of the latest movies, and more. But before you access any of these sites, you need to be clear about the threats they pose to your imminent and long-term well-being.

First, should you choose to download pirated files, keep the following firmly in mind:

It's illegal to have pirated files.   The odds of the FBI conducting a house-to-house search of your neighborhood for pirated files may seem low, but the penalties can be severe.

Anyone supplying pirated (or ostensibly pirated) files doesn't have much respect for the law.   So why would you think they respect your computer—or your wallet? Be very careful what buttons you click when exploring or downloading files from these sites. In particular, *never* run any EXE files. Use an up-to-date virus scanner to check the files you download before you try to use them, however harmless they may sound. Remember that file extensions under Windows are *not* an accurate indication of the file's contents. A file with a JPG extension or an MP3 extension could be an executable file waiting to damage your computer. Even files that bear their true extension can be dangerous. For example, DOC (Word document) files and XLS (Excel spreadsheet) files can contain macro viruses that can do anything from wiping out your documents and crucial files to attempting to format your hard drive.

Vulnerability Factor: Understanding the Dangers of Pirate Sites (*continued*)

Second, and more immediately: Apart from these dangers, you need to watch out for any suspicious signs on your computer. If the hard drive starts thrashing unexpectedly or the processor gets stuck in overdrive when you're putting minimal demands on it, you may have a problem. (It could also be Windows trying to update itself or Office 2000 trying to optimize itself.) If you suspect that someone is trying to access your computer—or has succeeded in doing so—drop the connection immediately.

Another time you may need to drop your connection is if you access a site that traps you in a welter of windows. By using a number of HTML and scripting tricks, a Web site can keep you entertained by opening a series of windows offering you (supposedly) more and more enticing items (usually culminating with the ultimate object of teenage lust: Britney Spears minus her Spandex). Every time you close one of these windows, it automatically opens another one; and every time you give it a moment, it opens another window to tempt you with more stuff.

Why is it doing this? You probably haven't insulted Odin or offended the Furies recently, so there's a mundane explanation: The site is trying to distract you and prevent you from leaving while it runs a script on your computer. This script might be doing anything from searching for personal details, passwords, and credit-card numbers to installing a virus, Trojan horse, or an attack program on your PC. You probably don't want to wait to find out which of these unlovely possibilities it is.

If you get caught by a site, these are your best shots at escape, in order of preference:

- Use the Alt+F4 key combination to try to kill all the browser windows. Using the keyboard like this is usually faster than trying to click the Close button on a multitude of windows of varying sizes open scattered across your screen.

Vulnerability Factor: Understanding the Dangers of Pirate Sites (*continued*)

☠ If you have work open in any other application, switch to it (by using the Taskbar or by pressing Alt+Tab), save the work, and close the application. Doing so may well seem like preparation for craven surrender—but you'll regret it if you don't. Close any other applications you can, even if they're not doing anything useful.

☠ Unplug your modem line (if you're using a modem) or your network connection (if you're connecting to the Internet via a network, a cable modem, or a DSL). If you're using an external modem, you can just switch it off instead, or unplug its power supply if it has no on/off switch. If it's a network connection, you'll probably need to pull the cable out of the back of the computer. (Hint: Squeeze the retaining clip first, or the computer will follow your arm.)

☠ Press Ctrl+Alt+Del to display the Close Program dialog box (in Windows 9*x* or Windows Me), the Windows NT Security dialog box (in Windows NT 4), or the Windows Security dialog box (in Windows 2000). Then (in Windows 9*x* or Windows Me), from the Close Program dialog box (shown below), select the offending instance of the browser and click the End Task button. Repeat as necessary. If that doesn't do the trick, click the Shut Down button to shut down your computer. From the Windows NT Security dialog box in Windows NT 4 or from the Windows Security dialog box in Windows 2000, click the Task Manager button to display the Task Manager dialog box. Display the Applications page if it's not already displayed, then select the offending instance of Internet Explorer in the Tasks list box, and click the End Task button. If Windows NT or Windows 2000 displays the Ending Task dialog box, click the End Now button. Repeat until each instance of Internet Explorer controlled by the site is closed.

Vulnerability Factor: Understanding the Dangers of Pirate Sites (*continued*)

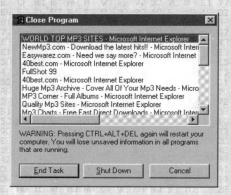

☠ If all else fails, reboot your computer. You may lose any configuration changes you've made in this Windows session, but if you suspect that the site is raiding your hard drive for information or attempting to damage it, the pain of a hard reboot pales in comparison.

Company and College Networks

The network was invented to simplify file sharing—and it has done so with a vengeance. Local area networks (LANs) provide high-speed connectivity over short distances—for example, within a building or several neighboring buildings. Campus area networks (CANs) and metropolitan area networks (MANs) connect longer distances, such as a college campus, at equally high speeds. Wide area networks (WANs) link LANs in different locations—for example, in different cities or on different continents—at lower speeds. And the Internet links all the wired parts of the planet.

> The terms LAN and WAN are universally accepted. Most people accept CAN and MAN as well, though both cause occasional amusement. Closer to home, two other terms are struggling to get established. For the home network, or home area network, the acronym HAN suggests itself. And for the personal area network—the network over which your PDA, cell phone, laptop, and pager will Bluetooth their information—the term PAN volunteers, though not without gathering scorn.

Most companies of any size and almost all colleges are networked these days. Both companies and colleges benefit greatly from coworkers and students being able to quickly and easily share files with each other. But company networks and college networks can also become hotbeds of digital piracy because they make it easy to share files illegally. Better yet, most companies and colleges have fast Internet connections, which enable the employees and students to transfer files at high speed.

Not that colleges or companies approve of digital piracy and illegal file sharing, of course. Every college and company worth its salt has an Internet access policy and a network policy to which students and employees must subscribe, or at least pay lip service.

Companies tend to have more restrictive policies than colleges, for a couple of reasons. First, it's usually much easier to terminate an employee than to get rid of a student. Second, companies tend to be more worried about being sued than colleges are. Most companies in the U.S. reserve the right to read their employees' e-mail without notice, and at the last count about 40 percent of U.S. companies did so regularly. The vast majority of companies regularly scan the files on network drives; many scan local hard drives as well. Many companies forbid personal use of the Internet. Most of those that permit employees personal use attach strict conditions to it to make sure that the employees neither goof off nor do anything that could get the company into trouble or harm its reputation.

Because this book is being published in the U.S.A., it concentrates on the situation in the U.S.A. As you'd imagine, things tend to be different in other countries, and you should investigate your local situation in light of the points raised in this book. Here's a quick example on the subject of companies reading their employees' e-mail. In the United Kingdom, the Regulation of Investigatory Powers Act (RIP for short—another slick and not-inappropriate acronym) gives companies sweeping rights to monitor their employees' e-mail. But the U.K.'s new Human Rights Act, part of European Community–wide legislation, explicitly gives U.K. citizens a right to privacy that appears to grant employees freedom from just this kind of monitoring. At this writing, it's not clear whether RIP scissors cut paper or whether HRA rock blunts RIP.

Even if your company or college has a free and easy policy on Internet access, keeping illegal files on a company network or college network is seldom a good idea. Your network folders may be protected from other users, but the network administrators and supervisors can and will access them. So if you feel compelled to keep illegal files there, you'll need to keep your wits about you.

Vulnerability Factor: Keeping Files on Network Drives

If you are keeping illegal files on a network at school or at work, be aware that most companies and colleges regularly back up the contents of their network drives to storage media such as digital tape or recordable DVD. (Digital tape is most popular because it has by far the largest storage capacity. For small network drives, recordable DVDs offer far greater retrieval speed and convenience than digital tape.)

The frequency of backup varies from institution to institution, but to be useful to man or beast, backups need to be frequent and regular. Many institutions run backups nightly to ensure minimal data loss should a network drive go down. Others run full backups less frequently (for example, weekly) but run incremental backups every day to record the changes that have taken place.

Vulnerability Factor: Keeping Files on Network Drives (*continued*)

Under either scenario, all the illegal files you've been keeping on your network drive are committed to a long-lasting medium and filed somewhere safe—probably off-site, probably fire-proof. The difference is that each full backup will contain a copy of all your files, while each incremental backup will contain only those that are new or that have been modified in the appropriate time period.

Some companies back up local hard drives as well. More of them encourage employees to keep all valuable files on the network drives. If your company doesn't back up local hard drives, your hard drive is a safer place for dubious files than the network drive.

Backup tapes are typically kept for a goodly length of time—in some cases, as long as five years. So if you store illegal files on network drives that get backed up, evidence of your piracy will be around for a long time.

In an encouraging development, many companies have begun to delete stored e-mail messages—and in some cases all backups—after a shorter period of time, such as a year. This is partly because of the Microsoft breakup case, in which the Department of Justice's case was heftily bolstered by indiscreet messages dug out of Microsoft's subpoenaed e-mail archive.

If your network administrators are dozy, incompetent, or loath to update antiquated software, you may be able to hide disapproved-of file types from the administrators by renaming them to innocuous or approved types. For example, most network administrators are deeply un-keen to have MP3 files on their networks, because so many MP3 files are illegal copies of copyrighted material. But if you rename the MP3 files with another extension often used for large files (for example, ZIP), you may be able to sneak them past cursory checks. Be aware, though, that many administration tools are smart enough not to believe everything they're told, and so these tools probe the files to make sure they're what they say they are.

WARNING

Never use EXE as an extension for files you want to disguise. Many EXE files *are* as large as an MP3 file or a small video file—but because unknown EXE files are prime suspects for carrying viruses, most network administrators and network-management utilities scan aggressively for EXE files and nuke any that aren't known and approved.

Even if you're able to pass a scan for file types, the size of the files is likely to give you away. Unless your administrator is sloppy or has been fired, they'll detect large stashes of music or video quickly—especially if you raise a flag by slopping over your allocated quota of network space.

Cynical Aside: Company Networks Increasingly Restrict Misuse

Have you noticed that as the years roll on, life seems to be getting more and more restricted? The laws and regulations go on piling up, restricting every step from birth to grave; the health police continue to battle the popular scourges of smoking, alcohol, and saturated fat; and the many conflicting squads of the morality police frantically condemn an ever-wider range of thoughts and activities that disagree with their (assorted) circumscribed moral compasses.

Am I overstating things? Perhaps. In any case, it's not too surprising that network policies are becoming more restrictive as well. Misuse of company networks was far more widely tolerated in the early to mid 1990s than it is today. Many an administrator of a small- or medium-sized network had no objection to vigorous games of DOOM or Quake taking place outside working hours. Many supervisors encouraged such games, either tacitly or by joining the fray, to help build teamwork, let employees vent aggression, and generally encourage them to work longer hours without demanding overtime pay.

Cynical Aside: Company Networks Increasingly Restrict Misuse (*continued*)

If you've read geek lit or are even moderately up-to-speed with hacker folklore, you'll know that Microsoft is famous for its culture of nerd activities and pranks. Some of these took physical form: For example, the original Windows NT team were renowned for letting off steam by playing hallway golf, Nerf bows-and-arrows, and "hoser ball," a game that involved hurling a tennis ball weighted with coins and sealed with duct tape at a pyramid of the soda cans the team had been drinking. Other activities were virtual, or at least electrical. Networked games were more than popular with the Microsofties, and when one group was forbidden to play networked games on the company LAN because they were disrupting work, they took matters into their own hands and built their own parallel, private LAN for games.

Nowadays, when traditional playground favorites such as slides and roundabouts are deemed too dangerous for America's precious and over-protected youth, network games are frowned upon too. Some of this stems from legitimate business reasons—24/7 connectivity is vital for an increasing number of businesses—but much of it is the killjoy attitude of modern America. Employees caught building a private LAN would be charged with the-deity-knows-what—criminal damage to the building, perhaps.

Zip and Other Removable Disks

If you need to deliver a quantity of files via sneakernet—walking them from computer A to computer B—you'll need to put them on physical media. This section discusses the assorted removable disks and similar media available in the 1990s. The next section discusses recordable CDs.

Zip Disk

In the mid 1990s, the Zip disk from Iomega Corporation quickly became the easiest way to move any file too big to fit on a floppy and smaller than about 100MB. Not surprisingly, Zip disks were widely used by digital pirates for transferring files via sneakernet.

The Zip disk derived its popularity from its capacity (95.7MB actual—100MB in marketing terms), ubiquity, and relative ease of use rather than from anything as trivial as aesthetics or superlative design. Apparently designed in an off-moment by someone who majored in industrial plastic molding, the external Zip drive came with an AC adapter the size of a pronged and flattened softball and was identifiable at 50 paces as an eyesore. The most basic (and most popular) model plugged into the parallel port and transferred files excruciatingly slowly. Subsequent models included SCSI models, which delivered decent if not blazing speed, and internal EIDE models, which masked the ugliness. Before too long, notebook manufacturers started producing custom internal Zip drives for their notebooks, signaling the Zip's industrywide acceptance as a standard.

An external Zip drive was fully portable, though you were fully aware of it all the time you were porting it (and its hefty AC adapter, or a battery pack almost the same size). But the disks were tough and, apart from an embarrassing technical episode called the Click of Death that destroyed all the data on a given disk, worked well. Within a couple of years of the Zip's introduction, you could send most anyone a Zip disk and be confident that they would be able to read it. This was great for business, great for home users, and great for pirates.

Precursors to Zip

The main precursors to the Zip were SyQuest drives from SyQuest Technology, Inc. These came in assorted capacities, such as 40MB, 80MB, and 200MB. SyQuests were effective and fast, but both the drives and their media were expensive, and the drives were awkward to configure. As a result, SyQuest drives were used primarily in corporate environments and by graphical artists who needed to transfer large files. SyQuests didn't go mainstream, and so they weren't widely used by pirates.

SyQuest Technology, Inc. went on to make the SyJet removable drive, a SCSI-driven screamer with 1.5GB capacity, before going bust and (in 1999) suffering the ultimate insult of having its assets purchased by Iomega Corporation.

Zip Challengers

In the mid and late 1990s, several competitors for the Zip emerged:

Shark drive   The late Shark drive (from Avatar Peripherals) is deeply lamented by travelers and pirates because it beat the Zip into a cocked hat on several counts. First, the Shark drive was much smaller than the Zip. You could put a Shark in your pocket without visiting Schwarzenegger's tailor first or enduring Mae West jokes. Second, the Shark drew its own power, so it needed no clunky AC adapter or battery pack. Third, Shark disks held 250MB—two and a half times as much as the original Zip disks. And fourth (surely the killer), the Shark drive actually looked halfway cool. Unfortunately, Zip had such a lock on the market that the Shark wasn't able to gain any significant traction, and it was discontinued after a couple of years.

LS-120 SuperDisk drive   Designed as a replacement for the humble floppy drive, the LS-120 managed to be backward compatible with floppy disks while offering 120MB capacity with LS-120 media. Floppy compatibility should have enabled the LS-120 to take over the world, or at least beat out the Zip disk, by becoming the standard drive in every computer. However, licensing problems, high cost, and the Zip's already established position in the market prevented the LS-120 from fulfilling its potential. At this writing, LS-120 drives and media are widely available but not widely used. As a result, LS-120 drives are popular for file sharing only with people who already have them.

HiFD drive   Like the LS-120, the HiFD was designed by Sony Corporation as a floppy-drive replacement that could read existing floppies. HiFD media held 200MB each, offering even greater capacity than the LS-120—so HiFD should have been able to beat out LS-120 and replace the floppy drive, shouldn't it? In theory, yes; but Sony was too greedy to provide attractive licensing terms, and the HiFD ended up making little impact on the market. At this writing, you can still get HiFD drives and media, but you'll have to look hard for them—and so few other people have them that you might as well not bother with them.

Bigger Than Zip

Once the Zip drive had shown the potential of the market for removable mass storage, the race was on to create higher-capacity drives that would enjoy similar success. Because Zip drives are still very widely used, and because recordable CDs (discussed in the next section) have picked up a large part of the market, none of the post-Zip drives have met with huge success. These are (or have been) the main contenders:

Zip 250 drive   The Zip 250 (as you'd guess, also from Iomega Corporation) increases the Zip's capacity to 250 marketing megabytes and is the natural successor to the original Zip drive.

Jaz drive   Also from Iomega Corporation, the Jaz removable drive comes in 1GB and 2GB versions. The Jaz uses a SCSI connection and delivers good performance. Jaz drives are great for backup. They're not so good for sharing files because relatively few people have them.

Orb drive   From Castlewood Technologies, the Orb drive offers larger capacity than Jaz (2.2GB) and good performance in its EIDE (internal), SCSI (internal and external), USB (external), and FireWire (external) incarnations. (The Orb also comes in a parallel-port incarnation that, because of its low speed, is best avoided unless parallel is the only port available to you.) Like the Jaz, Orb drives are great for backup and for sharing files with the relatively few people who own them.

SyJet drive   As mentioned a couple of pages ago, the SyJet was a high-performance 1.5GB SCSI drive produced by SyQuest Technology. Unfortunately, SyQuest went bust, and the SyJet achieved minimal market penetration. (Even more unfortunately, I still own one.)

SparQ drive   When it became clear that the SyJet was selling—how should I put this?—*disappointingly* against the Jaz in the bigger-than-Zip contest, SyQuest Technology tried to strike back by releasing the SparQ, a 1GB hard drive in a cartridge with impressive speed and a very low price. Unfortunately, they seem to have rushed the SparQ to market, and an intolerable number of the drives proved unreliable, especially suffering data loss from the cartridges. This unreliability killed the product and helped kill the company.

Smaller Than Zip

Zip disks are portable enough for conventional computer use—you can put one in any pocket you're not going to sit on—but they're not much good for portable consumer technologies such as MP3 players and digital cameras. (That said, see the following sidebar about film for filmless cameras.) Such pocketable consumer durables need smaller media.

These are the main contenders for the mini-storage market:

- PocketZip disks
- CompactFlash cards
- SmartMedia cards
- Memory Stick, um, *sticks*

The following sections discuss these media.

PocketZip Disks

The moment you read the name PocketZip, you probably guessed that it refers to a small portable disk from Iomega Corporation, the Utah-based company behind the Zip and Jaz. Small wonder that Iomega changed the name of the disk from its original Clik. (Iomega first positioned the Clik as a medium for digital cameras, then decided to switch it to more general use, including its own HipZip MP3 players.)

PocketZip disks hold 40MB each, which makes them more or less useful for music (about 40 minutes of MP3s at 128Kbps) or backing up small quantities of files. The disks are small, highly portable, and somewhat flimsy. The easiest way to load data onto the disks is to use the PocketZip PC Card drive, into which the PocketZip disks fit. PocketZip disks transfer data at up to 620Kbps, so in theory you can fill a disk in one to two minutes.

CompactFlash Cards

CompactFlash cards have been around longer than their competitors and, as a result, the technology is more widely used and more mature. A CompactFlash card is about the size of a short stack of the classic small size of Post-It™ note, or about a third of the size of a Type II PC Card. CompactFlash cards can be loaded via PC Card–sized readers or via external readers (typically USB or parallel port).

At this writing, CompactFlash cards are available with capacities up to 320MB. The main problem with CompactFlash cards is their cost, which typically runs between $2 and $3 per megabyte.

If possible, choose USB readers over parallel-port readers for CompactFlash cards and SmartMedia cards. USB is much faster.

Cynical Aside: Adventures in Innovative Marketing: Film for Filmless Cameras

You know how I just said that Zip disks were too big for use in portable consumer technologies such as digital cameras? Sadly, that's not entirely true—but for the wrong reasons.

Ironically enough, some of the hottest-selling digital cameras have been some of the clunkiest. Sony noticed that would-be digital photographers had trouble getting images from their cameras to their computers. Serial connections were awkward and slow, USB was flaky, and the existing mini-storage media not only needed clumsy docking stations but took half an eon to transfer each image.

(Cynical commentators have also suggested that Sony was responding to some photographers' shaky grasp of digital realities. Picture [yes, pun kinda intended] to yourself a conversation along these lines:

"So where are the pictures I just took?"

"They're in the camera."

"I know that—but *where* are they?"

Where reality is shaky, physical objects can come in handy.)

Anyway...the Sony Mavica still camera uses a floppy disk for storage, and the Sony Digital Mavica uses a Zip disk. Using such large media made the Mavicas far larger than most digital cameras—but people bought them because the disks provided easy (if slow) transfer of the images from the camera to a computer. Sony has now moved on to including a mutated CD-R in later Mavicas, thus ensuring a revenue stream despite the transition from film photography to digital photography. Mutated? Yes, this CD-R is proprietary—it's three inches wide instead of five, has a capacity of a relatively miserable 156MB, and costs about $4 a pop. As far as I can see, the only thing to be said for it is that it provides a revenue stream for Sony—I mean, it gives the customers a sturdy and glamorous physical medium on which to archive their photos.

SmartMedia Cards

SmartMedia cards have about the same footprint as CompactFlash cards, but they're much thinner, at about ³/₄ mm. So they're very portable, but they're also delicate; Unlike CompactFlash cards, you need to handle them with care. You can load them via PC Card adapters or external readers (typically USB or parallel port). As with CompactFlash, the PC Card adapters transfer data quickly, but the parallel readers are slow.

At this writing, SmartMedia cards are available with capacities up to 64MB. The main problems with SmartMedia cards are this relatively small capacity, high cost ($2 to $4 per megabyte), and delicacy.

Word to the Wise: CompactFlash Is Currently the Most Promising Mini-Medium

CompactFlash cards, SmartMedia cards, and Memory Stick sticks are shatteringly expensive, so you're unlikely to buy any more of them than you absolutely need. You're even more unlikely to want to give your CompactFlash or SmartMedia cards, or your Memory Stick sticks, to anyone else unless you love them pretty well.

At this writing, CompactFlash seems a smarter purchase than Smart-Media or Memory Stick. Memory Stick sticks have limited capacity, tend to be even more expensive than CompactFlash cards, and aren't widely used beyond Sony hardware. SmartMedia are more widely used than Memory Stick, but their capacity is small, and they're delicate enough to be easily damaged.

A 128MB CompactFlash card is painfully expensive, but you can amortize that cost by using the card in other technologies such as your Pocket PC, your Palm mutation (for example, a TRG Pro), or your digital camera. It can also serve as an effective and highly portable backup medium.

Memory Stick Sticks

Memory Stick is Sony's entry in the mini-medium stakes. Shaped like a stick of chewing gum, Memory Stick sticks slot into a special reader—typically one built into Sony hardware such as a laptop, a digital camera, or a digital-audio player (usually *not* an MP3 player; Sony doesn't like open formats). Some other companies are now starting to use Memory Stick technology, but it's most widely used by Sony products.

Sony touts Memory Stick as being suitable for digital photography, audio content, and video content. It's good for the first two, but at this writing, even the largest Memory Stick sticks (at 64MB) are too small for anything but the smallest video files. Memory Stick sticks cost between $2 and $3 per megabyte.

Recordable CDs

A great consumer favorite, recordable CDs have furthered the spread of piracy by making it trivial for anyone to transfer or back up a large number of files—up to 650MB for a regular CD-R, and up to 800MB for an extended CD-R. CD-R drives became borderline affordable in the mid 1990s, truly affordable in the late 1990s, and almost ubiquitous in 1999 and 2000. Extended CD-R media weren't widely available until 2000, but given that their increase in capacity over regular CD-R media is modest, and that most people were happy with the capacity of a regular CD-R, that didn't matter much.

Recordable CDs are especially popular with students, for reasons that are easy to understand. With an Internet connection and a computer equipped with a CD burner, the student need never buy a CD again. They can borrow CDs from friends and copy them or rip them. From the Internet, they can download MP3 files of just about everything ever released on CD. They can burn audio CDs from MP3 files if they need to listen to the music on audio CD players, or they can burn data CDs containing hundreds of MP3 files to carry their music easily or to trade it with their friends.

If you don't have a CD-R or CD-RW drive, cast your eye back at the section titled "CD Recorder or CD Rewriter" in Chapter 3, "The Pirate's Basic Tools," which outlines the criteria to keep in mind when choosing a drive.

Other Physical Media

At this writing, recordable CDs are the most convenient and affordable medium for making files portable and backing up files. Needless to say, though, many computer users crave portable media infinitely more capacious than recordable CD-R so that they can tote around (or back up) far greater volumes of files.

Such technologies are available, but for the moment, none has become widespread. This section discusses the possibilities for shifting large files from A to B or backing them up.

DVDs

Given the popularity of recordable CDs, recordable DVDs are a logical next step. There's just one problem: It ain't happened yet. But the technology is improving, and the cost is coming down, so recordable DVDs should go big in the next two or three years.

Recordable DVDs (DVD-RAM) can contain up to 4.7GB at this writing—a little over seven times as much as a regular recordable CD. But the media costs $35 a shot, or about 50 times as much as a CD-R—and it's WORM rather than WARM, so you can write it only once. Get it wrong, and you've got a truly expensive coaster… Unless you're needing to heave truly huge files about (we're talking video or databases, for this kind of file size), you're going to find more modest media much more sensible. The exception is corporate use, where recordable DVDs can come in handy in backing up large folders quickly.

Removable Hard Drives

If you need to move (or back up) a large number of gigabytes, you may want to get a removable hard drive. Removable hard drives come in with the full gamut of connections: parallel port, SCSI, USB, FireWire, and PC Card.

The pros and cons of each connection are pretty much as usual:

- Parallel-port hard drives can attach to any PC with minimal effort, but they're painfully slow. Unless you like watching cricket or holding paint-drying races, you've probably got better uses for the rest of your life.

- ☠ External SCSI hard drives offer good performance if each computer with which you want to use them has an external SCSI connector.

- ☠ USB external hard drives are good for any computer that has a USB port. (In other words, most modern computers.) They offer adequate if uninspiring performance.

- ☠ FireWire external hard drives offer better performance than USB drives—but your computer needs to have a FireWire port, which most computers don't. (You can always add one via a PCI card or a PC Card.)

- ☠ PC Card–*connected* external hard drives are great for laptops.

- ☠ PC Card hard drives (hard drives built inside a PC Card) are great for laptops, and extremely portable—but they have several disadvantages. First, their capacity is limited. Second, they're very expensive per megabyte (let alone gigabyte). And third, most of them take up two PC Card slots, the full complement for most laptops—so you won't be able to use any other PC cards at the same time.

Removable hard drives tend to be of little interest to pirates for file exchange for the simple reason that anyone who has paid $500 or so for a drive is unlikely to want to send it to someone else. But as an extension to adidasLAN, or for backup, they can come in very handy.

Portable MP3 Players

You can use some portable MP3 players for file backup and transfer, though you're unlikely to want to do this unless you're truly desperate. Most portable MP3 players have minimal capacity—the manufacturers affect to think that 64MB is a generous amount of storage for a player. (The manufacturers don't really believe this, but they want even less to price their players at $350 upwards, so they're kinda constrained on the amount of base memory they can afford to include.) And as soon as you start putting documents onto them, you're cutting into your music time. But if you need to carry around a backup of a file or two in case your house burns down, you may find a portable player a satisfactory solution.

> ## Word to the Wise: If You're Buying an MP3 Player, Consider CompactFlash
>
> If you're trying to decide which MP3 player to buy, keep in mind that removable and upgradable media give you far more flexibility than fixed media.
>
> Instead of buying an MP3 player with built-in storage, you may want to get one that takes removable media such as CompactFlash, Smart-Media, or even Memory Stick. That way, you can buy more media as necessary and store more music on them.
>
> As discussed earlier in this chapter, CompactFlash seems a better purchase at the moment than SmartMedia or Memory Stick.

Online Drives

Physical media (such as recordable CDs) and removable media are an effective means of transferring files to people with whom you have direct contact, either in person or via snail mail. But if your contact with the other party is virtual, and if snail-mail is out of the question for reasons of security or speed, you'll need to go virtual.

If transferring files directly from one computer to another (either using a P2P technology such as Napster or a direct connection such as NetMeeting) is unsatisfactory for whatever reason, consider using an online drive. An online drive is essentially an FTP site—masquerading as a Web site for ease of use—on which users can store files in their own virtual space. Typically, you create a password-protected account that you can access from any Web browser. (Some online drives use custom software, but most find it too unpopular to be sustainable.)

Online drives are good for transferring anything from a shipload to a boatload of files to one or more people that you trust enough to share an account name and a password. Some online drives provide shared folders that don't require you to reveal the account name and password in order for other people to use them. Depending on whom you're sharing files with, you need to balance security against convenience of use.

Most online drives demand some personal information and an undertaking to abide by their terms and conditions, all relevant laws, and so on. But most of them require little verification beyond a working e-mail address—when you sign up, they send you an e-mail to which you have to respond. So apart from that e-mail address, which can be a free online address (for example, a HotMail account), you can submit pretty much any information you want. And if you compromise an online drive, you can abandon it without compunction and start a new account.

Word to the Wise: Use Online Drives to Beat the Bandwidth Blues

Online drives are highly popular with digital pirates and people sharing files legitimately for two reasons:

- First, they're reasonably secure and discreet. Your ISP knows what you're doing; myplay knows what you're doing; and anybody you're sharing files with knows what you're doing. But you're not hanging your laundry out in private the way you are with, say, Napster.

- Second, online drives solve the problem not only of synchronous communications—the uploader and downloader needing to be online at the same time—but also of the downloader or downloaders having far greater bandwidth than the uploader. For example, say Susie has a 50MB AVI file she wants to share. But Susie has only a 56K connection, which gives 33.6K upstream, so it'll take Susie the best part of four hours to upload a single copy of the file. Anyone with a faster connection wanting to download that file from Susie will need to spend that same amount of time downloading it—and if more than one person is trying to download it at the same time, it'll take correspondingly longer. But once Susie has posted the file to an online drive, one or more people can download it at the full speed of each of their Internet connections. Susie's 56K connection is no longer a bottleneck.

WARNING Most online drives place cookie information on your computer—to help you use them, of course. Some may place registry entries—for your protection, you understand. This means that if you repeatedly create and abandon accounts using the same computer and same operating system, they'll know all about it. Whether they'll *do* anything about it, you'll need to find out for yourself....

Two of the most widely used online drives are FreeDrive (`www.freedrive.com`) and i-drive (`www.idrive.com`), each of which offers 50MB of space for free accounts and more if you pay more. There are many others. Even Yahoo gets into the game, offering 10MB of online-drive space to members.

But the killer at this writing is myplay, inc. (`www.myplay.com`), which offers users 3GB of space each. myplay is affiliated with Winamp.com among others and provides the My Winamp Locker feature.

I suggest reading myplay's terms and conditions closely, as some of them may make your eyebrows crawl into your hairline. Here's an example:

These rules may be modified from time to time, and each time you log on to the Service or use the Software you will be deemed to have accepted any such changes.

Eek. Here's another that may make your hairline retreat from your eyebrows:

Any time you upload User Content that originates with you (such as original recordings made by you of your own performances), *you grant myplay and its affiliates a royalty-free, perpetual, irrevocable, non-exclusive license and right (including any moral rights) to use that User Content in whole or in part*, on the Service itself and in connection with the advertising and promotion of the Service, throughout the world in any form, media, or technology now known or later developed. You understand that this right will embrace without limitation our use of the User Content on and in connection with our Service in the following ways: to reproduce it for use on our Service; to distribute, transmit, publicly perform and communicate it to the public on our Service; to modify and adapt it for technical purposes in connection with such uses on our Service; and/or to incorporate it in compilations of other works for such purposes. *You also warrant that any time you submit any other unpublished User Content originating with a third party, that the holder of any Rights in such original User Content has completely and effectively waived all such Rights and validly and irrevocably granted to you the right to grant the license stated above respecting the Service.*

Yes, you read that right. Anything original you post on myplay, myplay and its cronies can use without paying you a cent. You get all the blame, they get all the use. In other words, you may pay dearly for that 3GB of online space. (How myplay knows whether what you post is original is an interesting question.)

After all that, it comes pretty much as an aside that you're also expressly forbidden from sharing your password with others. But to use myplay to transfer files to other people, you'll probably want to do precisely that.

Up Next

This chapter has discussed how the pirate community grew as the Internet and the Web went mainstream. You've seen how Web sites and FTP sites remain effective means of transferring files to people you don't know. You've learned that newsgroups can still provide information for would-be pirates, but that the main activity these days takes place in the faster-paced environment of IRC. You're now aware (if you weren't before) of the illegal activity that takes place on many company networks and most college networks—and the dangers that network backups pose to such pirates.

This chapter has also discussed the merits of assorted removable media for backing up files or transferring them to people with whom you have direct contact. You've learned the advantages of online drives for relatively secure and very effective file sharing between two or more trusted parties.

The next chapter discusses the phenomenon of Napster, the pioneering P2P technology that brought piracy to the masses.

A Pirate Speaks: The Specialist Music Pirate

No argument, I pirate stuff. I download a shipload of music. But I still buy CDs. I still spend the same amount of money on music. And I'll tell you why.

Like I said, I spend the same amount of money on music now, but I spend it differently. I don't buy CDs from the big-name artists anymore. They've got the record deals. They've got the promotional budgets. And most of them have got more than enough money. Seriously, you think Metallica, say, or Aerosmith needs three bucks in royalties from me for a CD? Call the sandman in and dream on, baby!

The system favors the big guys. They've got it made. Some of them, their music's still good, but others, they're spinning their wheels, they just want to keep sucking from the tit. But I'm open-minded. I reckon I listen to a good half of all the rock that's released. I'm a sucker for new stuff, even if I never want to hear a lot of it again. Anything I like from a big-name band, I download. I've got about 20 gigs of MP3 files on my laptop and another 30 on a FireWire drive. Course, I ripped my CD collection first, so that makes up a chunk of it, and that's all legit. But I've downloaded a lot of tracks. I go for the highest-bitrate versions I can find because I've got a good sound card and great headphones. You can hear the difference. *You* can't? *I* can.

I told you I still buy CDs. I do. But the CDs I buy are from the little guys, the bands I like best and want to support. Most of these bands, you won't find their music on Napster or audioGnome—not unless I've put it there. You probably haven't even heard of half of them. But they're good, and they sure as hell appreciate my support. I know because I've talked to many of them. That's how small they are—they'll talk to their fans. Most of them, I'll buy every CD they put out. Sometimes I buy an extra CD to give to a friend. Spread the word a bit.

That's where most of my music money goes. But these days, I spend more money than I used to on going to concerts. In the old days, I had

A Pirate Speaks: The Specialist Music Pirate (*continued*)

to decide between buying CDs and going to concerts, and I usually figured the CDs would last longer. Now that I've stopped buying mainstream CDs, I can afford to go to more concerts.

When I do buy a CD, I rip it, encode it to MP3, and make it available via audioGnome and Freenet. I encode two copies of each track: one at 128Kpbs for the people who just want to know what the music sounds like, and who aren't prepared to download a big file, and one at 320Kbps for the true fans.

People I know well, I even share WAV files with. *Full* WAVs—30 to a hundred megs each. I've only got a dial-up connection with a couple of bonded 56K modems, so I'm not much good for Napster or audioGnome for big files. I get about 90K downstream—when the squirrels aren't mating with the junction box, anyway—but only about 60K upstream. So when I share WAVs, I've got to be creative. I put them up on myplay—that takes all night—then give my pals the account name and password. That way, my lame-ass phone lines aren't a bottleneck, and people can suck the files down as fast as their connection can handle it. And I don't have to worry about running my computer the whole time.

I guess you'd say I'm kinda obsessive about doing the MP3s right. I use MusicMatch Jukebox to add the lyrics and the band credits to the track tags. I don't usually add the art because I don't have a scanner, but the words and credits are key. Contact info for the band, that goes in there too.

One of the bands I'm really close to, they're just getting going. Produced their first two CDs themselves locally. They don't have an Internet connection between them. They were *thrilled* when some kids came to one of their gigs and told them they'd gotten to hear the music on the Net and liked it. The guy who writes the songs said I'd added a whole new dimension of marketing to the band. I felt real good about that. I'm enjoying the music I like and helping to spread it—and I'm not wasting my money on the big boys.

Chapter 6

Napster: Piracy for the Masses

Featuring

In this chapter, I'll show you how to use Napster, the wildly popular application that allows you to both find MP3 files online and share your own MP3 files online for others to download. I'll also show you some Napster-like technologies that stand ready to step in should Napster be closed down by legal challenges.

Napster creates MP3 communities on the fly from the users who log in to a server, enabling them to share MP3 files with one another. At this writing, Napster works only with MP3 and WMA files, although Napster may be changed to support other file formats, including graphics formats, in the future. Other P2P technologies support other file formats as well.

Napster was originally developed for Windows, but it's rapidly proved such a hit that it's been implemented on most currently used operating systems and graphical environments. In this chapter, I'll discuss Napster for Windows and the Mac and Gnapster (for Linux systems running the GNOME graphical environment). Other Napster clones, implementations, and related software include amster (for the Amiga); benapster and napster for beos (both for BeOS); jnap, jnapster, and java napster, multiplatform Java clients; and Napster/2 (for OS/2). For the latest URLs for these and other Napster-related software, check out the Napster FAQ at `faq.napster.com`.

I'll start by covering what Napster does and the issues it raises. After that, I'll recap the legal challenges that Napster is negotiating at this writing and the changes that seem likely. Then I'll discuss how safe Napster is to use, what information Napster users are exposing, and how easily illegal files can be detected. We'll then move on to the individual software implementations and look at each briefly in turn.

At the end of this chapter, I'll discuss Wrapster, which lets you disguise other files as MP3 files so that you can exchange them via Napster. In the next chapter, I'll show you some post-Napster P2P file-sharing technologies, including Gnutella, audioGnome, and Freenet.

Into the Valley of Lawyers...

In Chapter 2, "Crime and Punishment: Piracy and the Law," you learned about the legal issues surrounding Napster. Quick recap: Some legal experts think that Napster, Inc. has a good defense against accusations of inducing copyright infringement. Other experts think the opposite. Napster, Inc. is planning to appeal a February 2001 ruling supporting an injunction to shut the service down. Napster, Inc. has made an agreement with Bertelsmann to develop a new Napster service that would feature subscriptions and legal files. Napster, Inc. is trying to make similar deals with other record companies and their representatives. If it's successful in doing so, it may be able to distribute an attractive range of music legally.

So by the time you read this, Napster as it's discussed in this chapter may be no more. If Napster changes to a subscription service, or is closed down, you'll probably want to try software such as Gnutella, audioGnome, and Freenet instead of Napster. You might want to check the Napster Web site (`www.napster.com`) before reading this chapter.

Overview of Napster

This section discusses briefly what Napster is, what it does, and what you can do with it.

Napster's inventor, Shawn Fanning (who gave the software the nickname he received for his nap of short hair), created Napster to solve the two key problems of getting MP3 files online:

- There's no central way of searching for a particular MP3 file (though sites such as the Lycos Music MP3 Search site do their best), so you may not be able to find what you want, even if it exists.

- There's no easy way for artists to distribute their own music online other than signing up with sites such as Riffage.com or MP3.com.

Napster solves these problems by creating an ad-hoc virtual community for sharing MP3 files. Each user who has files to share designates one or more folders on his or her computer to be shared for uploads and, in turn, can search through and download any files that other people currently logged in are sharing.

When you start Napster, it contacts the central Napster server, which maintains a database of the available Napster member servers and hands your connection off to one of them. Typically, the handoff is automatic, with the central server performing load-balancing for the member servers and sending you to an available and convenient server. Some Napster clients and add-on programs (such as Napigator, available from www.napigator.com) let you specify a particular server to log into, which can be useful if you want to hang out with your friends at a particular virtual water cooler rather that being assigned to a server at the whim (so to speak) of the central server. Napster, Inc. has announced its intention to tie together all the servers eventually, creating one immense community. But given the circumstances Napster, Inc. is currently in, that may never happen.

Once you're logged in to the member server, Napster adds any MP3 files that you're sharing to its list of what's currently available. Other people logged in can then download the files that you're sharing, and you can download any of the files that everyone else is sharing. You can search through the list of files for ones that match specific criteria, and you can download multiple files at once if you feel so inclined. You can even chat with any of the other people who are logged on. When someone logs off, Napster removes their files from the list, so that they no longer appear to be available.

WARNING The main legal problem with Napster is that many of the files that people are sharing are ones that they cannot legally share. So if you use Napster to find music, be careful not to download any illegal MP3 files unwittingly. If you look in the right places, you should be able to find a good number of legal MP3 files.

At this writing, a number of universities have banned Napster, some for intellectual-property concerns, but more of them for the massive amount of bandwidth that it devours. Napster, Inc. has been working on adding features that allow administrators to allocate bandwidth effectively to reduce such problems.

The Future of Napster

At this writing, the future of Napster is far from clear. In Fall 2000, Napster, Inc. went to court to appeal against the injunction issued in July 2000 by Judge Marilyn Patel in San Francisco to shut down Napster. (The section titled "The Battle of Napster" in Chapter 2 discussed some of the legal arguments for and against Napster in layman's terms.) On February 12, 2001, the Ninth U.S. Circuit Court of Appeals issued a ruling upholding most of the aspects of the injunction but ordered Judge Patel to write a narrower injunction.

In October 2000, Napster, Inc. and the record giant Bertelsmann AG (the parent of BMG Entertainment) announced a strategic partnership by which Napster, Inc. would develop a new, subscription-based service that gave users access to Bertelsmann's huge catalog of music. Bertelsmann agreed to drop its participation in the RIAA's lawsuit when the new service was put in place. In the meantime (and at this writing), Napster, Inc. was negotiating with the other record companies to make similar deals and to put a more or less comprehensive service in place.

What's going to happen is far from clear. It seems almost certain that the new Napster service would be open to subscribers only. A subscription fee of $5 a month was mooted. Some reports suggested that there would also be a fee of $2 per track downloaded on top of the subscription fee.

So here's my speculation.

At the moment, users have three powerful motivations for using Napster. First, they can find more or less any music they want, if they search long, hard, or smart enough. Second, they can download the music for free. And third, because the files are in MP3 format, the users can use them freely—for example, putting them on portable MP3 players or using them on other computers. (Some users have a fourth powerful motivation—stealing music from the record companies, whom they perceive as having gouged them on CDs—but let's forget about that for the moment.) Because of these strong points, they're more than willing to put up with problems in the Napster service: low-quality music files encoded by the clumsy, truncated music files shared by the lazy, slow download rates, downloads terminated by the host, and so on.

When Napster moves to a subscription-based service, many of these problems should disappear. Instead of being shared by the millions of users, all the files will be stored on centralized server farms the size of Rhode Island. So all the files will be available all the time. The quality should be very high, and it should be consistent. Downloads should take place at the full speed of the user's Internet connection (be it speedy or snail-like) and should not be broken off unless the user's Internet connection collapses.

But unless Napster and Bertelsmann are careful, many users' motivations for using the Napster service may disappear with the problems. Unless Napster, Inc. can conclude deals with most of the major record companies or their representatives, the selection of music available will be limited. (If you are, or have been, a member of BMG and have searched in desperation for an appealing CD with which to fulfill your membership commitment, you'll understand the problem. To be fair, Bertelsmann's range is bigger than BMG, but it's anything but all-encompassing.) Depending on the fee structure Napster, Inc. ends up putting in place, the new service may wind up costing more than many members are prepared to pay. And whatever security arrangements are put in place to pacify the record companies and artists, users will need to have freedom in their personal use of the files: They will need to be able to download them to portable players and car players, burn them to CDs, restore them from backup, and perhaps use them on computers other than the computer onto which they downloaded them.

Let's consider the cost issue a bit more. I think that many current Napster users will be prepared to pay a modest subscription for all-you-can-eat access to a wide range of music. If the range of music is limited, all bets are off. And download fees for individual tracks will kill the service unless they're very small—on the order of 25 cents per track, perhaps. I can't see anybody beyond a very few people paying $2 a track for music available on the new Napster.

Napster, Inc. surely knows this. But the company clearly has powerful motivations for putting together a deal with the record companies. First, it has no desire to be nuked off the face of the planet by sheer megatonnage of lawyers. And second, the company wants to turn its massive membership into a profit center. Making a deal with the record companies may be the only way to continue Napster, and it's almost certainly the only way for the company to make a profit.

One of the biggest favors that Napster has done the music industry (beyond dragging it, kicking and screaming, into the 21st century) is expose millions of listeners to music they had never heard before and would never have heard through the radio, through MTV, or through their friends. In order to be effective in promoting music, the new Napster service will need to provide features that mimic this process. No doubt the new service will offer features such as previews of as many tracks as possible (in a format that ensures that anybody who wants to listen to them frequently will feel obliged to buy copies), the ability to create and save playlists and share them with friends, the ability to send recommendations to friends, and so on.

How Napster Users Can Be Tracked

When you use Napster, all your Napster actions can be tracked.

When you start Napster, or when you issue a Connect command after disconnecting or being disconnected, it contacts the central Napster server, which apportions you to a Napster member server within striking distance of you. (Striking distance is determined by your IP address and the number of hops you are from the available servers.) Napster then logs you on to the member server.

Each member server keeps track of who is connected to that server and their IP addresses. Because Napster works by establishing a direct connection between individual users, the packets of files transferred do not pass through the Napster system. (This is why you can usually continue a download when the user sharing the file moves to a different Napster server, but not when they quit Napster.) But Napster can track your searches, uploads, and downloads, and your ISP can link an IP address to a user account by the date and time. Napster can also track all the files you're sharing. And any Napster user connected to the same Napster member server as you can get a list of the files you're sharing by using the Hot List feature.

When Napster changes to a subscription-based organization, tracking will presumably be much tighter—but if all the files being downloaded by Napster users are legal, this shouldn't be too much of an issue. (Most likely, Napster users will need to be careful to opt out of any e-mail notifications that the new service offers, or they'll find their inboxes six feet deep in junk special offers.)

How Napster Can Be Closed Down

Napster can be closed down easily because Napster, Inc. forms a vulnerable central point. The central Napster servers, which receive logon requests and apportion them to the load-balanced network of Napster servers, are directly run by Napster, Inc., as are some of the servers to which the users are passed.

If Napster, Inc. is put out of operation because of legal challenges, the entire Napster network collapses. If Napster, Inc. changes Napster to a subscription-based organization, all Napster servers will change, and anyone who is not a subscriber will be unable to access the network.

Non-Napster servers attached to the Napster network (such as OpenNap servers) will still run if the Napster network is shut down. Non-Napster clients (for example, audioGnome) attaching to the servers would be unaffected.

Using Napster on Windows

This section discusses how to get, install, and use Napster itself, the young grand-daddy of the Napster clan.

Getting and Installing Napster

Start by downloading the latest version of Napster from `www.napster.com`. Once the download is complete, double-click the Napster distribution file to start the Setup routine, and then follow the prompts. You'll notice that the Software License Agreement that you have to accept warns you that "MP3 files may have been created or distributed without copyright owner authorization" and points out that "you are responsible for complying with all applicable federal and state laws applicable to such content, including copyright laws." If you read on (as you should), you'll also see that you consent to Napster automatically upgrading itself—and to Napster changing the terms and conditions of its software agreement by posting them on its Web site.

When Napster starts (which it does automatically by default at the end of the setup routine), you'll get to agree to the Software License Agreement and Disclaimer. Read (or scroll) to the end before clicking the Yes button. Then you'll see the Connection Information dialog box, shown in Figure 6.1.

Figure 6.1

Specify the details of your connection in the Connection Information dialog box.

If you want to, specify the speed of your Internet or network connection in the Connection Speed drop-down list. (See the nearby sidebar, "Should You Be Honest about Your Connection Speed?," for advice on whether to specify your true speed.) The choices go from 14.4K Modem to T3 or Greater. A T1 line is a fast dedicated line typically used for business; it delivers a constant 1.5 million bits per second (Mbps)—about the same as a DSL on a good day. A T3 line is a *very* fast line. If you're at a college, you may have a T1 or T3 connection. If you're at home, you're more likely to have a modem, cable, or a DSL connection.

Word to the Wise: Should You Be Honest about Your Connection Speed?

The speed you choose in the Connection Speed drop-down list controls the line speed Napster displays in the information it lists about you, not the line speed that Napster uses for transferring files. (Napster transfers files as fast as it can.)

The information Napster displays for you influences how other users interact with you—so you may choose to display disinformation rather than the truth. For example, if you have a 128K ISDN line, you'll get hit for downloads frequently because people will assume you'll deliver speedy downloads, whereas if you seem to have a slow modem connection, people may well shun you.

But if you choose to declare a slower connection than you have, don't claim a 14.4K modem—hardly anyone uses them anymore, so people will assume that you're hiding a fast connection and will try downloading files from you to find out if they're right. People also seem to assume that a connection whose speed is listed as Unknown may be fast, so that's not a great choice either.

If your computer connects to the Internet through a proxy server, click the Proxy Setup button to display the Proxy Setup dialog box (see Figure 6.2). (You're most likely to be behind a proxy server in a company or campus environment, in which case you may have to ask your network administrator for the details needed here.) Select the type of proxy server—SOCKS 4 Proxy Server or SOCKS 5 Proxy

Server—in the Proxy Type drop-down list, then fill in the server name in the Proxy Server text box and the port in the Proxy Port text box. If you're using a SOCKS 5 proxy server, fill in your user name in the Proxy Username text box and your password in the Proxy Password text box. In the File Transfer drop-down list, choose the Download Files through Proxy item or the Download Files Directly from Source item as appropriate. Then click the OK button to close the Proxy Setup dialog box and return to the Connection Information dialog box.

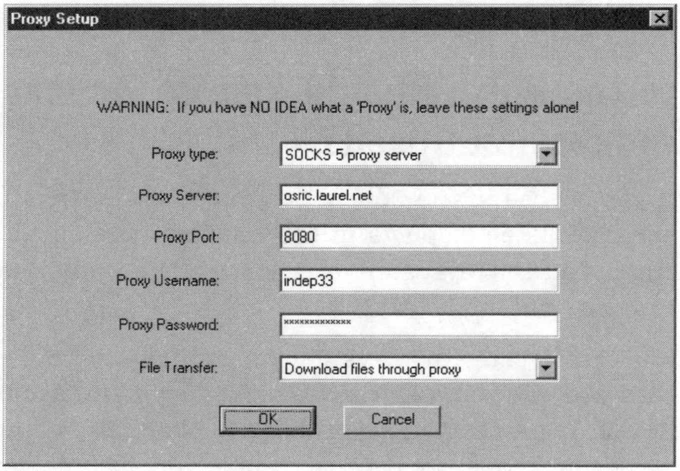

Figure 6.2

If your computer connects to the Internet through a proxy server, choose the appropriate settings in the Proxy Setup dialog box.

Proxy Setup		✕

WARNING: If you have NO IDEA what a 'Proxy' is, leave these settings alone!

Proxy type:	SOCKS 5 proxy server ▾
Proxy Server:	osric.laurel.net
Proxy Port:	8080
Proxy Username:	indep33
Proxy Password:	************
File Transfer:	Download files through proxy ▾

[OK] [Cancel]

NOTE   A *proxy server* is a computer that relays information, stores frequently accessed information in its cache, and applies filters to requests. For example, a proxy server on a company network might store parts of the critical Web sites accessed by company personnel but prevent anyone from accessing a smut site.

The next dialog box you'll see is the Napster Configuration dialog box, shown in Figure 6.3, in which you get to enter the username you want, password, and e-mail address, and choose whether to subscribe to the Napster newsletter. Try to choose a unique username (all the obvious ones have been taken by now). You can use any combination of letters, numbers, and the following characters: [ ] { } – _ ^ ! $. Be sure to choose a password that'll be hard to crack. (If the username you try is already in use, Napster displays first a dialog box warning you of the problem and then a dialog

box explaining you got the password wrong, before returning you to the Napster
Configuration dialog box so that you can try again.)

Figure 6.3

Enter your username and
details in the Napster Configuration dialog box.

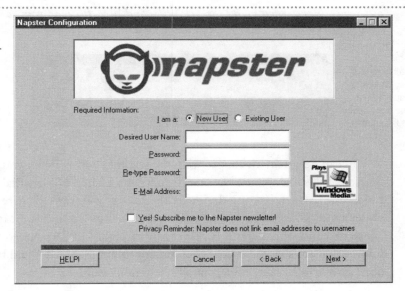

Once you've successfully chosen a username, Napster registers the name with the
Napster servers and displays the Optional Information dialog box (see Figure 6.4),
inviting you to supply your name, address, sex, age, income, and education. I can't
think why you'd want to give out this information, but you know best.

Figure 6.4

Supply your demographics
in the Optional Information
dialog box only if you really
want to.

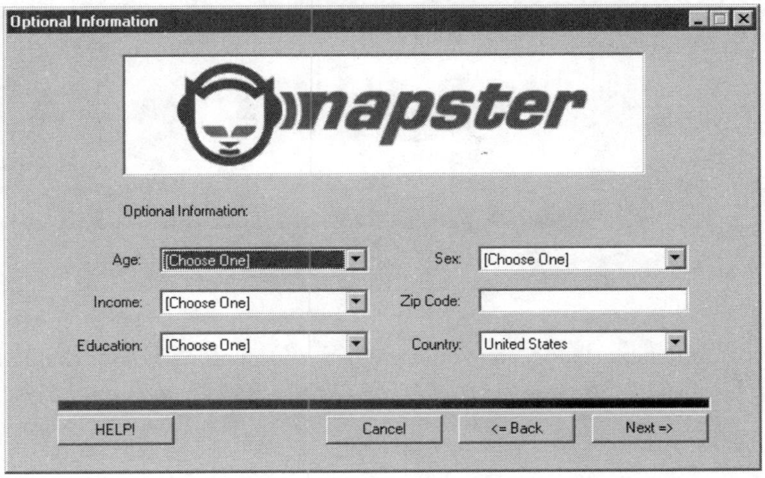

Next, you'll see the Scan for Files dialog box (see Figure 6.5), offering to scan your hard disks for MP3 and WMA files to share. *Unless you have no MP3 or WMA files on your computer except for files that you have the rights to distribute, click the No button— otherwise, Napster sets up all the MP3 files and WMA files on your computer for sharing.*

Figure 6.5

Don't let Napster scan your hard disks for audio files to share unless you have permission to share every audio file that's on your computer.

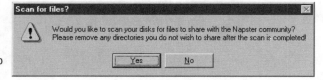

You can designate the appropriate folders for sharing when you dismiss the Scan for Files dialog box. Napster displays the Shared Folders dialog box (shown in Figure 6.6), which lets you designate the folders you want to share. Make sure you understand the legend and that you expand the tree so that you can see which folders are shared and which aren't. Be especially careful of folders shared by recursion— folders that are shared because their parent folder is shared—and be aware that you don't have to share any folders at all if you don't want to.

Figure 6.6

In the Shared Folders dialog box, make sure you're sharing only folders that contain MP3 and WMA files that you have the rights to distribute.

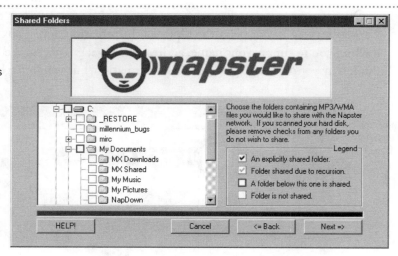

The next dialog box you'll see is the Download Folder dialog box (shown in Figure 6.7). *Be warned that by default this folder is shared with the Napster network.* It certainly shouldn't be, because there's no reason to assume that files that other people can legally distribute are ones that you can legally distribute as well—but shared it is. To prevent Napster from sharing this folder, select the Don't Share Files in Download Folder check box.

Figure 6.7

In the Download Folder dialog box, select the folder in which you want Napster to place downloaded files. Select the Don't Share Files in Download Folder check box if you don't want Napster to share the files you download.

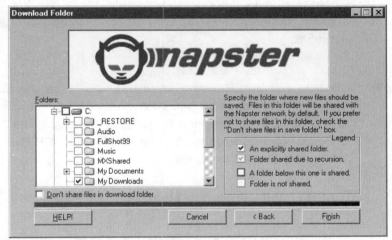

Next, if Napster experiences an error in determining your data port, it concludes that your computer is behind a firewall and displays the File Server Settings dialog box, shown in Figure 6.8.

Figure 6.8

Specify your firewall settings in the File Server Settings dialog box.

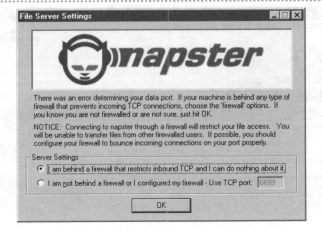

If you have no control over your firewall, select the I Am Behind a Firewall That Restricts Inbound TCP and I Can Do Nothing About It option button. (TCP is the Transmission Control Protocol, part of the TCP/IP protocol suite.) Napster cannot transfer files from other users whose computers are behind firewalls, but files from computers not behind firewalls transfer fine. If you have control over your firewall or are able to specify a TCP port for data use, select the I Am Not Behind a Firewall or I Configured My Firewall—Use TCP Port option button and specify the TCP port in the text box.

> At this writing, Napster sometimes displays the File Server Settings dialog box even when you're connecting via an ISP and no firewall is involved. If this happens to you, try selecting the I Am Not Behind a Firewall or I Configured My Firewall—Use TCP Port option button and using the default port, 6699.

After that, Napster displays its Home page (see Figure 6.9).

Figure 6.9

When Napster starts, it displays its Home page.

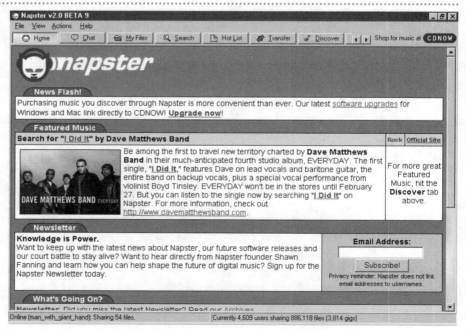

Before you start using Napster, you should probably choose a few more settings—ones that do not appear in the current setup routine. To set these settings or to change any of the Napster settings you chose during setup, choose File ➤ Preferences to display the Napster Preferences dialog box, which gathers together all the changeable information that you entered during setup. (You can't change your username without reinstalling Napster.)

The Napster Preferences dialog box contains six pages: Personal, Chat, Schemes, Sharing, Downloading, and Proxy. The following sections discuss the extra options that you'll probably want to set.

Personal Page

The Personal page of the Napster Preferences dialog box (see Figure 6.10) contains text boxes for your username (which you cannot change without uninstalling and reinstalling Napster) and your e-mail address and password (which you can change). You can change your ostensible connection speed in the Connection Type drop-down list, and you can choose between the Napster Internal Player and your Default Media Player in the Media Player drop-down list.

Figure 6.10

You can change your e-mail address, password, connection type, and media player on the Personal page of the Napster Preferences dialog box.

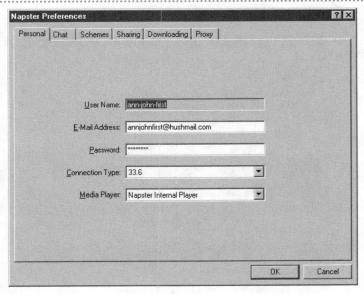

Chat Page

The Chat page of the Napster Preferences dialog box (see Figure 6.11) has four options that you'll probably want to set:

Automatically Join My Previous Channels When Signing On to Napster check box   This check box lets you automatically join the chat channels you were using at the end of your last Napster session.

Do Not Display Offensive Words in Private Messages or Public Chat Rooms check box   This check box switches on and off the "swear filter"—whether Napster bleeps out any offending words (starting with "suck"), substituting symbols instead.

Display My Incoming Private Messages in Separate Windows check box This check box controls whether Napster displays incoming private messages in separate windows or in the main chat window.

Display Notification When a User Enters or Exits a Chat Room check box This check box controls whether Napster notifies you when users enter and leave chat rooms. Because Napster chat can get busy, you may want to clear this check box to keep down the amount of noise you're subjected to.

Figure 6.11

Choose chat options on the Chat page of the Napster Preferences dialog box.

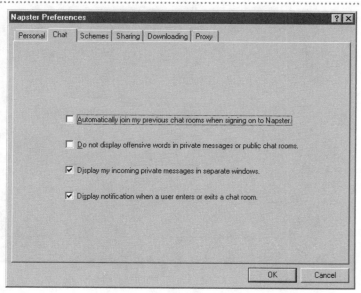

Schemes Page

The Schemes page of the Napster Preferences dialog box (see Figure 6.12) lets you use different color schemes for Napster. (The screen shots shown in this chapter use the default color scheme.)

Figure 6.12
Choose color schemes for Napster on the Schemes page of the Napster Preferences dialog box.

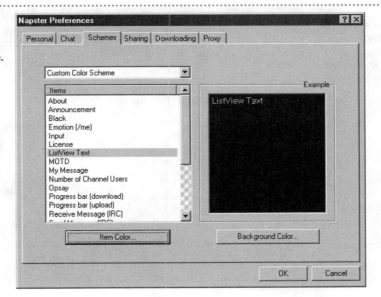

Sharing Page

The Sharing page of the Napster Preferences dialog box (see Figure 6.13) lets you change the folder or folders you're sharing with the Napster community, change the TCP port you're using, and force Napster to search your hard disks for MP3 and WMA files to share via Napster.

It also contains the Maximum Simultaneous Outbound Transfers Per User text box, which controls the number of files each Napster user can download from you simultaneously. Make sure this setting is appropriate for your line speed: If you have a modem connection, reduce the outbound transfers per user to 1 in order to give visitors the maximum speed possible. (If multiple visitors connect at the same time, they'll still get low speeds—but the speeds will be lower still if you let each user have multiple uploads.) If you have a heavy-duty connection such as a T1, you may want to choose a larger number, perhaps between 2 and 10. But bear in mind that usually it's best to transfer each file as quickly as possible rather than transferring several files more slowly at the same time.

Figure 6.13

Set the maximum number of simultaneous uploads per user on the Sharing page of the Napster Preferences dialog box.

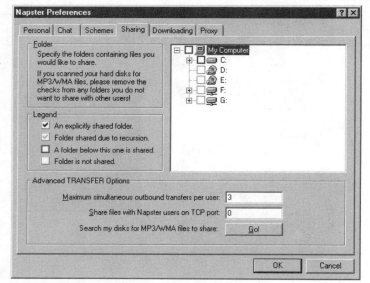

If you don't want others to be able to download any files that you're sharing, set the Maximum Simultaneous Outbound Transfers text box to 0 (zero). When you do this and click the OK button to close the Napster Preferences dialog box, Napster displays the File Server Shut Down dialog box warning you that others will not be able to download your shared files and asking you to confirm that you want to take this step. Click the Yes button if you do—but remember that in general it's more sensible not to share files than to share them but not allow people to download them.

When you have the Maximum Simultaneous Outbound Transfers text box set to 0, Napster asks you if you want to enable the file server each time you start Napster.

Downloading Page

The Downloading page of the Napster Preferences dialog box (see Figure 6.14) lets you change your download folder and offers these three options:

Max Simultaneous Inbound Transfers text box   This text box controls the number of simultaneous downloads that Napster performs (if you've selected multiple files). If you have a fast connection, enter a number between 5 and 10 (or between 5 and 25) so that you can pull down a number of songs at the same time from lower-bandwidth sites. If you have a modem, keep the number low— perhaps 2 or 3—so that each song you're downloading gets a significant chunk of your bandwidth and none takes too long to download. Also, the longer a download takes, the more chance that the Napster user you are downloading it from will go offline, leaving you stuck with an incomplete file.

If you have a modem connection, you'll often want to change your Max Simultaneous Inbound Transfers number to find the connections you need and maximize your download speed. When searching for files you want, set a figure around five so that Napster tests multiple connections at once and you can quickly see which users you can download from and which you can't. (You can also issue a Force Transfer command to get a similar effect.) Once you get a couple of downloads running, lower the Max Simultaneous Inbound Transfers number to the number of connections, so that they go faster. And if you hit a user who's the mother lode of files you're after and from whom you can download files successfully, drop the Max Simultaneous Inbound Transfers number to 1 so that you get each track as quickly as possible, in case the user goes offline. Then queue all the tracks you want to download from the user, and Napster will download them one by one at your top speed.

Delete Partial Files When Download Fails drop-down list   Select Yes in this drop-down list if you want Napster to automatically delete any file that isn't fully downloaded. The default setting is No, and there's also a Prompt Me setting that's useful if you'll be monitoring your Napster sessions closely. (I'd like to see a partial setting, where you could automatically delete anything of which you got, say, less than a third or a half, but keep anything of which you got more than that.)

Remove Successful Downloads from Transfer Window drop-down list Select Yes in this drop-down list instead of the default No if you want Napster to automatically remove the entries for successfully downloaded tracks from the Download page. This option is useful for heavy downloading sessions on a fast line.

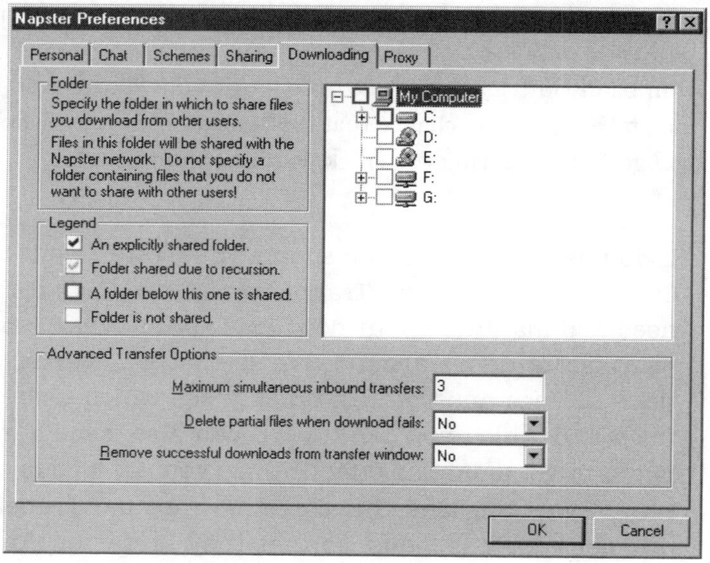

Figure 6.14

Choose download preferences on the Downloading page of the Napster Preferences dialog box.

Proxy Page

The Proxy page of the Napster Preferences dialog box (see Figure 6.15) offers a half-dozen settings for people connecting to the Internet through a proxy server. You'll recognize these settings as those that appear in the Proxy Setup dialog box, which we covered earlier in the chapter.

If you don't use a proxy server, you don't need to mess with these settings; if you do use a proxy server, you need to get them right. If you don't know the details of your proxy server, ask your network administrator—but if you're running Napster in a business setting, make sure you have a valid business reason for needing to know the proxy server information (unless you own the business, of course.)

Figure 6.15

If you're connecting through a proxy server, you can tweak the settings on the Proxy page of the Napster Preferences dialog box.

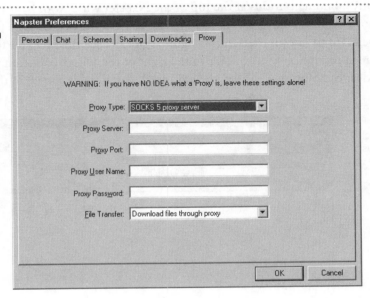

 If you don't have a good reason to query the local network guru for proxy server settings, check to see if the information you need is residing in the bowels of your browser. In Internet Explorer, choose Tools ➤ Internet Options to display the Internet Options dialog box, click the Connections tab to display the Connections page, and click the LAN Settings button to display the Local Area Network (LAN) Settings dialog box, whose Proxy Server group box may be able help you. In Netscape Navigator, choose Edit ➤ Preferences to display the Preferences dialog box, expand the Advanced category, click the Proxies entry, and see what you find. This information won't necessarily be exactly what you need, but it may put you on the right track.

Finding Music with Napster

The Napster interface consists of eight pages—Home, Chat, My Files, Search, Hot List, Transfer, Discover, and Help—which you navigate between by clicking the eight corresponding buttons at the top of the Napster window or by pressing Ctrl+Tab (to move from left to right). As you'd guess, you use the Search page (shown in Figure 6.16) to find music. (In this figure, you can't see the Help button because of the screen resolution used, but it's to the right of the Discover button.) Click the Advanced button to display the advanced search fields shown in the figure.

Figure 6.16

Use the Napster Search page to search for music.

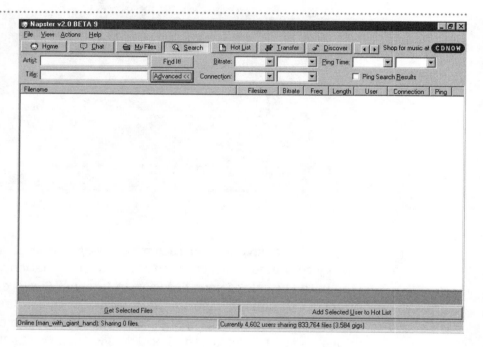

Specify your search criteria by using the text boxes and drop-down lists at the top of the window. You can search by up to six criteria, which gives you good flexibility in finding the music you're looking for. For example, to search for any MP3 files by a given artist, you would specify only the artist's name in the Artist text box. To search for a particular track by that artist, you would specify the artist's name and either the track's name or any keywords in the track in the Title text box. To search for only copies at or above a certain bitrate (say, 128K) and available on ISDN or faster connections, you would click the Advanced button to display the Bitrate, Connection, and Ping Time fields, and then specify those criteria as well.

To exclude a word from a search, enter it with a hyphen before it. Doing so can be useful when an artist or band is best known for a track that you're not interested in. For example, if you search for tracks by the Boomtown Rats, you're likely to get 100 results of "I Don't Like Mondays" and no other tracks. But if you search for **Boomtown Rats –Mondays**, Napster excludes the word "Mondays" from the search, and you should see only tracks without the word. (Note that this is an example only. Any Boomtown Rats MP3 files being shared are most likely illegal.)

Use the three advanced fields to restrict the search as much as you want. Each of the drop-down lists in the left-hand column offers four settings: the default blank setting (meaning that the field is not used), AT LEAST, EQUAL TO, and AT BEST.

If you want to get MP3 files of only good quality or better, set the Bitrate row's first drop-down list to AT LEAST and the second to the minimum quality you want—for example, 128kbps. (If you have a slow connection or a portable player with a small amount of storage and don't want to download any files of a bitrate higher than your chosen acceptable bitrate, select the EQUAL TO item instead of the AT LEAST item.)

Use the Connection row and the Ping Time row to make sure you only get hits that should download at a decent speed:

- You can specify a minimum, exact, or maximum line speed in the Connection row. If you use this field, you'll usually want to specify a minimum connection speed. For example, you might choose AT LEAST ISDN-128K to get hosts with two-channel ISDN or better. It seldom makes sense to specify an exact connection speed unless you feel you must have T3 connections only. And there's no sense in specifying a *maximum* connection speed—unless you're very strange, you'll want the fastest connection you can find.

- *Ping time* is the time, measured in milliseconds (ms), it takes for a packet of information to get from your computer to the host computer and back. A longer ping time usually means there are more *hops* (stages) in the connection between your computer and the host, which translates to a greater burden on the Internet and a potentially longer download time. Usually you won't need to specify a ping time; instead, you can sort your search results by ping time (provided you keep the Ping Search Results check box selected) and take the fastest relevant result. (If you do want to try setting a ping time, you might choose AT BEST 500 ms to avoid ultra-slow connections.) To use pings at all, you need to select the Ping Search Results check box.

Remember that 56K modems, DSLs, and cable connections have much slower upstream speeds than downstream speeds. A 56K modem delivers a maximum of 33.6K upstream, and many DSL and cable connections (depending on the carrier and the service plan) deliver only 128K maximum upstream. In particular, don't scorn ISDN connections—they deliver the data rate advertised, and an ISDN-128K connection often outperforms a DSL or cable on the upload. And if you're prepared to use modem connections, set a minimum of 33.6K or even 28.8K rather than 56K—33.6K is the maximum speed you'll get when downloading from a 56K modem, so there's no sense in excluding 33.6K modems, which will deliver the same speed; and 28.8K is only about 15 percent slower than 33.6K, so it's still worth using. Also, remember that a number of Napster users will be deliberately hiding speedy connections in order to avoid downloads—so you may want to try downloading from some ostensible 14.4K connections or Unknown speed connections to see if they're really faster than they claim.

Often, you'll do best to start by performing a search with only one or two criteria, to see if you get some results. If you get plenty of results, apply further criteria and search again until you get a smaller number of results that more closely match your needs. In particular, you may want to leave the Bitrate field open on your first search so that you see all the available copies of tracks. If there are plenty of copies, you can then add in the bitrate criterion to narrow the field to your chosen bitrates; if not, you will at least be aware of low-bitrate versions of the tracks you're looking for rather than missing them altogether.

Keep an eye on the track length of the songs returned in your Napster searches. Some of the songs listed may be incomplete, because Napster downloads get broken off if the host goes offline. If you can figure out by consensus what the track length is for the song you're interested in, you'll be able to avoid wasting your time and bandwidth on downloading someone else's incomplete version.

When you've set your search criteria, click the Find It! button. Napster searches through the songs available in the libraries and returns a list of what it has found. Figure 6.17 shows Napster having found 100 tracks that match the search criterion "Cure." Most are tracks by the band The Cure (as you'd expect), but others are tracks with the word "Cure" in them (including tracks from Ashford + Simpson, Morphine, A Perfect Circle, and Denis Leary). The tracks are being supplied by a number of different users.

Figure 6.17

The Search page lists all matching songs found, with colored circles indicating the connection speed.

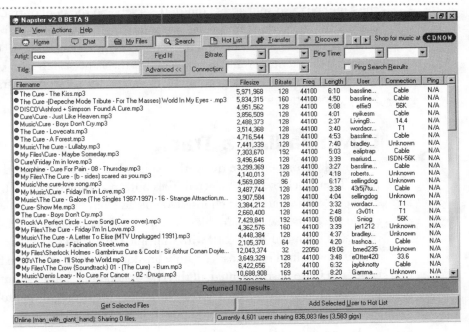

Most of the fields in the results list on the Search page are easy enough to understand: Filename, Filesize, Bitrate, Freq (frequency), Length (time in minutes and seconds), User (the host's name), Connection, and Ping (the ping time). The colored circles next to the filenames provide a quick guide to the line speed:

- A red circle denotes a 33.6K or slower modem, or an unknown speed. Remember that unknown speeds can be high—as can lines that the users have chosen to hide as low-speed modems.

- A yellow circle denotes anything from a 56K modem to a 128K ISDN line.

- A green circle denotes anything faster than a 128K line—a cable modem, a DSL, a T1, or a T3.

Something else to try: Instead of searching for particular titles by the artists you're interested in, search for words like "rare," "bootleg," and "live." Doing so may turn up some true treasures—along with more Grateful Dead tracks than the average human can handle.

The Napster community is not only dynamic (with people logging on and off all the time) but also split across multiple servers. So the pool of tracks available changes constantly. If you don't find what you're looking for, disconnect from your current server (File ➤ Disconnect) and immediately connect again (File ➤ Connect) until you get a different server. Alternatively, try the same search later on the same server—different people may be logged on by then, and the selection of tracks available is likely to be different.

Downloading a Track

To download one or more tracks that you've located, select it or them on the Search page. Then click the Get Selected Files button at the bottom of the page, or right-click one of the tracks and choose Download from the context menu. To download a single track, you can also double-click the track name. Napster displays the Transfer page, as shown in Figure 6.18 with multiple Cure tracks being downloaded. Note that at this point I'm almost certainly breaking the law, as (to the best of my knowledge) the Cure hasn't granted all these people permission to shunt their copyrighted material around on the Internet. So these files are illegal: illegal to share and illegal to download. (You'll be relieved to know I didn't keep them.)

As each download runs, Napster shows you its status (Getting Info, Queued, Remotely Queued, Downloading, File Complete, Canceled, Unavailable, or Transfer Error), the line speed, a progress bar for it, the download rate (as in Figure 6.18), and the time left on the download. Here's what the status terms mean:

Getting Info   This means that Napster is contacting the host offering the file for download. If there's a problem with transferring the file, the transfer may get stuck at the Getting Info stage, in which case you'll need to cancel it. The transfer will eventually time out, but if you're at your computer, you'll probably nuke it for non-performance long before Napster times it out.

Figure 6.18

The Transfer page shows you the status of all your current downloads.

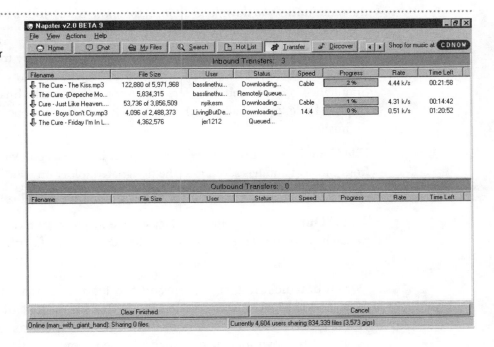

Figure 6.18

The Transfer page shows you the status of all your current downloads.

Downloading   This indicates that Napster has established a satisfactory connection to the host and is downloading the file. The bar in the Progress column shows you the progress of the download visually.

Unavailable   This typically indicates that the download has failed, either because of firewalling problems or because the host has gone offline. It may also mean that the host has deliberately killed the download.

Transfer Error   This typically indicates that the host has disconnected from or exited Napster. It may also indicate that the host has removed the file from the folder in which Napster has it listed, or that the host has renamed the file, and has not refreshed their Napster library.

Queued   This indicates that you're currently downloading your maximum number of tracks (set in the Max Simultaneous Downloads text box on the Downloading page of the Napster Preferences dialog box), so the track is waiting for one of the current downloads to finish. If you want to download more tracks at once, increase the Max Simultaneous Downloads number—but remember that the more tracks you download at once, the more thinly your bandwidth is spread, and the longer each download will take.

Remotely Queued   This indicates that the host is currently transferring its maximum number of tracks to you and other Napster users (as set in their Max Simultaneous Outbound Transfers Per User text box on the Sharing page of the Napster Preferences dialog box), so the track is waiting for one of those transfers to finish.

File Complete   This indicates that Napster has finished downloading the file from the host and has saved it to the designated folder on your hard drive.

Canceled   This indicates that you have canceled the download.

Timed Out   This indicates that Napster has given up on trying to get a response from a host. Napster then moves on to the next download that you have queued.

When downloading, try to spread the load as much as possible: Don't try to download multiple files from the same host at the same time unless both you and the host have fast connections. For example, if you try to download ten tracks at once from a host that has a 56K modem, you'll get a miserable transfer rate of a few hundred bytes a second and each track will take several hours to download (assuming that the host allows each user to download that many tracks at once). Instead, hit multiple 56K hosts for a track apiece, and you'll get them much quicker (provided you have the bandwidth yourself). This strategy of not overburdening a host may be foiled by other people hitting the same host and downloading files, but at a minimum, you should make sure that you don't throttle any host by yourself.

When you try to download a file that has the same name as a file that's currently in your library, Napster displays the File Exists! dialog box (see Figure 6.19), which lets you overwrite the existing file or (if you can access the remote machine) rename the remote file. Usually, you won't be able to rename the file on the remote machine (and even if you could, it's bad Netiquette), so you'll do better to open an Explorer window, rename the existing file with that name, and then tell Napster to overwrite the existing file (which won't be there any more, but Napster won't notice).

Figure 6.19

The File Exists! dialog box warns you that you're downloading a track with the same name as one already in your download directory and lets you decide how to solve the problem.

While downloading, you can use the two buttons at the bottom of the Transfer page to cancel or clear finished transfers:

- Click the Cancel button, or right-click the transfer and choose Cancel from the context menu, to cancel a transfer. Canceling a transfer leaves the entry in your Transfer list, so you can try it again later; aborting the entry removes the entry from your Transfer list.

- Click the Clear Finished button to remove completed transfers from the Transfer page. Clearing finished transfers also removes from the Transfer page files that were unavailable or that were canceled.

The context menu for the Inbound Transfers list box on the Transfer page gives you several more options:

- Choose the Play Song! item to play the track even as you're downloading it. You'll be able to hear only as much of the track as you've downloaded, but this feature can help you identify tracks that you don't want to continue downloading (for example, if you're getting a different track than you thought or if the track is low quality or damaged).

- Choose the Force Transfer item to force the transfer of a queued item. Forcing a transfer temporarily overrides your Maximum Simultaneous Downloads setting.

- Use the Prioritize submenu (which has items for Move Up, Move Down, Move to Top, and Move to Bottom) to improve the order in which you're downloading tracks. First, promote the tracks you're most interested in to the top of the list, so that you get them before the hosts who are providing them go offline. Second, if you're downloading a number of tracks from a couple of hosts at about the same speed, you might want to alternate queued tracks so as to balance your demands on each host.

☠ Choose the Cancel Transfer item to cancel a transfer but keep it on the Transfer page, and the Delete/Abort Transfer item to cancel a transfer and remove it from the Transfer page.

☠ Choose the Clear Finished item to remove completed or impossible transfers from the Transfer page.

Napster stores the files for incomplete transfers in the \Napster\ Incomplete\ folder. Visit this folder from time to time to retrieve lost partial gems and to clear out the residue.

Playing Music in Napster

Any MP3 files in the folders you've designated for sharing via Napster and in your download folder are listed on the My Files page (shown in Figure 6.20). You can play these files directly or add them to your playlist.

The lower-left corner of the Library page contains the controls for Napster's internal audio player: a volume control, a position slider, and the standard buttons—Play, Pause, Stop, Previous, and Next. If you chose to use your default MP3 player instead of Napster's internal audio player, clicking the Play button launches (or switches to) your default player.

To play a song quickly, double-click it in the library. Otherwise, create a playlist by using the Add button to add tracks selected on the Library page to the playlist and then rearranging them into the order you want. Use the Save button and the resulting Save As dialog box to save a playlist you want to keep, and the Load button and resulting Open dialog box to open a saved playlist.

To delete a track from your library, right-click it and choose Delete (From Disk) from the context menu, and then choose the Yes button in the resulting Delete File dialog box.

Figure 6.20

The Library page contains all the files you've shared and those you've downloaded.

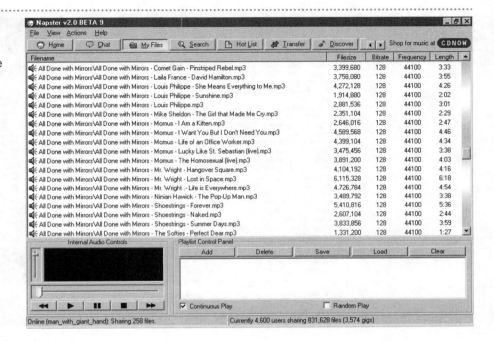

To refresh your library when you've made changes to it by using Explorer, right-click in it and choose Refresh Library from the context menu. (Napster automatically adds tracks you've downloaded to the library, so you don't need to refresh it on their account.)

Chatting on Napster

To keep you entertained while searching for the MP3 files you want or letting people download the MP3 files you can legally share, Napster supports multiple chat channels that you can join and leave at will. The chat channels allow both public and private messaging—although at this writing, relatively few Napster users seem to spend much time chatting, presumably because they're there primarily for the music.

The Chat page, shown in Figure 6.21, is easy to navigate. You start off with a Private channel that remains open the whole time. The Private channel displays the Napster message of the day when you log on and also displays any private messages that are sent to you. (Private messages are also displayed on the current Chat page.)

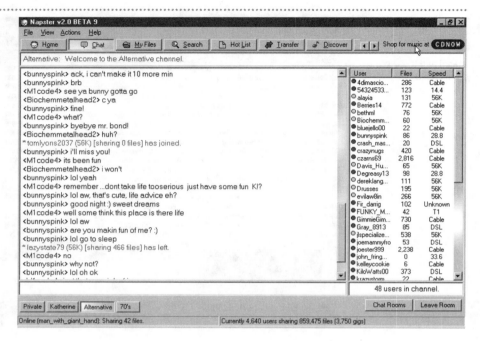

To join another channel, click the Chat Rooms button. (If you joined any chat channels after running Napster the first time, you may already have other channels available.) Napster displays the Channel List dialog box with the root list of channels selected (see Figure 6.22). To display the full list of channels available on the server, including user-created channels, click the View All button. (To restore the view to the root list, click the resulting View Root button.)

Select the channel or channels you want to join (Shift+clicking and Ctrl+clicking work for multiple selections), and then click the Join button to join them. You can join up to five channels at a time (on top of the Private channel).

You can create your own chat channel by clicking the Create >> button to display an extra part of the Napster Chat Rooms dialog box, entering the name in the Channel to Create text box, and clicking the Create button. This channel will then be available to other users connected to the same server as you. To view the channel, users will need to click the View All button to display the full list of channels. User-created channels appear with a smiley-face icon next to them, like the GreenRoom and IndustroGoth channels shown in Figure 6.23.

Figure 6.22

Use the Napster Chat Rooms dialog box to join and create chat rooms.

Figure 6.23

User-created channels are identified by a smiley-face icon instead of the Napster icon.

Each channel you join appears as a button across the bottom of the screen below the Chat text box. You can move from one chat channel to another by clicking the appropriate button, or you can move from one channel to the next (from left to right) by pressing Ctrl+X.

You can view the information available about a user by right-clicking their entry in the user list and choosing View Information from the context menu. Napster displays the Finger Information dialog box for the user, as shown in Figure 6.24.

Figure 6.24

Use the View Information command and the resulting Finger dialog box to get information about another Napster user.

To send a private message to someone, right-click their entry in the user list and choose Private Message from the context menu. Napster displays the Instant Message window (see Figure 6.25). Type the message and press Enter to send it.

Figure 6.25

Sending an instant message

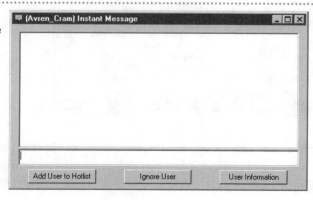

TIP You can also send a private message by typing **/tell <*username*>** and the message in the text box at the bottom of a chat page.

If someone's bothering you with private messages, you can ignore them by clicking the Ignore User button on the Instant Message window. You can also ignore somebody in a chat room by right-clicking their entry in the user list and choosing Ignore from the context menu. Napster displays "Ignored user <*username*>'s channel and private messages" in the chat pane. The person being ignored receives no notification of the ignorance.

To un-ignore someone whose handle you can remember, right-click their entry in the user list in chat and choose Unignore. Napster displays "Removed <*username*> from ignore list" in the chat pane. If you've been ignoring a bunch of people and have forgotten who they all are, choose Action ➤ View Ignore List to display the Ignore List dialog box (see Figure 6.26). Use the Remove button to remove selected users from your ignore list, or use the Clear button to forgive everyone their trespasses in one fell swoop. Then click the Close button to close the Ignore List dialog box.

Figure 6.26

Use the Ignore List dialog box to un-ignore people whose names you've forgotten.

To find out information about a user listed in chat, use the Information feature. Right-click the user in the user list in a chat pane and choose View Information from the context menu to display the Finger Information box for the user.

If you know that someone is online with the Napster server you're using, you can find out what channel (or channels) they're in by using the Information command. Choose Actions ➤ Get User Information `finger` command in the Chat text box. For example, to find out which channel (or channels) the user Mustang999 is in, you could use the following command:

`/finger Mustang999`

If the user is online with this server, you'll see the Finger Information dialog box for the user; this dialog box includes the user's current channel or channels. If the user is not currently online with this server, Napster doesn't display the Finger Information dialog box, but instead displays the message "user *<username>* is not a known user" in your chat pane. (This message is not visible to other participants in the chat room.)

Even if you care nothing for chat, you can use it to find out who's online and interested in the same types of music as you, the number of songs they're sharing, and the speed of their connection. Then check out interesting people by using the Hot List feature as described in the next section.

Beyond the swear filter (which substitutes symbols to bleep out common obscenities and offensive words in chat), Napster has two levels of punishment for people caught transgressing against community standards of etiquette in chat. First, an administrator may "muzzle" you to shut you up for the time being; they then get to decide when to unmuzzle you later. Second, if you're still offensive after repeated muzzling, an administrator may "kill" you—disconnect you from the server.

Maintaining a Hot List

Apart from searching for a particular artist or track, Napster provides a great way of finding out what music people are sharing: the hot list. This feature lets you browse through all the files that a particular user is offering—letting you discover little-known music that people are sharing. And once you find a gem, you can see what else that same person is sharing. Chances are good they'll have more music that interests you.

At this writing, with the Napster pool of music split across many servers, the hot list is not as compelling a feature as it will become if Napster integrates all servers into a common pool. You can add to the hot list any user whose name you encounter online or whose name you happen to know, but there's no guarantee that any person you add to your hot list in one session will log into the same Napster server as you the next session—nor that they'll even be online in the first place. Napster, Inc. has of course no control over who is online when, but they've been working on the server problem, and you can now see hot-list users across servers and exchange messages with them—but you cannot yet see the files they're sharing unless you're both connected to the same server.

One easy way to add a user to the hot list is from the Chat page, whose right-hand pane lists the users in your current chat channel, together with the number of songs they're sharing and their connection speed. (There's no list of users for the Private channel, of course.) By default, this pane is sorted alphabetically by user, but you can sort by the Songs column or by the Speed column by clicking the column heading. Click a column heading a second time to sort the column in reverse alphabetical order.

You can add a user to the hot list from the Chat page, the Search page, or the Transfer page by either right-clicking a listing featuring them and choosing Add to Hot List from the context menu or by selecting the user and choosing Actions ➤ Add User to Hot List. On the Hot List page, you can add a user by clicking the Add User to Hot List button, entering the user's name in the User to Add text box, and clicking the OK button.

When you add a user to the hot list from the Chat page or the Search page, Napster displays the Hot List page. Figure 6.27 shows a hot list with seven of the members online (in the Online pane) and rather more offline (in the Offline pane).

To see what one of the users on your hot list is currently offering, double-click their entry in the Online box. If Napster is slow to show the user's list of files, right-click the entry and choose Refresh File List from the context menu. If you see the Napster Notification dialog box telling you that Napster is unable to transfer the file because both users are firewalled, you need to find another host or change your configuration so that incoming TCP packets can get through the firewall to your computer.

To remove a user from your hot list, right-click their entry in the Online pane or the Offline pane and choose Delete User from the context menu. Napster displays the Remove User dialog box (see Figure 6.28). Click the Yes button to complete the eviction.

Figure 6.27

Use the Hot List page to browse through the list of MP3 files that another user is sharing.

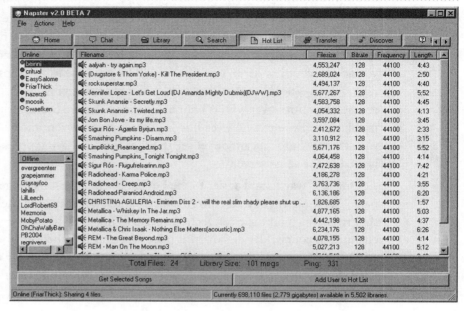

Figure 6.28

When you sicken of someone, remove them from your hot list.

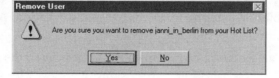

Sharing Music with Napster

If you have music that you have the right to distribute, Napster provides you with an effortless mechanism for sharing it: Just place the tracks in the folder (or in one of the folders) you've designated for sharing, and start Napster. If the tracks don't appear in your library, right-click and choose Refresh Library from the context menu to make Napster rescan the shared folders.

Before you start sharing tracks with Napster, make sure that you've chosen an appropriate number for simultaneous uploads per user in the Max Outbound Transfers Per User text box in the Napster Preferences dialog box (File ➤ Preferences). For a modem connection, you'll probably want to limit each user to 1 upload at a time;

any more than this will deliver a lame data rate that will make the tracks take hours to transfer—and that's if only one user is downloading from your computer at a time. For a 64K ISDN connection, you might try 2; for a 128K ISDN line, a DSL, or a cable connection, perhaps 3; and a higher number for a T1, depending on whether you have the whole line to yourself (unlikely). If you have a T3 to yourself, you'll be able to enter much higher numbers and still deliver a good data rate to a number of people. But keep in mind, as I mentioned before, that in most cases it's best to transfer each track as quickly as possible in case the connection collapses at one end or the other. So there's an argument for using a setting of 1 for Max Outbound Transfers Per User even if your Internet connection is stout enough to transfer the entire contents of the Library of Congress every hour.

Once you've shared the files, anybody logged onto the same Napster server as you can access them, either by turning them up in a search or by adding you to their hot list and explicitly scanning your shared files.

When someone is downloading a file from your computer, you'll see the entry appear in the Outbound Transfers pane on the Transfer page, marked *Transferring*, as in Figure 6.29. If tracks are queued for upload from your computer, these do not appear in the Outbound Transfers pane until they become active.

Figure 6.29

Tracks being downloaded from your computer appear in the lower pane on the Transfer page.

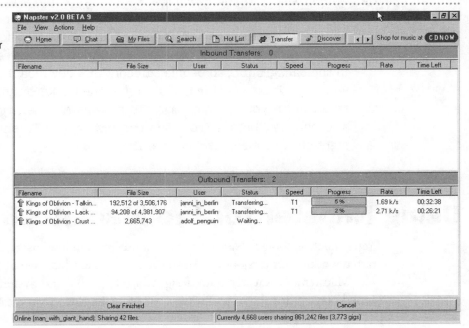

You can cancel a transfer by selecting it and clicking the Cancel button. Alternatively, right-click the transfer and choose Cancel Transfer from the context menu to cancel the transfer, or choose Delete/Abort Transfer to delete it and remove it from the Transfer page. In either case, the track is listed as a Transfer Error or as Unavailable to the would-be downloader. Canceling a transfer isn't the greatest of Netiquette, and if you're concerned about your karma, you might want to message people to warn them that you're about to take an ax to their download. But as things stand with Napster, they won't be able to tell the difference between your canceling a transfer manually and Napster disagreeing with itself or with the Internet, so only your conscience benefits from your messaging them. The resulting truncated file will be useless or unsatisfactory either way. Likewise, you won't know which of the many Transfer Error and Unavailable messages you get are the result of malice and which are the result of natural Internet phenomena.

If you exit Napster while someone is downloading a track from your computer, the downloader will get a Transfer Error message for the track. If you disconnect from Napster but keep your Internet connection open, Napster can usually continue uploads that are in progress. (This is because Napster establishes a one-to-one connection between users rather than connecting them through the Napster server.)

WARNING

When exiting Napster, use the File ➢ Exit command rather than clicking the Close button in the upper right-hand corner of the window or using the control menu. Exit ends your Napster session, but clicking the Close button gets rid of the Napster window but leaves Napster running in the background, so people can continue downloading files that you're sharing. While Napster is running in the background, you'll see a Napster icon in your system tray. To restore Napster, right-click this icon and choose Restore from the context menu. To shut down Napster, right-click the icon and choose Exit.

Using Napster for the Macintosh

Pretty much as soon as Napster became a hit for Windows users, Mac programmers started working on versions of Napster to run on the Mac. Two of the leading versions were Macster and Rapster, both designed for System 8 and System 9, and a version named Napster for the MacOS X—as its name implies—was created for System X.

In late 2000, Macster was adopted as the official Napster client for the Macintosh, was renamed Napster for the Mac, and was released as a beta version.

This section discusses Napster for the Mac.

Getting, Installing, and Configuring Napster for the Mac

Download the latest version of Napster for the Mac from the Napster Web site, www.napster.com. Unstuff what you download if it doesn't unstuff itself automatically, and then double-click the Napster Installer item to start the setup routine running.

The Napster Installer walks you through the steps of the setup routine.

The first Napster Installer dialog box (shown in Figure 6.30) lets you select the folder in which to install Napster for the Mac. Do so (or accept the default choice) and click the Install button to proceed.

Figure 6.30

In the first Napster Installer dialog box, you can choose the folder in which to install Napster for the Mac.

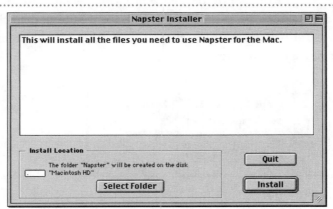

You'll then see the Installing dialog box (shown in Figure 6.31) as the Napster Installer installs Napster.

Figure 6.31

The Napster for the Mac installation proceeds apace.

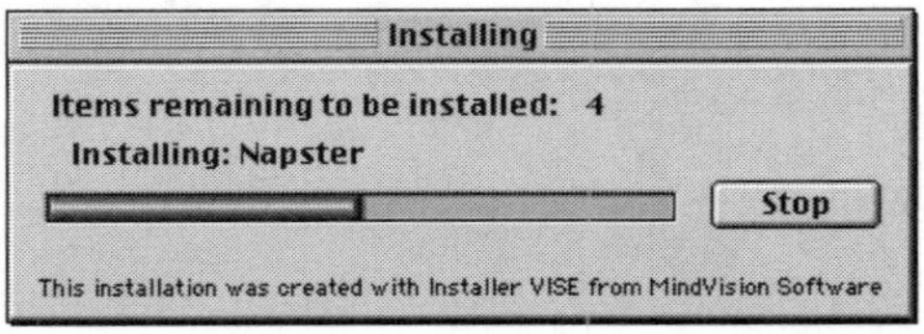

When the installation is complete, you'll see the "Installation was successful" dialog box shown in Figure 6.32. From this dialog box, you can click the Continue button to install further copies of Napster on the same computer (for example, so that you can have two or more Napster accounts on the same Mac). More likely, you'll want to click the Quit button to exit the Napster Installer.

Figure 6.32

The Napster Installer lets you install further copies of Napster on your computer if you want.

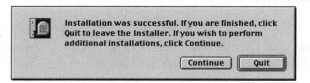

Once you've finished installing copies of Napster, double-click the Napster icon in the Napster folder (or in one of the Napster folders) to run the Napster Setup Assistant.

First, you get to accept (or decline) a license agreement. Read (or scroll) to the end of the license agreement to enable the right-arrow button, then click this button. The Napster Setup Assistant displays the untitled dialog box shown in Figure 6.33, asking whether you agree to the terms.

Figure 6.33

Agree to the terms if you want to use Napster.

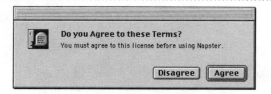

Click the Agree button if you want to proceed. You'll then see the Napster Setup Assistant: Introduction dialog box (shown in Figure 6.34).

Click the right-arrow button. You'll see the Napster Setup Assistant: Account Type dialog box (shown in Figure 6.35), which lets you create a new account or use an existing account (for example, an account you've set up with Napster or one of its clones).

Figure 6.34

The beginning of the Napster Setup Assistant's performance

Figure 6.35

The Napster Setup Assistant: Account Type dialog box lets you either register a new Napster account or set up an existing Napster account.

If you choose to set up a new account, you'll follow these steps:

- In the first of the two Napster Setup Assistant: Optional Information dialog boxes (shown in Figure 6.36), you can enter details of your age, sex, and education level. In the second of these dialog boxes, you can specify a favorite music genre, the city where you live, and your zip code. Supplying this information is optional, so don't feel obliged to divulge it—or to tell the truth if you do give information.

Figure 6.36

The Napster Setup Assistant asks you for a lot of optional information. Give it only if you feel so inclined.

In the Napster Setup Assistant: Account Information dialog box (shown in Figure 6.37), enter a login name and the password you want to use. The login name needs to be unique within the Napster system, which means you'll need to be creative. Consider using symbols or multiple underscores to make a unique version of a name that has already been taken. Make sure that your password is creative enough that it can't be cracked easily.

Figure 6.37

In the Napster Setup Assistant: Account Information dialog box, enter a unique user name and an unguessable password.

In the Napster Setup Assistant: Connection Settings dialog box (shown in Figure 6.38), enter the e-mail address you want Napster to know for you (this might not be your real e-mail address) and the speed as which you want your network connection to be listed. (Again, this may not be the real speed—but as mentioned earlier in the chapter, beware of listing a suspiciously low modem speed to hide a high-speed connection. (Most people—rightly—don't believe that anybody is really using a 14.4kbps modem any more.)

Figure 6.38

In the Napster Setup Assistant: Connection Settings dialog box, enter the e-mail address you want to share with Napster and specify the speed as which you want your network connection to be listed.

🕱 In the Napster Setup Assistant: Download Folder dialog box (shown in Figure 6.39), click the Choose Download Folder button. Use the resulting Choose a Folder dialog box to select the folder you want to store downloaded MP3 files in, and then click the Choose button.

Figure 6.39

In the Napster Setup Assistant: Download Folder dialog box, specify the folder in which you want Napster to store MP3 files you download.

🕱 In the Napster Setup Assistant: Network Options dialog box (shown in Figure 6.40), use the Yes and No option buttons to let Napster know whether your computer connects to the Internet through a firewall and whether you want Napster to connect automatically to Napster when you run it.

Figure 6.40

In the Napster Setup Assistant: Network Options dialog box, specify whether your computer connects to the Internet through a firewall.

In the Napster Setup Assistant: Proxy Server dialog box (shown in Figure 6.41), choose proxy server settings if your network uses a proxy server. If you don't connect to the Internet through a firewall, you probably don't use a proxy server.

Figure 6.41

If your computer connects to the Internet through a firewall, you might also need to specify proxy server settings in the Napster Setup Assistant: Proxy Server dialog box.

In the Napster Setup Assistant: Registration dialog box (shown in Figure 6.42), click the Register Account button and wait while Napster registers your account and logs you in to it.

Figure 6.42

The Registration dialog box

Once you've successfully created a unique username and logged in, Napster for the Mac displays a Welcome message box. Click the OK button to dismiss this message box, and you'll see the Napster panel, shown in Figure 6.43, and the Console window, which shows current messages.

Figure 6.43

Use the Napster panel to navigate the various Napster for the Mac windows.

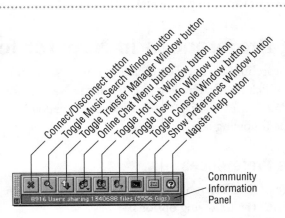

Here's what the buttons do:

Connect/Disconnect button   Click this button when disconnected to connect to a Napster server. When connected, click this button to break the connection.

Toggle Music Search Window button   Click this button to display the Music Search window.

Toggle Transfer Manager Window button   Click this button to toggle the display of the Transfer Manager window.

Online Chat Menu button Click this button to display a menu containing a Join item and a list of the chat windows you're currently in.

Toggle User Info Window button Click this button to toggle the display of the User Information dialog box.

Toggle Hot List Window button Click this button to toggle the display of the hot list.

Toggle Console Window button Click this button to toggle the display of the Console window.

Preferences button Click this button to display the Preferences dialog box.

Napster Help button Click this button to access Napster for the Mac's online help.

Community Information panel This panel displays three pieces of information about the Napster server you're currently connected to: the total number of tracks available, the number of libraries available (in other words, the number of users), and the data size (in gigabytes) of those tracks.

Choosing Preferences in Napster for the Mac

Before you start searching for and downloading music, set your preferences in Napster for the Mac. Click the Preferences button on the Napster for the Mac panel, or choose Edit ➢ Preferences, to display the Preferences dialog box, then set preferences as described in the following subsections.

General Page Preferences

The General page of the Preferences dialog box (shown in Figure 6.44) in Napster for the Mac contains the following options:

MP3 Player group box Use the controls in this group box to identify to Napster for the Mac the MP3 player you want to use. In the Default Players drop-down list, either select one of the players listed by name (for example, MACAST or GrayAMP) or select the Other option, use the resulting Choose a File dialog box to identify the player, and click the Choose button.

Filter Mature Language check box Select this check box (which is selected by default) if you want Napster to bowdlerize "mature" (in other words, adult) language in chat channels.

Show Join/Leave in Chat check box   Select this check box (which is selected by default) if you want Napster to indicate when users join and leave the chat channels you're in.

Connect on Startup check box   Select this check box if you want Napster to automatically connect to a Napster server when you run it. (Most people find this feature useful.)

Show Tooltips check box   Select this check box (which is selected by default) if you want Napster to display ToolTips when you hover the mouse over its buttons.

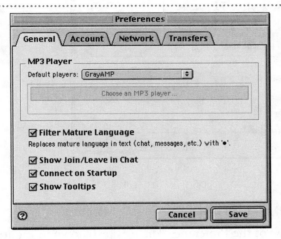

Figure 6.44

Identify your MP3 player on the General page of the Preferences dialog box.

Account Page Preferences

The Account page of the Preferences dialog box (shown in Figure 6.45) contains the following options:

User Account ID text box   This text box contains your user ID for Napster. You shouldn't need to change this.

Password text box   This text box contains your password for Napster. You shouldn't need to change this, either.

Email Address text box   This text box contains the e-mail address that Napster supplies to Napster. You may want to use a secondary e-mail address or a fictional e-mail address instead of your primary e-mail address.

Connection Speed drop-down list   Use this drop-down list to set the connection speed Napster lists for you. This is the speed that other users see when viewing search results and that Napster uses for searches that specify a connection speed. This speed need bear no relation to your actual connection speed and does not affect the speed at which you can download or upload information.

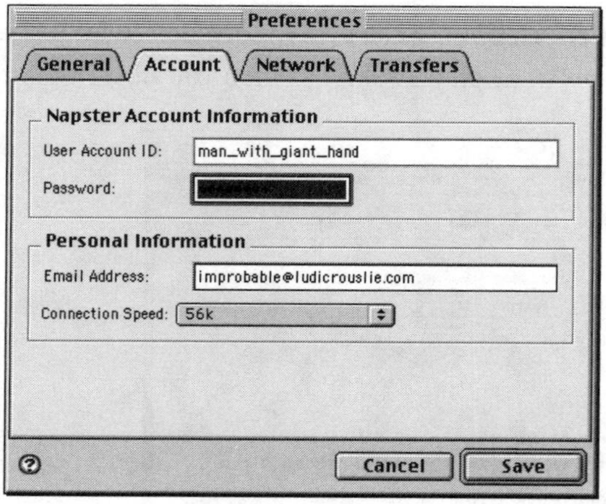

Figure 6.45

On the Account page of the Preferences dialog box, check the e-mail address and connection speed that Napster lists for you.

Network Page Preferences

The Network page of the Preferences dialog box (shown in Figure 6.46) contains the following options:

I Am behind a Firewall check box   Select this check box if your Mac connects to the Internet through a firewall or if you're not sure whether it does. If you chose the correct setting while configuring Napster, you shouldn't need to change it.

SOCKS v4 Proxy check box   If your Mac connects to the Internet through a proxy server, select this check box and enter the address of the proxy server in the Address text box. As with the previous check box, if you set this option correctly while configuring Napster, you shouldn't need to change it (unless your proxy server changes).

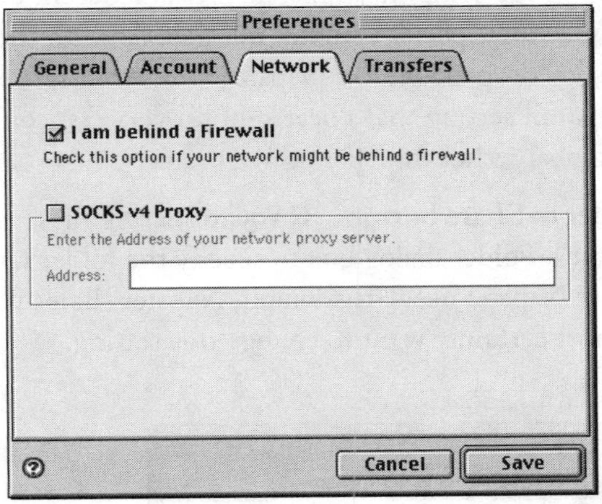

Figure 6.46

If necessary, specify firewall and proxy settings on the Network page of the Preferences dialog box.

Transfers Page Preferences

The Transfers page of the Preferences dialog box (shown in Figure 6.47) contains the following options:

Max Simultaneous Inbound Transfers drop-down list   Use this drop-down list to specify the largest number of files that you want Napster to download at once. The default setting is 1, which works well for modem connections but which you'll want to increase if you have a broadband connection. Napster offers settings from 1 to 10 files and a No Limit setting that's best kept for very fast connections.

Choose a Download Folder button   Use this button and the resulting Choose a Folder dialog box to specify the folder in which you want Napster to store downloaded files.

Allow Sharing check box   This check box controls whether Napster shares any files on your computer. *Select this check box only if you have files that you have the right to distribute.* This check box is selected by default, so you may well need to clear it.

Max Simultaneous Outbound Transfers drop-down list   If you're sharing files, use this drop-down list to specify the maximum number that Napster should try to transfer at once. If you have a modem connection, keep the default setting, 1, so that your computer transfers files at a decent clip. If you have a broadband connection, specify a higher number. As with the Max Simultaneous Inbound Transfers drop-down list, Napster offers transfer settings from 1 to 10 files and a No Limit setting that's best kept for very fast connections. Note that this setting is global rather than per user.

Choose a Folder to Share button If you're sharing files, use this button and the resulting Choose a Folder dialog box to specify the folder you want Napster to share with other Napster users. By default, Napster shares your downloads folder, so you will almost certainly want to change this setting.

Figure 6.47

Choose downloading and file-sharing options on the Transfers page of the Preferences dialog box.

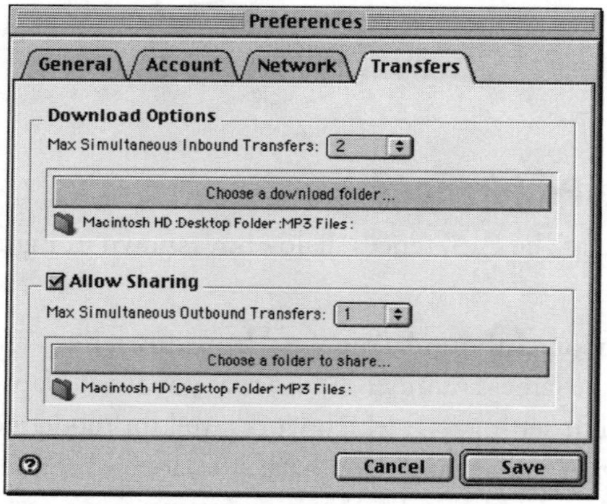

Finding and Downloading Music with Napster for the Mac

To search for music with Napster for the Mac, display the Music Search window by clicking the Toggle Music Search Window button on the Napster panel, pressing Apple+F, or choosing Find ➤ Find Music. Figure 6.48 shows the Music Search window with a search item entered.

Specify criteria for the search as necessary. If you want to specify a bitrate, frequency, or line speed, click the Show Advanced Search Options arrow. Napster displays an extra panel of options, as shown in Figure 6.49.

Figure 6.48

Use the Music Search window to find the music you're interested in.

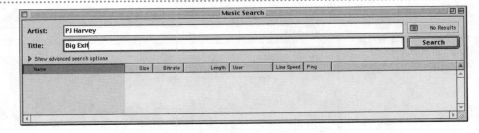

Figure 6.49

The Music Search window hides Napster's advanced search features until you click the Show Advanced Search Options button.

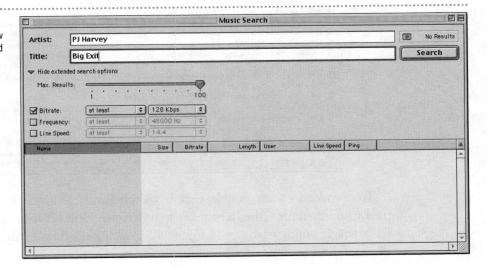

Click the Search button to set the search running. Napster searches the Napster server, changes the title of the Music Search window to "Search Results," and displays the results in it, as shown in Figure 6.50. In this figure, I've sorted the results by the Ping column, putting the closest connections at the top of the list.

If you don't find the track you're looking for, try disconnecting from your current Napster server and connecting to another server. The easiest way to do this is to double-click the Connect/Disconnect button on the Napster toolbar. The first click disconnects you from the current server, and the second click requests a new connection. But you can also press Apple+D (or choose File ➢ Disconnect) to disconnect, and press Apple+K (or choose File ➢ Connect) to reconnect.

Figure 6.50

You can sort the results in the Search Results window by any of its columns by clicking the column heading.

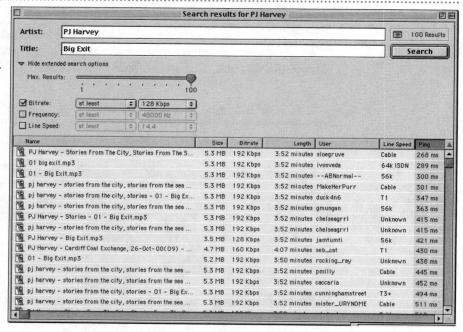

To download a track, double-click it. (Alternatively, Shift+click to select multiple tracks, and then press the Return key to download them.) Napster displays the Transfer Manager window (shown in Figure 6.51) listing the downloads, the progress, the file size, the download speed, and the time remaining.

When you're downloading tracks, Napster displays status information in the Progress column. These are the terms used and their meanings:

Waiting for Info   This status means that Napster is getting information from the Napster server about the host offering the file for download.

Connecting   This status means that Napster is contacting the host offering the file for download. If there's a problem with transferring the file, the transfer may get stuck at the Waiting Connection stage, in which case you'll can either cancel it manually or wait for it to time out.

Waiting Connection   This status means that Napster is trying to establish a connection with the host offering the file.

Timed Out   This status indicates that Napster has given up on trying to get a response from a host. Napster then moves on to the next download that you have queued.

Figure 6.51

The Transfer Manager dialog box lists your downloads and shows their progress.

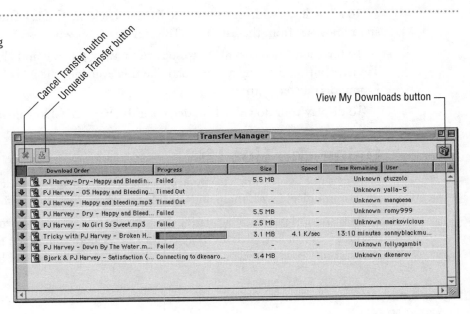

File Complete   This indicates that Napster has finished downloading the file from the host and has saved it to the designated folder on your hard drive.

Queued   This indicates that you're currently downloading your maximum number of tracks (set in the Max Simultaneous Inbound Transfers text box on the Transfers page of the Preferences dialog box), so the track is waiting for one of the current downloads to finish. If you want to download more tracks at once, increase the Max Simultaneous Inbound Transfers number—but remember that the more tracks you download at once, the more thinly your bandwidth is spread, and the longer each download will take.

Delayed by User   This indicates that the host is currently transferring its maximum number of tracks to you and other Napster users (as set in their Max Simultaneous Outbound Transfers text box on the Transfers page of the Preferences dialog box), so the track is waiting for one of those transfers to finish.

Failed   This typically indicates that the download has failed, either because of firewalling problems, because the host has deliberately canceled the download, or because the host has gone offline.

The progress bar appears when a download is running and shows you the progress of the download.

To kill a download, select it in the list and click the Cancel Transfer button. Napster removes it from the list in the Transfer Manager window.

To force a queued download to start right away, select it and click the Unqueue Transfer button. Forcing a download like this overrides the Max Simultaneous Inbound Transfers setting.

To display your downloads folder, click the View My Downloads button.

Using the Hot List

Napster's hot list feature lets you keep a list of users that you want to track so that you can communicate with them and quickly see which files they're sharing.

As with most parts of Napster for the Mac, the hot list has its own window. To display the Hot List window, click the Toggle Hot List Window button on the Napster panel, choose Tools ➤ Hot List, or press Apple+J. Figure 6.52 shows the Hot List window.

Figure 6.52

Use Napster's hot list to keep track of users you're interested in.

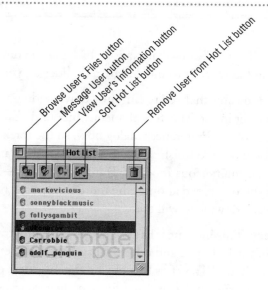

Users who are currently connected to the same Napster server as you appear in black. Users connected to other servers or not connected to Napster at all appear in gray.

To add a user to your hot list, select their name in one of the Napster windows that shows user names (for example, the Transfer Manager window) and choose User ➤ Add to Hot List or press Apple++ (in other words, Apple+Shift+=).

To remove a user from your hot list, select the user's name in the Hot List window click the Remove User from Hot List button or choose User ➤ Delete.

Browsing a User's Library

One of the prime purposes of the hot list is to browse another user's library to find files that interest you. To browse a user's library from the Hot List window, select the user and click the Browse User's Files button. To browse a user's library from another window, select an item identifying the user (for example, a file listing in the Search Results window) and choose User ➤ Browse Library or press Apple+B.

Figure 6.53 shows an example of browsing a library.

Figure 6.53

Napster lets you browse another user's library to see which files they're sharing.

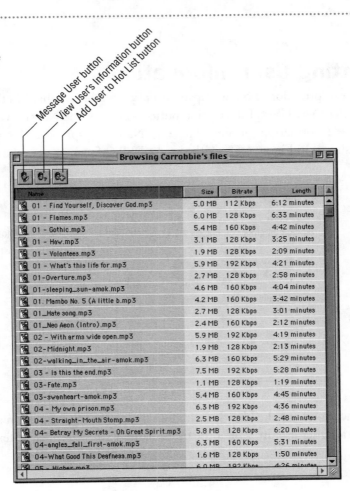

As in the Search Results window, you can double-click a file to download it. Click the Message User button to start an instant message to the user. Click the View User's Information button to view information about the user. Or click the Add User to Hot List button to add the user to your hot list.

If both your computer and the computer you're trying to access are firewalled, you'll see the error message box shown in Figure 6.54.

Figure 6.54

Napster warns you if it's not able to transfer files from the user you're interested in.

Getting User Information

To get information about a Napster user, select a listing that has the user's name and click the View User's Information button in one of the Napster windows or choose User ➢ Information (or press Apple+I). Napster displays the User Information dialog box (shown in Figure 6.55) with the available information on the user.

Figure 6.55

The User Information dialog box does its best to give you information about a selected user.

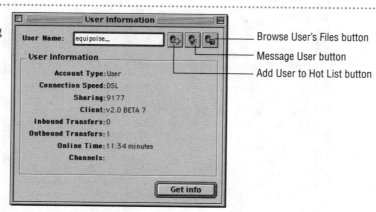

Once you have the User Information dialog box open, you can get information about another user by typing the user's name in the User Name text box and clicking the Get Info button. This technique is useful for finding out information about a user who's not currently listed in one of the Napster windows. You can also use it to add to your hot list a user who is not currently listed in a Napster window.

Sending a Message to a User

To send a message to a user listed in one of the Napster windows, click the Message User button in that window or choose User ➤ Message (or press Apple+'). Napster displays the Private Message To dialog box (shown in Figure 6.56). Enter the message in the text box and click the Send button to send it.

Figure 6.56

Use the Private Message To dialog box to send a private message to another Napster user.

Browse User's Files button
View User's Information button
Add User to Hot List button

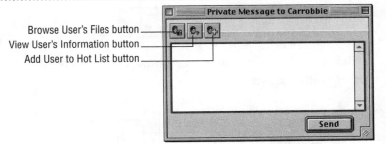

When someone sends you a message (or a reply), Napster displays it in the Incoming Message From dialog box (shown in Figure 6.57).

Figure 6.57

When you receive a message, Napster displays the Incoming Message From dialog box.

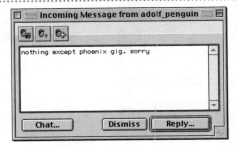

If you don't want to reply, click the Dismiss button to dismiss the Incoming Message From window. To reply to the message, click the Reply button. Napster displays the Reply Message To dialog box (shown in Figure 6.58).

Figure 6.58

Use the Reply Message To dialog box to reply to a private message.

Click the Chat button to open a private chat window (shown in Figure 6.59) for chatting with the user.

Figure 6.59

To take your relationship to the next stage, open a private chat window.

Chatting

Napster provides a full-fledged implementation of chat. Not only can you join any of the channels that already exist on the Napster server to which you're connected, but you can also create new chat channels of your own.

To join a chat channel, click the Chat button on the Napster toolbar and choose Join from the resulting drop-down menu. (Alternatively, choose Channels ➤ Channel List or press Apple+H.) Napster displays the Select a Channel window (shown in Figure 6.60), taking a moment to download the latest list of chat channels from the Napster server you're currently connected to.

Figure 6.60

Use the Select a Channel window to choose the chat channel you want to join.

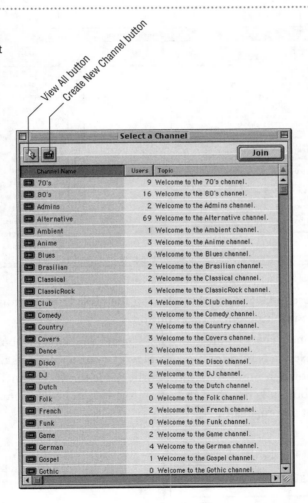

To join a channel, select it in the list box and click the Join button. Napster displays the chat window for the channel you chose. Figure 6.61 shows an example of chatting with Napster.

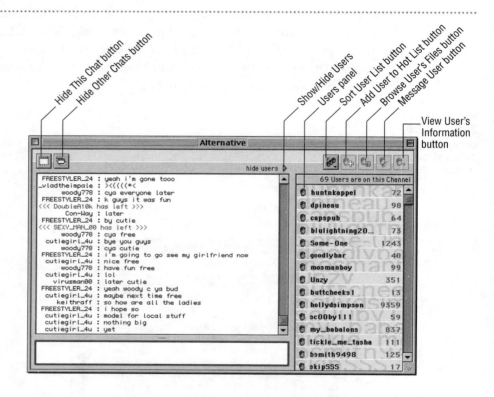

Figure 6.61

Chatting with Napster

You can close the Users panel by clicking the Hide Users button, and redisplay it by clicking the resulting Show Users button.

To create a new chat channel, click the Create New Channel button or choose Channels ➤ New Channel (or press Apple+N). Napster displays the New Channel dialog box (shown in Figure 6.62). Enter the name for the channel in the Name the Channel text box and click the OK button to create it. Napster creates the chat channel and joins it automatically.

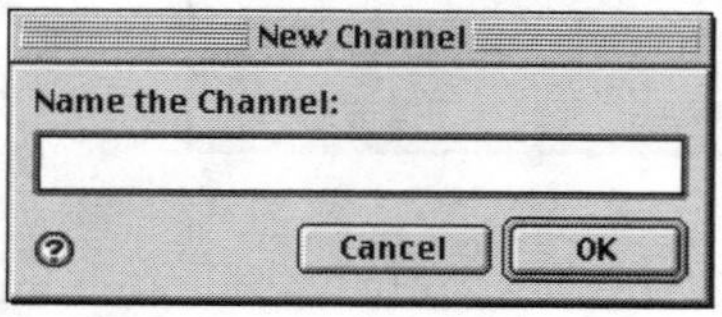

Figure 6.62

You can create new chat channels by using the New Channel dialog box.

Using Napster on Linux

At this writing, there are multiple Linux versions of Napster being developed, including gnap, Gnapster, GNOME-Napster, and knapster. Gnapster, gnap, and GNOME-Napster are for the GNOME environment, and knapster is for the KDE environment.

In this section, I'll discuss Gnapster briefly. I'll expect you to have read the general sections earlier in this chapter, so that you know what Napster is and what it does.

Gnapster is a relatively full implementation of Napster for the GNOME desktop environment. It supports most of the "regular" Napster features, including searching for tracks, downloading and uploading them, and chatting with other users. Gnapster doesn't support a hot list as such, but it lets you easily browse another user's files—which, as you'll see, can be more useful than a hot list. What's more, you can create and use multiple accounts on Gnapster.

At this writing, Gnapster does not show you the ping time or frequency when you search. Because most people rip music from CD-quality sources—44.1kHz—the frequency isn't usually a big issue. But not seeing the ping time to hosts means that you won't be able to tell which hosts are close and which are far—so you may get slower downloads than you'd like.

Using Gnapster

In this section, I'll run through the key points of Gnapster, one of the implementations of Napster for the GNOME desktop environment.

Getting, Installing, and Configuring Gnapster

Download the latest version of Gnapster from `www.faradic.net/~jasta/Gnapster.html`. Get either the source (if you feel like compiling the application or you need to compile it) or a suitable distribution package for the version of Linux you're using. Then install Gnapster using the standard installation procedure for the version of Linux you're running.

The first time you run Gnapster, it automatically displays the Gnapster Properties dialog box. Figure 6.63 shows the User Information page of this dialog box.

Figure 6.63

Enter your user information on the User Information page of the Gnapster Properties dialog box.

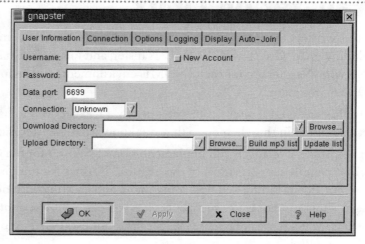

Enter your username and password in the text boxes. If this is a new account, select the New Account check box. If you're transferring an existing account to Gnapster, make sure this check box is cleared.

In the Data Port text box, leave the default setting, 6699, alone unless you know you need to use a different data port.

In the Connection drop-down list, select the connection speed you want to have listed. Remember that this setting doesn't affect the speed of your connection, just the speed that is reported to other users.

Specify your download directory in the Download Directory text box and your upload directory in the Upload Directory text box, and then click the Build MP3 List button to have Gnapster create a list of the MP3 files in your upload directory.

On the Connection page of the Gnapster Properties dialog box (shown in Figure 6.64), specify any firewall and SOCKS information necessary for your connection. If your computer is behind a firewall and cannot accept inbound connections, select the Firewalled without the Ability to Accept Connections check box. If you use a SOCKS proxy server, select the SOCKS Proxy check box, specify the server's IP address and port, choose between the SOCKS 4 and SOCKS 5 option buttons, and enter your username and password.

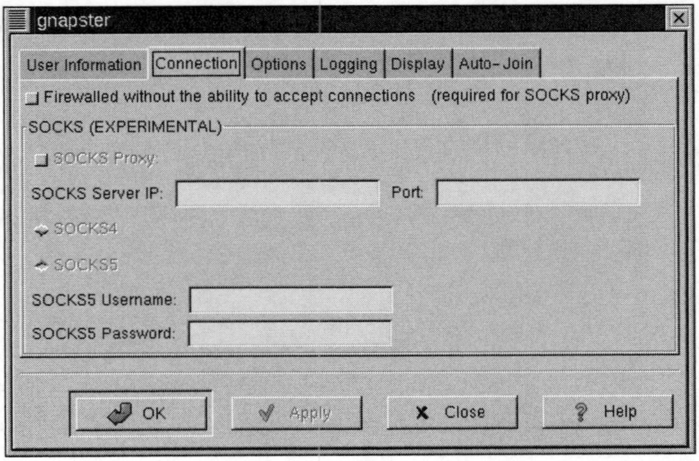

Figure 6.64

Specify any necessary firewall and SOCKS information on the Connection page of the Gnapster Properties dialog box.

On the Options page of the Gnapster Properties dialog box (shown in Figure 6.65), make your choices for the following options:

Auto-Query a User upon Incoming Message check box   Select this check box to have Gnapster automatically get information about each user who sends you a message. If you find yourself checking the information for people who contact you, this option can prove useful.

Convert Spaces to Underscores? check box   Select this check box to have Gnapster change spaces in filenames to underscores.

Auto-Hide Userlist on Channel Join check box   Select this check box if you want Gnapster to automatically hide the user list of a channel when you join it. (Otherwise, the user list is displayed by default.)

Hide Join/Part Messages check box   Select this check box if you want Gnapster to suppress the automatic messages generated when users join a channel and leave a channel.

Reject Uploads While Downloads Are Active check box   You can select this check box if you want to prevent uploads from happening while a download is running. Unless you're running a very underpowered computer with a high-bandwidth connection, uploading and downloading at the same time should not be a problem.

Figure 6.65

Choose options on the Options page of the Gnapster Properties dialog box.

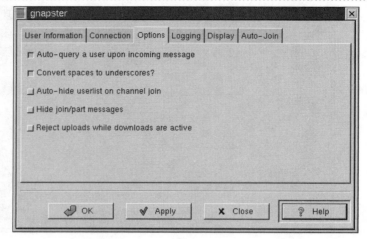

On the Logging page of the Gnapster Properties dialog box (shown in Figure 6.66), select or clear the Log Messages to Disk check box to specify whether you want Gnapster to log messages to disk. This option is selected by default.

Figure 6.66

The Logging page of the Gnapster Properties dialog box

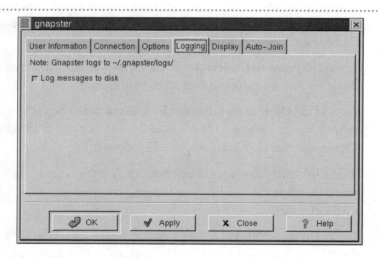

On the Display page of the Gnapster Properties dialog box (see Figure 6.67), choose options for how you want Gnapster to appear. You can specify the font you want Gnapster to use. (You will need to restart Gnapster to apply the new font.) You can also apply transparency effects and themes.

Figure 6.67

The Display page of the Gnapster Properties dialog box

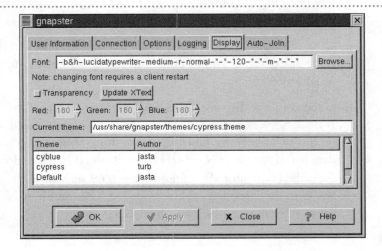

On the Auto-Join page of the Gnapster Properties dialog box (see Figure 6.68), you can specify the channels you want to join automatically when you connect to a Napster server.

Figure 6.68

On the Auto-Join page of the Gnapster Properties dialog box, specify the channels you want to join automatically.

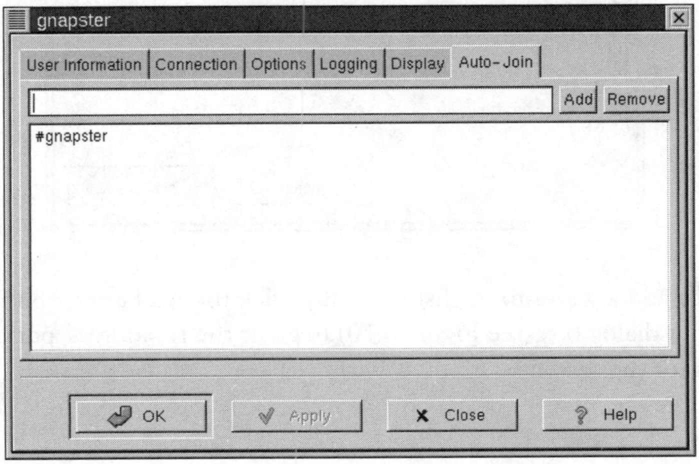

Apply your preferences and close the Gnapster Properties dialog box. Then use one of the following options on the File menu to connect to a server:

- Choose File ➤ Connect to Last Server (or press Ctrl+C) to connect to the last Napster server to which you were connected.

- Choose File ➤ Connect to Official Server (or press Ctrl+O) to connect to the Napster server and be doled out to one of the Napster servers in the usual way.

- Choose File ➤ Browse OpenNAP Servers (or press Ctrl+B) to display the Browse Servers dialog box. When you first display this dialog box, its list of servers will be empty. Click the Refresh List button to download an up-to-date list of the OpenNAP servers available. (Gnapster downloads this list from the Napigator Web site.) Figure 6.69 shows the Browse Servers dialog box with the latest list of servers loaded. Use the Show Network drop-down list to filter the list of servers displayed.

Figure 6.69

Use the Browse Servers dialog box to identify the server you want to connect to.

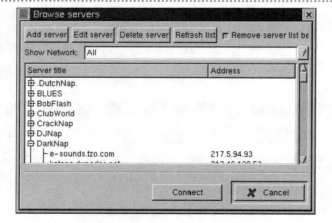

To add a server to the list manually, click the Add Server button and use the Add Server dialog box (see Figure 6.70) to enter the IP address, port number, and description for the server.

Figure 6.70

You can add a server to the Gnapster list manually by using the Add Server dialog box.

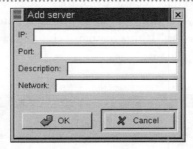

You can edit a server's entry by selecting it in the list box and clicking the Edit Server button, then working in the Edit Server dialog box (see Figure 6.71).

Figure 6.71

The Edit Server dialog box lets you edit a server entry in the Browse Servers list.

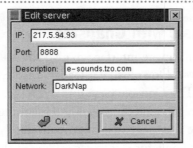

To connect to a server, select it in the list box and click the Connect button.

If you see the Error dialog box shown in Figure 6.72, you'll know that the username you created was already in use. Return to the User Information page of the Gnapster Properties dialog box and choose another. (If you already have the username registered to you, chances are you've entered your password incorrectly.)

Figure 6.72

If you see this Error dialog box, it means either that the new username you're trying to create has already been taken or that you entered your password incorrectly for your existing username.

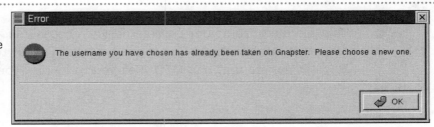

When you restart Napster, you may see the Error message box shown in Figure 6.73 telling you that "Your ~/.gnapster/shared file is outdated, please use the preferences menu to rebuild your list." If this happens, choose Napster ➤ Update Shared File or press Ctrl+U to update it.

Figure 6.73

If you see this Error message box, update your shared file by choosing Napster ➤ Update Shared File or pressing Ctrl+U.

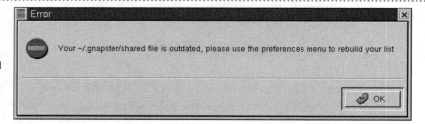

Finding and Sharing Music with Gnapster

Like Napster, Gnapster uses a multipage interface to give you quick access to its features, providing Search, Browse, Download, Upload, Console, and Message of the Day pages (at this writing). The Console page displays textual information about what's happening in Gnapster, including chat and incoming and outgoing file requests. The Message of the Day page displays the message of the day from Napster. When there's something new for you to see on one of the pages, the text on its tab appears in white. The rest of the time, the tab text appears in black.

As usual, you can move from page to page by clicking the tabs on the pages. Alternatively, make sure the focus is on the tabs, then press the Tab key to highlight each tab in turn (from left to right) or Shift+Tab (from right to left), and then press the spacebar or the Enter key to display the page for the highlighted tab.

Figure 6.74 shows the Gnapster window.

To disconnect from your current server, choose File ➤ Disconnect. You may want to disconnect and connect again in order to be assigned to a Napster server that has MP3 files you're looking for.

Figure 6.74
The Gnapster window uses
a multipage interface much
like Napster's.

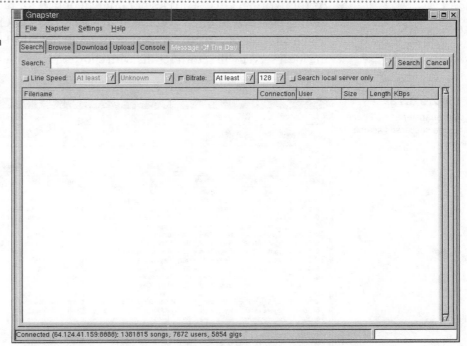

Figure 6.74
The Gnapster window uses
a multipage interface much
like Napster's.

Searching for MP3 Files

To search for MP3 files, you use Gnapster's Search page (shown in Figure 6.75 after
a successful search). The process is very similar to the Napster process, with these
main differences:

- Instead of providing a text box for the artist's name and a text box for the
  track name, Gnapster provides only the Query text box. Enter the text that
  you want to search for—either the artist or the track name, or both, in any
  order you want.

- While the search is running, you'll see the indicator in the right-hand panel
  of the status bar moving to the left and right, and the word "Searching"
  appears at the left-hand end of the status bar. If the search is successful, the
  results are displayed.

☠ At this writing, Gnapster does not offer an option for pinging the search results. However, it offers you the Search Local Server Only check box, which lets you specify that you want to search only the local server. Typically, the local server will return results with shorter ping times, but fewer results.

Figure 6.75

The Gnapster Search page after a successful search

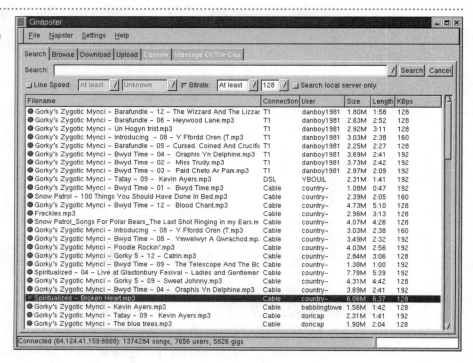

Downloading MP3 Files

To download a track, double-click it on the Search page or right-click it and choose Download from the context menu. Gnapster submits a download request to the host and, on getting a positive answer, begins the download. Unlike Napster, Gnapster doesn't automatically display the Download page when you submit a download request.

Once you've chosen to download one or more tracks, click the Download tab to display the Download page. Figure 6.76 shows the Download page with one track being downloaded, one being requested, one connecting, and several queued in the lower panel.

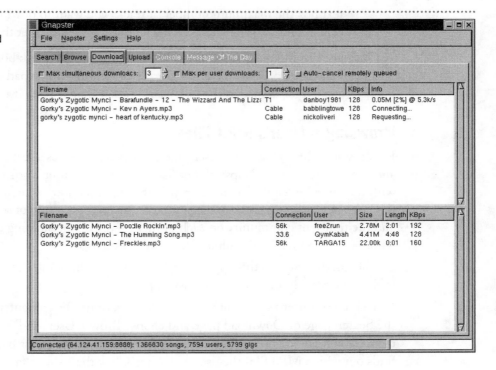

To cancel a download, right-click it on the Download page and choose Cancel Download from the context menu. To delete a download, right-click it and choose Cancel and Remove File from the context menu. To move an active download to your queue, right-click it and choose Move to Queue from the context menu.

To keep your downloads running smoothly, choose appropriate settings for the Max Simultaneous Downloads and Max Per User Downloads features:

☠ Use the Max Simultaneous Downloads feature to make sure you're not trying to force too much data at once through your connection. Select the Max Simultaneous Downloads check box and enter in the text box the maximum number of tracks you want to download at once. For a 56K modem connection, a number of 1–3 usually works best.

☠ Use the Max Per User Downloads feature to make sure you're not slowing your download speed by demanding too many files from a single user at the same time. Select the Max Per User Downloads check box and enter in the text box the maximum number of tracks you want to download from a single user at once. To transfer each track as fast as possible, set this number to 1.

Gnapster also offers an Auto-Cancel Remotely Queued check box. When you select this check box, Gnapster automatically cancels any download that is remotely queued (queued for upload at the host's end) rather than leaving it to languish.

Browsing a User's MP3 Files

For browsing through another user's files, Gnapster provides a feature that's simpler and more effective than Napster's hot list. You identify a user who's currently online with the same server as you and then rifle through that user's shared folders. Unlike the hot list, this feature is impermanent, like the Napster group of separate servers and the transient community on each of them—you're not building up a list of people whom you'll be unable (or unlikely) to contact ever again.

The disadvantage to this approach is that you can check out only one user's shared folders at once—but this failing is easy to put up with.

To browse a user's shared library of MP3 files, right-click an entry for the user on the Search page or Download page and choose Browse User's MP3s from the context menu. You'll see the message "Retrieving MP3 List" in the status bar as Gnapster finds out which MP3 files the user is sharing. Click the Browse tab to display the Browse page, which displays a list of the user's shared MP3 files (see Figure 6.77). When something catches your fancy, you can download it or queue it as usual.

You can also browse a user's library by entering the user's name in the Username text box on the Browse page and clicking the Browse User button.

If nothing happens when you try to browse a user's shared library, check the Console page. If you see the message "Error: Parameter is unparsable," it means that your request has gone off into the ether. Try browsing a different user's library.

Getting Information on a User

To get information on a user, right-click a listing featuring the user on the Search page and choose Whois User from the context menu. Then switch to the Console page to view the result.

Figure 6.77

Gnapster lets you easily browse a list of the MP3 files that another user is sharing.

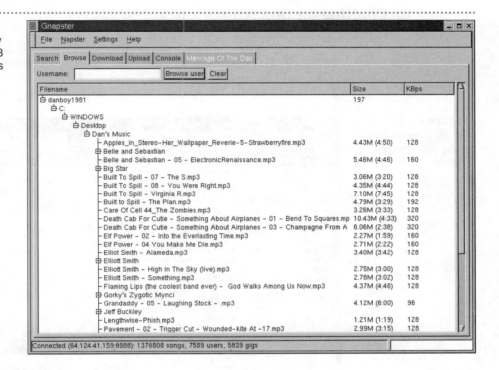

Sharing MP3 Files

All you need to do to share MP3 files via Gnapster is place them in the upload directory you designated on the User Information page of the Gnapster Properties dialog
box. (To change the upload directory, display this dialog box by choosing Settings ➤
Preferences.)

Once the MP3 files are in the shared folder, they're available to anybody who's
logged into the same Napster server as you are. When someone starts to download a
file from your computer, you'll see it appear in the list box on the Upload page,
together with details about who is downloading it and the line speed they're using.

If you see that users are downloading too many files at once for the connection
you're using, change the number of simultaneous uploads by selecting the Max
Uploads check box on the Upload page and entering an appropriate number in the
text box. If any one user is hogging your bandwidth, throttle them back by selecting
the Max Per User Uploads check box and entering a modest figure (for example, 1)
in the text box.

Chatting on Gnapster

Gnapster implements chat on its Console page via subpages.

To display a list of chat channels, choose Napster ➤ List Channels. Gnapster displays the Channel Listing dialog box (see Figure 6.78).

Figure 6.78

Use the Channel Listing dialog box to join chat channels.

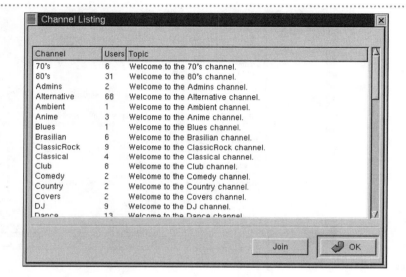

To join a channel, select it and click the Join button. Gnapster adds a chat page for the channel, as you can see in Figure 6.79. You can then participate in the chat by typing into the text box at the bottom of the chat page and pressing the Enter key. To leave the chat channel, select it by clicking its tab, and then choose Napster ➤ Part Channel.

To chat with a user, choose Napster ➤ Query User. Napster inserts a query stub—/query—in the text box. Type the user's name and press the Enter key. Gnapster opens a private chat channel with the user, with its own tab for access.

To stop chatting with a user, select the tab for the private chat and choose Napster ➤ Unquery User.

You can also use text commands if you find them easier. Here are the basics:

☠ Use the /join or /j commands to join a channel. For example, the following commands join the Alternative channel:

```
/join alternative
/j alternative
```

Figure 6.79

Chatting on Gnapster

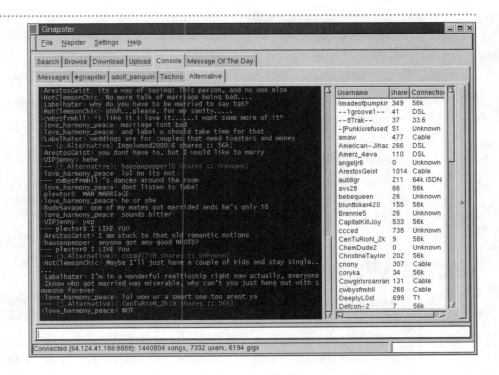

- Use the /part command to leave a channel. For example, the following command leaves the Alternative channel:

  /part alternative

- Use the /msg or /m commands to send a private message to a user. For example, the following command sends the message "Are you in Houston?" to the user LiveHerald:

  /m LiveHerald Are you in Houston?

- Use the /raw command to send a message to everyone in the channel. For example, the following command sends the message "The Cleaners from Venus rule!" to everyone in the current channel:

  /raw The Cleaners from Venus rule!

- Use the /whois command to display information about a user. For example, the following command displays information about the user voodoosweeney:

  /whois voodoosweeney

A regular message shows up in the list box on the Console page preceded by the name of the user who sent it, enclosed in angle brackets. For example, a message from the user voodoosweeney would appear like this:

```
<voodoosweeney> Anyone got Metallica live MP3 files?
```

A private message shows up on its own subpage on the Console page. The subpage bears the name of the user who sent it.

Exiting Gnapster

To exit Gnapster, choose File ➤ Exit or press Ctrl+Q. Alternatively, you can perform a "safe exit"—making sure Gnapster closes all files currently being transferred—by choosing File ➤ Safe Exit or pressing Ctrl+S.

Using Wrapster and Wrapintosh

As you saw in the Napster section, Napster is built to share MP3 files—and only MP3 files. If you put other file types in the Napster folder, Napster ignores them.

If you want to transfer files other than MP3 files using Napster, you need to disguise the files as MP3 files. Wrapster is software that lets you do this disguising; Wrapintosh is a Mac version of Wrapster. Wrapster marks the files as being encoded at a special bitrate (32kbps) and frequency (32kHz), so that you can search for them by using Napster. You can put one file or multiple files in a Wrapster archive.

At this writing, the creators of Wrapster have abandoned the project, but Wrapster is still available, together with its source code (should you feel the urge to read it or tinker with it) and patches for hacking Napster's MP3-validation routines.

At this writing, a Linux Wrapster client is under development. This client is called Dewrapster. You can find it at woggo.org/users/theo/.

Using Wrapster

Download the latest version of Wrapster from the Wrapster Web site (at this writing, `notoctawian.cjb.net/`). Then double-click the Wrapster distribution file to start the setup routine. Choose the installation location and the Start menu folder as usual, and then launch Wrapster from the Start menu folder you specified.

To use Wrapster, create a new archive by choosing File ➢ New Archive or pressing Ctrl+N, specifying the name and location for the archive in the New Wrapster File dialog box, and clicking the Save button. Then, in the Wrapster window (shown in Figure 6.80 with an archive underway), you add files to the archive by choosing Actions ➢ Add Files (or pressing Ctrl+A) and using the resulting Open dialog box to specify the files. If you need to remove files, choose Actions ➢ Remove Files ➢ All (or press Ctrl+R) or Actions ➢ Remove Files ➢ Selected (Ctrl+Shift+R). When you've got the archive lined up to your satisfaction, choose Actions ➢ Commit to Disk to create the archive file and save it to disk.

Figure 6.80

Wrapster lets you create archive files disguised as MP3 files and share them via Napster.

Then you put the archive in one of your shared Napster folders, and users logged into the same Napster server as you can search for it. To find Wrapster files yourself, specify any relevant artist or song information, then set the bitrate to be equal to 32Kbps and the frequency to be equal to 32kHz, and perform the search. When you find a file that interests you, download it as usual.

Wrapster files can contain *anything*, including executable files, viruses, and worms. Run a virus checker on any Wrapster files you download, both before and after you extract them.

To extract files from a Wrapster archive:

1. Choose File ➢ Open Existing Archive to display the Open Wrapster File dialog box.

2. Select the file and click the Open button to open it.

3. Choose Actions ➢ Extract Files ➢ All (or press Ctrl+E) or Actions ➢ Extract Files ➢ Selected (Ctrl+Shift+E). Wrapster displays the Extract Files To dialog box.

4. Enter the target folder in the text box, either by typing it in or by clicking the ... button and using the resulting Browse for Folder dialog box to identify the folder.

5. Click the OK button in the Extract Files To dialog box. Wrapster extracts the file or files.

If you find yourself using Wrapster frequently, you'll want to change its default options settings. Choose View ➢ Options to display the Options dialog box (shown in Figure 6.81).

Figure 6.81

If you use Wrapster frequently, change the settings in the Options dialog box to suit you.

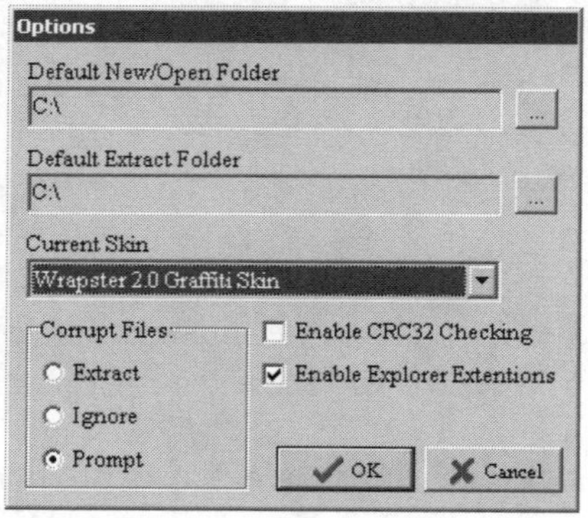

Then choose options as follows:

Default New/Open Folder text box   In this text box, specify the default folder in which to create new Wrapster files and look for Wrapster files to open. You can either type into the text box or click the ... button and use the resulting Browse for Folder dialog box to identify the folder.

Default Extract Folder text box   In this text box, specify the default folder to which you want Wrapster to extract files. Again, you can either type into the text box or click the ... button to display a Browse for Folder dialog box.

Current Skin drop-down list   This drop-down list lets you choose different skin-like looks for Wrapster.

Corrupt Files group box   The option buttons in this group box let you specify what you want Wrapster to do when it encounters corrupt files in an archive: Extract (extract them anyway), Ignore (ignore them), or Prompt (prompt you to decide whether to extract them or ignore them). Prompt is usually the best bet, because it lets you know what's going on and doesn't clutter up your drives with corrupt files without your knowledge.

Enable CRC32 Checking check box   This check box enables 32-bit cyclic redundancy checks (CRC32) on the files in the Wrapster archive. Usually it's a good idea to perform CRC checks on the files to make sure they haven't been mangled. When you use this option, Wrapster places a green check mark next to files that have checked out okay and a red X next to those that failed the CRC. When you don't use this option, Wrapster displays an uninformative blue question mark next to each file in the archive.

Enable Explorer Extentions check box   This check box enables the Wrapster extensions in Explorer: Wrapster adds to your Explorer context menu items for opening files with Wrapster, extracting them to recent folders you've used with Wrapster, and so on. If you find these extensions useful, leave this check box selected.

Wrapster offers a New Archive Wizard that lets you specify the details of the archive real or putative contents. You get to choose an archive type: App, Application, Game, Games, or Porn. And you can adjust the mask and description of the file. To start the New Archive Wizard, choose File ➤ New Archive Wizard (well, what else?).

To exit Wrapster, choose File ➤ Exit or press Ctrl+X or Alt+F4.

Using Wrapintosh

As mentioned earlier, the Mac version of Wrapster is called Wrapintosh. At this writing, you can download Wrapintosh from `users.ap.net/~jeffm/wrapintosh/`. (You'll find PPC and FAT versions of Wrapintosh; choose appropriately for your Mac.) Unstuff the archive if it doesn't unstuff automatically, and then run Wrapintosh by clicking the resulting Wrapintosh icon.

As you can see in Figure 6.82, Wrapintosh has one of the less cluttered user interfaces in the history of recent software. Leave both the Check CRC32 check box and the Create CRC32 check box selected unless you have a good reason to unwrap or wrap files without performing a cyclic redundancy check.

Figure 6.82

Wrapintosh is extremely easy to use.

To wrap a file, click the Wrap File button. In the resulting Open dialog box, select the file to wrap, and click the Open button. Wrapintosh then displays the Save dialog box. Specify the name and location for the wrapped file—Wrapintosh suggests the same name with an MP3 extension, which may well not suit you—and then click the Save button to create the wrapped file.

To unwrap a wrapped file you've downloaded, click the UnWrap File button. In the resulting Open dialog box, select the file you want to unwrap, and then click the Open button. Wrapintosh creates an auto-numbered folder named Extracted Archive n (Extracted Archive 1, Extracted Archive 2, and so on) and puts the extracted files in it.

Up Next

In this chapter, I've discussed the Napster technology, the Napster clients for Windows and the Macintosh, and the Gnapster client for Linux. You now know what Napster is, what it does, and how to use it. You've seen how you can use Wrapster and Wrapintosh to disguise other files as MP3 files so that you can use Napster to share and transfer them. And you're aware of how easily Napster users and their actions can be tracked.

I've also discussed the uncertainty of Napster's future: how the company is trying to cut a deal with the record companies to create a new, secure, subscription-based Napster; and how, if it can't cut a deal, Napster could be closed down very quickly.

If you're a fan of exchanging music via Napster, you'll probably be looking for a way of continuing to do so even if Napster is closed down. The good news is that many post-Napster technologies stand ready to take up the slack if Napster is closed down. The next chapter investigates the most promising of these post-Napster technologies.

A Pirate Speaks: The Accidental Pirate

I guess I'm a pirate. Here's what happened.

I'd been on Napster for three or four months. I'd downloaded some albums and tried out some new music and things. But as I looked around, I noticed that there were a lot of good albums from the 60s and early 70s that weren't even available. I checked CDNow and CD Universe: None of these things were still in print. But it was obvious from chatting with people on Napster and seeing what people were looking for that there was a lot of interest in some of the old music that was out of print.

So I took one of my 38-year-old record albums and I digitized it. I ran *The Trip* soundtrack recording on a great—but decades unused—Onkyo turntable into my sound card, recorded WAVs with the Creative Wave Studio program that came with my Sound Blaster, and then encoded the WAVs to MP3s with MusicMatch Jukebox. Real easy. Then I put the tracks up on Napster.

Well, you know, when you've played an LP for a long time, it picks up some clicks and pops and nicks and scratches. So when I put the album up there, the first person that downloaded it *berated* me for putting something up in that condition. I said, "Sorry, but I just really don't have anything that's capable of fixing up the files." And he said, "Hey, that's not a problem. You just get SoundForge by Sonic Foundry." I asked how much that was. He said, "You don't have to *pay* for it. It's all here on Napster. You just *search* for it."

He explained that Wrapster is a product that wraps a program in a sheath of MP3-ness so that it can be transferred on Napster. I didn't really have to do anything. He told me who to go to and how to download SoundForge. So I did. And then he suggested that I have some add-ons and some click- and hiss-removers, sound equalizers, and things like that. So I downloaded them too. I put them on my machine and ran my files through it, and they sounded a million times better. It was an amazing program.

A Pirate Speaks: The Accidental Pirate (*continued*)

Then I got to thinking about it: How many times am I actually going to use this program? It's like a $300 program. The add-ons make it a couple of thousand dollars. All I wanted to do was clean up my old files so that other people could enjoy these out-of-print records that I had. So I didn't really feel like I was a professional that needed to buy this program and spend all these hundreds of dollars—or thousands of dollars—to use the product because I'm not really using it professionally. I'm just sort of cleaning some files. And it's available for casual users.

So I guess I'm a pirate, but I really don't feel that way: I've just used this product a couple of times. If Sonic Foundry had some sort of usage license and I could pay them by use, well, maybe I'd do that. But given the fact that it's so readily available and the fact that I use it so little, I really don't feel too bad about being a "pirate."

Chapter 7

Post-Napster Technologies

Featuring

- audioGnome
- Gnutella
- iMesh
- SpinFrenzy
- CuteMX
- Aimster
- Freenet

In the previous chapter, you saw how Napster brought about an explosion of piracy by implementing point-and-drool sharing of MP3 files.

Napster is a wonderful idea, a great implementation (even at the late-beta stage), and immensely cool. But it's facing almost as many lawyers as the Light Brigade faced cannons. (You know: Lawyers to left of them, lawyers to right of them, lawyers in front of them volleyed and thundered…) Almost worse, Napster, Inc. has made a deal with Bertelsmann to create a new pay-per-download Napster service and is trying to conclude deals with other major record companies.

All in all, the prognosis for Napster as we know it ain't good. This chapter picks up where the last chapter left off and discusses the P2P technologies designed to pick up from Napster if and when it stumbles, falls, or disintegrates into a paid shadow of itself. This chapter also examines the P2P technologies designed to share files other than music files.

We'll start by looking at audioGnome, because it's a powerful client that's also extremely easy to use. Like Napster, audioGnome is set up for sharing music files only—MP3, WMA, and WAV files— though you'll also find a lot of Wrapster files masquerading as MP3 files. audioGnome ties into the Napster network and integrates it with the open OpenNap network, giving you almost unparalleled access to a wide range of Napster and Napster-like servers.

At this writing, audioGnome is available only for Windows. If you want a post-Napster P2P technology for Linux or the Mac, you'll need to look further—but not that much further.

Gnutella is a P2P client and server technology that's available for a wide variety of platforms, including Windows, Linux, and the Mac. Gnutella works for all kinds of files—broadly speaking, if the data is saved as a file, Gnutella can share it. Most of the available Gnutella clients (and there are many) work with all file types, though some restrict themselves by specializing in music files.

Moving back to the Windows-only side of the fence, there are three Napster-like services—iMesh, Spinfrenzy.com, and CuteMX—that work for music, video, pictures, software (some services, but not all), and other files (again, some services only). Each of these services is implemented through a central point, so they're vulnerable to legal attack. That said, iMesh is located in Israel, where U.S. law can be brought to bear only indirectly.

Next is Aimster, a hot P2P technology based on instant messaging. At this writing, Aimster runs on Windows only, but a Mac version is in the works.

The last P2P technology that we'll look at in this chapter is Freenet, a loose structure designed to withstand the legal holocaust that may subsume Napster. At the moment, Freenet is under heavy development. As a result of that, it's changing rapidly, rough if not jagged around the edges, and difficult to use. As a result of *that*, relatively few people appear to be using Freenet compared to the other P2P technologies discussed in this chapter. But if the dogs of law are unleashed and Judgments Day comes to P2P technologies, you can bet that Freenet will receive a tremendous influx of nuked Napsterites and audioGnomics.

Using audioGnome

audioGnome is a post-Napster user-to-user file-sharing technology designed at the time Napster seemed in imminent danger of being shut down and first released in July 2000. Should Napster be shut down, audioGnome would be unlikely to follow, because it doesn't use its own servers.

audioGnome has several other advantages apart from being harder to close down than Napster:

- audioGnome lets you specify which server or servers to connect to rather than doling you out to whichever server is best equipped to take on another client.

- audioGnome lets you connect to multiple servers at once, which means that you can access a wide variety of files.

- audioGnome also lets you connect directly to individual users who are running its PNN feature, so that you can operate independently of the servers.

- audioGnome lets you resume broken or paused downloads. This feature can be very valuable when you need to transfer large files over a slow connection.

- audioGnome gives you control over the amount of bandwidth it uses, so you can prevent it from monopolizing your entire Internet connection.

Installing audioGnome

Download the latest version of audioGnome from the audioGnome Web site (www.audiognome.com) and install it by running the distribution executable.

At this writing, the setup routine is unremarkable. Double-clicking the distribution executable extracts the files it contains to a temporary folder of your choosing. You're then invited to run the setup.exe file. When you do so, you get to choose the destination folder and Start menu group to which you want to add audioGnome, and that's it.

Vulnerability Factor: audioGnome

As I mentioned, audioGnome will be much more difficult to shut down than Napster because it is not controlled at a single point. But that doesn't mean that audioGnome is entirely safe for users.

audioGnome's PNN feature, which offers direct user-to-user connections that bypass the server network, provides good security. But when you're connected through a server, anyone able to tap into that server can see all the actions you take. And even with PNN, because audioGnome lets you browse a user's shared files, it's easy for anyone to get a list of the files you're sharing.

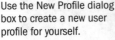 Create your music repository and the folder you intend to share before starting the audioGnome setup. At this writing, audioGnome does not refresh the listing in the Browse for Folder dialog box, so you cannot create a new folder and then select it once the Browse for Folder dialog box has been displayed.

The first time you run audioGnome, you have to agree to a license agreement in which you essentially agree not to do anything illegal with the software. After that, the Pick User Profile dialog box appears. Click the Add button to display the New Profile dialog box (see Figure 7.1).

Figure 7.1
Use the New Profile dialog box to create a new user profile for yourself.

Enter the name for your profile in the text box and click the OK button. audioGnome creates the profile and adds it to the Pick User Profile dialog box (shown in Figure 7.2 with two profiles created).

Figure 7.2
From the Pick User Profile dialog box, you can create a new user profile for yourself, select the existing profile you want to use or rename or delete an existing profile.

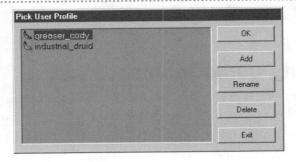

With your profile selected, click the OK button. audioGnome then walks you through the creation of a default nickname and a default password for your profile. After that, it displays the Browse for Folder dialog box once for you to specify which folder on your computer to share with other users and a second time for you to specify a download folder.

After that, you see the audioGnome window (see Figure 7.3), which has a multipage interface for audioGnome's various functions—search, file transfers, chat, and so on.

Figure 7.3

The audioGnome interface has multiple pages for audioGnome's various functions.

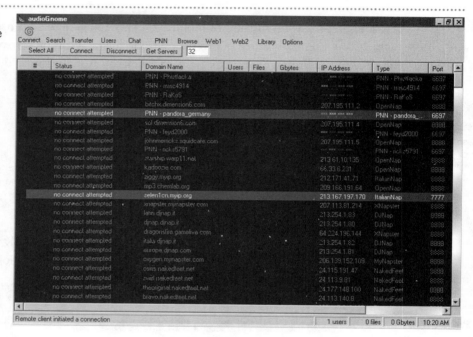

Configuring audioGnome

Once you've completed the setup routine, audioGnome will be ready for use with default settings—but you should change some of these default settings immediately.

First, make sure that audioGnome isn't sharing your download folder. Click the Library tab to display the Library page (see Figure 7.4). In the upper list box, select the entry for your download folder (if there is one) and click the Delete button to remove it.

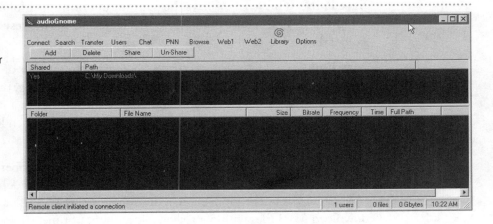

Figure 7.4

Before you do anything else, make sure audio-Gnome isn't sharing your download folder.

Next, click the Options tab to display the Options page (shown in Figure 7.5; you'll notice that I've blanked out my password, which otherwise appears in plain text). Then choose settings for the options as appropriate:

Data Listen Port   This setting controls the port on which audioGnome listens for data. Don't change the setting unless you're sure that you need to use a different port.

Greeting   This setting controls the greeting sent by audioGnome. Change this to something that amuses you—and change it frequently if you hope to amuse others. (The default setting, *Hello Banana!*, has ceased to be amusing.)

Share MP3   This drop-down list controls whether audioGnome shares MP3 files in your shared folder. Unless you have MP3 files that you can legally distribute, choose No.

Share WMA   This drop-down list controls whether audioGnome shares WMA files in your shared folder. Unless you have WMA files that you can legally distribute, choose No.

Share WAV   This drop-down list controls whether audioGnome shares WAV files in your shared folder. Unless you have WAV files that you can legally distribute, choose No.

Shared Path   This label displays the path to the folder you're sharing. To change the folder, move your mouse pointer over the label and use the resulting Browse for Folder dialog box to choose the new folder.

Save Path   This label displays the path to your download folder. To change the folder, move your mouse pointer over the label and use the resulting Browse for Folder dialog box to choose the new folder.

Max Uploads   This setting controls the maximum number of files that audioGnome uploads at once from your computer. At this writing, the default setting is 5. If you have a modem connection, reduce the number to 1 or 2. (Remember that even a 56K modem delivers only 33.6K upstream—much less than a single 56K modem at the other end can suck down.)

Max Downloads   This setting controls the maximum number of files that audioGnome tries to download at once. At this writing, the default setting is 5. If you have a modem connection, reduce the number to 1, 2, or 3 so that you can download MP3 files within a reasonable amount of time. (If you try to download too many files at once over a modem connection, each will take a long time.)

Max Concurrent Downloads from One User   This setting controls the maximum number of files that audioGnome tries to download at once from any one user. The default setting is 1. There's not much reason to change this setting: If the user supplying the files has a faster connection than you, your connection will be the limiting factor; if your connection is faster than theirs, their connection will be the limiting factor. But either way, it makes most sense to transfer each file as quickly as possible rather than running multiple downloads more slowly.

Max Concurrent Uploads from One User   This setting controls the maximum number of upload requests from any one user that audioGnome tries to execute at one time. As with the Max Concurrent Downloads from One User setting, there's little reason to change this setting from its default value, 1.

Max Transfers   This setting controls the maximum number of transfers (uploads and downloads together) that audioGnome tries to execute at one time. The default setting is 6. Increasing this number significantly may bog down the performance of all transfers. If you have a modem connection, you might want to lower the number.

Max Upload Rate   This setting controls the maximum speed at which audioGnome uploads data from your computer. The setting allows you to prevent audioGnome from using the whole of your available bandwidth. For example, if you have a fractional T1 connection that can transfer 50 kilobytes (KBps) per second, you might want to set a Max Upload Rate of 25KBps so that audioGnome doesn't use more than half of the bandwidth at any one given time. (Note that these figures are *kilobytes*—KB—rather than *kilobits*, Kb.) If you have a modem, you probably won't want to worry about this setting. You *can* use the setting to throttle down audioGnome on a modem connection—for example, by setting a Max Upload Rate of 2KBps compared to the approximately 3.5KBps that a 56K modem delivers upstream—but the resulting uploads will be painfully slow.

Transfer Timeout Interval (seconds) This setting specifies the number of seconds it takes for a transfer to time out (and be canceled). The default setting is 180 seconds—three minutes. Valid settings are from 20 seconds to 180 seconds.

Show Opennap Controls This drop-down list controls whether audioGnome displays Opennap controls. The default setting is No.

Auto Change to Transfer Tab This drop-down list controls whether audioGnome automatically displays the Transfer page when you set a download running. The default setting is Yes, which lets you see immediately whether audioGnome succeeds in establishing the connection and getting the transfer going.

Auto Change to Users Tab This drop-down list controls whether audioGnome automatically displays the Users tab when you perform an action such as adding a user to your list of users. The default setting is Yes.

Connection Type (Speed) Use this drop-down list to specify the connection type and speed that other users see for you. This setting has no effect on the speed of your uploads and downloads. The default setting, Unknown, is suitably uninformative.

IRC Nickname If you want audioGnome to know your IRC nickname so that you can use its IRC features, enter it here.

IRC Password If you enter your IRC nickname, enter your IRC password here.

List Ignored at Connection This setting controls whether audioGnome automatically clears your Ignore list (the list of users you have chosen to ignore) when you connect. The default setting is Yes.

Auto Clear Ignored at Connection This setting controls whether audioGnome loads your Ignore list when you connect. The default setting is No.

Enable PNN This setting controls whether PNN is enabled or disabled. (PNN is a direct network connection between two users.)

Local Domain Name   This label contains the local domain name or IP address of the computer running audioGnome.

Enable Re-connect on Recoverable Errors   This setting controls whether audioGnome automatically tries to reestablish a connection with the server if it is disconnected.

Enable Debug Mode   This setting controls whether audioGnome displays or suppresses error messages when it runs into an error. Unless you want to see the error messages, leave the default setting, No.

Figure 7.5

Use the Options page to configure audioGnome.

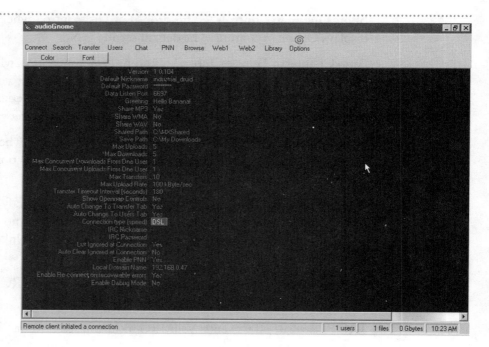

Connecting to a Server

To connect to a server, click the Connect tab to display the Connect page. Then either double-click a server to connect, or select one or more servers and click the Connect button.

Figure 7.6 shows audioGnome with connections established to a bunch of servers. For each active server, Active appears in the Status column, and the Users, Files, and Gbytes columns show the number of users, files, and gigabytes of data available on those servers.

Figure 7.6

audioGnome with a bunch of connections established

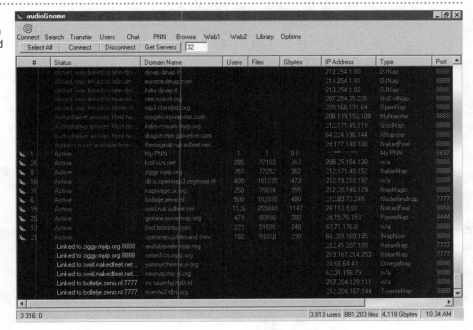

 To connect to as many servers as possible, click the Select All button and then click the Connect button. Because there are a large number of servers, trying to connect to all of them isn't usually a good idea, but you may want to try it in desperation. You'll typically end up connected to a good number of servers, but not to anything like all of them.

To disconnect from a server you're connected to, select the server and click the Disconnect button, or right-click the server and choose Disconnect from Server from the context menu.

NOTE   Some audioGnome server operators will kill (disconnect) you if they feel you're not sharing enough files or if you don't join a chat channel. You'll see messages such as *You have been killed by SlaYa: Auto Leech Kill: Share more files* or *You have been shot!! by Bri: I won't say I told ya so, but I told ya so! You've been warned!*

Click the Get Servers button to refresh the list of servers. You may want to do this once you've been online for a while.

Finding Music with audioGnome

Once you've connected to one or more servers, you're ready to start searching. Here's what to do:

1. Click the Search tab to display the Search page. Figure 7.7 shows the Search page with search criteria specified and a search executed.

Figure 7.7

The audioGnome Search page after a successful search

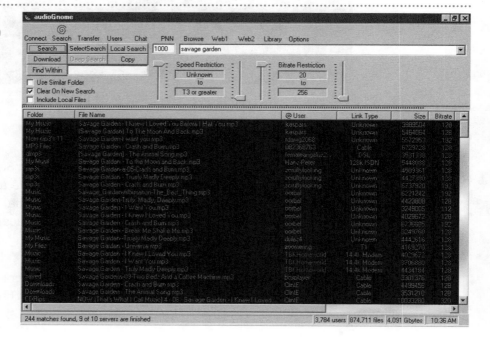

2. Enter your search term in the Search box.

   ☠ To exclude a word from a search, put a minus sign in front of it. For example, if you want to find tracks by Dido other than her collaboration with Eminem, you could use `Dido -Eminem`.

   ☠ You can retrieve search terms that you've used earlier in the audioGnome session by using the drop-down list.

   ☠ Most Wrapster files are tagged with the word *Wrapster* to avoid confusion, so you can find Wrapster files by entering **Wrapster** in the Search box. Usually, you'll want to add something more specific (for example, **ebook** or part of a word identifying what you're looking for) because searching on **Wrapster** alone will return too large a number of entries for handy viewing.

3. In the Number Space, enter the maximum number of search results you want. (The default setting is 1000.)

4. If you want, use the Speed Restriction sliders to set the range of connection speeds that you're interested in. The left-hand slider controls the speed in the upper text box, which sets the slower end of the range. The right-hand slider controls the speed in the lower text box, which sets the faster end of the range.

   ☠ To get the most results, don't set any speed restrictions: Leave the range set to its default Unknown to T3 or Greater.

5. Use the Bitrate Restriction sliders to specify the bitrate or the range of bitrates that you find acceptable. The left-hand slider controls the bitrate in the upper text box, which sets the lower end of the range. The right-hand slider controls the bitrate in the lower text box, which sets the faster end of the range.

   ☠ If you want, you can set the upper and lower bitrates to be the same—for example, set a range of 128 to 128 if you want to find only files encoded at 128Kbps.

   ☠ If you're searching for Wrapster files, remember to include the 32Kbps bitrate in your range—or set a range of 32 to 32.

6. Select the Use Similar Folder check box if you want audioGnome to put the downloaded file in a folder with the same name as the folder that contains it on the host machine. This check box is cleared by default, but you may want to experiment with this feature.

7. Leave the Clear on New Search check box selected (as it is by default) if you want audioGnome to clear the current search results when you execute a new search.

8. Select the Include Local Files check box if you want to search through your local files as well. (You won't usually want to do this.)

9. Click one of the Search buttons to execute the search:

   - Click the Search button to search all the servers you're currently connected to.

   - Click the Select Search button to search only those servers (of those you're currently connected to) that you've selected on the Connect page.

   - Click the Local Search button to search files on your Library page.

   - Click the Deep Search button (if it's available) to search 11 times over all the servers you're currently connected to. Performing a deep search takes much longer than performing a regular search, but it can turn up many more results.

TIP To narrow down your search results, enter further criteria in the Find Within text box and click the Find Within button.

Downloading Files with audioGnome

To download a file with audioGnome, double-click it on the Search page. Alternatively, select multiple files and click the Download button. audioGnome displays the Transfer page, shown in Figure 7.8 with a number of e-book downloads happening.

Figure 7.8

The Transfer page shows the files you're uploading and downloading.

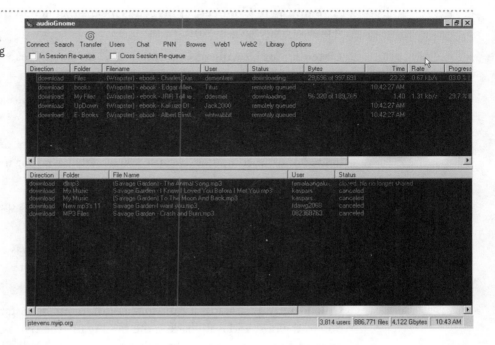

As you can see in the figure, the Transfer page contains two list boxes. The upper list box displays current transfers, and the lower list box displays transfer history—transfers that have been completed (for example, "finished receiving data") and transfers that cannot be completed (for example, "timeout resolving remote port"). Each of the list boxes contains a number of columns, most of which you can see in the figure. Here's what the columns show:

- The Direction column shows whether you're downloading or uploading a file.
- The Folder column shows the folder in which the MP3 file is stored.
- The Filename column shows the filename of the MP3 file.
- The User columns show the name of the user supplying the file.
- The Status column shows the status of the download or upload, using the following terms:

Resolving Remote Port　This status means that audioGnome is resolving the port connection with the host.

Attempting to Connect   This status means that audioGnome is trying to establish a connection with the host.

Listening for Download Connection   This status means that audio-Gnome is waiting to start the download.

Listening for Upload Connection   This status means that audioGnome is waiting to start the upload.

Queued   This status means that the track is queued for download or upload on your computer (because you already have your maximum number of uploads or downloads running).

Remotely Queued   This status means that the track is queued for download on the host's computer.

Downloading   This status means that audioGnome has established a connection to the host and is downloading the file. The Bytes column, Rate column, and Progress column show the progress of the download.

Uploading   This status means that audioGnome has established a connection to the host and is uploading the file. Again, the Bytes column, Rate column, and Progress column show the progress of the upload.

Timeout Resolving Remote Port   This status means that audioGnome has timed out while trying to resolve the port on the remote machine.

Timeout Listening for Download Connection   This status means that audioGnome has timed out while trying to establish a connection for download.

Dormant   This status means that the download or upload is still active, but nothing much is happening.

Canceled   This status means that you have canceled the download or upload.

Finished Receiving Data   This status means that audioGnome has finished downloading the file.

Finished Sending Data   This status means that audioGnome has finished uploading the file.

Closed by Error   This status means that an error has occurred that has caused audioGnome to terminate the download. You may also seen *Closed by error: connection is forcefully rejected.*

- The Bytes column shows the number of bytes in the file and the number of bytes transferred so far. This information appears only when the download is running (or dormant).

- The Time column displays the length of time left on a running download. When a download is not running, it displays the time at which the file was queued.

- The Rate column displays the rate of a running download in kilobytes per second.

- The Progress column displays a percentage and a visual indicator showing the progress of a running download.

- The Server# column displays the number of the server to which the user supplying the file is connected.

- The Server Name column displays the name of the server to which the user supplying the file is connected.

Word to the Wise: Throttle Greedy Users to Benefit Others

As you saw earlier, audioGnome lets you specify how much of your bandwidth to devote to its activities. But it goes even further than that: It also lets you throttle back any user who's monopolizing your bandwidth. By doing so, you can prevent a user from hogging your upload capability. (Also, if you decide you don't like someone, you can give them frustratingly slow downloads. For example, if they consistently cancel your downloads, you might want to throttle them back. Actually, you'll probably want to plain throttle them as well.)

To throttle back a user, right-click an upload listing, select the Set Upload Transfer Rate Limit item on the context menu, and choose an appropriate setting from the sub-menu that appears. Your choices run from 1.0kByte/sec to 100kByte/sec, which gives good flexibility over everything from a modem connection to a T1.

To cancel a transfer, right-click it and select Cancel/Remove Transfer(s) from the context menu.

To copper your bet against your download being broken off, you can select the In Session Re-queue check box, the Cross Session Re-queue check box, or both. These two check boxes cause audioGnome to attempt to re-queue a broken-off download when the remote user resurfaces, either during the current session (the In Session Re-queue check box) or during subsequent sessions (the Cross Session Re-queue check box). These features don't always work, but you may well find them worth trying.

Browsing a User's Library

Like Napster, audioGnome lets you browse the files that other users are sharing. The easiest way to browse a user is to right-click a listing on the Search page that features them and choose Browse User from the context menu. audioGnome displays a list of the user's shared files on the Search page. From there, you can download the files as usual.

Figure 7.9 shows an example of browsing a user's shared files. As you can see (if you can decipher the small print), this user is sharing an eclectic selection of files—everything from *War and Peace* to software (including the BlackICE Defender software and a beta of Adobe Photoshop) to games to music.

Figure 7.9

audioGnome lets you browse another user's library to see which files they're sharing.

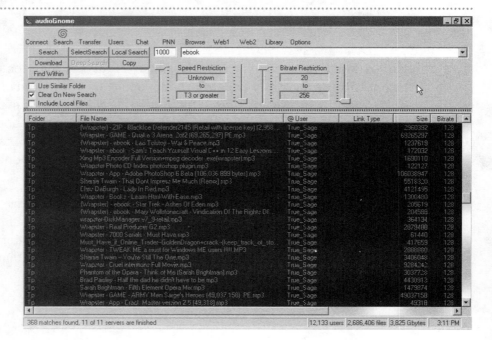

Sharing Files

To share files with audioGnome, place them in your shared folder and make sure the Share MP3 drop-down list on the Options page is set to Yes. (If you're sharing WMA files and WAV files as well, make sure the Share WMA drop-down list and the Share WAV drop-down list are also set to Yes.) The files will then be visible to other users, who will be able to download them.

To quickly see what's in your shared folder or folders, click the Library tab to display the Library page. In the default colors, shared folders and files appear in green, while non-shared folders and files appear in yellow. Figure 7.10 shows the Library page.

Figure 7.10

Use the Library page to see which folders and files you're sharing.

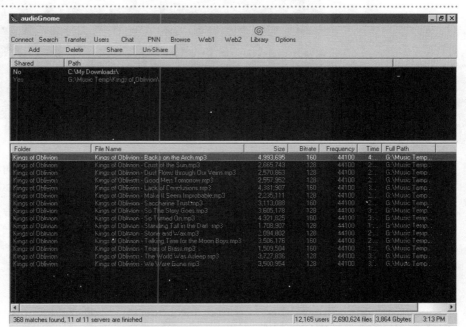

Chatting on audioGnome

As you'd guess, chatting on audioGnome takes place on the Chat Rooms page. Display the Chat Rooms page by clicking the Chat Rooms tab, then click the List All button to get the current listing of chat channels available. Figure 7.11 shows the Chat Rooms page with a listing of servers.

Figure 7.11

The Chat Rooms page of audioGnome

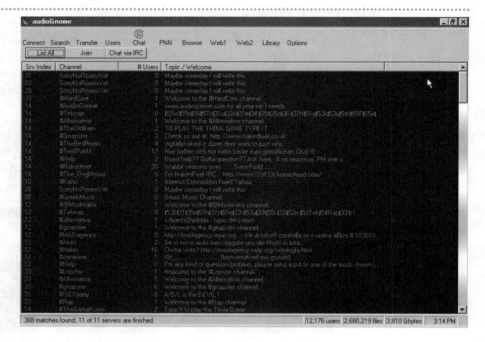

To join a channel, select it in the list and click the Join button. (You can join multiple chat channels if you like.) audioGnome opens a chat window. Figure 7.12 shows an example of a chat window.

To leave a chat channel, click the Close button on its window.

PNN

audioGnome's PNN feature lets you connect directly to one or more other users—or one or more other users to connect directly to you—without going through the server. This means that you can transfer files when not connected to the server. It also gives you greater privacy in your transactions.

PNN listings display PNN and the user's name (for example, PNN – Jill2001) on the Connect page. You can connect to them (or, to be more accurate, *attempt* to connect to them) in the same way as any of the other servers. If you're using PNN and you issue a Select All command on the Connect page, audioGnome will select the PNN servers as well as the regular ones.

Figure 7.12

Chatting on audioGnome

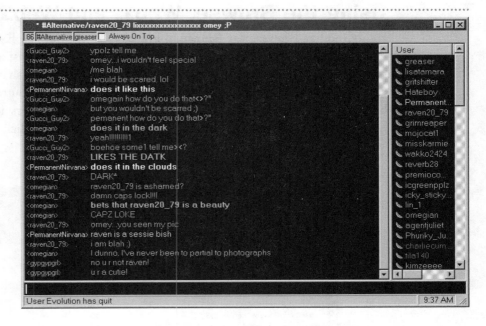

To run PNN, set the Enable PNN option on the Options page to Yes. Then add each user to the Users page as usual (for example, by issuing an Add User(s) to List command from the Search page or the Transfer page).

The PNN page shows the details of your PNN connections. Figure 7.13 shows an example of the PNN page. As you can see, most of the columns are self-explanatory: the number of the socket being used for PNN, your user name, the port audioGnome is using, the client type, your connection details (for example, a 56K modem), and the number of files you're sharing. The user number is an ID number that audioGnome assigns dynamically at the start of each session.

Figure 7.13

The PNN page of audioGnome

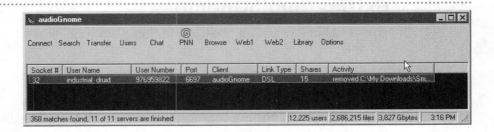

Using the Browse, Web1, and Web2 Pages

audioGnome's Browse page (shown in Figure 7.14) provides an Explorer-style window for managing your audioGnome folders. The drop-down list at the top of the page initially provides access to your download folder and your shared folder, but you can type in other paths as necessary, and you can use the Back button and Forward button to navigate from folder to folder. The context menu offers a variety of common commands. For example, to see details of the files, right-click and choose View ➢ Details from the context menu.

Figure 7.14

Use the Browse page to explore, manage, and rename your files.

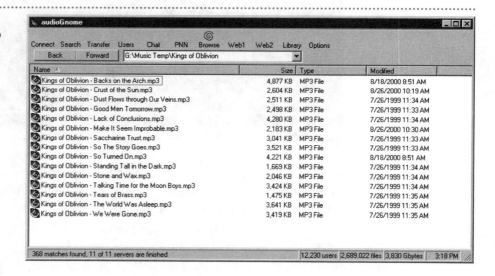

The Web1 page and the Web2 page provide access to audioGnome support, updates, and information. These pages are self-explanatory, so I won't show them here.

Exiting audioGnome

To exit audioGnome, click the Close button on its window.

Using Gnutella

As I've mentioned, Napster is being sued by the RIAA and Metallica for encouraging copyright infringement. In the Napster setup, users log in to the individual Napster servers, which are coordinated by the master server, and can then share files directly with each other. The centralization provides an easy and effective target for the lawsuit: Close down the Napster servers, and nobody will be able to trade MP3 files (or other files disguised as MP3 files) via Napster.

Enter Gnutella. Gnutella is a networking and file-sharing protocol implemented in a way that doesn't use a central server. Instead, people who install Gnutella can establish their own connections to one another, setting up and tearing down virtual networks at will. This makes Gnutella more resilient—more Internet-like, you might say—and so harder to target and harder to shut down than Napster. (The Gnutella site claims that Gnutella is designed to survive a nuclear war and that it can withstand an even-more-destructive band of hungry lawyers.) Besides, where Napster and audioGnome are designed to share only MP3 files at this writing, Gnutella can be used to share any type of file.

Gnutella was initially developed by some of the programmers at Nullsoft (makers of Winamp) after Nullsoft was bought by America Online (AOL). Gnutella appeared on AOL for all of one day before being withdrawn because of intellectual-property, uh, *concerns*, but that day was enough to get it into the wild. Since then, Gnutella versions have been developed by a loose army of volunteers.

A wide range of Gnutella clients are available on the Web for different operating systems including Windows, MacOS, Linux, and BeOS. If you're looking for a Gnutella client, the best place to start is the Gnutella Web site, `gnutella.wego.com`, which keeps links to the assorted client sites.

At this writing, there are so many Gnutella clients for Windows and Linux that it doesn't make sense for me to pick one to present here, because you'll probably choose a different client. (On the Mac, things are different—there's only Mactella at the moment.) So here's what I'll do: In the next section, I'll discuss in general how Gnutella works. Then I'll discuss the standard features of most Gnutella clients. Then I'll provide brief details of some of the clients available for Windows and Linux—and of Mactella, of course.

As you'll see, Gnutella is a bit harder to use than Napster and audioGnome, it doesn't let you browse in the same way that Napster and audioGnome do, and because of the nature of the network, performance can be poor. These limitations perhaps explain why, at this writing, Gnutella seems to be much less widely used than Napster and audioGnome. However, should Napster (and perhaps audioGnome) be closed down, you can bet that Gnutella use will soar.

How Gnutella Works

Before you start trying to use Gnutella, it helps to have an idea of how the technology works, because it's substantially different from Napster.

Like Napster, Gnutella has both a client aspect and a server aspect. But unlike Napster, in Gnutella, both the client and the server are designed to act without central control: Instead of linking to a server that coordinates sharing, searches, and downloads and uploads (as in Napster), Gnutella is designed as a fully peer technology and links from one peer to the next. Also unlike Napster, which (at this writing) is constrained to sharing MP3 files, Gnutella is designed for sharing all kinds of files. So if you've got *any* material you want to share, you can use Gnutella to make it available to the whole wide world directly from your computer.

In theory, Gnutella can be used for sharing the original files that people have created and that they can distribute freely: things they've written (thoughts, recipes, diatribes, screeds, and love poems that will make any sentient reader chew off their left leg), drawn, photographed (including their own bodies doing interesting things), or recorded. But in reality, Gnutella is widely, though not exclusively, used for sharing illegal copies of copyrighted material. You *will* find files being shared legally via Gnutella, but you'll also find far more pirated material.

Because Gnutella is implemented as a peer-to-peer technology, it can be much harder to attach to the Gnutella network than to a network that uses central servers, such as Napster or audioGnome. In order to attach to the network, you need the IP address of one or more nodes currently on the network. Once you're connected to that computer, you're connected to the rest of the network through it, and Gnutella can search recursively through the network, starting with the computer to which your computer is connected.

In the early days of Gnutella clients, you used to have to connect manually by supplying the IP address of a computer connected at that time to gnutellaNet. Nowadays most Gnutella clients come with auto-connection features loaded with a list of IP addresses that they speed-dial (as it were) automatically until they manage to establish your desired number of connections.

With some Gnutella clients, you still need to supply an IP address. And even with auto-connecting clients, you may want to specify a particular IP address to connect to rather than taking the luck of the draw. It's not too hard to come up with an IP address. If you can't hit up a friend who's currently on gnutellaNet, one of the best ways to find a current IP address is by checking the #Gnutella group on the EFNet channels on IRC. This group usually shows a current IP address in its topic and often evicts people who fail to notice it and ask for an IP address.

> You'll also find Gnutella host listings at the Clip2 DSS Web site, gnutellahosts.com.

Once your computer has glommed onto one or more nodes of gnutellaNet, it needs to find out about the computers out there. To do so, the Gnutella client pings each connected computer (sending a *ping* packet) to tell them you're on the network. On receiving the ping, each node sends back a different type of packet, a *pong*, giving the computer's IP address and details of the files it's sharing. The pong packets travel back along the route the ping packets took, bouncing from node to node until they reach your computer.

> When you execute a search, your computer sends out query packets that are forwarded from node to node. On receiving the query packet, the computer compares it to the files that it is sharing *and* transmits the query packet to all the computers it's connected to. If there's a hit on the computer, it sends back a query-hit packet giving the its IP address and details of the matching file or files. Your client builds a list of files for you to look at and decide which you want.

> At this writing, gnutellaNet has no browse capability for finding out what files are available: You have to search by specific criteria each time.

As I just mentioned, each node that receives the query packet sends it on to the computers it's connected to—but not for ever, or the Internet would gradually silt up with packets bouncing around for the half-life of coal. Each packet has a Time To Live setting—a TTL, if you like your TLAs—that tells the Gnutella client whether to forward it or to kill it. Most clients set a default value of 5, 6, or 7 for TTL; any value above 7 makes the packets travel through an uncomfortably large number of nodes before expiring. Generally speaking, a high TTL increases the size of the Gnutella network you're attached to, but it slows performance; a low TTL gives better performance over a smaller network.

Word to the Wise: Realities of Peer-to-Peer Networking

In Gnutella, all information is passed from peer to peer for searches, search results, and simply building and maintaining the Gnutella network. This has three results worth remembering:

- First, Gnutella can be very slow compared to P2P technologies that use a central server, such as Napster and audioGnome. A search in Gnutella may take 10 minutes to execute rather than 10 seconds. Be patient. Also, results crawl in gradually rather than arriving in a bunch as they do with Napster. Be more patient.

- Second, you'll often see a high level of activity on your Internet connection even when you're not uploading or downloading any files yourself. Normally this degree of activity on an otherwise apparently inactive connection would suggest that something is amiss with your computer, but with Gnutella it doesn't necessarily indicate a problem. (It *can* indicate a problem—someone could be filching files from your computer without your being aware of it, and the Gnutella activity might mask the unusual amount of information transfer taking place. It's hard to tell the difference, especially given that Gnutella's actions can be misinterpreted as hostile by firewall software.) Usually, it just means that you're an active part of the gnutellaNet, and your computer is busily passing ping, pong, query, and query-hit packets back and forth with its peers.

- Third—and obviously enough—because a chunk of your bandwidth is being devoted to gnutellaNet, you have less bandwidth available for downloading and uploading files, so each activity takes longer. If you have cable or DSL, this probably won't worry you too much. But if you have single-channel ISDN or a dial-up connection, you may find your patience being tried.

When you request a download, Gnutella tries to use an HTTP Get command to download the file directly from the node that has it (*not* through the node-to-node route that the pings, pongs, and query packets have been traveling). If the other computer is behind a firewall, the Get command may not work, because most firewalls block incoming connection attempts for security. In this case, your Gnutella client communicates to the node that has the file that your computer wants to get the file, but cannot, and asks it to push the file out through the firewall.

When you make your computer a node on the Gnutella network, you're essentially inserting it into a giant virtual web of other computers. Your computer connects to one or more (usually several) existing nodes on the network. Other computers then connect to your computer, so you have both outgoing connections (your computer attaching to another computer) and incoming connections (other computers attaching to your computer). Computers within range of your computer are said to be within your Gnutella horizon. Computers beyond that are, naturally enough, beyond your horizon. Your horizon can be near or far, but for a typical Gnutella setup, there are a large number of nodes within it. Say you attach to six nodes, each of which is attached to five other nodes, each of which is attached to five other nodes, etc. Using a TTL of 7, you'll have the best part of 100,000 computers within your horizon. And then you've got incoming connections as well.

General Features and Options of Gnutella Clients

As I mentioned, there are too many different Gnutella clients for Windows and Linux to discuss them individually in any depth. So this section presents an overview of the features and options you'll usually find on Gnutella clients so that you'll be able to get going with whichever Gnutella client you choose. Some Gnutella clients *don't* have some of these features, which you may find a blessing or a hindrance. Other Gnutella clients have these features and more—in which case you'll have to work out the other features on your own.

Most Gnutella clients arrange their interface as four or five pages, each representing one major area of Gnutella's functions. Some Gnutella clients use windows rather than pages. These pages or windows go by different names but are usually a gnutellaNet page, a search page, an uploads page, a downloads page, and a configuration page (or a configuration dialog box).

Vulnerability Factor: Gnutella and gnutellaNet

Technologically speaking, gnutellaNet's way tough. As I mentioned, it was designed as a robust P2P technology that would survive both physical assaults and copyright-law assaults.

So gnutellaNet's less than vulnerable. But what about *you*, when you're using it?

gnutellaNet doesn't use centralized servers (each node is its own client and server), so there's no central log of the computers attached at any one time. To list all the computers attached to gnutellaNet would be almost impossible, though by attaching a large number of nodes and comparing the results, it might be possible to build a partial picture.

Searching for files on gnutellaNet is relatively safe, because information is passed from one connected computer to another. This makes it very difficult to tell where the search originated, though in theory it would be possible to trace the search back to its source. In practice, it's highly doubtful that anyone would bother—and searching for something is in itself an innocent activity.

Downloading and uploading files via Gnutella is less safe. For downloading and uploading, a direct connection is established between the computer supplying the file and the computer downloading it. This is necessary for performance—it wouldn't make sense for the millions of bytes in a download to follow the tortuous path of the ping and pong packets. So when you download or upload a file, the computer at the other end knows your IP address, and they know which file you're sending or receiving.

Gnutella does not support browsing a user's shared files, so the only way that someone can build up a list of the files you're sharing is by searching and registering hits.

gnutellaNet Page

One feature that most Gnutella clients supply in one form or another is monitoring of connections and statistics, letting you see what's going on. Here are a few examples:

☸ Figure 7.15 shows the gnutellaNet page of gtk-gnutella.

Figure 7.15

Most Gnutella clients have a gnutellaNet page or window that lets you monitor what's happening. This example is from gtk-gnutella.

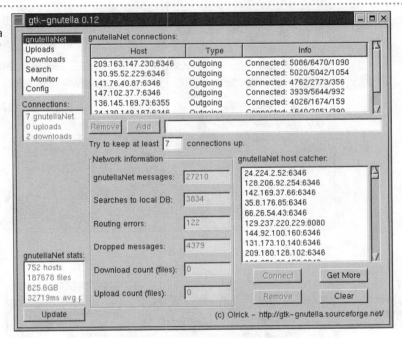

☸ Figure 7.16 shows the four pages—Connections, Files, Messages, and Packets—of the Toadnode Statistics window.

☸ Figure 7.17 shows the Net Stats page of the Mactella client.

Search Page

Even more important than the gnutellaNet page is the search page or search window, because this is the only way that you'll be able to find files via Gnutella.

Figure 7.16

Toadnode breaks this information across the four pages of the Toadnode Statistics dialog box.

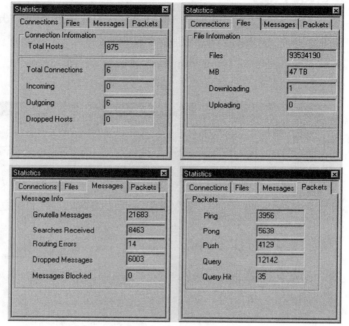

Figure 7.17

The Net Stats page of the Mactella client shows a huge amount of information.

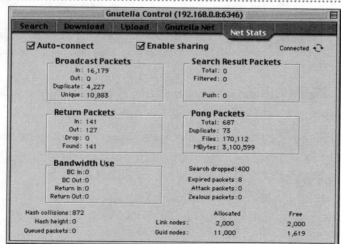

Most search pages (or search windows) are relatively simple, providing a text box for specifying the search criteria, start and stop buttons (often integrated into a single button), a list box for results, and a download button. Here are a couple of examples:

☠ Figure 7.18 shows the Search page of the Mactella client.

Figure 7.18

Mactella has a nicely implemented Search page.

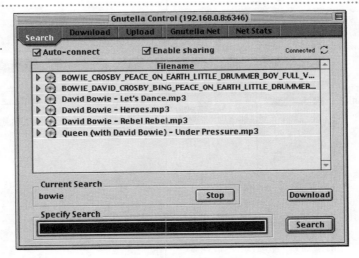

☠ Figure 7.19 shows the Search page of the Gnubile client.

Figure 7.19

The Gnubile Client lets you sort search results by filename, size, server, and link speed.

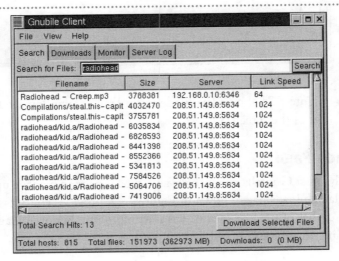

Downloads Page

Once you've found a file you want, you'll need to download it. All Gnutella clients I've seen have a downloads page or window that shows the progress of downloads and lets you cancel them. Some also let you pause and resume downloads.

Here are a couple of examples:

☠ Figure 7.20 shows gtk-gnutella's Downloads page.

Figure 7.20

gtk-gnutella's Downloads page lets you easily change your maximum number of simultaneous downloads.

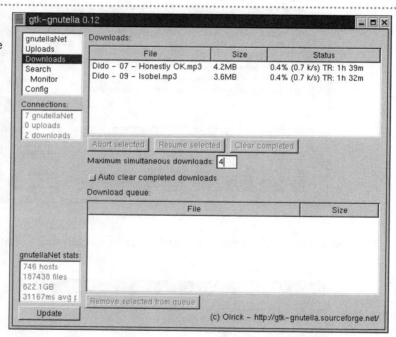

☠ Figure 7.21 shows Toadnode's File Transfer window (in the lower-left corner of the screen).

Uploads Page

Similarly, most Gnutella clients have an Uploads page to manage uploads. For example, Newtella's Uploads page, shown in Figure 7.22, provides controls for setting the maximum number of uploads overall, the maximum number of uploads per user, and for controlling the amount of bandwidth used.

Figure 7.21

Toadnode provides a File Transfer window that includes Pause and Resume buttons.

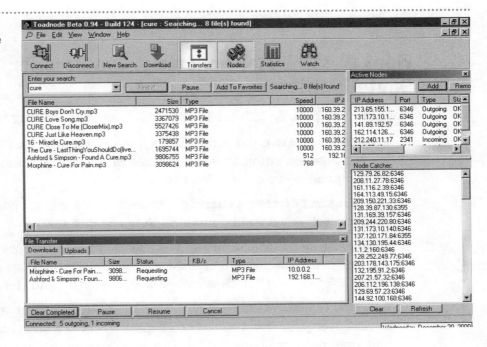

Figure 7.22

Newtella's Uploads page lets you manage both uploads and bandwidth.

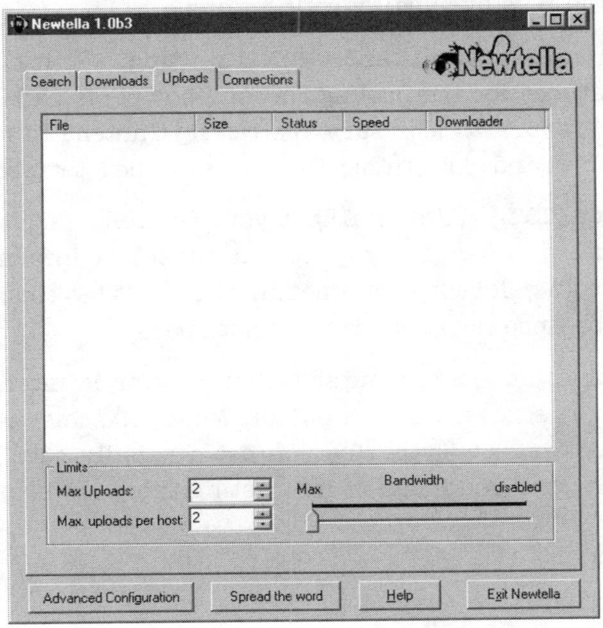

Word to the Wise: Important Features for Gnutella Clients

When you're choosing a Gnutella client, look for the following features:

Automatic *and* manual connections   Your Gnutella client should let you connect automatically for ease *and* connect manually for close management of connections.

Enabling and disabling sharing   Your Gnutella client should provide controls for enabling and disabling sharing easily.

Sharing filter   Some clients let you specify which file types in your shared folders to share. For example, you might choose to share only MP3 files and ZIP files rather than everything in the folders.

Download queue management   Your client should give you tight control over your downloads. Look especially for the ability to pause and resume downloads, which can save you hours when downloading large files over balky connections.

Upload management and bandwidth throttling   Your client should provide features for controlling the number of uploads your computer delivers and, if necessary, restricting Gnutella to only part of your available bandwidth rather than hogging the lot indiscriminately.

Time to Live (TTL)   It's vital that your Gnutella client let you set the TTL, the number of computers a packet of information can travel through before it is stopped. If you can't set this, you won't be able to balance network size against speed.

Another feature that some Gnutella clients offer is monitoring the terms that other people are searching for. What *good* this actually does you is anybody's guess: Typically, you get a rapidly scrolling list of terms that may give you ideas of interesting things to search for but

Word to the Wise: Important Features for Gnutella Clients (*continued*)

will more likely remind you that a lot of people are searching for pornography, warez, and distressingly bad music. The illustration below shows an example of a search monitor from gtk-gnutella.

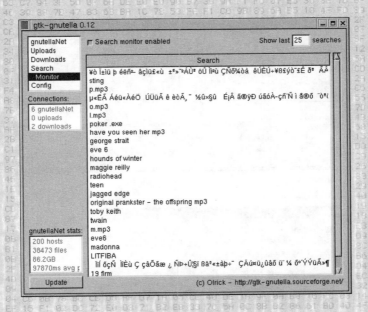

Configuration Page or Configuration Dialog Box

The last page that most Gnutella clients have is a configuration page or dialog box for letting you manipulate the various options. Figure 7.23 shows the gtk-gnutella Config page.

Given how many options there are, dialog boxes tend to be more popular than configuration pages. Figure 7.24 shows the Toadnode Options dialog box.

Figure 7.23

gtk-gnutella uses a Config page for setting options.

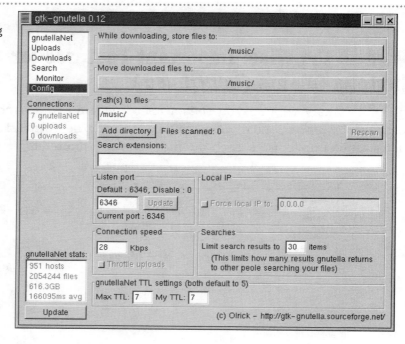

Figure 7.24

Toadnode uses an Options dialog box in fine Windows style.

Windows Clients

Not surprisingly, there's an impressive number of different Windows clients for Gnutella. The list below details some (but far from all) of the current ones, but you'll no doubt find others have sprung up by the time you read this. Some of these clients have their own Web sites, but you should find links to them all at the Gnutella Web site (again, gnutella.wego.com).

- Newtella (www.newtella.com) is a Gnutella client that's restricted to MP3 files. (You'll find a lot of Wrapster files as well.) Figure 7.25 shows Newtella's Connections page, which provides an auto-connection feature and easy management of your connections.

Figure 7.25

Newtella is a Windows client for Gnutella that's restricted to MP3 files (and files that masquerade as MP3 files).

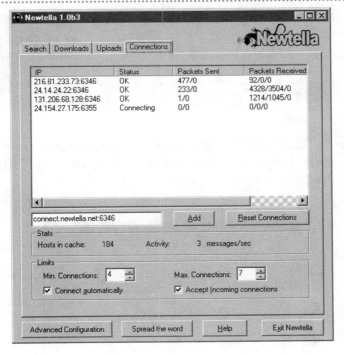

- Toadnode (www.toadnode.com) offers a selection of European languages from Finnish to Magyar. Toadnode (shown in Figure 7.26) offers good features for searching for all types of files.

Figure 7.26

Toadnode is a slick
Gnutella client with a
colorful interface.

Figure 7.26

Toadnode is a slick
Gnutella client with a
colorful interface.

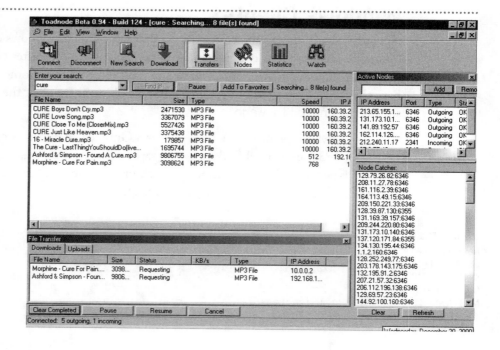

☠ N-Tella (shown in Figure 7.27) is a stripped-down client that works effectively. Despite its relative lack of features, somehow N-Tella manages to be harder to use than some of its competitors.

Figure 7.27

N-Tella has a nice interface
but isn't as easy to use as
it appears.

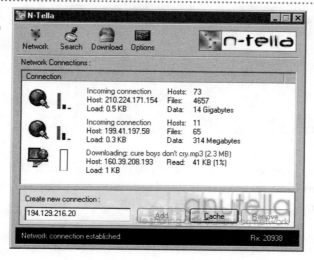

Gnucleus (shown in Figure 7.28) is a powerful Gnutella client that uses a multi-window interface.

Figure 7.28

Gnucleus uses a multi-window interface that cries out for a higher screen resolution than this.

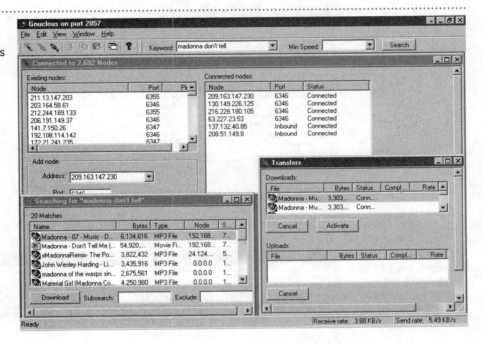

Linux Clients

Linux clients for Gnutella aren't as numerous as Windows clients, but at this writing, plenty are in development, including the following:

- The Gnubile Client has a neat and uncluttered interface arranged on four pages. Figure 7.29 shows the Gnubile Client after a successful search.

- gtk-gnutella offers the "classic" Gnutella-client look and has a full-ish implementation of features. Figure 7.30 shows gtk-gnutella.

- gnut is a text-based client—but a GUI is in the works.

Figure 7.29

The Gnubile Client

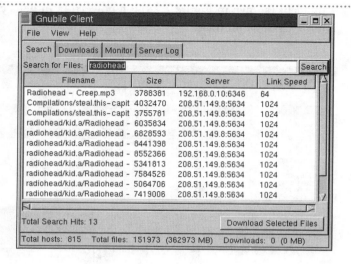

Figure 7.30

gtk-gnutella has the classic Gnutella-client look and offers impressive functionality for downloading.

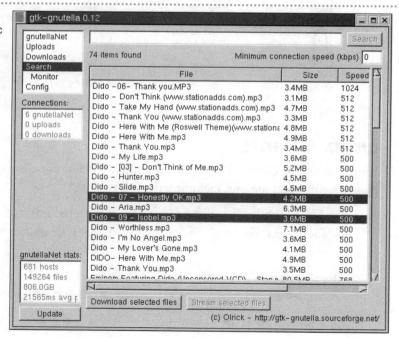

    ☠ Gnucleus is based on the Gnubile Client but offers options for protecting files. Figure 7.31 shows the Search page of Gnucleus. Note the Protected tab at the right-hand end of the row of tabs.

Figure 7.31

Gnucleus is based on the Gnubile Client but adds a Protected page for protecting files.

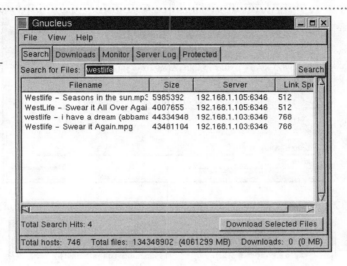

Mac Client: Mactella

If you use the Mac, you'll know that your choice of software tends to be much more limited than that for Windows or Linux users. Gnutella clients are no exception: There's only one Gnutella client for the Mac—Mactella. But it's a good one: Mactella is relatively mature, lets you set a large number of options, and gives good feedback about what's happening.

Each of Mactella's five pages—like the Search page, shown in Figure 7.32 —provides an Auto-Connect check box for instructing Mactella to connect automatically to whichever Gnutella nodes it can find and an Enable Sharing check box that lets you toggle sharing on and off at will.

Mactella marshals most of its configuration options into its Preferences dialog box (shown in Figure 7.33).

Figure 7.32

Mactella provides an Auto-Connect check box and an Enable Sharing check box on each page of its interface.

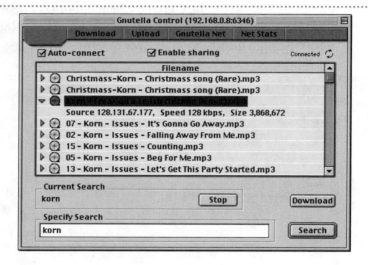

Figure 7.33

Mactella's Preferences dialog box provides good control over Mactella's options.

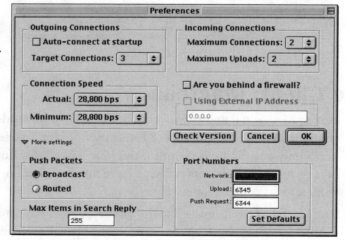

Gnutella Web Sites

If you can't (or won't) install Gnutella client software on your computer, all is not lost, because there are assorted Web sites that implement Gnutella clients through a Web interface. With most of these clients, you can only search and download files—you cannot upload files—but this is enough to satisfy many people.

At this writing, Gnutella Web sites include the following:

- ☠ gnutello (**www.gnutello.com**)
- ☠ gnute Network Search (**gnute.com**)
- ☠ TellaSeek (**techdevelopers.com/tellaseek/**)
- ☠ MP3Board (**www.mp3board.com**)

Most of these Web sites have a straightforward search interface that acts as an interface for gnutellaNet; some can search Napster servers as well. You enter the parameters for a search, submit it, and get one or more pages listing results (if any). To download a file, you click its listing. Transfers take place like a standard download from a Web site.

When you're accessing Gnutella Web sites, all standard cautions for Web sites apply. In particular, be suspicious of Web sites that open extra windows with enticing blandishments to distract you while they attempt to ransack your computer.

Using iMesh

iMesh is a search tool for music, video, and graphics files. iMesh supports skins (of which you can download a number from **www.imesh.com**) and plug-ins, such as a plug-in for Winamp that lets you search for files from Winamp.

At this writing, the iMesh software is in beta and is highly unstable. Back up your system files before installing and running iMesh.

Getting and Installing iMesh

To get iMesh, steer your browser to the iMesh Web site, **www.imesh.com**. Follow the Download link and download the latest version of the client software, then run the downloaded file to start the installation routine.

iMesh has a straightforward installation routine: You agree to a license agreement, select a program folder, specify a download folder, and choose whether to create an iMesh icon on your Desktop.

The first time you start iMesh, the Registration Wizard runs. Fill in the information in the text boxes in the Personal Details group box: your iMesh nickname (which needs to be unique), your first and last names (real or otherwise), and the e-mail address to which you want iMesh to send your password should you lose it. Then click the Next button to move along to the second screen of the Registration Wizard, which requests information about your location.

None of the fields in the Location Details group box is required information, so you can leave these fields blank if you prefer. Click the Next button to proceed to the third screen of the Registration Wizard (shown in Figure 7.34 with settings chosen), which contains settings that require more attention than those on the second screen.

Figure 7.34

The third screen of the Registration Wizard includes required information and some important choices.

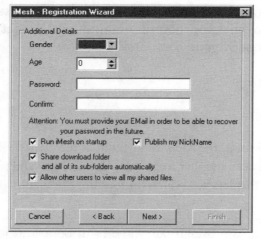

Use the Gender drop-down list and the Age drop-down list to specify your gender and age if you want to. You'll need to specify an age of 13 or older: If you leave the Age drop-down list set to its default setting of 0, or if you set an age younger than 13, iMesh displays the iMesh dialog box shown in Figure 7.35 telling you that, in accordance with the Children's Net Privacy Law (also known as COPPA), it will not allow ages under 13 to be registered. If iMesh displays this dialog box, click the OK button to return to the third screen of the Registration Wizard. You can specify an age as old as you like, but iMesh reduces any age over 120 to 120.

Figure 7.35

If you give an age under 13 (or if you leave the default setting of 0 in the Age drop-down list), iMesh displays this dialog box telling you that it will not allow ages under 13 to be registered.

Also on the third screen, enter an unguessable password in the Password text box and in the Confirm text box. Then specify settings for these four check boxes, all of which are selected by default:

Run iMesh on Startup check box   Leave this check box selected if you want iMesh to run every time you start Windows. Otherwise, clear this check box.

Publish My NickName check box   Leave this check box selected if you want iMesh to publish your nickname on its network. Clear this check box if you want to remain a little more private.

Share Download Folder and All of Its Subfolders Automatically check box
Leave this check box selected if you want iMesh to share your designated download folder and any subfolders it contains. *Sharing your download folder is almost always a bad idea, because it may cause you to commit a felony by unwittingly sharing copyrighted material that you do not have the right to distribute.* Clear this check box.

Allow Other Users to View All My Shared Files check box   Select this check box if you want other users to be able to view all the files you're sharing as opposed to only files that you share explicitly. Clear this check box too.

Click the Next button to move on to the fourth (and final) screen of the Registration Wizard (shown in Figure 7.36).

In the Connection drop-down list, specify the speed of your Internet connection if you want to. This speed is the connection speed that other users will see listed for you. It doesn't affect the speed at which you can upload and download files. So you can leave the setting at its default, I Don't Know, if you want.

If you know that your computer connects to the Internet through a proxy server, select the I Am behind a Proxy check box and enter the proxy server's details in the Proxy Address and Proxy Port text boxes. (If you don't know the details of your network's proxy server, ask your network administrator.)

Figure 7.36

Choose connection settings on the fourth screen of the Registration Wizard.

Click the Finish button to finish the registration process and to dismiss the Registration Wizard. iMesh starts the Share Wizard. Figure 7.37 shows the first screen of the Share Wizard.

Figure 7.37

The first screen of the Share Wizard

In the Search on Drives drop-down list, select the drive or drives that you want to search for files, and then click the Next button. iMesh searches for files you may want to share (such as MP3 files) and displays a list of them in the second screen of the Share Wizard (shown in Figure 7.38).

Figure 7.38

On the second screen of the Share Wizard, clear the default check marks from any folders that you don't want to share.

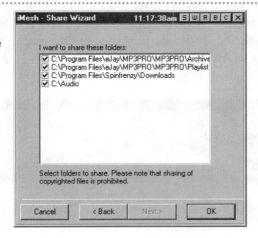

By default, iMesh selects the check box for each folder it lists—but it tells you "Please note that sharing of copyrighted files is prohibited." How kind. Clear the check boxes from all folders except those that contain files that you have the right to distribute. Then click the OK button.

iMesh then appears in its default, "tab style" look (shown in Figure 7.39).

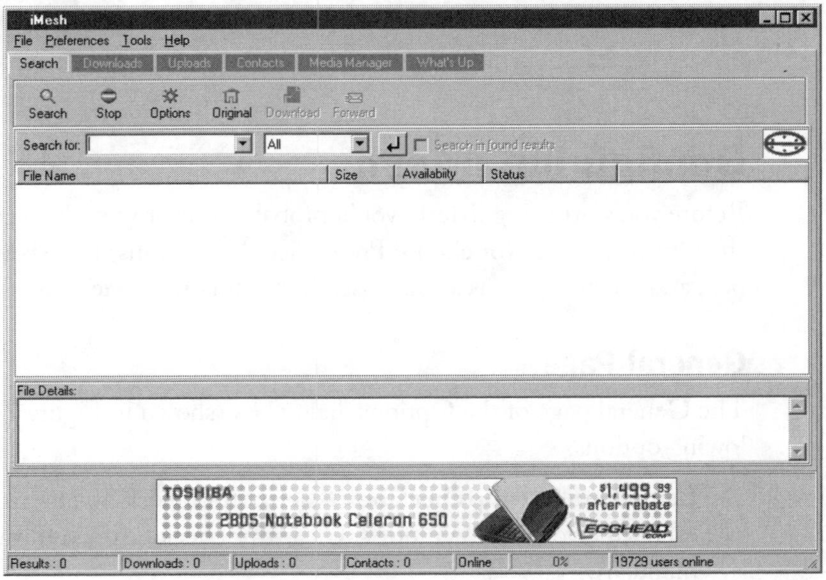

Figure 7.39

iMesh offers two different looks. This is the default, "tab style" look.

iMesh also offers an "Outlook style" interface (shown in Figure 7.40) that you can apply by choosing Preferences ➢ Select Appearance ➢ Outlook Style or by pressing Alt+1. (To get back to the tab-style interface, choose Preferences ➢ Select Appearance ➢ Tab Style or press Alt+2.)

Figure 7.40

The "Outlook style" interface is iMesh's second option at this writing.

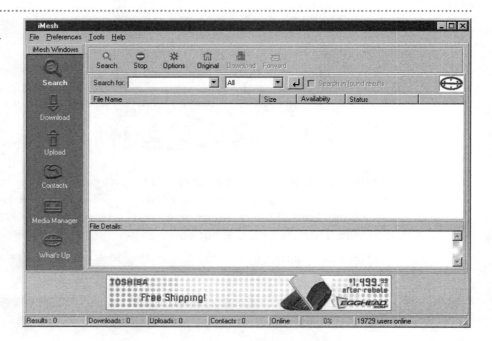

Configuring iMesh

Before you start using iMesh, you'll probably want to tweak its configuration. Click the Options button (or choose Preferences ➢ Options) to display the Options dialog box, and choose options as discussed in the following sections.

General Page

The General page of the Options dialog box (shown in Figure 7.41) contains the following options:

Launch on Startup check box   Select this check box to make iMesh launch each time you start Windows. Clear this check box if you want to launch iMesh manually.

Always on Top check box   Select this check box if you want to run iMesh on top of any other active application. To run iMesh as a "normal" application window, clear this check box.

Show Splash check box   Select this check box if you want to see the iMesh splash screen (the opening graphical logo) each time you run iMesh. Clear this check box to skip the splash screen.

Show Desktop icon check box   Select this check box if you want to have an iMesh icon (a shortcut) on your desktop. If you don't want a shortcut, clear this check box.

Sticky Window check box   Select this check box if you want iMesh to remember the position of the Uploads window and the Downloads window each time it displays them. Clear this check box if you prefer to position the windows manually.

Show Main Menu check box   Leave this check box selected if you want the iMesh window to show the menu bar, as it does by default. Clear this check box to get rid of the menu bar.

Mini Toolbar check box   Select this check box to display the toolbar as small buttons without text. Leave this check box cleared (as it is by default) to display the toolbar as large buttons with text.

Disable Status Messages check box   Select this check box if you want to prevent iMesh from displaying status messages. Leave this check box cleared (as it is by default) if you want to see the status messages.

Figure 7.41
The General page of the
Options dialog box

Locations Page

The Locations page of the Options dialog box (shown in Figure 7.42) lets you specify the folder in which you want iMesh to save files you download via iMesh. To change the folder, either type directly into the Default Location text box or click the Change button, use the resulting Browse for Folder dialog box to navigate to and select the folder, and click the OK button.

Figure 7.42

The Locations page of the Options dialog box

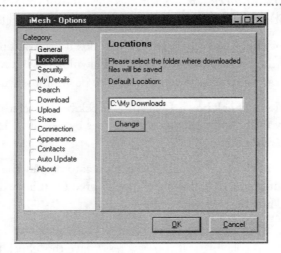

Security Page

The Security page of the Options dialog box (shown in Figure 7.43) provides the following options:

Set Password group box The Password text box and Confirm text box contain the password you entered during setup of iMesh.

Publish My NickName check box Select this check box if you want iMesh to publish your nickname on its network. Clear the check box to maintain somewhat greater privacy. (People from whom you download files, and people who download files from you, will of course see your nickname whatever the setting in this check box.)

Ask for Password on Program Startup check box Select this check box if you want iMesh to prompt you for your password when you start it. If your computer is shared (even in a family location), you might want to select this check box.

Antivirus Protection group box   To use an antivirus program on files you download, select the Use Antivirus Protection Program check box and identify the program in the Antivirus Protection Program Located In text box. (To navigate to the program, click the … button and use the resulting Choose Antivirus Protection Program dialog box to select the program.)

Figure 7.43

The Security page of the Options dialog box

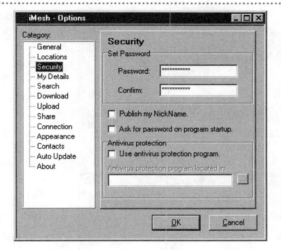

My Details Page

The My Details page of the Options dialog box (shown in Figure 7.44) contains three pages that store the information you entered during the registration process. You can change this information as necessary by working on the My Details page.

Search Page

The Search page of the Options dialog box (shown in Figure 7.45) contains only two options:

Show Only Available Results check box   Leave this check box selected (as it is by default) to have iMesh show you only results that are available. Select this check box if you want iMesh to display unavailable results as well. (Unavailable results may be useful for showing you other files that you may want to search for later.)

Clean Search History button   Click this button to clear the information that iMesh has stored on the searches you have performed.

Figure 7.44

The My Details page of the Options dialog box

Figure 7.45

The Search page of the Options dialog box

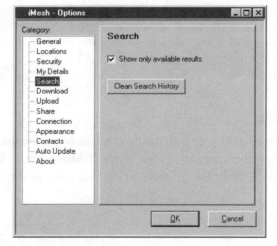

Download Page

The Download page of the Options dialog box (shown in Figure 7.46) contains the following four options:

Maximum Concurrent Downloads text box In this text box, enter the maximum number of downloads you want to have running at the same time. The default setting is 3, but if you use a modem connection, you may want to set 1 or 2 instead. If you have a very fast connection and typically find yourself downloading from several much slower connections, try setting a higher number.

Message Alert check box   Select this check box to have iMesh display a notification message when a file finishes downloading.

Tray Icon Alert check box   Select this check box to have iMesh display a notification in the system tray when a file finishes downloading.

Sound Alert check box   Select this check box to have iMesh play a sound to get your attention when a file finishes downloading.

Figure 7.46

The Download page of the Options dialog box

Upload Page

The Upload page of the Options dialog box (shown in Figure 7.47) contains these two options:

Maximum Concurrent Uploads text box   In this text box, enter the maximum number of uploads you want to have running at once. The default setting is 20, which is far too high for a modem connection; a setting of 1 or 2 is much more suitable. For a fast connection, such as an ISDN, cable, or a DSL, try a setting of between 3 and 5.

Ports Restricted for Use by iMesh text box   In this text box, you can enter the numbers of ports that you want to prevent iMesh from using. For example, if you don't want iMesh to use ports 80 and 8080, you would enter **80, 8080** in the text box. (If you don't know what different ports do, leave this text box empty.) To apply these settings, click the OK button to close the Options dialog box, then exit iMesh and restart it.

Figure 7.47

The Upload page of the Options dialog box

Share Page

The Share page of the Options dialog box (shown in Figure 7.48) contains these options:

Scan for Changes in Shared Directories group box   Use the settings in this group box to specify how you want iMesh to scan for changes in your shared directories. (For example, when you add music files to a shared folder, or remove files from a folder, iMesh won't be aware of the changes until it performs a scan of the folder.) In the Period drop-down list, choose the interval at which you want iMesh to scan the directories: 1 hour, 3 hours, 6 hours, 12 hours, 1 day, or 3 days. Select the Tray Animation While Scanning check box if you want iMesh to display an animation in your system tray to indicate that scanning is taking place. Click the Scan Now button to perform a scan immediately.

Allow Other Users to View All My Shared Files check box   Select this check box if you want other users to be able to view all the files you're sharing.

Figure 7.48

The Share page of the Options dialog box

Connection Page

The Connection page of the Options dialog box (shown in Figure 7.49) lets you update the connection and proxy server information you supplied during the registration process.

Figure 7.49

The Connection page of the Options dialog box

Appearance Page

The Appearance page of the Options dialog box (shown in Figure 7.50) lets you choose the look for iMesh and specify whether to display the iMesh skin. Click the link at the bottom of the page to download more skins from the iMesh Web site.

Figure 7.50

The Appearance page of the Options dialog box

The iMesh skin is a small window (shown in Figure 7.51) that gives you information and access to iMesh's different functions. Clear the Hide Skin check box (which is selected by default) to display the iMesh skin.

Figure 7.51

The iMesh skin

Contacts Page

The Contacts page of the Options dialog box (shown in Figure 7.52) contains the following options:

Accept Instant Message from Other Users check box   Select this check box if you want to receive instant messages from other iMesh users. Clear this check box if you want to be left alone.

Incoming Message Notification group box In this group box, specify the type or types of notification you want iMesh to give you when you receive an instant message. Select the Popup Message Dialog check box, the Sound Alert check box, and the Tray Icon Alert check box as appropriate.

Figure 7.52

The Contacts page of the Options dialog box

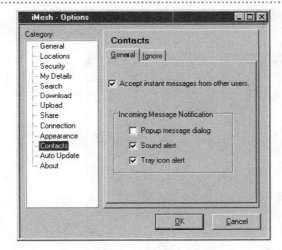

The Ignore subpage of the Contacts page (shown in Figure 7.53) lets you maintain the list of iMesh users you're ignoring. Use the Remove button to remove a selected contact from the Ignore list. Use the Move to Contacts button to move a selected contact from the Ignore list to the Contacts list.

Figure 7.53

The Ignore Subpage of the Contacts page of the Options dialog box

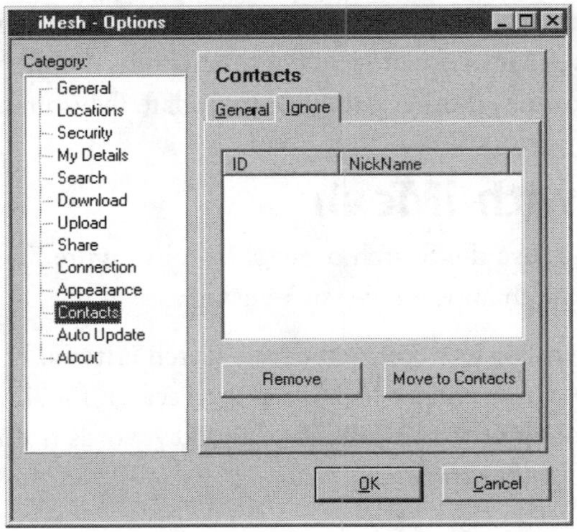

Auto Update Page

The Auto Update page of the Options dialog box (shown in Figure 7.54) lets you specify whether and (if so) how frequently iMesh should try to update itself automatically. Leave the Automatically Check for a New Version check box selected (as it is by default) to have iMesh check automatically, and use the Every drop-down list to specify your chosen interval in days.

Figure 7.54

The Auto Update page of the Options dialog box

About Page

The About page of the Options dialog box (shown in Figure 7.55) contains information about the version and build of iMesh you're using and your iMesh ID number. If you chose not to have iMesh update itself automatically, use the version and build information to determine whether you need to update iMesh manually.

Searching with iMesh

To search with iMesh, use the Search page (shown in Figure 7.56) or the Search window, depending on which appearance you're using.

1. In the Search For text box, enter your search criteria. For example, if you're looking for music, enter a band's name to search for all available tracks by that band, or enter the band's name and key words from a track title to search just for that track.

Figure 7.55

The About page of the Options dialog box shows you which version of iMesh you're using.

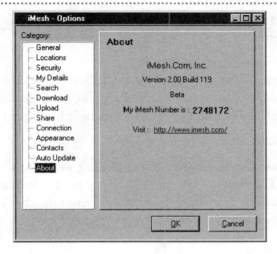

Figure 7.56

The iMesh Search page

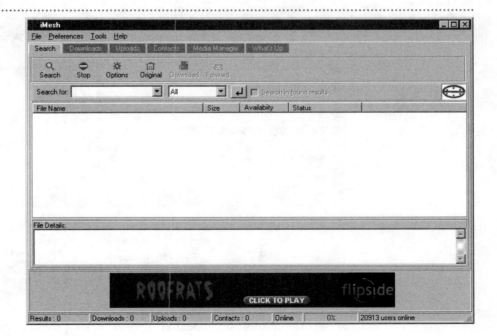

Once you've performed some searches, you can select one of your previous searches from the Search For drop-down list.

2. In the drop-down list to the right of the Search For drop-down list, choose the category of file to search for: All, Audio, Video, Images, Software, or Documents. For example, to search for music files, select Audio.

3. Click the ↵ button to execute the search.

Figure 7.57 shows the Search page of iMesh after a successful search for Smashing Pumpkins tracks. The pink stars in the Availability column indicate the relative availability of the tracks: The more stars there are, the better the chance of your being able to download the track.

Figure 7.57

The Search page showing the results of a successful search

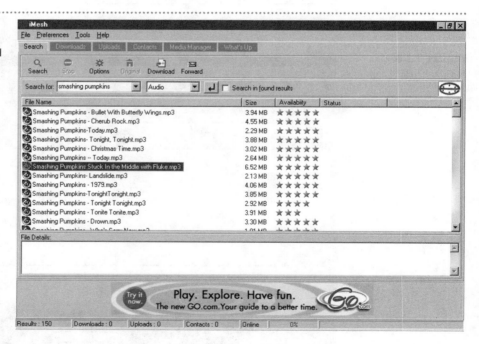

You can sort the results on the Search page by clicking the column headings. For example, you might want to sort by the File Name column so that you can see what's available, or by the Availability column so that you can assess the relative availability of the tracks.

> If you get a lot of results, you can refine a search. Select the Search in Found Results check box, specify additional criteria in the Search For text box, and click the Search button. iMesh searches through the search results for the criteria you've specified and returns any matches.

Forwarding Information about a Track to a Friend

To forward the information about a track you've located to a friend, select the track and click the Forward button. iMesh launches your e-mail client (or activates it if it's already running) and starts a canned message with information about the track included as an attachment. Figure 7.58 shows Outlook Express with such a message underway.

Figure 7.58

iMesh makes it easy to forward the information about a track to a friend.

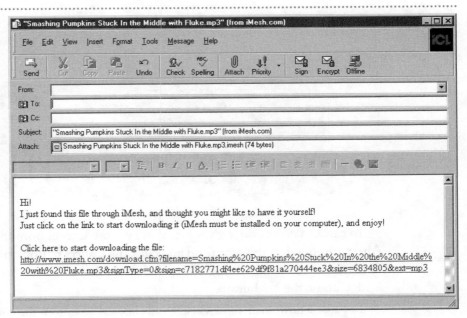

Edit the message as appropriate, address it, and send it on its way.

Downloading with iMesh

To download a track, select it on the Search page and click the Download button. (To download multiple tracks, Shift+click or Ctrl+click to select them.) Alternatively, to download a single track, double-click it. The Status column on the Search page shows Added to Downloads.

Figure 7.59 shows the Downloads page with one download running and a second download getting connected.

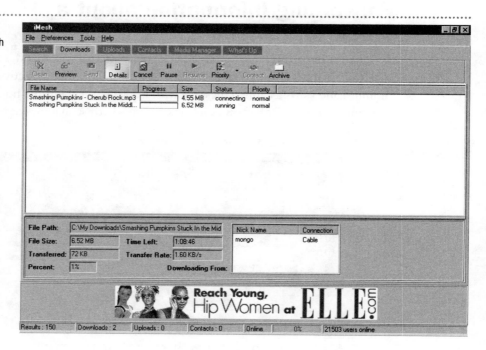

To cancel a download, right-click it and choose Cancel from the context menu. Alternatively, select the download and click the Cancel button on the toolbar. iMesh displays a confirmation dialog box to make sure that you want to cancel the download. Choose the Yes button.

To pause a download, right-click it and choose Pause from the context menu, or select it and click the Pause button on the toolbar. iMesh displays *Paused* in the Status column. You can then resume the download by right-clicking it and choosing Resume from the context menu or by selecting it and clicking the Resume button on the toolbar.

To preview a download (for example, to make sure you're getting the track you hoped for), right-click it and choose Preview from the context menu. Alternatively, select the download and click the Preview button on the toolbar. iMesh starts as much of the track as it has downloaded playing in your default music player.

By default, iMesh assigns each download Normal priority. To raise the priority of a download, right-click it and choose Set Priority ➤ High from the context menu. (To return the priority to Normal, right-click and choose Set Priority ➤ Normal from the context menu.) Alternatively, select the download and click the Priority button on the toolbar to toggle the priority between Normal and High.

When iMesh has finished downloading files, it displays the iMesh dialog box shown in Figure 7.60.

Figure 7.60

Until you tell it to desist, iMesh displays this iMesh dialog box after it finishes downloading a file.

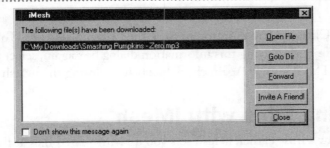

From this dialog box, you can take the following actions:

- ☠ To open one of the files you've downloaded, select it in the list box and click the Open File button. Opening a music file starts it playing in your default music player.

- ☠ To open an Explorer window showing the folder into which the track was downloaded, select it in the list box and click the Goto Dir button.

- ☠ To forward the information on the track to a friend, select the item and click the Forward button. iMesh will start an e-mail message in your default e-mail application, as discussed in the previous section.

- ☠ To send a recommendation for the track to a friend, click the Invite a Friend button and use the resulting Invite a Friend dialog box (shown in Figure 7.61) to specify the friend (or friends), then click the OK button.

Figure 7.61

Use the Invite a Friend dialog box to send information about an item you've downloaded to a friend.

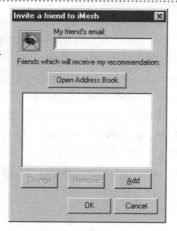

☠ Click the Close button to close the iMesh dialog box. To prevent iMesh from displaying this information dialog box again, select the Don't Show This Message Again check box before closing the iMesh dialog box.

Sharing Files with iMesh

As you saw a little earlier, iMesh sets you up with shared files at the end of the setup and registration routine—but you may want to change the files and folders you're sharing later.

To do so, click the Media Manager tab to display the Media Manager page (shown in Figure 7.62). Expand the tree on the left-hand side to reveal the folder you want to share (or stop sharing), then select its check box (to share the folder) or clear the check box (to stop sharing the folder).

WARNING

If you want to set up all media files on your computer for sharing, click the Run Sharing Wizard in the Share dialog box and follow its prompts. Remember that for most people, sharing all media files is a bad idea because it is very likely to violate other people's copyrights.

Uploading Files

When other iMesh users download files that you're sharing, you'll see the details on the Uploads page. From here, you can add a user to your list of contacts (discussed in the next section), send a message to a user, or cancel an upload.

Using Contacts

iMesh provides features for building a list of contacts with whom to exchange messages or files.

To add a user to your list of contacts, right-click an entry featuring the user on the Downloads page or the Uploads page and choose Add to Contacts from the context menu. iMesh adds the user to your list of contacts and displays the Contacts page (shown in Figure 7.63).

Figure 7.63

Use the Contacts page to manage your contacts.

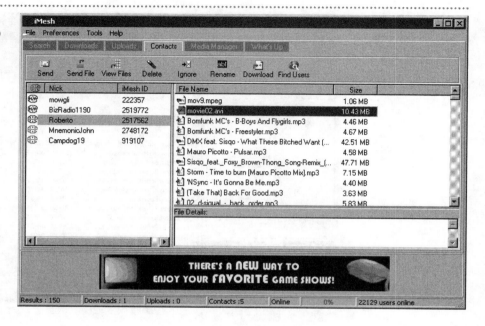

You can take the following actions with contacts on the Contacts page:

- To remove a contact from your list of contacts, right-click their name and choose Delete from the context menu. Alternatively, select the contact and click the Delete button on the toolbar.

- To ignore a contact, right-click their name and choose Move to Ignore List from the context menu. Alternatively, select the contact and click the Ignore button on the toolbar.

NOTE   To rescind your ignoring of a contact, use the Move to Contacts button on the Ignore subpage of the Contacts page in the Options dialog box.

- To view a contact's files, right-click the contact on the Contact page and choose View Files from the context menu. (Alternatively, select the contact and click the View Files button on the toolbar.) iMesh retrieves the list of files the user is sharing and displays it on the Contacts page. You can then download a file by right-clicking it and choosing Download from the context menu.

- To rename a contact (for example, to give them a name that makes it easier for you to identify them), right-click the contact and choose Rename from the context menu. (Alternatively, select the contact and click the Rename button on the toolbar.) iMesh displays an edit box around their name. Enter the new name and press the Enter key. (The renaming happens only at your end, of course; the contact's name remains the same for everybody else.)

- To send a message to a contact, right-click the contact's name and choose Send a Message from the context menu. (Alternatively, select the contact and click the Send button on the toolbar.) iMesh displays the Send Message to iMesh User dialog box (shown in Figure 7.64). Enter the message in the text box and click the Send button.

Figure 7.64

Sending a message to a contact

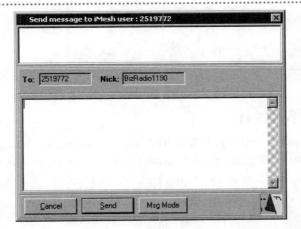

- To send a file link to a contact (so that they can download it easily from you), right-click the contact's name and choose Send a File Link from the context menu. (Alternatively, select the contact and click the Send File button.) iMesh displays a different Send Message to iMesh User dialog box (shown in Figure 7.65). Click the … button to display the Choose File You Want to Recommend to Your Friend dialog box, navigate to and select the file, and click the Open button to enter its details in the File Name text box. Enter a description in the File Description text box so that your contact knows what you're sending, and click the Send button to send the file link.

If the folder that contains the file you recommend is not shared, iMesh prompts you to share it.

Figure 7.65

Sending a file link to a contact

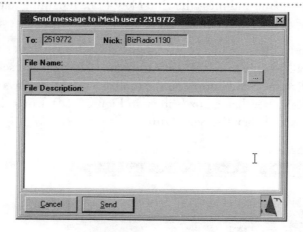

Exiting iMesh

To exit iMesh, right-click the iMesh icon in your system tray and choose Exit from the context menu. (Clicking the Close button—the X button—on the iMesh window closes the iMesh window but does not exit iMesh.)

Vulnerability Factor: Using iMesh, Spinfrenzy.com, or CuteMX

Using iMesh, Spinfrenzy.com, or CuteMX leaves you widely exposed. Each time you log in, the service knows your IP address and can track every move you make: all your chat, all your searches, and (more to the point) each file you download or upload.

Because each of these three services is centralized, each can easily be shut down by the forces of the law. If any of these services is required to share their activity logs, the copyright cops will have libraries-ful of information on who has been trafficking in illegal files.

Using Spinfrenzy.com

Like CuteMX and iMesh, Spinfrenzy.com is a search tool for music, video, and graphics files. As you'd guess from its name, Spinfrenzy.com is implemented as a Web site, but you need to install the SpinFrenzy Xchange client component to be able to download and upload files.

On the upside, Spinfrenzy.com offers strong features and (at this writing) a reasonable variety of content. On the downside, Spinfrenzy.com blasts you with enough ads and pop-up windows to try the patience of a saint.

To use Spinfrenzy.com, you sign up at the Spinfrenzy.com Web site (www .spinfrenzy.com), create a user ID and password, and download and install the SpinFrenzy Xchange software. The SpinFrenzy Xchange setup routine offers to automatically scan your hard disk for audio and video files to share (see Figure 7.66); resist this offer by clicking the Don't Scan, I Will Specify button.

Figure 7.66

Don't let SpinFrenzy Xchange automatically scan your hard disk for audio and video files to share.

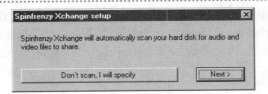

Then choose options for sharing in the resulting SpinFrenzy Xchange – Options dialog box (shown in Figure 7.67):

- In the I Want to Store Downloaded Files in This Folder group box, the Ask Me When I Download option button is selected by default. If you want SpinFrenzy to put all the files you download in the same folder, select the unnamed option button, click the Change button, and use the Browse for Folder dialog box to specify the folder you want to use.

- In the I Am a Registered User of Spinfrenzy.com group box, you can enter your SpinID and password so that you don't need to enter them each time you connect to SpinFrenzy. If you share a computer with others, you may prefer to leave these text boxes empty for security—but if you use the Auto-Connect on Startup option (discussed below), SpinFrenzy Xchange will automatically log you into SpinFrenzy as a visitor. You then won't be able to do any uploading or downloading until you log on as yourself.

- In the Share Media Files group box, select the Video check box, the Pictures check box, and the Other Media check box as appropriate. Make sure that the From These Folders Only option button is selected, then click the Add button and use the Browse for Folder dialog box to specify each folder in turn.

- In the Share All Files group box, you can specify folders from which you want to share all files or all files except for certain types. To specify the folders, click the upper Add button and the Browse for Folder dialog box. To specify the file types you want to exclude, click the lower Add button and use the resulting Open dialog box to select a file of the appropriate type. For example, if you want to share all files except JPGs, click the Add button, select a JPG file in the Open dialog box, and click the Open button.

- In the Network Settings group box, use the Internet Connection drop-down list to indicate the speed of your Internet connection (from Dunno to T3). This is the speed that other SpinFrenzy users will see listed for you, so you may choose to be deliberately inaccurate. However, this setting affects the Download and Upload Limit of NN Files at a Time setting, so you'll need to choose a number here appropriate to the real speed of your Internet connection.

- In the lower-right corner of the SpinFrenzy Xchange – Options dialog box, there are two more check boxes and a command button. Leave the Let Other Users Send Chat Requests to Me check box selected if you want to be available for chat; otherwise, clear it. Leave the Auto-Connect on Startup check box selected if you want SpinFrenzy to connect automatically to the server when you start it up. Click the Refresh Library button to force SpinFrenzy to reload the list of files you're sharing in the assorted folders.

Before you install SpinFrenzy Xchange, you can search for items on the SpinFrenzy Web site, but you can't download the items you find, and you can't share items on your drive. Once you've installed SpinFrenzy Xchange, downloading and sharing snap into place.

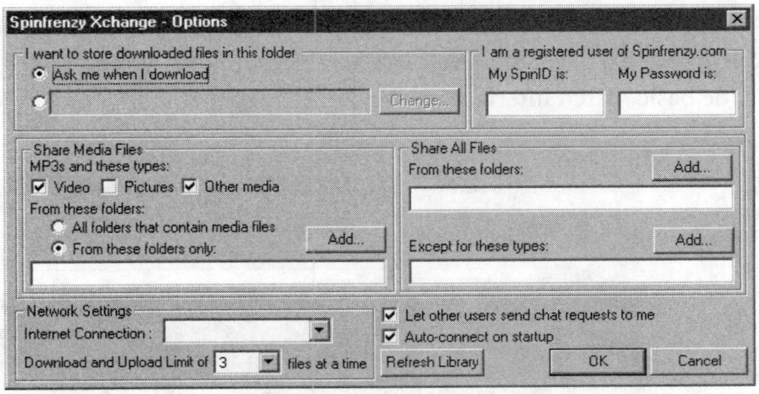

Figure 7.67

Set up sharing manually in the SpinFrenzy Xchange – Options dialog box.

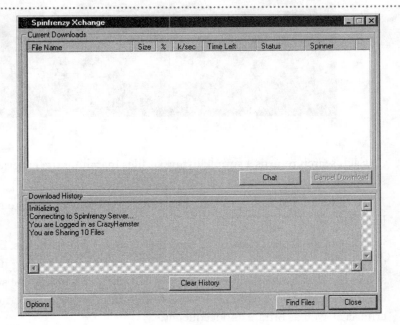

Once you close the Options dialog box, SpinFrenzy Xchange automatically logs you into Spinfrenzy.com (see Figure 7.68).

Figure 7.68

SpinFrenzy Xchange automatically logs you into Spinfrenzy.com.

Once you've set up SpinFrenzy Xchange, you can download and share files via Spinfrenzy.com. At this writing, Spinfrenzy.com uses a simple search interface that lets you search for all items, MP3s, videos, photos, or other files. Figure 7.69 shows the basic search interface for MP3 files.

Figure 7.69

The Spinfrenzy.com search interface for MP3 files.

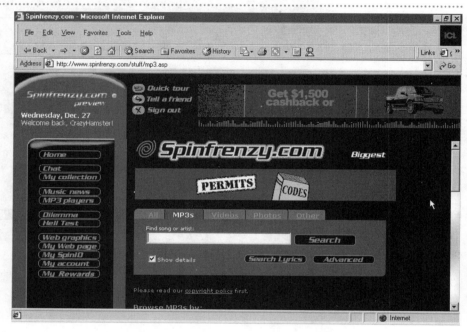

Each search returns a simple listing of files matching the criteria. Figure 7.70 shows an example of search results.

To download a track, you click its listing. SpinFrenzy Xchange manages the download (shown in Figure 7.71).

You can also specify advanced search criteria for your searches, including the name of the file you're looking for (if you know it) and the user sharing it. Figure 7.72 shows the advanced search page. As you can see in the figure, the strongest features are for MP3 files, for which you can specify song criteria, artist criteria, and album criteria as well as bitrate and frequency.

Figure 7.70

The result of searching for MP3s of Madonna's track Music.

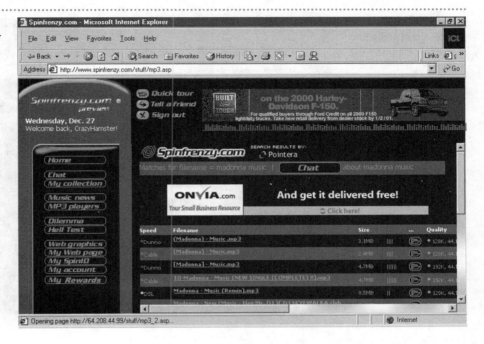

Figure 7.71

SpinFrenzy Xchange manages each download from Spinfrenzy.com.

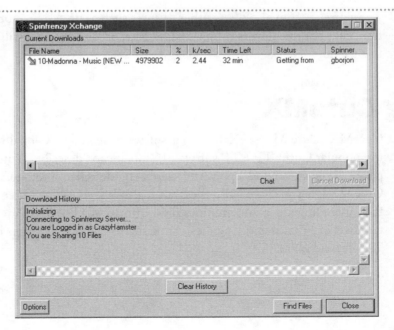

Spinfrenzy.com also offers other features such as browsing another user's collection, chat in three flavors (HTML, Java Lite, or Java), and e-mailing details of a file to a friend.

Using CuteMX

CuteMX (Cute Media eXchange) is software created by GlobalScape, the makers of the popular CuteFTP FTP software. GlobalScape describes CuteMX as "your own personal file server and a powerful search engine rolled into one." Like Napster, CuteMX lets you share MP3 files, but it also lets you share other types of media files, including video and graphics files. Instead of a hot list, CuteMX lets you maintain lists of Friends and Enemies. At this writing, CuteMX runs on Windows 95, 98, Me, and 2000.

WARNING

At this writing, CuteMX forces you to share files in order to download files from other users. This is bad because it may encourage people to share files that they don't have the legal right to share, pushing them toward breaking the law. (As I mentioned earlier, I don't have any problem with your sharing files illegally, provided that you know what you're doing is illegal, you're aware of the consequences, and you're breaking the law of your own free will.) If you want to use CuteMX but don't have any files that you can legally share, I suggest you create some by firing up Sound Recorder and recording several short WAV files of microphone noise. Save each under a creative name such as "Sound of Silence 1," and you'll have original files that you can legally share. (Alternatively, you might write a few original poems.) You'll probably get flamed by anyone who downloads them, but hey, that's the price of pleasure with CuteMX if you want to stay on the right side of the law.

Download the latest version of CuteMX from www.cutemx.com, double-click the distribution file, and follow the setup routine for creating a new user account (or setting up an existing account, if you have one), specifying your connection speed (for which it claims that an accurate answer helps increase performance), selecting a shared folder and a default download folder (shown in Figure 7.73), and specifying the file types you want to share. At this point, switch to Explorer and put your newly created WAV files there if necessary, before CuteMX can object that you're not sharing any files and therefore force you to use Browse mode.

In the Registration Complete! dialog box (shown in Figure 7.74), clear the Start CuteMX When Windows Starts check box unless you have a permanent Internet connection *and* you're sure you want CuteMX trying to run itself each time you start (or restart) Windows. You'll probably also want to use the Edit Shared File Types button and the Security Options button to tweak the CuteMX settings before running CuteMX for the first time.

Figure 7.73

When setting up CuteMX, make sure you don't share your default download folder.

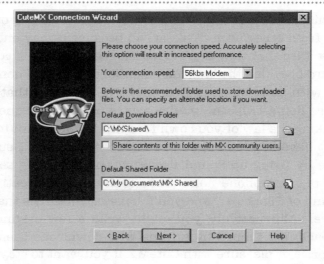

Figure 7.74

You'll probably want to clear the Start CuteMX When Windows Starts check box in the Registration Complete! dialog box.

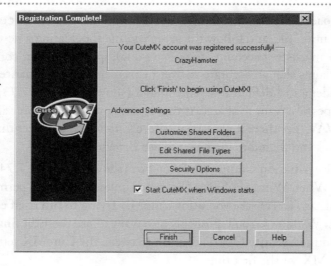

Once you've finished setting CuteMX up, you'll find it easy to use. The CuteMX interface features a button panel on the left-hand side for navigating between the different pages. Figure 7.75 shows the Search page after a successful search for Limp Bizkit files.

Figure 7.75

CuteMX lets you search for MP3, video, and graphics files.

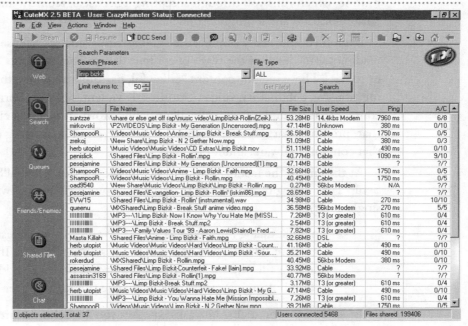

Figure 7.75

CuteMX lets you search for MP3, video, and graphics files.

Using Aimster

Aimster is a file-sharing technology that works via instant messaging. At this writing, Aimster works only with Instant Messenger and its own instant messaging layer, but the Aimster team is working on plug-ins for MSN, ICQ, Napster, and other instant messaging technologies.

This section discusses how to get Aimster, install it, configure it, and use it for finding and sharing files. I'll let you find out the instant-messaging and chat features on your own; if you're into instant messaging already, they'll probably be second nature to you.

Getting and Installing Aimster

Download the latest version of Aimster from the Aimster Web site, `www.aimster` `.com`. Run the distribution executable to launch Aimster's straightforward installation

routine, which runs you through accepting a license agreement and selecting a destination location and a program folder.

Even if you normally skip license agreements, Aimster's license agreement is worth
reading for its detail of the types of content that you agree not to "distribute, link to,
or solicit." These include content "unlawful, harmful to minors, threatening, harassing, abusive, defamatory, vulgar, gratuitously violent, obscene, pornographic, libelous,"
content that "includes personally identifiable information about children," content
that "promotes participation in multi-level or pyramid marketing initiatives," content
that contains malware, and more.

At the end of the installation routine, you see a series of InstallShield Wizard:
Setup Type dialog boxes (which I won't show you here), each of which asks you a
single question:

- The first dialog box asks whether you want to allow guest access to the files
  you share. The default setting is the Yes option button. If you want to confine your file-sharing via Aimster to people on your buddy list, select the No
  option button instead. (You can change this setting later if necessary.)

- The second dialog box asks whether you are behind a firewall. The default
  setting is the No option button. If your computer connects to the Internet
  through a firewall, select the Yes option button. If you're not sure, Aimster
  suggests leaving the No option button selected. (Again, you can change this
  setting later if necessary.)

- The third dialog box asks whether you want to install the Aimster instant
  messaging layer. At this writing, you need to install this item if you want to
  share files with your buddies. (When plug-ins are available for other instant
  messaging technologies, you won't need to install this item.) Choose the
  Install option button or the Do Not Install option button as appropriate.
  You may also need to install Instant Messenger, which you can download for
  free from www.aol.com.

NOTE If Instant Messenger is running when you run Aimster for the first
time, Aimster may volunteer to close Instant Messenger, change its settings to work with Aimster, and restart it. Allow Aimster to do this.

The first time you run Aimster, you see the Connect to Aimster dialog box (shown in Figure 7.76):

☠ If you already have an account, enter your username and password in the text boxes.

Figure 7.76

If you have an Aimster account, specify your username and password in the Connect to Aimster dialog box.

☠ If you don't have an account, click the New User button. Aimster displays the Create a New User dialog box (shown in Figure 7.77). Enter a unique username of up to 20 characters in the Username text box, enter the next in your list of unbreakable passwords in the Password text box and Confirm Password text box, and click the OK button. Aimster then connects to Aimster, creates the account (if the username is unique), and returns you to the Connect to Aimster dialog box, in which it displays a message that it has successfully created the account. (If the username isn't unique, you get to try again.)

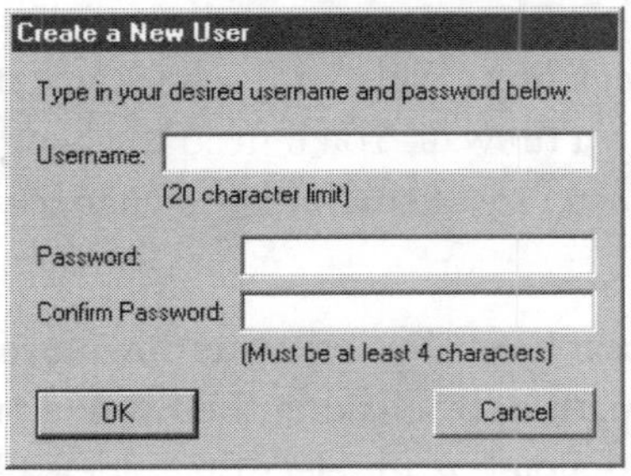

Figure 7.77

If you don't have an Aimster account, create one in the Create a New User dialog box.

Select the Remember My Password check box if you want Aimster to store your password so that you don't need to enter it next time, but remember that storing passwords like this can compromise your security.

Click the Connect button to connect to Aimster. You'll probably see an Aimster Info dialog box when you log on. Read it for pertinent information and click the OK button to dismiss it.

Aimster then initializes itself and displays the Aimster Settings dialog box, in which you can choose settings for Aimster as described in the next section.

Configuring Aimster

Before you run Aimster, check your configuration settings in the Aimster Settings dialog box. This dialog box is displayed automatically when you've logged on to Aimster for the first time, and you can display it at any time by clicking the Configure button or the Settings button in the Aimster Control Panel.

Aimster Page Settings

Figure 7.78 shows the Aimster page of the Aimster Settings dialog box, which offers the following settings:

Remember My Password check box   Select this check box if you want Aimster to remember your password. (Before you do this, consider the risks of storing passwords.)

Connection Speed drop-down list   Specify the connection speed that you want Aimster to display to other users.

File Sharing Listening Port text box   In this text box, you can change the port on which Aimster listens for file-sharing. You shouldn't need to change this setting unless Aimster isn't working.

I Am Behind a Firewall check box   Select this check box if your computer connects to the Internet through a firewall. You'll need to change this setting only if you got it wrong during Aimster installation or you change your computer's network connection.

Save Files I Download In text box   Specify your download directory in this text box, either by typing in the path or by clicking the Browse button and using the resulting Browse for Folder dialog box to select the folder. The default path is `Aimster\Users\`*`username`*`\Download\`.

Allow Guest Access to My Files check box   Select this check box if you want to allow guests access to your files. Clear this check box if you want only your buddies to be able to access your files.

Max Aimster Uploads text box   In this text box, enter the maximum number of files that Aimster should try to send at the same time. The default setting is 5, but you should probably use a lower number unless you have a fast Internet connection. For a modem connection, a setting of 1 is best; for ISDN, cable, or DSL, 2 or 3; and for a full T1, 5 to 10.

Figure 7.78

Choose settings for Aimster on the Aimster page of the Aimster Settings dialog box.

Windows Page Settings

Figure 7.79 shows the Windows page of the Aimster Settings dialog box, which offers the following settings:

Remember Window Sizes and Positions check box   Leave this check box selected (as it is by default) to have Aimster restore each window to its previous size and position at each new session.

Make Windows Always on Top check box   Select this check box if you want the Aimster windows to appear on top of all other running applications. Leave this check box cleared (as it is by default) to allow other applications to appear in front of Aimster when they are active.

Toggle Buttons Do Not Close Windows check box Select this check box (which is cleared by default) if you want the Control Panel's toggle buttons not to close the windows from which they are removing the focus. For example, with this check box cleared, clicking the Buddies button in the Control Panel with the Buddy List window already displayed closes the Buddy List window. With this check box selected, clicking the Buddies button removes the focus from the Buddy List window but leaves it displayed.

Auto Switch to Transfers check box Leave this check box selected (as it is by default) if you want Aimster to automatically switch focus to the Transfers window when you start a transfer. Clear this check box if don't want to switch focus like this.

Flash Instant Messages check box Leave this check box selected (as it is by default) if you want Aimster to flash instant messages at you. Clear this check box to enhance your visual peace.

Flash Chat Rooms check box Leave this check box selected (as it is by default) if you want Aimster to flash chat room messages at you. Clear this check box if you prefer to examine chat rooms in your own time.

Figure 7.79
Choose settings for
Aimster's windows
on the Windows page
of the Aimster Settings
dialog box.

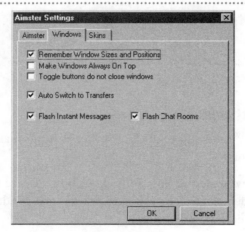

Skins Page Settings

The Skins page of the Aimster Settings dialog box offers a choice of the skins you have installed. Aimster comes with several skins, but you can download other skins from the Aimster Web site and from skins sites.

The screen shots in the rest of this section use the Slate skin rather than the default skin, because the default skin, while attractive in color, is almost unreadable in grayscale.

When you've finished choosing settings, click the OK button to close the Aimster Settings dialog box.

Navigating the Aimster Interface

The Aimster interface consists of a half-dozen windows, four of which are shown in Figure 7.80.

- The Control Panel provides quick access to the various windows via its row of buttons, a listing of the active channel, and information about the user status (online or offline) and the number of plug-ins loaded.

- The File Search window provides tools for searching for files.

- The Buddy List window lets you keep a list of your buddies.

- The Chat Manager window lets you join, leave, and create chat channels.

- The File Library window (not shown in the figure) lets you manage the files you're sharing.

- The Transfers window (not shown in the figure) lets you monitor and cancel file transfers.

Figure 7.80

The Aimster interface uses a half-dozen windows, of which these four are key.

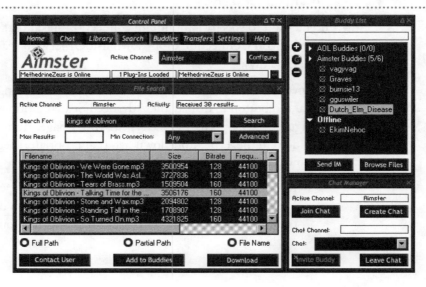

Searching for Files with Aimster

To search for files with Aimster, follow these steps:

1. Click the Search button in the Control Panel to display or activate the File Search window (shown in Figure 7.81 after a successful search).

Figure 7.81

The Aimster File Search window

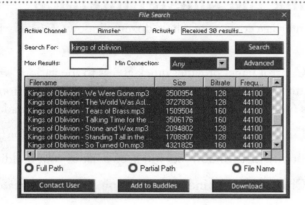

2. Enter your search term or terms in the Search For text box.

3. If you want to limit the maximum number of results Aimster retrieves (for example, in order to reduce search time), enter a maximum number in the Max Results text box.

4. If you want to specify a minimum connection speed that's acceptable, select it in the Min Connection drop-down list. Otherwise, leave this drop-down list set to Any.

5. To specify the file type or the bitrate that you're searching for, click the Advanced button to display the Advanced Search Options dialog box (shown in Figure 7.82). Specify the file type (MP3, Image, Audio, Application, Text, or Video) in the Type drop-down list. If appropriate, specify the bitrate in the lower two drop-down lists.

   ☠ Remember to clear these advanced search criteria when you no longer need them. Because the Advanced Search Option dialog box keeps these criteria out of sight, it's easy to forget that you've set them.

Figure 7.82

Use the Advanced Search Options dialog box to specify the file type and the bitrate you're searching for.

6. Click the Search button to perform the search. Aimster consults its current database and returns a list of results.

You can use the Full Path option button, the Partial Path option button, and the File Name option button at the bottom of the File Library window to toggle the view among full paths, partial paths (the directory containing the file and the file name), and the file name only. These options typically aren't useful for file search results, but they are useful in the File Library window, from which they seem to have been borrowed.

Downloading Files with Aimster

Once you've found a file you were looking for, you can download it by selecting it in the list box in the File Search window and clicking the Download button. By default, Aimster displays the Transfers window (shown in Figure 7.83) when you start a download so that you can watch it happening.

Figure 7.83

The Transfers window shows the progress of your downloads and uploads.

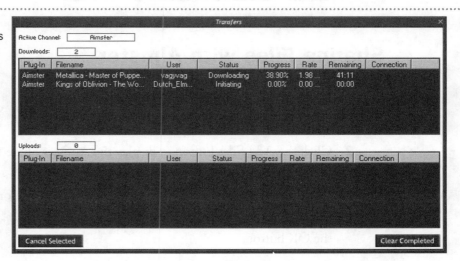

To cancel a download or upload, select it and click the Cancel Selected button. To clear the listings of all completed and failed transfers, click the Clear Completed button.

Browsing a User's Files

To browse a user's files, right-click their entry in the Aimster Buddies list in the Buddy List window and choose Browse Files from the context menu. Aimster lists the user's files in the Browse Files window, with the user's name in the User text box, as shown in Figure 7.84. From here, you can download the files as usual.

Figure 7.84

Aimster lets you browse a user's files.

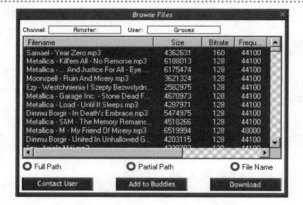

Sharing Files with Aimster

To share files with Aimster, add them to your File Library:

1. Click the Library button in the Control Panel to display or activate the File Library window.

2. Click the Add Files button to display the Aimster Shared Directories dialog box (shown in Figure 7.85).

3. Click the Add Directory button to display the Browse for Folder dialog box.

4. Navigate to and select the first directory you want to share, and then click the OK button.

Figure 7.85

Use the Aimster Shared Directories dialog box to add and remove shared directories.

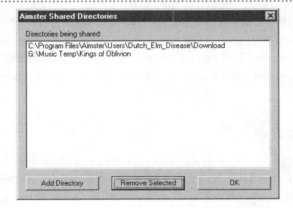

5. Repeat steps 3 and 4 for each other directory you want to add.

☠ To remove one or more directories that you've been sharing, select them in the Directories Being Shared list box in the Aimster Shared Directories dialog box and click the Remove Selected button.

6. When you've finished adding files, click the OK button to close the Aimster Shared Directories dialog box.

Aimster adds the files in the directory or directories to the list in your File Library. Figure 7.86 shows a File Library that contains a healthy number of files.

Figure 7.86

Aimster's File Library lists the files you are sharing with the world or with your buddies.

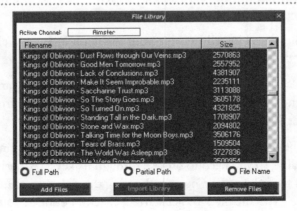

Use the Full Path option button, the Partial Path option button, and the File Name option button at the bottom of the File Library window to toggle the view among full paths, partial paths (the directory containing the file and the file name), and the file name only. The Partial Path option button and the Full Path option button are primarily useful for discovering which folder contains a particular file.

Using Freenet

Freenet is an ambitious file-sharing project that's currently under heavy development. Unlike Napster, Freenet does not use a centralized system of servers, being designed to be hard (perhaps impossible) to shut down by human intervention. Freenet also uses encryption to provide privacy for the nodes on its network, allowing users of Freenet to become anonymous.

Compared to technologies such as Napster, Gnutella, and audioGnome, Freenet is more difficult to set up. This section outlines the general steps for getting Freenet up and running—but because the project is being developed at a cracking pace, this section does not give specifics that are likely to change. At this writing, implementations of Freenet are available for Windows, Linux, and assorted Unixes, with a couple of Mac implementations trying to catch their coattails.

The general steps for setting up Freenet are as follows:

- Download and install the Java 2 Runtime Environment (JRE) from the Sun Java site, `java.sun.com`, unless you have the JRE or a full version of Java installed already.

- Download and install Freenet from the main Freenet Web site, `freenet.sourceforge.com`.

- Download and install a GUI for Freenet (if you don't want to run Freenet from the command line). You'll find links to the GUIs from the main Freenet Web site.

- Find the files you want, and download them. At this writing, Freenet is not searchable, so you need to browse through its keys. (A *key* is a kind of description of the information posted. By using the right key, a Freenet user can retrieve a specific file.) To get started, check `freenet.sourceforge.net` for information on *key servers*—servers that list available keys.

- Insert into Freenet any files that you want to share.

 Freenet is designed for sharing all kinds of files without restriction or oversight. You'll find a lot of music files on Freenet, but you'll also find politics, philosophy, software, videos, and pornography—among other things.

Up Next

In this chapter, you've seen how to use the best—or at least the most promising—of the post-Napster P2P technologies: audioGnome for music and Wrapster files; Gnutella for any kind of files; iMesh for music, graphics, and video files; Freenet for whatever you may find there; Aimster for sharing files while instant messaging; and CuteMX if you must.

These P2P technologies are right there on the cutting edge of Internet piracy—but the older and wiser pirates prefer to stay away from sharp edges and public fora. In the next chapter, I'll show you the tools the pros use: NetMeeting for Windows and HotLine for the Mac.

Turn the page. You've waited long enough.

A Pirate Speaks: The Porn Pirate

I've been pirating porn for years. It's free. It's discreet. And it's so simple, a kid could do it. Actually, lots of kids do.

Mostly, it's a matter of going on the right newsgroups, looking through them, and downloading the JPEGs and the GIFs and the MPEGs that are out there. Thousands of JPEGs or hundreds of MPEGs fit on a CD, so I don't need to worry about keeping them on my computer where other people might run into them.

Most of the MPEGs I have are only a couple of minutes each, because I don't have enough bandwidth to actually pull down full movies or any big amount of video. But it's easy to take down a 10K or a 100K still picture, and it's amazing how many of them I can download in a two- or three-hour session, even at 56K. And people are posting thousands of new pictures every day.

Like I was saying, I go to the newsgroups for a lot of stuff. I avoid the Web sites—some of them have good stuff, but they all want a credit-card number and an adult certificate before they'll display anything worth having. And they try to stick cookies all over every computer that visits them.

I find the best newsgroups are the alt.binaries.erotica and alt .binaries.pictures hierarchies. Underneath pictures there are any number of amazing and perverse things: There's erotica, there's sex, there's contortion.nude, there's fetish.diapers—literally scores and scores of different types of pornography. It's amazing the things some people like. Some of them are gross, and some of them are really sick—you know, stuff that's illegal. Under alt.binaries.pictures, there are voyeurs and supermodels and tasteless, to name just a few. There's also alt.binaries.sex, but I find it's not so good.

A Pirate Speaks: The Porn Pirate (*continued*)

So what I do is simply subscribe to these newsgroups, go on them, and start downloading pictures. I download all the headers in the newsgroups, then sort the posts by size in descending order, biggest files at the top, smallest at the bottom. That way, I can usually get all the pictures with the best resolution up on top and all the spam messages, all the advertising crap, on the bottom. There's an incredible amount of spam and some of the pictures are labeled like GLORIOUS EXPLICIT COED SEX and so on, but all they've got is some stupid little picture with an advertisement for a porn site. So I just get rid of this crap. Anything under 10K, I just do a block Delete. Nothing that size is going to be worth looking at.

Then I take a look at the top of the list, where the biggest files are, and see what's there. After I delete all the text files, the spam, and the ads at the bottom, I rearrange what's left so I can see what's what. Sometimes I sort by the date, because people post things in sequence. Sometimes I sort by the person that submitted them, because often people are submitting blocks of pictures from various series of pornography. There's the Admiral Krag series of famous porno pictures. They're all numbered AKX: AKX-0001 and so on to like AKX-1987. There are thousands and thousands of pictures in there. And people actually collect them like they collect books. Some people trade them like they were baseball cards or Pokémon. You could call it Pornomon, I guess.

It's so easy—and it's free. I just download the pictures, take a look at them, discard the bad ones, keep the good ones. The pictures I keep, I put in various folders for the different types of stuff I like. I guess all these pictures must be copyrighted but, well, they're available, and it's not like anybody knows I've got them.

A Pirate Speaks: The Porn Pirate (*continued*)

Some of the pictures are grainy. They're just captures from motion pictures. Other pictures are really, really high quality. Obviously they're from sets of still pictures that were made for magazines or porno books. In the 100K range, the quality of the JPEGs is usually quite amazing. Down in the 15K, 20K range, the pictures are usually small and grainy, so they're not worth having. There's also a lot of amateurs, too, putting up pictures of themselves and their wives. If it says "amateur" on it, I stay away from it because it'll be a bunch of crap.

Every now and then someone will lay up a minute or two of a video, usually an MPEG, in the newsgroups. Because they're big, MPEGs are generally broken up into many, many files: 1 through 15, 1 through 25, that kind of thing. Often—and this is really annoying—there'll be 10 of the 15 but not the other five. I'm not sure why that happens, but I find if I stay on the newsgroup for a couple of weeks and check back every day, generally the entire series of files will appear. Then I can combine them with Outlook Express into a single MPEG file and play it with Windows Media Player. Sometimes I can only get most of the component files, like 13 out of 15 or 20 out of 25. That usually works okay: The file will be jerky, but it'll assemble, and I can watch it okay.

Most of these MPEGs are captures of the key scenes from commercial porno movies. Some of them are new—it's easy to make them from DVDs, and some people even post all the different angles for people who've got time to download them. But I run across a lot of old favorites as well, like scenes from *Deep Throat* or *The Devil in Miss Jones* and Traci Lords' movies.

Recently I've been using audioGnome and Napster to download pictures and movie clips. People wrap the pictures and clips up into Wrapster archives so they look like MP3 files and then share them. I just search by **wrapster**—or even **porn**—or by the 32kbps bitrate.

A Pirate Speaks: The Porn Pirate (*continued*)

What I like about Wrapster is that it lets me download a whole bunch of stuff in one archive. But there are a couple of problems too. First, there's no way to tell what's in an archive until it's finished downloading, and I can unwrap it. Some of the archives contain some real crap—a hundred pictures of feet in wooden clogs, or a five-minute video of rubber gloves, or medical-fetish stuff. And second, many of the worthwhile files are password protected. The bastards who made the archives want people to sign up at their Web site before they'll give out the password to the zip file in the archive. I never do these sign-ups, because I never know whether the site's gonna try to run a script on my computer. Instead, I look around for messages of Wrapster passwords posted by people who hate this trick and want to help people out. There are a few passwords, like *successfully* and *Congratulations*, that work for a lot of files (even the non-porn ones).

I've got hundreds of CDs of JPEGs and MPEGs. They don't cost a cent beyond the media. I don't sell them or anything. I just keep them so I can look at them occasionally, that's all. It's no big deal. Lots of people do it. It doesn't hurt anyone.

Chapter **8**

NetMeeting and HotLine—the Tools of the Pros

Featuring

- ☠ Installing NetMeeting
- ☠ Making calls with NetMeeting
- ☠ Hosting a meeting with NetMeeting
- ☠ Sharing files via NetMeeting
- ☠ Chatting via NetMeeting
- ☠ Sharing applications via NetMeeting
- ☠ Installing HotLine Client
- ☠ Installing HotLine Server
- ☠ Sharing files via HotLine
- ☠ Chatting via HotLine

This chapter discusses the tools that the pro pirates use to share files—NetMeeting for Windows and HotLine for the Mac. NetMeeting and HotLine provide secure and effective file-sharing and chat capabilities, and are very popular with legitimate users as well.

There's a simple reason that NetMeeting and HotLine are the pros' favorite tools. It's that no lawyer can touch them.

NetMeeting is a collaboration, file-sharing, and videoconferencing package for Windows. It's entirely aboveboard—so much so that it's essentially built into Windows and Internet Explorer, which means that you'll find it on just about every Windows PC.

HotLine is a client and server application for sharing files, chatting, and reading news. HotLine is most popular on the Macintosh, but a full implementation is available for Windows as well.

We'll start with NetMeeting.

NetMeeting

This section discusses NetMeeting, Microsoft's collaboration, file-sharing, and video-conferencing package for Windows.

NetMeeting is most pirates' favorite tool for sharing files for two reasons: first, because Windows is so widely used (if also widely hated), NetMeeting can be used for communicating with almost anyone; and second, because NetMeeting is powerful, effective, and very secure.

What Is NetMeeting and What Can You Do with It?

NetMeeting is a collaboration and remote-control application from Microsoft—and one of the most powerful tools in a pirate's arsenal.

These are the basic things you can do with NetMeeting:

- Transfer files from one computer to another
- Chat with other users
- Share audio and video
- Share an application—or your entire desktop—with another user
- Remotely control another user's computer
- Remotely control your own computer (essentially the same as controlling another user's computer, but with slight security differences)
- Share ideas via a whiteboard (Microsoft Paint)

For pirates, the most useful capabilities are chat (for finding out who's got which files) and file transfer (getting them from A to B and from B to A).

NetMeeting's audio- and video-sharing features are of interest primarily to users who either are on the same local area network (or campus area network) or have exceptionally fast Internet connections. Over dial-up, ISDN, DSL, or cable connections, NetMeeting's audio-sharing features can be tolerably useful, like Internet telephony applications. Over anything but the most robust connection, video sharing (or videoconferencing) tends to be disappointing—unless you're content with a small window and a single-digit frame rate.

Another problem is that you can share audio or video with only one other user at a time, so neither is of any use if you're conferencing with multiple people. Chat, on the other hand, can be shared among pretty much any number of people since it is text based and takes up very little bandwidth.

A bigger problem is that while NetMeeting can encrypt data (including chat and whiteboarding), it cannot encrypt audio and video, so any call involving audio or video is insecure.

Getting NetMeeting

If you're running any semi-recent version of Windows, you probably have NetMeeting installed. If you haven't seen it, check the Communications submenu of the Start menu (Start ➤ Programs ➤ Accessories ➤ Communications) for a NetMeeting item. Failing that, choose Start ➤ Run to display the Run dialog box, type **conf** in the Open text box, and click the OK button.

Vulnerability Factor: Using NetMeeting

As I mentioned at the beginning of the chapter, NetMeeting is popular with pirates because it can be highly secure. If you establish point-to-point connections without going through a server (such as a directory server), you can only be tracked from your ISP (as you always can). Unlike with server-based applications (such as Napster), you're not exposing yourself in a public forum, so you're much less likely to attract unwelcome attentions.

For security, *never* use NetMeeting's audio-conferencing and videoconferencing features, because audio and video prevent you from using NetMeeting's security features. Stick with data-only calls and require security for each call so that you can use certificates to make sure of the identity of each participant in your calls or meetings. Assign a different password to each meeting you set up and communicate it securely to each participant.

Even on secure calls, never use any of NetMeeting's features that give someone else control of your computer. These features can be lethal to your computer, even if the guilty party is only horsing around rather than being actively bent on inflicting damage.

If you do seem to lose control of your computer, disconnect the network or Internet connection first, then power down your PC—if necessary, by switching it off rather than shutting down Windows. If you don't shut down Windows, it will want to scan your hard disk when you restart it. Let it do so, and follow up with a comprehensive virus scan for anything unpleasant that the attacker may have installed to give them control of your PC.

TIP

Because the various versions of NetMeeting don't entirely agree with each other, check which version of NetMeeting you have. You'll find the number in the About Windows NetMeeting dialog box (Help ➢ About Windows NetMeeting). Visit the Microsoft Web site (www.microsoft.com) and see if there's a later version available; if there is, download it and install it. That'll optimize your chances of being able to communicate with other people.

Installing and Configuring NetMeeting

This section discusses how to set up NetMeeting (when you install it) and how to configure it after installation.

Setting Up NetMeeting

The first time you run NetMeeting on a computer (or the first time any given user with a distinct user profile runs NetMeeting), you need to configure it. As usual, there's a Wizard to walk you through the configuration.

Here are the steps:

1. Choose Start ➢ Programs ➢ Accessories ➢ Communications ➢ Net-Meeting to start the configuration process. NetMeeting displays the Net-Meeting dialog box shown in Figure 8.1.

Figure 8.1
NetMeeting's opening greeting

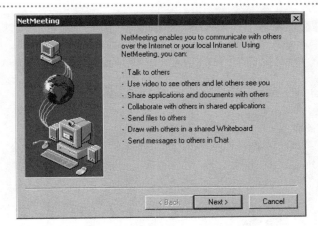

2. Click the Next button to proceed to the second NetMeeting dialog box (shown in Figure 8.2).

Figure 8.2

In the second NetMeeting dialog box, enter such personal information as you want made public.

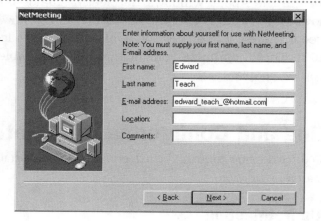

3. Enter whatever information you find appropriate in the First Name text box, the Last Name text box, and the E-mail Address text box. All three are required fields, but you can supply bogus information if you so choose. The Location text box and Comments text box are not required, but you can fill them in if doing so amuses you or will provide information useful to others.

4. Click the Next button to move on to the third NetMeeting dialog box (shown in Figure 8.3).

Figure 8.3

In the third NetMeeting dialog box, specify whether you want to log on to a directory server automatically.

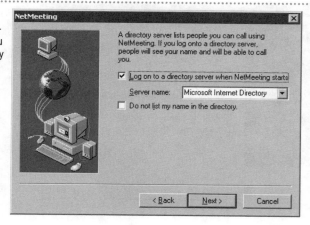

5. If you want NetMeeting to log you on to a directory server when you start NetMeeting, leave the Log On to a Directory Server When NetMeeting Starts check box selected and choose the server in the Server Name drop-down list. If you don't want to log on automatically, clear the check box. (You can log on manually at any time that suits you.) If you don't want Net-Meeting to list your name in the directory when you log on (automatically or manually), select the Do Not List My Name in the Directory check box; otherwise, leave it cleared, as it is by default.

6. Click the Next button to display the fourth NetMeeting dialog box (shown in Figure 8.4).

Figure 8.4

In the fourth NetMeeting dialog box, specify your connection speed.

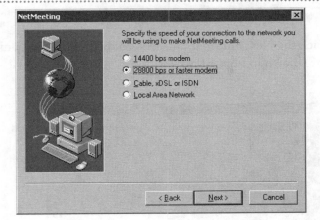

7. Select the option button that most closely matches your connection speed: 14400 bps modem; 28800 bps or faster modem; Cable, xDSL, or ISDN; or Local Area Network. This setting controls how NetMeeting tries to handle heavy data streams such as audio and video, so don't choose a misleading speed the way you might with Napster or a similar technology.

8. Click the Next button to proceed to the fifth NetMeeting dialog box (shown in Figure 8.5).

9. Select or clear the check boxes to tell NetMeeting whether to put one of its shortcuts on your desktop and/or on your Quick Launch toolbar. (If you use the Quick Launch toolbar, that is typically the most useful place to have the shortcut.)

Figure 8.5

In the fifth NetMeeting dialog box, tell NetMeeting where to install its shortcuts.

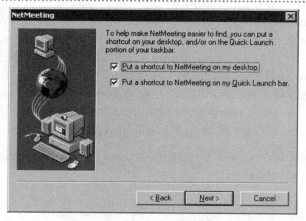

10. Click the Next button to move on to the first Audio Tuning Wizard dialog box (shown in Figure 8.6).

Figure 8.6

The Audio Tuning Wizard enjoins you to turn off all audio programs.

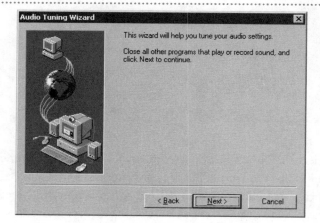

11. If you're planning ever to use NetMeeting's audio features, close all sound-producing or audio-recording programs. (Yes, you need to stop the MP3s playing for a minute or two.) If you have a microphone, make sure it's plugged in, not muted, and (if applicable) switched on.

12. Click the Next button to display the second Audio Tuning Wizard dialog box (shown in Figure 8.7).

Figure 8.7

Next, the Audio Tuning Wizard tests your speakers or headphones.

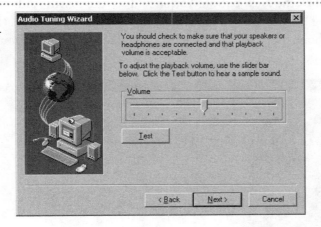

13. Click the Test button. The Audio Tuning Wizard starts playing a sound sample. Adjust the volume as necessary to get the signal comfortably audible. Then click the Next button to display the third Audio Tuning Wizard dialog box (shown in Figure 8.8 with the volume being set).

Figure 8.8

The Audio Tuning Wizard then sets your microphone volume.

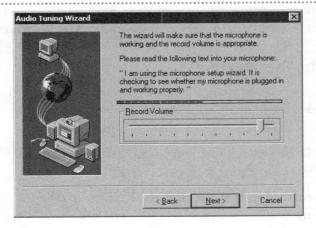

14. Speak into your microphone for 20 to 30 seconds at normal volume. (If you want, read the sample text shown in the third Audio Tuning Wizard dialog box, but it's nothing magical, so declaim poetry or curse fluently if you prefer.) The Audio Tuning Wizard adjusts the Record Volume slider to an appropriate level.

15. Click the Next button. You should see the fourth Audio Tuning Wizard dialog box, shown in Figure 8.9, telling you that all is well. (If you had a microphone problem, you'll see instead a dialog box telling you that.)

Figure 8.9

The final Audio Tuning Wizard dialog box

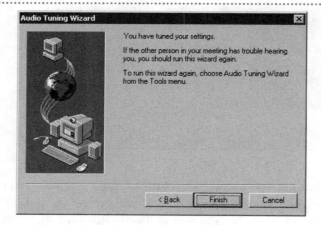

16. Click the Finish button. NetMeeting then starts.

NetMeeting is now adequately configured for basic use—but you'll do well to change some settings immediately, as discussed in the next section.

Configuring NetMeeting

As usual with Windows applications, most of NetMeeting's options appear in the Options dialog box. Choose Tools ➢ Options to display the Options dialog box and choose options as discussed in the following subsections.

General Page Options   These are the options on the General page of the Options dialog box (shown in Figure 8.10):

My Directory Information group box   Enter in the First Name text box and Last Name text box the name by which you want NetMeeting and other users to know you. You may well not want to use your real name, but please don't call yourself Edward Teach. In the E-mail Address text box, enter the e-mail address you want to appear. This might be a real account or a bogus account, but you need to enter something—the field is required. You don't have to enter anything in the Location text box and Comments text box, but do so if you want to.

Figure 8.10

The General page of the Options dialog box

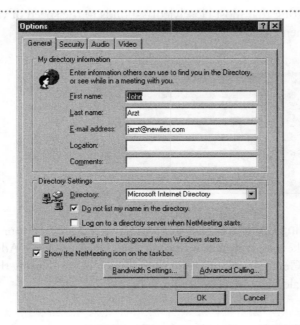

Directory Settings group box In the Directory drop-down list, choose the directory server you want to use. To prevent NetMeeting from listing you in the directory—for example, if you want to lurk on a public server—you can select the Do Not List My Name in the Directory check box. Select the Log On to a Directory Server when NetMeeting Starts check box if you want NetMeeting to automatically log you on to a directory server when you start it.

Run NetMeeting in the Background When Windows Starts check box Select this check box (which is cleared by default) if you want to start Net-Meeting automatically with each session of Windows.

Show the NetMeeting Icon on the Taskbar check box Select this check box if you want to have a NetMeeting icon in your system tray (*not* on the Taskbar—the option is misnamed).

Network Bandwidth Dialog Box If you need to check or change your bandwidth setting, click the Bandwidth Settings button on the General page of the Options dialog box to display the Network Bandwidth dialog box (shown in Figure 8.11).

Choose the setting that most closely corresponds to the speed of your network connection, and then click the OK button.

Figure 8.11

Use the Network Bandwidth dialog box to check or change your bandwidth setting.

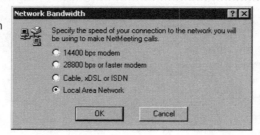

Advanced Calling Options Dialog Box   If you need to place your NetMeeting calls through a gatekeeper computer or through a gateway, click the Advanced Calling button on the General page of the Options dialog box to display the Advanced Calling Options dialog box (shown in Figure 8.12).

Figure 8.12

If your NetMeeting calls need to go through a gateway, choose the appropriate options in the Advanced Calling Options dialog box.

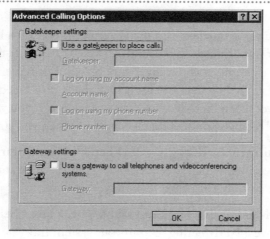

To use a gateway, select the Use a Gatekeeper to Place Calls check box and enter the gatekeeper computer's IP address or name in the Gatekeeper text box. You can then select the Log On Using My Account Name check box or the Log On Using My Phone Number check box as appropriate, and enter the account name in the Account Name text box or the phone number in the Phone Number text box.

To use a gateway, select the Use a Gateway to Call Telephones and Videoconferencing Systems check box and enter the gateway's IP address or name in the Gateway text box.

Security Page Options The Security page of the Options dialog box (shown in Figure 8.13) offers choices that are important for keeping your NetMeeting meetings secure and private. But before you choose them, you need to know the basics of NetMeeting security. See the following sidebar for a quick briefing.

Figure 8.13

Choose security options on the Security page of the Options dialog box.

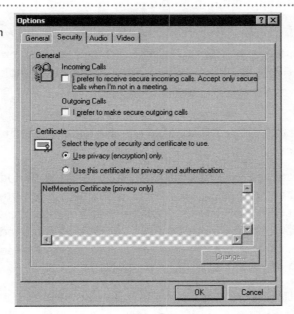

These are the options on the Security page of the Options dialog box:

I Prefer to Receive Secure Incoming Calls. Accept Only Secure Calls When I'm Not in a Meeting check box Select this check box if you want to receive only secure calls. The part about accepting calls when you're not in a meeting refers to Remote Desktop Sharing, a feature that lets you access your own computer remotely when NetMeeting is not running. (The section "Using Remote Desktop Sharing to Access Your Own Computer," later in this chapter, discusses how to use Remote Desktop Sharing.)

Word to the Wise: NetMeeting Security

To choose the right security options, you need to understand the basics of NetMeeting security. By default, any NetMeeting call you place is not secure, which means that (theoretically) it can be eavesdropped on by anyone determined enough. So you probably want to use security for your calls as much as possible.

NetMeeting offers some good security features:

- You can use passwords to restrict access to meetings. This is a vital step that everyone should take unless they're planning to host a free-for-all. You specify the password when setting up the meeting.

- You can encrypt the data transferred during a meeting. Again, you'll almost always want to do this.

- You can use authentication certificates to check the identity of callers. On the face of it, this feature seems attractive—and for business settings it's crucial. But because an authentication certificate conclusively identifies the individual involved (in theory—they might have given their certificate to someone else), you may find people unwilling to use this feature.

Unfortunately, NetMeeting's security is limited in that it cannot encrypt audio and video: If you want to videoconference or transmit audio, you need to place an insecure call. (This is why NetMeeting calls are not secure by default: NetMeeting is built to try to transmit audio and video until you prevent it from doing so.) As you saw earlier in the chapter, this failing is one of the reasons that most pirates choose not to use NetMeeting's audio and video features.

I Prefer to Make Secure Outgoing Calls check box   Select this check box to use NetMeeting's security features for all your outgoing calls. (If you prefer, you can choose manually to make some calls secure and other calls not secure.) Remember that any call that includes audio or video is not secure.

Certificate group box   In this group box, choose the type of security you want to use. The default setting is the Use Privacy (Encryption) Only option button. Leave this option button selected if you want to use NetMeeting's security features to encrypt data but you don't want to authenticate meeting participants. If you do want to use authentication, select the Use This Certificate for Privacy and Authentication option button. Then click the Change button to display the Select Certificate dialog box, choose the certificate to use, and click the OK button.

Audio Page Options   The Audio page of the Options dialog box (shown in Figure 8.14) contains the following options:

If your computer does not have a sound card, the Audio page does not appear in the Options dialog box.

Enable Full-Duplex Audio So I Can Speak While Receiving Audio check box Mostly self-explanatory. Select this check box to enable full-duplex audio—input and output at the same time. The only problem here is if your sound card doesn't support full-duplex audio; in this case, this check box will be dimmed and unavailable. Most modern sound cards do support full-duplex audio, so if yours doesn't, take the hint and upgrade it.

Enable Auto-Gain Control check box   Select this check box if you want NetMeeting to work with your sound card and audio driver to automatically adjust the microphone volume to a workable level. Provided your sound card supports auto-gain, it's a good idea to use it, because you'll then be able to vary your speaking volume and your distance from your microphone without blasting your co-meeter or fading away. If your sound card doesn't support auto-gain, this check box will be dimmed and unavailable.

Automatically Adjust Microphone Volume While in a Call check box   This option picks up where the previous option leaves off: If your sound card doesn't support auto-gain, select this check box so that NetMeeting can adjust the microphone volume to keep you audible during a call. Even if your sound card does support auto-gain, there's no harm in keeping this check box selected, as it is by default.

Figure 8.14

Choose audio options on the Audio page of the Options dialog box.

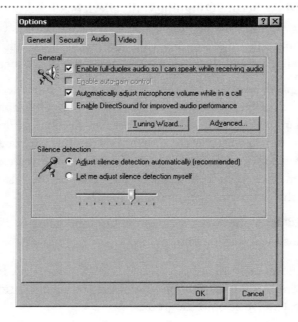

Enable DirectSound for Improved Audio Performance check box Select this check box if you want to use DirectSound to improve audio performance.

Silence Detection group box Use the two option buttons and the slider in this group box to specify how you want silence detection to be adjusted. The default setting is to have the Adjust Silence Detection Automatically (Recommended) option button selected, which gives NetMeeting control over detecting when silence has broken out. If you find that NetMeeting's silence detection gives you unsatisfactory results, such as chopping off your voice when you're speaking softly, select the Let Me Adjust Silence Detection Myself option button and move the slider to an appropriate position.

In addition to the options described above, the Audio page of the Options dialog box has two command buttons: a Tuning Wizard button and an Advanced button. As you'd imagine, clicking the Tuning Wizard button runs the Audio Tuning Wizard, which you can use to help you adjust your audio and microphone levels.

Clicking the Advanced button displays the Advanced Compression Settings dialog box (shown in Figure 8.15), in which you can specify a codec for compressing and decompressing the audio you transfer with NetMeeting. Select the Manually Configure Compression Settings check box (it's cleared by default) and select the appropriate codec in the Preferred Codec for Audio Compression drop-down list.

Figure 8.15

Use the Advanced Compression Settings dialog box to configure your audio compression settings manually.

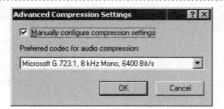

Video Page Options   The Video page of the Options dialog box (shown in Figure 8.16) contains the options for videoconferencing. As mentioned earlier, NetMeeting supports video only on two-person meetings and only on insecure connections—so if you want to conference with multiple people at the same time, or if you want to use only secure connections, you'll probably want to turn these features off.

Figure 8.16

Choose videoconferencing options—or turn them all off—on the Video page of the Options dialog box.

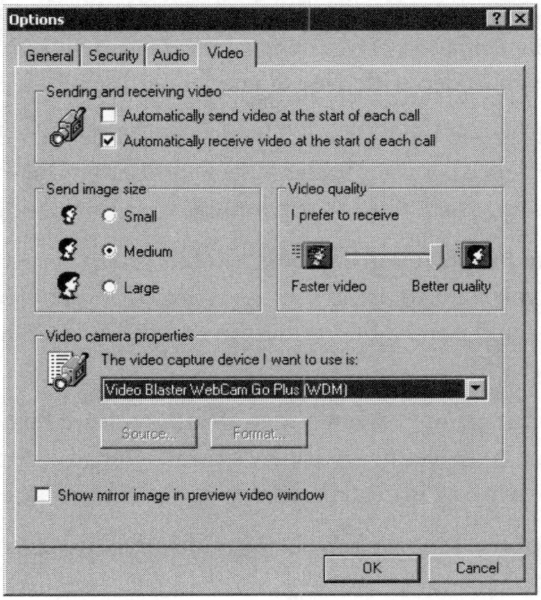

Anyway, these are the options open to you:

Automatically Send Video at the Start of Each Call check box   Select this check box if you want NetMeeting to send video at the start of every call. Unless you're heavy into videoconferencing, you won't want to select this check box. And if you don't have a video camera, this check box won't be available to you.

> If you choose not to send video automatically, you can start to send video at any time during a two-person non-secure call by clicking the Start Video button.

Automatically Receive Video at the Start of Each Call check box   Select this check box if you want NetMeeting to automatically receive incoming video. Clear this check box if you have no interest in video.

Send Image Size group box   If you'll be sending video, specify the image size to send by selecting the Small option button, the Medium option button, or the Large option button. As you'd expect, unless you establish a very fast connection with the other participant in the meeting, you're trading off image size against frame rate: You can have postage-stamp–sized video with a decent frame rate or more easily visible video with a lower and jerkier frame rate.

Video Quality group box   If you'll be receiving video, set the I Prefer to Receive slider to the balance between Faster Video and Better Quality that most pleases you. (Chances are, you'll need to experiment with this setting.)

Video Camera Properties group box   In this group box, you can select the video camera you want to use in the The Video Capture Device I Want to Use Is drop-down list and use the Source button and the Format button (if they're available) to configure it.

Show Mirror Image in Preview Video Window check box   Select this check box if you want NetMeeting to display a mirror image of the video you're sending in the preview window instead of displaying it the real way around.

That's enough options for the time being. Click the OK button to close the Options dialog box.

Setting Your Downloads Folder   Next, specify your downloads folder—or, as Net-Meeting prefers to term it, your *received files folder*. By default, NetMeeting uses a folder named \Received Files\ under the \NetMeeting\ or \NetMeetingNT\ folder. You'll probably want to use a folder in a handier location—for example, in your data folders rather than in your application folders.

Here's how to specify the downloads folder:

1. From the main NetMeeting window, press Ctrl+F or choose Tools ➢ File Transfer to display the File Transfer window.

2. Choose File ➢ Change Folder to display the Browse for Folder dialog box.

3. Navigate to and select the folder you want to use.

4. Click the OK button.

Placing and Receiving Calls

Once you've got NetMeeting set up, you'll probably want to start making calls. Here's how to proceed.

Finding Out Who's Available

First, you'll need to find out who's available. One way of finding out who's available is to use a directory server (such as the MSN Messenger service that you can use if you have a HotMail account or a Passport account).

Most self-respecting pirates won't go anywhere near a directory server (unless they run their own). Instead, they'll set up calls either via e-mail or via private chat messages. Chat is usually the best bet, as it tends to be quicker, and participants can easily check their current IP address.

Placing a Call

NetMeeting gives you several ways to place a call.

Here's the way of placing a call that gives you most control:

1. Choose Call ➢ New Call, or press Ctrl+N, to display the Place a Call dialog box (shown in Figure 8.17).

Figure 8.17

The Place a Call dialog box gives you the most control over the call you're placing.

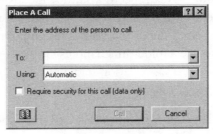

2. In the To text box, enter the designator of the person or computer you're calling. This can be an e-mail address (for example, `jane_bigfoot@hotmail.com`), an IP address (for example, `206.13.31.12`), a telephone number, or a computer name.

   ☠ Once you've placed a few calls, you'll be able to choose previous recipients from the To drop-down list.

3. In the Using drop-down list, choose Automatic, Network, or Directory as appropriate. Automatic puts the onus on NetMeeting to decide whether to connect via the network or via a directory.

4. If you want to place a secure, data-only call, select the Require Security for This Call (Data Only) check box.

5. Click the Call button to place the call.

A quicker way of placing a call, but one that does not let you specify security (NetMeeting goes by your choice on the Security page of the Options dialog box) or choose between Automatic, Network, or Directory placement, is to enter the address in the Place Call text box of the NetMeeting window and press Enter or click the Place Call button. If you're calling someone you've called before, you'll be able to choose the address from the Place Call drop-down list instead.

While the (as it were) phone is (as it were) ringing at the other end, you see the NetMeeting dialog box shown in Figure 8.18.

Figure 8.18

NetMeeting displays this NetMeeting dialog box while waiting for the other party to pick up.

If the other person accepts the call (or if they've set up NetMeeting to accept calls automatically, and it does so), their name and your name will appear in the Name list box, as in Figure 8.19. If you've chosen to send or receive audio or video at the beginning of a non-secure call, that'll start happening too.

Figure 8.19

When the other party picks up the call, you see their name and yours listed in the Name list box.

If the person you're calling does not pick up your call, or if they reject it, Net-Meeting displays the NetMeeting dialog box shown in Figure 8.20.

Figure 8.20

When the other party does not pick up or rejects your call, you'll see this Net-Meeting dialog box.

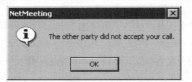

You can then add further people to the call by calling them using the same procedure.

Keeping a SpeedDial List

Most people tire quickly of typing IP addresses and complex directory entries. To help out, NetMeeting provides a SpeedDial feature that lets you build a list of the people you want to contact most frequently.

Creating a SpeedDial Entry   To create a SpeedDial entry:

1. Choose Call ➤ Create SpeedDial. NetMeeting displays the Create Speed-Dial dialog box (shown in Figure 8.21).

Figure 8.21

Create SpeedDial entries for the people you contact most frequently.

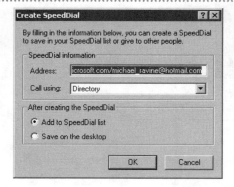

2. In the Address text box, enter the address of the person or computer. This can be an IP address, the computer name, or a directory server listing (for example, `ils.microsoft.com/edwardteach666@hotmail.com`).

3. In the Call Using drop-down list, select Directory for a SpeedDial entry that will connect through a directory or Network for a connection through a LAN or over the Internet.

4. In the After Creating the SpeedDial group box, select the Add to SpeedDial List option button if you want NetMeeting to store the new SpeedDial entry in your SpeedDial list or the Save on the Desktop option button if you want NetMeeting to create the SpeedDial entry on your desktop. If you have a lot of SpeedDial entries, you'll probably want to store them in the SpeedDial list, but if you have just a few, or you have a few that you want to be able to access instantly from outside NetMeeting, you may want to store them on the desktop instead.

By default, NetMeeting stores SpeedDial entries under names based on their addresses, which—whether directory entries, e-mail addresses, or IP addresses—are friendlier for computers than for humans. To make things easier, rename your SpeedDial entries by using conventional Windows renaming techniques. The SpeedDial entries on your desktop should be easy to find; the ones stored in your SpeedDial list will be in the \NetMeeting\SpeedDial folder, which should be in your \Program Files\ superstructure.

Using Your SpeedDial List   SpeedDial entries that you've stored on your desktop are easy to access: Display the desktop, and there they should be.

The SpeedDial entries stored in your SpeedDial list aren't as easy to access as they might be. To get to them, click the Find Someone in a Directory button to display the Find Someone window, then choose SpeedDial in the Select a Directory drop-down list, as shown in Figure 8.22.

Figure 8.22

You can access your SpeedDial list from the Find Someone window.

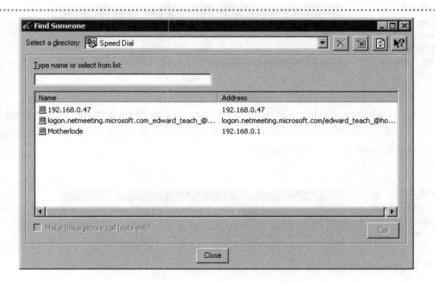

Select your victim, select the Make This a Secure Call (Data Only) check box if appropriate, and then click the Call button to place the call.

Receiving a Call

Receiving a call is simplicity itself. When someone calls you, NetMeeting displays the NetMeeting – Incoming Call dialog box (shown in Figure 8.23).

Figure 8.23

The NetMeeting – Incoming Call dialog box alerts you to an incoming call.

If you want to accept the call, click the Accept button. (Otherwise, obviously enough, click the Ignore button. They won't know whether you've rejected the call or if you just weren't there to take it.)

If the caller is using NetMeeting's security features, the NetMeeting – Incoming Call dialog box displays a Details button as well as the Accept button and Ignore button. Figure 8.24 shows an example.

Figure 8.24

When the incoming call is using security, a Details button appears on the NetMeeting – Incoming Call dialog box.

Click the Details button to expand the NetMeeting – Incoming Call dialog box and see details of the certificate the caller is using with NetMeeting. Figure 8.25 shows an example of this.

Figure 8.25

Click the Details button to see details of the certificate the caller is using with NetMeeting.

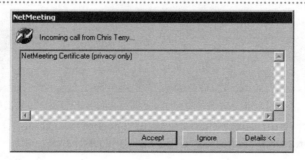

If you want to keep NetMeeting running, but also want to make sure you don't receive any calls, choose Call ➤ Do Not Disturb. NetMeeting then suppresses any incoming calls. Choose Call ➤ Do Not Disturb again to return to the world of modern communications.

Word to the Wise: Finding Out Your IP Address

Directory servers work surprisingly well, but the easiest way to establish a connection with another computer is to use its IP address.

If you have a permanent connection to the Internet (for example, if you have a DSL), you probably have a fixed IP address. But if you connect via dial-up, your ISP probably assigns you a free IP address dynamically each time you connect. That means you'll need to find out your IP address before you try to get someone to call you via NetMeeting.

On computers that have Winsock 2 installed (most of them), the easiest way to find out your IP address is to choose Help ➤ About Windows NetMeeting to display the About Windows NetMeeting dialog box (shown below).

The IP Addresses line at the bottom to the About Windows NetMeeting dialog box shows all current IP addresses associated with your computer.

Word to the Wise: Finding Out Your IP Address (*continued*)

In this case, the first IP address is that of the dial-up adapter, while the second address is that of the adapter on the local network. If your computer has multiple network cards or network connections, you will see more IP addresses here.

If your computer does not have Winsock 2 installed, you won't find your IP address in the About Windows NetMeeting dialog box. Read on.

If you're running NT 4, open a command prompt window, type **ipconfig**, and press Enter. NT displays a listing of all IP-addressed devices on your computer and their IP addresses.

If you're running Windows 9*x* or Windows Me, choose Start ➢ Run to display the Run dialog box. Type **winipcfg** in the Open text box and click the OK button. Windows opens the IP Configuration dialog box, an example of which is shown below. The IP Address text box (or IP Autoconfiguration Address text box if you're using Internet Connection Sharing) shows the IP address for the network adapter selected in the drop-down list. You can click the More Info button to display further information, including the IP address of your DNS server.

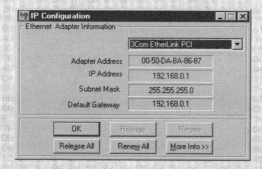

Hosting a Meeting on Your Computer

Placing and receiving calls is easy enough, but for more flexibility, you'll want to host a meeting. You can then specify a password for the meeting, require security for it, and restrict the actions that the participants can take.

Here's how to host a meeting:

1. Choose Call ➤ Host Meeting to display the Host a Meeting dialog box (shown in Figure 8.26).

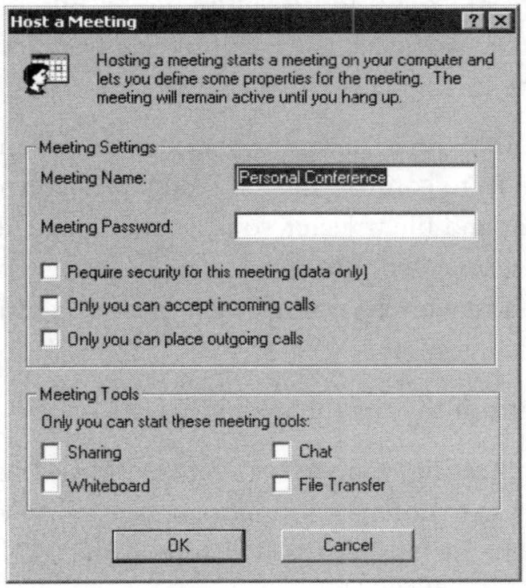

Figure 8.26

Use the Host a Meeting dialog box to set up the details of a meeting you plan to host.

2. Enter a name for the meeting in the Meeting Name text box. (You can accept the default name, Personal Conference, but you'll probably want something more descriptive so that those trying to get into the meeting know they're in the right place.)

3. Enter the password for the meeting in the Meeting Password text box. As usual, make the password good—more than six characters long, no recognizable word in any known language, and so on. Unless you establish a small and very secure group, you'll do best to create a new password for each meeting you host.

4. Choose restrictions for the meeting:

   ☠ Select the Require Security for This Meeting (Data Only) check box. The only reason for not using security is if you must use video or audio—which, you'll remember, are restricted to two participants only, so they're not much use in a group situation.

   ☠ Select the Only You Can Accept Incoming Calls check box if you want to prevent other people from joining the meeting by placing calls to the participants.

   ☠ Select the Only You Can Place Outgoing Calls check box if you want to prevent the participants in the meeting from letting other people into the meeting by calling them once they're connected to the meeting.

5. In the Meeting Tools area, select the check boxes for any of the NetMeeting tools that you want to control yourself. You'll probably want to allow anybody to start chat and file transfer, so leave the Chat check box and the File Transfer check box cleared. But if you want to prevent other people from starting sharing and whiteboarding, say, select the Sharing check box and the Whiteboard check box.

6. Click the OK button to start the meeting.

When people join the meeting, you see the NetMeeting – Incoming Call dialog box as usual, and can choose to accept it or ignore it as usual. If you chose to require security for the meeting, the Details button will appear on the NetMeeting – Incoming Call dialog box, and you will be able to view the information on the certificate the caller is using with NetMeeting.

To end the meeting, click the End Call button or choose Call ➤ Hang Up.

Joining a Meeting

To join a meeting, place a call as usual to the host. Usually, you'll do best to use the Place a Call dialog box so that you can specify a security setting other than your default if necessary.

When your computer has established a connection with the meeting host, Net-Meeting displays the Enter Password dialog box (shown in Figure 8.27). Enter the password and click the OK button. If you enter the correct password, the meeting host will see the NetMeeting – Incoming Call dialog box and will be able to accept or ignore the call as usual.

Figure 8.27

To join a meeting, you need to supply its password.

If the host accepts the call, you see the Meeting Properties dialog box, of which Figure 8.28 shows an example. As you can see in the figure, I'm entering a high-security meeting: Security is required; I cannot accept incoming calls or place outgoing calls; and I cannot start the sharing and whiteboard tools. Click the OK button to dismiss the Meeting Properties dialog box.

Figure 8.28

The Meeting Properties dialog box shows you the restrictions on the meeting.

NetMeeting then appears as usual. If there are restrictions on the tools you can use, their buttons appear grayed out and disabled. If the call is secure, the words *In a secure call* and a padlock icon are displayed at the bottom of the window.

Using Remote Desktop Sharing to Access Your Own Computer

For those times when you're on the road and need to access your home (or office) computer, NetMeeting provides a feature called Remote Desktop Sharing. Remote Desktop Sharing is essentially an automatically hosted meeting that will accept only a single connection. (If you want, you can use Remote Desktop Sharing to let someone else access your computer, but it's usually not a good idea; because Remote Desktop Sharing is designed to run without being monitored, you get no warning about incoming connections and no chance to decline them.)

You can only use Remote Desktop Sharing when you're *not* running NetMeeting, so you don't need to worry about Remote Desktop Sharing starting when you're using NetMeeting. Depending on your needs, you can set Remote Desktop Sharing to start automatically when you exit NetMeeting or start it yourself manually only when appropriate. Most people find it best to configure Remote Desktop Sharing not to start automatically.

Configuring Remote Desktop Sharing

Before you can use Remote Desktop Sharing, you need to configure it. To do so, you use the Remote Desktop Sharing Wizard as follows:

1. Choose Tools ➢ Remote Desktop Sharing to start the Remote Desktop Sharing Wizard. Figure 8.29 shows the first Remote Desktop Sharing Wizard dialog box.

Figure 8.29

If you need to access your computer from elsewhere, Remote Desktop Sharing may be right up your street.

2. Click the Next button to move on to the Remote Desktop Sharing Wizard—Set Password dialog box (shown in Figure 8.30).

Figure 8.30

Specify an original password in the Remote Desktop Sharing Wizard—Set Password dialog box.

3. Enter an original and unguessable password in the New Password text box and the Confirm New Password text box. Don't use any of your existing passwords, no matter how good you may think them. Make a careful note—preferably mental—of this password.

   ☠ If you're reconfiguring Remote Desktop Sharing, you'll need to enter your original password in the Old Password text box before you can proceed.

4. Click the Next button to proceed to the next Remote Desktop Sharing dialog box (shown in Figure 8.31), which suggests you enable a password-protected screen saver in order to protect your computer from the attentions of people who happen to be around when you're not. (You may have enabled a password-protected screen saver already; the Remote Desktop Sharing Wizard doesn't check before asking.)

Whether you use a screen saver or not, everything you do in your Remote Desktop Sharing session will be visible on your monitor—so turn your monitor off if anybody else will be able to see it. Use the screen saver password to prevent anybody else from taking control of your computer locally while you're away.

Figure 8.31

It's best to enable a password-protected screen saver to protect your computer from people on site when you're remote.

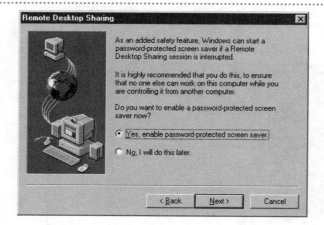

5. Choose the Yes, Enable Password-Protected Screen Saver option button or the No, I Will Do This Later option button as appropriate. Then click the Next button. If you chose the Yes option button, the Wizard displays the Screen Saver page of the Display Properties dialog box so that you can choose and enable a screen saver. Click the OK button when you're done, and the Wizard displays the final Remote Desktop Sharing Wizard dialog box (shown in Figure 8.32), to which it will have taken you directly if you chose the No option button. This dialog box tells you that you've finished setting up Remote Desktop Sharing.

6. Click the Finish button to close the Remote Desktop Sharing Wizard dialog box.

Figure 8.32

Configuring Remote Desktop Sharing is all over bar the congratulations.

Activating and Deactivating Remote Desktop Sharing

To activate Remote Desktop Sharing, close NetMeeting if it's running. Then right-click the NetMeeting Remote Desktop Sharing icon in the system tray and choose Activate Remote Desktop Sharing from the context menu. Nothing visible happens, but NetMeeting starts Remote Desktop Sharing running. (To make sure, click the NetMeeting Remote Desktop Sharing icon in the system tray again. You'll see that the Activate Remote Desktop Sharing item is unavailable and that the Turn Off Remote Desktop Sharing item is available.)

To deactivate Remote Desktop Sharing, click the NetMeeting Remote Desktop Sharing icon in the system tray and choose Turn Off Remote Desktop Sharing from the context menu.

Accessing Your Computer via Remote Desktop Sharing

To access your computer from another computer via Remote Desktop Sharing:

1. Call ➤ New Call to display the Place a Call dialog box (shown in Figure 8.33).

Figure 8.33

When calling to a computer running Remote Desktop Sharing, you must select the Require Security for This Call (Data Only) check box in order to connect.

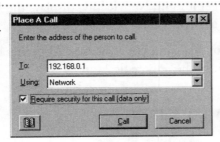

2. Enter the name or IP address of the host computer in the To text box as usual.

3. In the Using drop-down list, select Automatic, Network, or Directory as appropriate as usual.

4. Select the Require Security for This Call (Data Only) check box. *You must select this check box in order to make a connection to a computer that's running Remote Desktop Sharing.*

5. Click the Call button. NetMeeting then places the call as usual.

6. When NetMeeting makes the connection, it displays the Remote Desktop Sharing Password dialog box (shown in Figure 8.34).

Figure 8.34

To make a connection via Remote Desktop Sharing, you need to enter the Remote Desktop Sharing password for the remote computer.

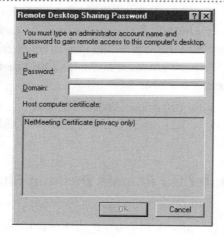

7. Enter your user name in the User text box and your password and click the OK button. If you get it right, NetMeeting displays the Meeting Properties dialog box (shown in Figure 8.35).

8. Click the OK button to dismiss the Meeting Properties dialog box. You'll then be able to control the remote desktop.

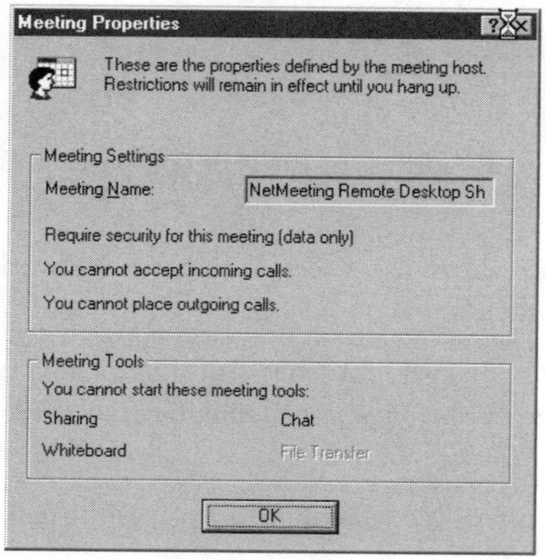

Figure 8.35

NetMeeting displays the Meeting Properties dialog box to let you know the details of the Remote Desktop Sharing meeting you've joined.

When you end your Remote Desktop Sharing session (by clicking the End Call button or choosing Call ➤ Hang Up), NetMeeting activates the screen saver on the remote computer (assuming a screen saver is enabled).

Changing Your Remote Desktop Sharing Setup

To change your Remote Desktop Sharing setup after you've configured it using the Remote Desktop Sharing Wizard, choose Tools ➤ Remote Desktop Sharing. Net-Meeting displays the Remote Desktop Sharing Settings dialog box (shown in Figure 8.36). You can then clear the Enable Remote Desktop Sharing on This Computer check box to disable Remote Desktop Sharing, click the Wizard button to run the Remote Desktop Sharing Wizard again, or click the Change Password button and use the resulting Password dialog box to change your password. Click the OK button when you've finished.

Figure 8.36

Use the Remote Desktop Sharing Settings dialog box to change your Remote Desktop Sharing settings once you've configured Remote Desktop Sharing.

Transferring Files

Not surprisingly, file transfer is the NetMeeting feature that pirates use the most. This section discusses how to use it to move files back and forth. Obviously enough, for either operation, you'll need to be connected to one or more other NetMeeting users, so establish a connection first if you're not currently connected.

Sending a File to Another User

To send a file to another user:

1. Click the Transfer Files button in the NetMeeting window to display the File Transfer window (shown in Figure 8.37 with some files already added). Alternatively, press Ctrl+F or choose Tools ➤ File Transfer.

Figure 8.37

Use the File Transfer window to get files from A to B.

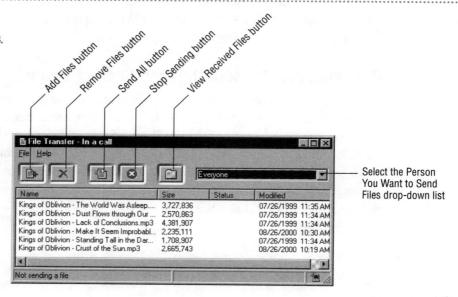

2. Line up the files you want to transfer. Click the Add Files button to display the Select Files to Send dialog box (shown in Figure 8.38). Navigate to and select the files you want to send, and then click the Add button to add them to the File Transfer window. Repeat this process until you've arranged all the files you want to send. Use the Remove Files button to remove from the list any files that you add by accident.

Figure 8.38

In the Select Files to Send dialog box, identify the files you want to transfer.

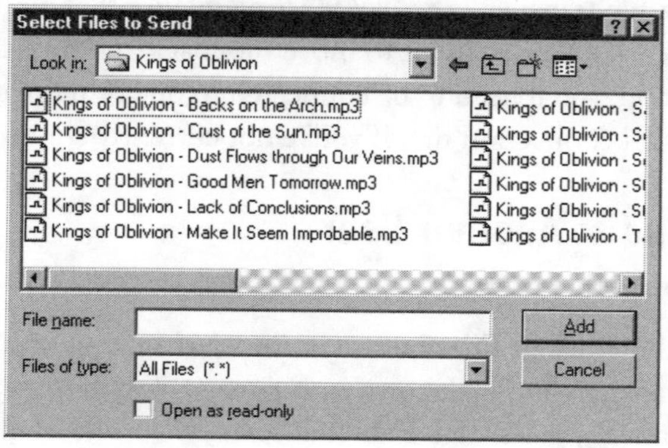

3. In the Select the Person You Want to Send Files drop-down list, choose the recipient of the files. The default selection is Everyone, which you'll probably want to change.

4. If you want to transfer all the files in the File Transfer window to the recipient, click the Send All button or choose File ➤ Send All. If you want to transfer just some of the files, select them in the File Transfer window and choose File ➤ Send a File.

5. NetMeeting starts to transfer the files one by one. As it does so, the Status column shows the file status: blank until an action is taking place, Sending while the file is being sent, Sent once the file has successfully been transferred, or Canceled if you or the recipient cancel the transfer. Figure 8.39 shows the File Transfer window with file transfer underway.

Figure 8.39

The Status column of the File Transfer window tells you how the file-transfer operation is proceeding.

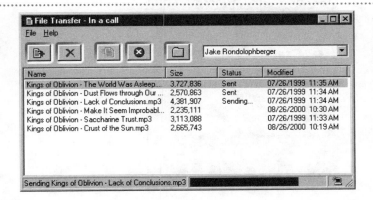

If the recipient cancels the transfer of a file, you'll see the File Transfer message box shown in Figure 8.40 telling you so. NetMeeting then cancels any pending file transfers.

Figure 8.40

You'll see this File Transfer message box if the recipient cancels an incoming transfer.

To prevent you from wasting time by transferring multiple copies of the same file, NetMeeting lets you send each file listed in the File Transfer window only once. To send a file again (for example, if the transfer fails, or if you have to cancel it), remove the file from the File Transfer window, then add it again.

Receiving a File from Another User

When another user sends you a file, NetMeeting displays a window such as the one shown in Figure 8.41. The title bar of the window bears the name of the file or (as in the figure) as much of it as will fit.

Figure 8.41

NetMeeting displays a separate window for each incoming file.

While the file is being transferred, the window offers you an Accept button and a Delete button, together with a dimmed and unavailable Open button. You can click the Accept button to dismiss the window or simply let it ride until the transfer is complete or you want to deal with it. Because this is a window rather than a dialog box, its presence on screen does not block any subsequent file transfers; instead, their file-transfer windows will stack up on top of this one, so you can deal with each in turn.

If you don't want to receive the file, click the Delete button. NetMeeting disposes of however much of the file you've received, cancels any subsequent transfers, and closes the file-transfer window.

When the transfer is complete, the Accept button changes into a Close button and the Open button becomes available. Because the file has now arrived and been saved to disk, you can no longer reject it, but you can delete it by clicking the Delete button.

If you're running anti-virus software that monitors each download and automatically warns you of problems, it may be safe to use the Open button to open the file. Clicking this button triggers the Windows application associated with the file type. For example, if the file you've received is an MP3 file, clicking the Open button will activate or launch your default MP3 player or jukebox. But it's safer to try to open the file from an application designed to run it. That way, if the file is a renamed EXE file that your anti-virus software has missed, the application will return an error when it is unable to open it, whereas triggering the Windows association would have run the file.

If you're using anti-virus software that requires manual intervention, don't use the Open button. Instead, click the Close button to close the file-transfer window, and then tell your anti-virus software to scrutinize the file. The files you receive go into the downloads folder (the "received files folder") you designated. To see what you've received, choose File ➢ Open Received Folder from the File Transfer window. NetMeeting opens an Explorer window to your downloads folder.

If you receive two or more files with the same name (for example, two copies of the same file), NetMeeting names the second copy Copy (1) of and the filename.

Chatting

After file transfer, the pirate's second-favorite NetMeeting feature is chat, because it's useful for socializing, for learning who's around, and for finding out which files everyone has and wants.

To chat with NetMeeting, click the Chat button, choose Tools ➢ Chat, or press Ctrl+T. NetMeeting displays the Chat window (shown in Figure 8.42). To send a message, enter it in the Message window and press Enter or click the Send Message button. You can send a message to everybody currently in the chat session or restrict it to a particular participant by using the Send To drop-down list.

Figure 8.42

NetMeeting includes a straightforward implementation of chat.

Whiteboarding

Whiteboarding tends to be of less interest to the average pirate than file transfer and chat, but it can be useful for showing people how to do things.

To use the whiteboard feature, click the Whiteboard button or choose Tools ➤ Whiteboard. Figure 8.43 shows an example of using the Whiteboard to convey an image, with the remote pointer (View ➤ Remote Pointer) used to indicate a particular part of the screen.

Figure 8.43

You can use NetMeeting's whiteboard feature for visual illustrations of techniques.

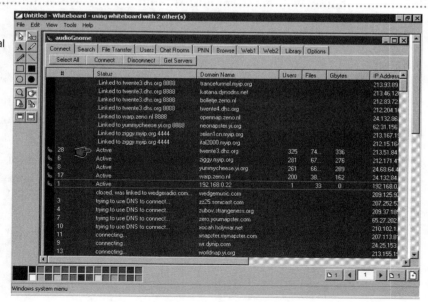

Sharing an Application—or Your Desktop

If you want to, you can share one or more applications—or your desktop—with another NetMeeting user. This can be useful for demonstrating an application.

If you're feeling trusting, you can even allow another NetMeeting user to control an application or your entire desktop. Most pirates don't do this for several compelling reasons:

- First, NetMeeting's file-transfer and chat capabilities are adequate for most of their needs.

- Second (and as a result), they have nothing to gain by letting another user control their desktop.

- Third, ceding control of your desktop is usually an impressive security risk. It may occasionally be useful, and tolerably safe, to let someone share an application or two—for example, when you're collaborating on a document. But give someone control of your desktop and they have free rein to do whatever they want to your system—start applications, rummage through your files, delete anything they want, or install applications or viruses.

All that said, under extreme circumstances, you may want to give control of your desktop to someone you're sure is trustworthy so that they can show you how to do something tricky.

To share your desktop or an application, click the Share Program button, choose Tools ➢ Sharing, or press Ctrl+S. (This peculiar usage of the pan-Windows keystroke for the Save command seems ill-advised—but since NetMeeting is Microsoft software, I suppose it must be okay in some way I can't grasp.) NetMeeting displays the Sharing window (shown in Figure 8.44).

In the list box, select the application you want to share and click the Share button. You can then unshare the application by selecting it and clicking the Unshare button or by clicking the Unshare All button.

The other user (or users) see a window titled with your NetMeeting name and "Programs," as in Figure 8.45. The windows appear on a featureless gray desktop in the positions in which you currently have them. If you place an unshared window over one of the shared windows, it blocks the other user's view of the shared window, but its contents aren't transmitted. When you're setting up sharing, the NetMeeting window and the Sharing window often block the view of the other windows, so you need to remember to move them out of the way or minimize them once you've arranged the sharing.

Figure 8.44

Use the Sharing window to share your desktop or an application.

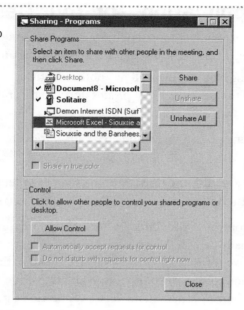

Figure 8.45

How the other NetMeeting user (or users) see the applications you're sharing.

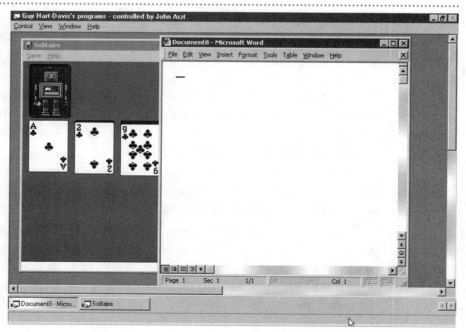

To let the other user (or users) control your shared applications, display the Sharing window and click the Allow Control button. Clicking this button makes available the Automatically Accept Requests for Control check box and the Do Not Disturb with Requests for Control Right Now check box, which you can use to automatically accept and to disable requests for control. Once you've clicked the Allow Control button, it changes into a Prevent Control button that you can click to prevent control of the shared applications.

Usually, you'll want to retain manual control over allowing other users control of your applications. When you click the Allow Control button but leave the Automatically Accept Requests for Control check box cleared, NetMeeting displays the Request Control dialog box (shown in Figure 8.46) to alert you to incoming requests for control.

Figure 8.46

NetMeeting displays the Request Control dialog box to let you decide whether to grant control or deny it.

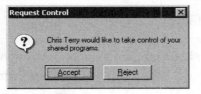

If you accept the request for control, the user is able to control the application much as if it were on their own desktop. You see every action they take, and your mouse pointer takes on the initials of the user controlling it. You can regain control temporarily by clicking your mouse in one of the shared windows or regain control permanently by clicking the Prevent Control button in the Sharing window or by unsharing the application.

If you reject the request for control, or do not respond to it within the timeout period, the user requesting control sees one of the Request Control Failed dialog boxes shown in Figure 8.47.

Figure 8.47

When you reject a request for control or allow it to time out, the requesting user sees one of these Request Control Failed dialog boxes.

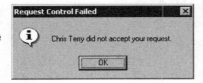 

To share your desktop and all open applications, select the Desktop item at the top of the Share Programs list box. If you allow control of your desktop, the other user can take more or less any action that Windows supports—bar anything that closes NetMeeting, of course. Again, you see the actions they take, and their initials appear on the mouse pointer.

When you're sharing your desktop with NetMeeting, you can't change display properties. For example, you can't change your screen resolution or color depth.

HotLine

NetMeeting is a component of Internet Explorer, but although Microsoft makes a version of Internet Explorer for the Macintosh, it doesn't contain NetMeeting. Given how deeply NetMeeting has to hook into the Windows API in order to do its tricks, this perhaps isn't surprising—but it does mean that people wanting to share files, chat, and videoconference on the Mac need to look elsewhere for their software.

For file sharing and chat, one of the most popular applications is HotLine, a P2P program created by HotLine Communications Ltd. of Canada. HotLine also supports news, though most pirates use this component far less than file sharing and chat.

HotLine Communications Ltd. also makes a version of HotLine for Windows, but HotLine is primarily popular on the Mac.

Unlike NetMeeting, Hotline comes in separate client and server components—HotLine Client and HotLine Server. As you'd guess, you use the HotLine Client to connect to a HotLine Server for file-sharing, chat, and maybe news. If you have files to share yourself, you can run the HotLine server and let other people connect to it to share files and chat. You can also run a news server, but since this feature seems less popular, I won't cover it in this section.

If HotLine doesn't agree with you, two other file-sharing programs for the Mac that you might want to investigate are Carracho and Zombie.

Vulnerability Factor: Using HotLine Client and HotLine Server

HotLine can be highly secure (with one dangerous limitation)—or it can be lethally insecure. The choice is yours.

Private servers without guest accounts are the safest way of using HotLine. If you create a private server and allow only a few trusted users to access it, you're unlikely to draw attention to yourself.

Public servers with guest accounts are the most dangerous way of using HotLine. If you make your HotLine Server public, list it with trackers, and allow guests to connect, all bets are off.

HotLine provides impressive control over users. You can allow access to your server only to users who have established accounts with you. You can assign a different and unguessable password for each account. You can control the actions that users can take by assigning privileges to their accounts. And the moment anyone misbehaves, you can boot them off your server.

As usual, you can be tracked by your ISP, but this is always the case. The really bad news on the vulnerability front is that both HotLine Client and HotLine Server pass information (including the user's IP address) to Hotline Communications Ltd. So anyone using HotLine for piracy is putting considerable faith in Hotline Communications Ltd. not to divulge their dirty deeds.

Getting and Installing HotLine Client

Here's how to get started with HotLine Client.

First, download the latest version of HotLine Client. You'll find it at the HotLine Communications Web site (www.bigredh.com) and at major software sites, such as CNET. The HotLine Communications site is the best place to start, because it'll have the latest version of HotLine Client and links to mirror sites that have it.

If the distribution file doesn't unstuff itself automatically, unstuff it manually. Then run the HotLine Client Installer to install the client. Click the Continue button in the first HotLine Client Install dialog box, and you're on your way.

Next, you see the License Agreement dialog box. Read the license agreement carefully and click the Accept button if you want to proceed. In case you're feeling lazy: The license agreement has a couple of key provisions that you probably ought to know about. First, you're allowed to distribute the software unmodified—not a big deal, but it might help you make the odd HotLine connection, so go for it if you feel the urge. Second, you agree to HotLine collecting information about your use of the software, including your IP address, length of sessions, and some system information. This provision may make you feel a bit queasy. And third, you're responsible for the digital content and any offensive material you run into—as usual.

The Installer then displays the Readme file detailing the latest bug fixes and new features. Browse these and note anything of interest.

You then see the first HotLine Client Installer dialog box (shown in Figure 8.48), in which you can use the Select Folder button and its resulting dialog box to select a different installation folder if you want.

Figure 8.48

In the first HotLine Client Installer dialog box, select an installation folder if you don't want to use the default folder.

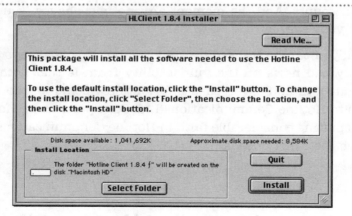

Click the Install button. You then get to choose a folder in which to install the HotLine documentation. After that, the Installer installs the files and displays a message box telling you so. Click the Quit button to dismiss the message box.

Now run HotLine Client by double-clicking the HotLine Client icon. The first time you run HotLine Client, you need to configure it.

In the first Welcome to HotLine dialog box, click the Next button. In the second Welcome to HotLine dialog box (shown in Figure 8.49), enter the name you want to use for HotLine. Then click the Next button.

Figure 8.49

In the second Welcome to HotLine dialog box, enter the HotLine username you want.

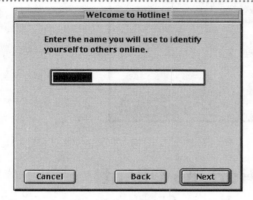

In the third Welcome to HotLine dialog box (shown in Figure 8.50), choose the icon that you want to appear next to your name. Then click the Next button.

Figure 8.50

Next, choose an icon to give color or character to your username.

In the fourth (and final) Welcome to HotLine dialog box (shown in Figure 8.51), click the Finish button.

Next, HotLine Client displays the Agreement dialog box. Read (or scroll) to the bottom of the text to find the Agree button, and click it if you can bring yourself to. You then see the HotLine Client windows.

Figure 8.51

The end of the HotLine Client configuration process. Click the Finish button.

Configuring HotLine Client

Before you get going with HotLine Client, you need to configure it a bit. Click the Options button or choose Hotline ➤ Options to display the Options dialog box, then proceed as discussed in the following sections.

General Page Options

The General page of the Options dialog box (shown in Figure 8.52) provides the following options:

Your Name text box This text box shows the name you entered during HotLine Client setup. You can change it as you want.

Queue File Transfers check box Leave this check box selected (as it is by default) if you want HotLine Client to queue file transfers for you.

Show Join/Leave in Chat check box Leave this check box selected (as it is by default) if you want the Chat window to show notices of people joining and leaving the chat room. To skip these notices, clear this check box.

Show Date/Time check box Leave this check box selected (as it is by default) to have HotLine Client display the date and time.

Figure 8.52

The General page of the Options dialog box

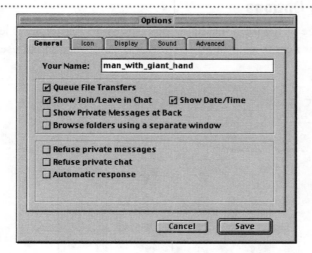

Show Private Messages at Back check box   Select this check box if you want to prevent private message windows from being displayed in front of other windows. If you leave this check box cleared, as it is by default, incoming private messages pop up on top of other windows.

Browse Folders Using a Separate Window check box   Select this check box to make HotLine Client display a separate window for each folder you open when browsing. Leave this check box cleared (as it is by default) if you prefer to do all your browsing in a single window.

Refuse Private Messages check box   Select this check box to have HotLine Client refuse private messages sent to you.

Refuse Private Chat check box   Select this check box to have HotLine Client refuse private chat requests sent to you.

Automatic Response check box   To have HotLine Client respond automatically to private messages and private chat, select this check box and enter the text for the automatic response in the text box that appears below the check box.

Icon Page Options

The Icon page of the Options dialog box (shown in Figure 8.53) lets you select an icon to appear next to your name in HotLine windows that list users.

Figure 8.53

The Icon page of the Options dialog box

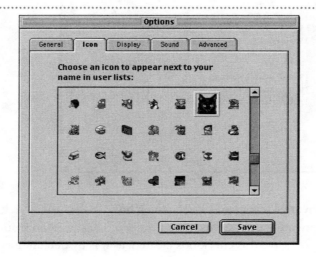

Display Page Options

The Display page of the Options dialog box (shown in Figure 8.54) provides the following options:

Text sizes, colors, and background colors   Use the Size text box, Text Color panel, and Back Color panel for the Public Chat, Private Chat, View Text, and News Post items to specify text size, text color, and background color of your likings. Clicking one of the Text Color or Back Color panels displays a Choose a Color dialog box that you can use to select just about any color.

Toolbar Buttons on Top check box   Select this check box to have the toolbar buttons appear above the banner ad instead of below it.

Magnetic Windows check box   Select this check box if you want the HotLine Client windows to stick to each other when you move them so that their edges touch.

Show ToolTips check box   Leave this check box selected (as it is by default) to make HotLine Client display ToolTips when you hover the mouse pointer over a button. Clear the check box to suppress ToolTips.

Figure 8.54

The Display page of the
Options dialog box

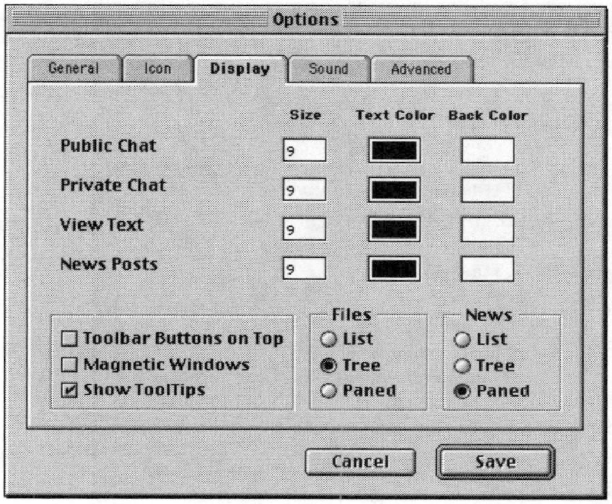

Files group box   Select the List option button, the Tree option button, or the
Paned option button to specify how you want files to be displayed in windows.
The default setting is Tree.

News group box   Select the List option button, the Tree option button, or the
Paned option button to specify how you want news to be displayed in windows.
The default setting is Paned.

Sound Page Options

The Sound page of the Options dialog box (shown in Figure 8.55) lets you choose
whether to have HotLine Client play sounds for different events and actions. You can
turn sounds on and off globally by selecting and clearing the Play Sounds For check box.

Advanced Page Options

The Advanced page of the Options dialog box (shown in Figure 8.56) offers the following options:

SOCKS Firewall text box   If you connect to your intranet or the Internet via a
SOCKS firewall, enter the address in this text box.

Tunnel through HTTP Proxy check box   Select this check box if you connect
to the Internet through an HTTP proxy server.

Figure 8.55

The Sound page of the Options dialog box

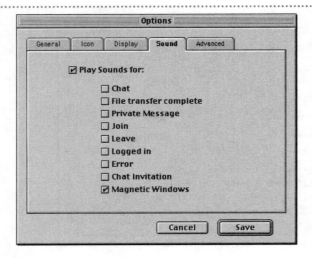

Don't Save Cookies check box   Leave this check box selected (as it is by default) to prevent HotLine Client from saving cookies. If you want to save cookies, clear this check box. Saving cookies may give you easier return access to some HotLine servers, but cookies can compromise the security of your computer.

Figure 8.56

The Advanced page of the Options dialog box

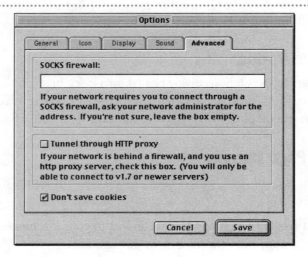

Click the Save button to save your chosen option settings and to close the Options dialog box.

The HotLine Client Windows

Once you've chosen configuration options to your satisfaction, you should be ready to get up and running with HotLine Client.

HotLine initially seems a little overwhelming because it has a toolbar and six main windows: Servers, Files, Chat, Users, News, and Tasks. The first three of these windows you'll meet in due course as you learn to put HotLine Client into action, but we'll visit quickly with the HotLine Client Toolbar, and the Users, News, and Tasks windows here before we go on.

The HotLine Client Toolbar

The HotLine Client Toolbar (shown in Figure 8.57) provides quick access to the various features of HotLine Client.

Figure 8.57

The HotLine Client Toolbar provides access to the various areas of the HotLine Client.

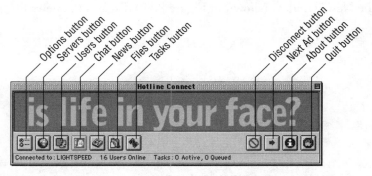

The Users Window

The Users window (shown in Figure 8.58) provides a list of all the users currently attached to the server you're attached to. The Users window contains buttons for private chat, private messages, getting client information, and (when you're logged in as admin) for disconnecting users. It displays a listing for each user currently online, with their chosen icon and icons indicating their privileges, whether they're refusing private messages or refusing private chat.

The privilege indicators appear in the Status column to indicate the approximate level of privileges that the user enjoys on this server. A silver icon indicates a user who has all privileges enabled. A red icon indicates a user with the privilege to disconnect other users. A yellow icon indicates a user who has some privileges (but not the privilege to disconnect other users). A green icon indicates a user who has no privileges.

Figure 8.58

The Users window

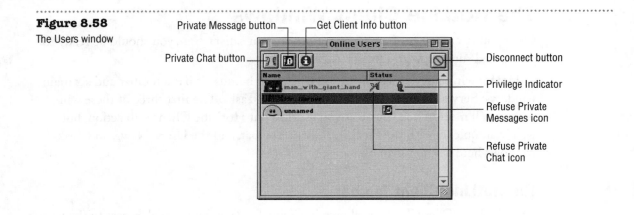

Private Message button

Get Client Info button

Private Chat button

Disconnect button

Privilege Indicator

Refuse Private Messages icon

Refuse Private Chat icon

The News Window

The News window (shown in Figure 8.59) displays the news for the server.

Figure 8.59

The News window

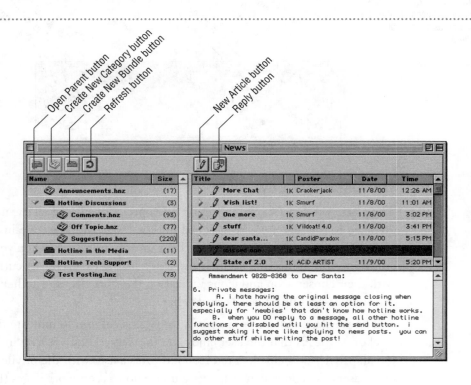

Open Parent button

Create New Category button

Create New Bundle button

Refresh button

New Article button

Reply button

    Ammendment 982B-8360 to Dear Santa:

6. Private messages:
        A. i hate having the original message closing when
    replying. there should be at least an option for it.
    especially for 'newbies' that don't know how hotline works.
        B. when you DO reply to a message, all other hotline
    functions are disabled until you hit the send button. i
    suggest making it more like replying to news posts. you can
    do other stuff while writing the post!

The Tasks Window

The Tasks window (shown in Figure 8.60) provides a running display of the tasks that HotLine Client is currently performing. Usually, you won't need to display or monitor the Tasks window, but if things seem to get stuck, you can use its Kill Task button and Begin Task button to try to kill off stuck tasks and begin other tasks.

Figure 8.60

The Tasks window provides a running display of all the tasks HotLine is working on.

Begin Task button

Kill Task button

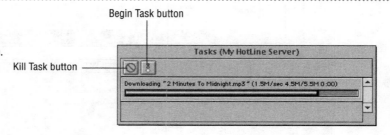

Connecting to a Server

The first step, naturally enough, is to connect to a HotLine server. The HotLine Client Servers window comes complete with entries for Hotline Communications Ltd. and a tracker or two, but you'll doubtless want to add to these.

To find servers, you can either use a tracker (a directory of HotLine servers and a listing of their contents) or visit a Web site that lists servers. You'll find various tracker sites on the Web, including the Tracker-Tracker site at www.tracker-tracker.com. To add a tracker to your Servers window list, click the Add Tracker button in the Servers window and use the New Account dialog box to supply the details of the tracker.

Once you know the address of a server, you can connect to it as follows:

1. Click the Servers button on the HotLine Client Toolbar (or choose Hotline ➢ Show Servers, or press Apple+R, or press the F1 key) to display or activate the Servers window (shown in Figure 8.61).

Figure 8.61

Figure 8.61

The Servers window

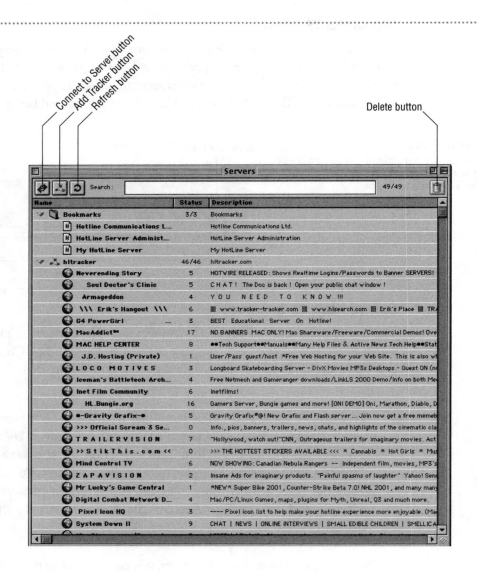

2. Click the Connect to Server button to display the Connect dialog box (shown in Figure 8.62).

3. Enter the IP address or the name of the server in the Server text box.

Figure 8.62

Use the Connect dialog box to connect to a server

4. Enter your login name in the Login text box. If you don't have an account with the server, try connecting as **guest**.

5. If you have an account with the server, enter the password in the Password text box. If you're trying to connect as a guest, try leaving the password blank. (A guest account can have a password, but most guest accounts don't.)

6. If you will want to connect to this server regularly, save a bookmark for it. Click the Save button in the Connect dialog box. Enter the name for the server in the Save Bookmark As text box in the resulting dialog box (shown in Figure 8.63) and click the Save button.

Figure 8.63

Save a bookmark for any server you'll want to connect to repeatedly.

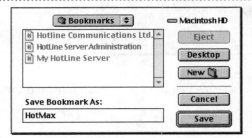

7. Click the Connect button in the Connect dialog box.

HotLine Client now attempts to connect to the server. If all goes well, you're likely to see an Agreement dialog box such as the one shown in Figure 8.64. Scroll down to reach the Agree button, click it, and you should be in.

Figure 8.64

To access a server, you almost always need to accept its agreement.

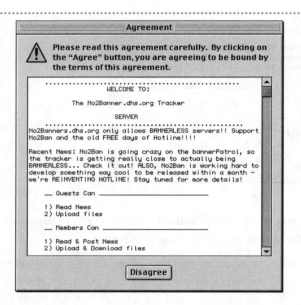

If the server isn't available, you may see the Connection Closed dialog box shown in Figure 8.65.

Figure 8.65

The Connection Closed dialog box indicates that a connection with the server isn't available.

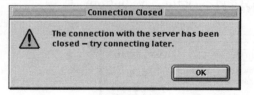

To disconnect from a server, click the Disconnect button on the HotLine Client Toolbar.

Downloading and Uploading Files

Provided you have the appropriate privileges, downloading and uploading files with HotLine Client is easy. To download or upload files:

1. Click the Files button on the HotLine Client Toolbar, or choose Hotline ➤ Show Files, or press Apple+F, to display the Files window (shown in

Figure 8.66). The Delete button appears only if you have delete privileges for the folder.

Figure 8.66

The Files window

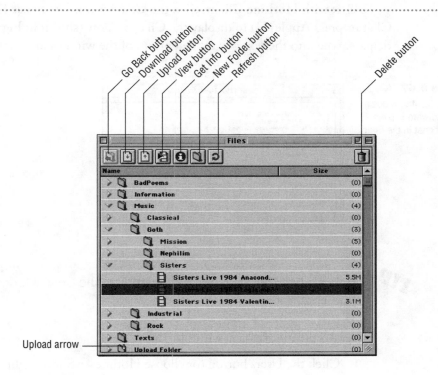

 Upload arrow

2. Navigate down the folder structure until you find what you want.

TIP

To perform a type-down search, click the title bar of the Files window and type the first few letters of what you're looking for.

3. To download a file, select it and click the Download button.

4. To upload a file, double-click an upload folder, then click the Upload button. In the resulting dialog box, select the file to upload, and then click the Open button.

Communicating with HotLine Client

HotLine Client supports both chat and private messages.

To chat with HotLine Client, click the Chat button (or choose Hotline ➤ Show Chat or press Apple+H) to display the Chat window (shown in Figure 8.67). To participate, type into the text box at the bottom of the window and press Enter.

Figure 8.67

HotLine Client provides a straightforward implementation of chat in the Chat window.

```
Chat (192.168.0.8)
<<<   Mr_Gurper has left    >>>
<<<   10/13/04 8:30:22 PM   >>>
<<<   Mr_Gurper has joined  >>>
<<<   10/13/04 8:30:58 PM   >>>
     Mr_Gurper:  hey yall
man_with_gian:  MorF?
     Mr_Gurper:  M 18
     Mr_Gurper:  you?
man_with_gian:  guess!
<<< godlivesinfaxes is now known as faxmydog >>>
```

TIP You can use the Private Chat button on the Chat window to enter a private chat room.

To send a private message with HotLine Client:

1. Click the Users button (or choose Hotline ➤ Show Online Users or press Apple+U) to display the Online Users window.

2. Select the user and click the Private Message button. HotLine Client displays a Send Message window (shown in Figure 8.68).

3. Type the text of your message.

4. Click the Send button.

When someone sends you a private message, it appears in a Private Message From window like that shown in Figure 8.69. Click the Reply button to reply or the Dismiss button to dismiss the message.

Figure 8.68

You can also send private messages by using the Send Message window.

Figure 8.69

An incoming private message appears in a Private Message From window.

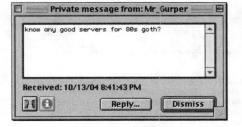

Installing and Configuring HotLine Server

Download the latest version of HotLine Server from the HotLine Communications Ltd. Web site (www.bigredh.com) or from a Mac software site. Generally speaking, your best bet is to go to the HotLine Communications Web site, which will farm you out to a mirror site that has the latest version of the software.

If you don't already have HotLine Client installed, download the latest version of that too. You'll need this in order to get HotLine Server configured and running.

Installing HotLine Server

Unstuff the HotLine Server distribution file if it doesn't unstuff itself. Then run the HotLine Server Installer.

First, you see the License dialog box. If you've read the license agreement for Hot-Line Client, much of this will seem familiar. As with HotLine Client, you can distribute HotLine Server in its unmodified form to anyone you choose as long as you don't sell it, and you agree to HotLine collecting information about your use of the software, including your IP address, length of sessions, and some system information. Also as before, you agree that anything illegal that you manage to do with the software is entirely your own fault.

Next, the Installer displays the Readme file. Read it, save it for reference if you want, and then proceed.

You then see the first HLServer Installer dialog box (shown in Figure 8.70), in which you can use the Select Folder button and its resulting dialog box to select a different installation folder if you want.

Figure 8.70
In the first HLServer Installer dialog box, select an installation folder if you don't want to use the default folder.

Click the Install button. The Installer creates the folder and installs HotLine Server into it. Double-click the HotLine Server icon in the folder to start HotLine Server.

The first time you run HotLine Server, you need to configure it. HotLine Server displays the Set Admin Password dialog box (shown in Figure 8.71).

Enter the password in both the New Admin Password text box and the Verify New Password text box and click the OK button. This password is crucial to keeping your HotLine server secure, so make it a good one. *Do not reuse any of your existing passwords, no matter how good you think they may be.*

Figure 8.71

The first time you run Hot-Line Server, you need to create an admin password.

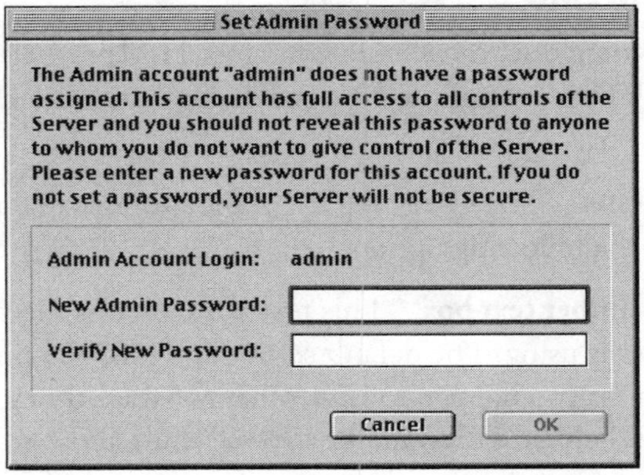

| Set Admin Password |

The Admin account "admin" does not have a password assigned. This account has full access to all controls of the Server and you should not reveal this password to anyone to whom you do not want to give control of the Server. Please enter a new password for this account. If you do not set a password, your Server will not be secure.

Admin Account Login: admin

New Admin Password:

Verify New Password:

[Cancel]   [OK]

Once you dismiss the Set Admin Password dialog box, you see HotLine Server. Figure 8.72 shows an example with three windows: the HotLine Server Log window, the Statistics window, and the HotLine Server Toolbar. Your arrangement of windows will probably look different than this.

Figure 8.72

The HotLine Server Tool-bar, the HotLine Server Log window, and the Statistics window.

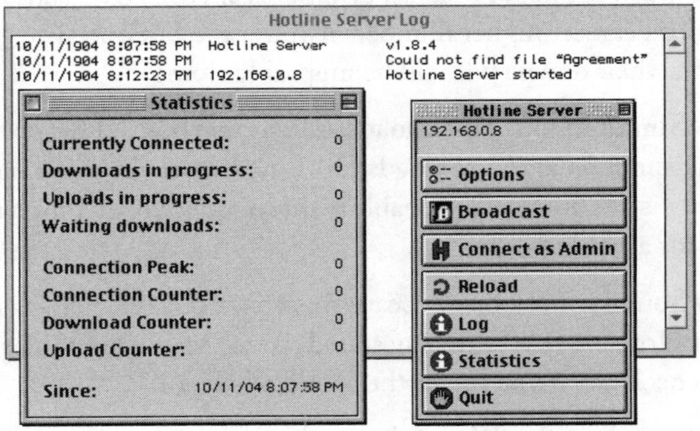

Hotline Server Log
10/11/1904 8:07:58 PM Hotline Server   v1.8.4
10/11/1904 8:07:58 PM   Could not find file "Agreement"
10/11/1904 8:12:23 PM 192.168.0.8   Hotline Server started

Statistics

Currently Connected: 0
Downloads in progress: 0
Uploads in progress: 0
Waiting downloads: 0

Connection Peak: 0
Connection Counter: 0
Download Counter: 0
Upload Counter: 0

Since: 10/11/04 8:07:58 PM

Hotline Server
192.168.0.8
⟐ Options
📄 Broadcast
🖥 Connect as Admin
↻ Reload
❶ Log
❶ Statistics
✋ Quit

You may see that, as in the figure, the HotLine Server Log window is complaining *Could not find file "Agreement."* This is fine—you'll create the agreement in a little while.

Configuring HotLine Server

Before you do anything else, you should configure HotLine Server. This means taking a blaze through the pages of the Options dialog box. Click the Options button to display this dialog box.

General Page Options   The General page of the Options dialog box (shown in Figure 8.73) contains the following options:

Server Port Number text box   This text box contains the port number that HotLine Server is using. The default setting is 5500. You probably won't need to change this unless you happen to have other software trying to use the same port. If your server is behind a firewall, the firewall must allow inbound connections on the specified port and the next three ports (for example, 5500, 5501, 5502, and 5503) and outgoing UDP traffic on the previous port (for example, 5499).

Maximum Simultaneous Downloads text box   This text box controls how many simultaneous downloads HotLine Server permits. The default setting is 100, which is appropriate only if you have your own T3. For a modem connection, change the setting to 1 or 2. For ADSL or cable, experiment with a setting of between 2 and 5. For a fast symmetrical DSL, try a setting of between 5 and 10. (You can set higher numbers if you want, but once you get more than a few clients, their downloads will be miserably slow.)

Max Simultaneous Downloads/Client text box   This text box controls how many simultaneous downloads HotLine Server allows each client. The default setting is 10, but you'll probably want to reduce it to 1 for a modem connection or 2 for anything faster.

Play Sounds check box   Leave this check box selected (as it is by default) if you want HotLine Server to play sounds to tell you when things are happening. Clear this check box if you prefer the sound of silence.

Confirm Quit check box   Leave this check box selected (as it is by default) if you want HotLine Server to double-check that you want to quit. This setting is especially useful if your mouse or your brain is not fully under your command.

Log Downloads to File check box   Select this check box if you want HotLine Server to write a log of all files downloaded. Logging downloads will help you see what's popular with whom.

Log Uploads to File check box   Select this check box if you want HotLine Server to write a log of all files that users upload to your server. Logging uploads is a good way of monitoring incoming files, though you can also do this by trawling through your upload folders regularly.

Log Connects to File check box   Select this check box if you want HotLine Server to write a log of all connections. Logging connections will help you spot troublesome users.

Log Account Changes to File check box   Select this check box if you want HotLine Server to write a log of all account changes. Having such a log typically helps with account administration.

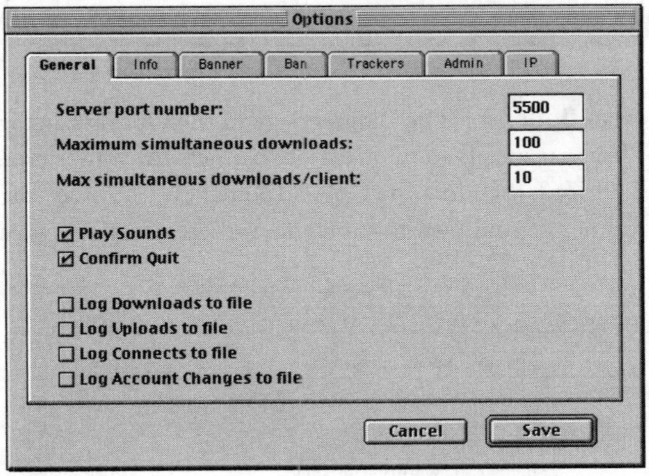

Figure 8.73

The General page of the Options dialog box for Hot-Line Server

Info Page Options   The Info page of the Options dialog box (shown in Figure 8.74) contains two text fields for information about your server:

Name text box   Enter the name for your server in this text box. Be original.

Description text box   Enter the description for your server in this text box. Be descriptive rather than original here: An inaccurate description will draw disappointed users and flames. Above all, don't promise—or even imply—that the server offers a broad wealth of treasure when in fact it has only a nugget or two.

Figure 8.74

The Info page of the Options dialog box for Hot-Line Server

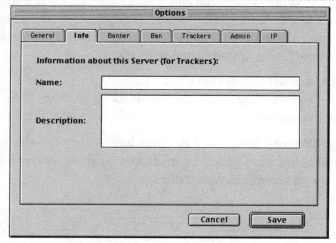

Banner Page Options   The Banner page of the Options dialog box (shown in Figure 8.75) lets you specify local or remote banners for your server. As you'll undoubtedly have noticed, the HotLine Client Toolbar cycles ads at you relentlessly. You can add in a banner of your own to supplement these ads, but you cannot get rid of them.

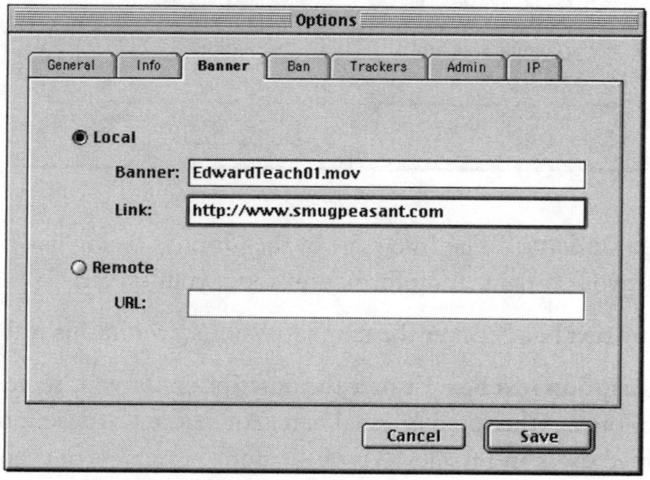

Figure 8.75

The Banner page of the Options dialog box for Hot-Line Server

To use a local banner, select the Local option button and enter the name of the banner in the Banner text box. The banner can be a GIF, a SWF, a JPG, or a MOV. It needs to be smaller than 256K, cannot have spaces in its filename, and must be placed in the same folder as HotLine Server. If you want the banner to open a URL when the user clicks it, enter the URL in the Link text box.

If you've signed up with a banner site (such as ValueClick or Adsmart), you can use a remote banner instead. To do so, select the Remote option button and enter the URL for the banner in the URL text box.

> You need to restart HotLine Server in order to get your new banner working. When you restart, check the HotLine Server Log window to make sure it's not telling you that it could not find the file. (If you do get this message, put the file in the right folder and restart HotLine Server.)

Ban Page   The Ban page of the Options dialog box lets you keep a list of banned IP addresses. I'll show you how to do this later in the chapter.

Trackers Page   The Trackers page of the Options dialog box lets you list your server with HotLine Trackers. I'll discuss this later in the chapter.

Admin Page   The Admin page of the Options dialog box lets you specify an admin account and reset it if necessary. I'll discuss these actions later in the chapter.

IP Page   The IP page of the Options dialog box (shown in Figure 8.76) lets you specify which IP address HotLine should bind to. This capability is useful only if you have multiple IP addresses for your computer. If you have a single IP address, as most people do, leave the Server IP text box set to 0.0.0.0. (0.0.0.0 isn't your computer's IP address, but it causes HotLine Server to bind to the computer's IP address.)

Click the Save button to apply your changes and to close the Options dialog box.

Creating Your Agreement

Next, you remember that the HotLine Server Log window was complaining that it couldn't find the agreement file. That's because you need to create one.

Figure 8.76

The IP page of the Options dialog box for HotLine Server

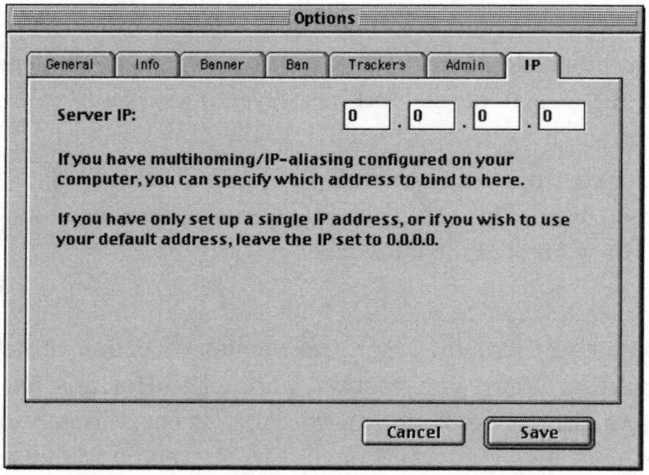

Open SimpleText and type the text you want for your agreement. You can enter pretty much anything you want; you'll probably draw some inspiration from the agreements you've encountered as a HotLine Client user.

Save the file under the name **Agreement** in the HotLine Server folder. Then click the Reload button on the HotLine Server Toolbar to reload the server. You should see the line *Loaded file "Agreement"* appear in the HotLine Server Log window. (If not, chances are you saved the file under the wrong name or in the wrong place. Try again.)

Now that the agreement has been loaded, anyone trying to connect to your server for the first time will see it and will need to click its Agree button to connect.

Setting Up Folders for Sharing

Next, you need to set up folders for the files you want to share and one or more upload folders for files that you'll receive. To set up folders, you can use either Hot-Line Client or the Mac Finder.

If you're creating a lot of folders, you'll probably find the Finder easier. Create the folder structure you want within the `Hotline Server : Files` folder.

To create an upload folder, create a folder as usual but include either the word *upload* or the words *drop box* in its name. HotLine Server treats such folders as upload folders.

If you're creating a small number of folders, you can use HotLine Client instead as follows:

1. Click the Files button on the HotLine Client Toolbar (or choose Hotline ➤ Show Files or press Apple+F) to display the Files window. Figure 8.77 shows the Files window with the beginnings of a folder structure in place.

Figure 8.77

Use the Files window to set up folders for sharing.

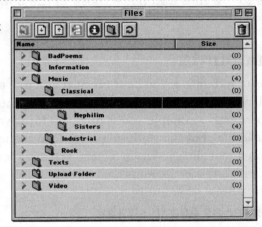

2. To create a folder within the currently selected folder, click the New Folder button. HotLine Client displays the Create Folder dialog box (shown in Figure 8.78).

Figure 8.78

Enter the name for the new folder in the Create Folder dialog box.

3. Enter the name for the folder in the text box and click the Create button to create it.

4. Click the Refresh button to refresh the display in the Files window, and the new folder appears.

Adding Files to the Folders

Once you've set up your folder structure for sharing, populate the download folders with files. You'll find this easiest to do by using the Finder.

Rather than copying files into the download folders, you may want to create aliases to the files and place those in the download folders.

Creating Accounts

Next, you need to create accounts. If you have a regular group of people that you share files with, you'll do well to create individual accounts for them with privileges appropriate to each person. For example, you may choose to allow some people only to download and upload files, but allow others to download and upload both files and folders. Others yet you might allow to create folders. You might even create other administrators who can create user accounts themselves.

Log into Your Server as Administrator

In order to create accounts, you need to log into your server as administrator. Here's how to do so:

1. Start HotLine Client.

2. Click the Connect to Server button on the Servers window to display the Connect dialog box (shown in Figure 8.79 with settings chosen).

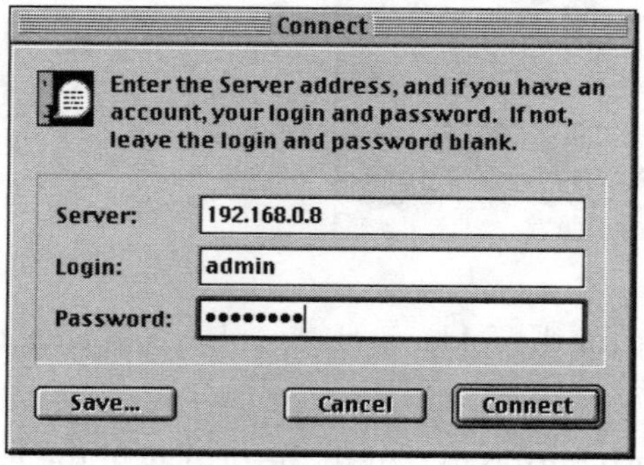

Figure 8.79

Connect to your server as admin.

Connect

Enter the Server address, and if you have an account, your login and password. If not, leave the login and password blank.

Server:	192.168.0.8
Login:	admin
Password:	••••••••

Save...   Cancel   Connect

3. In the Server text box, enter the IP address of the server. (Remember that this address is displayed at the top of the HotLine Server Toolbar.)

4. Enter **admin** in the Login text box and your admin password in the Password text box.

5. If you want to be able to access your server easily (as is likely), click the Save button to display the dialog box shown in Figure 8.80. Enter a descriptive name in the Save Bookmark As text box (HotLine Server suggests your IP address, but you can probably improve upon this) and click the Save button. HotLine Server saves the bookmark and closes the dialog box, returning you to the Connect dialog box.

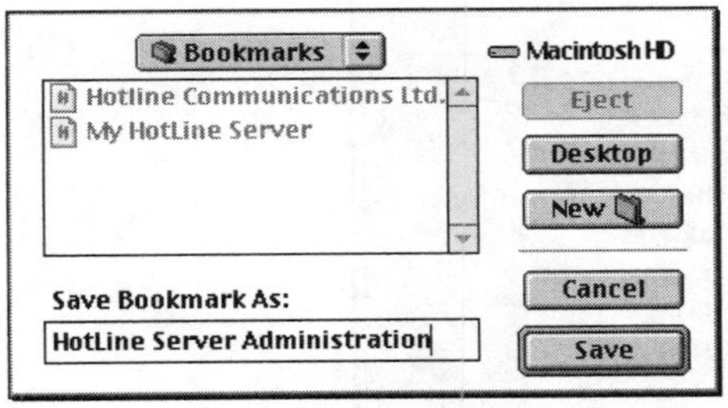

Figure 8.80

Create a bookmark for your server so that you can access it quickly to administer it.

6. Click the Connect button in the Connect dialog box to connect to your server. HotLine Server displays the Agreement dialog box.

7. Click the Agree button.

You're now logged into your server as admin and can perform administrative actions. The HotLine Client Toolbar displays two additional buttons, the New User button and the Open User button, as shown in Figure 8.81.

Figure 8.81

When you're logged into your server as admin, the HotLine Client Toolbar displays two extra buttons for administrative tasks.

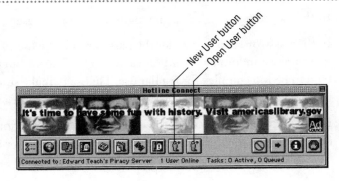

Creating User Accounts

To create a user account, you need to be logged into your server as admin, as described in the previous section. Then follow these steps:

1. Click the New User button on the HotLine Client Toolbar to display the New User dialog box (shown in Figure 8.82 with some information entered).

Figure 8.82

Creating a new user by using the New User dialog box

New User

Name: Ethelred Unready

Login: EthelReady

Password: 8BT1aIrHQIL2nGhEcYJ2

Access:

File System Maintenance
- ☑ Can Download Files
- ☑ Can Download Folders
- ☑ Can Upload Files
- ☑ Can Upload Folders
- ☐ Can Upload Anywhere
- ☐ Can Delete Files
- ☐ Can Rename Files
- ☐ Can Move Files

Cancel   Save

2. In the Name text box, enter the name for the account. This is a descriptive name for your use, so you may want to base it on the name—or some characteristic—of the user to help you remember it. (You can force the user to use this name rather than a name of their choice, but usually you won't want to do so.)

3. In the Login text box, enter the login name for the user.

4. In the Password text box, enter the password for the user. HotLine Server suggests a new random password for each user you create, but these passwords tend to be too complex for regular use. That said, make sure that your password is hard to crack—and use a different password for each user you create.

5. In the Access list box, select the check boxes for the actions you want the user to be able to take and make sure the check boxes for all other actions are

cleared. The actions are divided into six categories: File System Maintenance, User Maintenance, Messaging, News, Chat, and Miscellaneous.

- For most users, assign a basic set of permissions such as the following (the default for HotLine Server at this writing): Can Download Files, Can Download Folders, Can Upload Files, Can Upload Folders, Can Send Messages, Can Read Articles, Can Post Articles, Can Initiate Private Chat, Can Read Chat, Can Send Chat, and Can Use Any Name.

- Restrict actions such as commenting files, creating, moving, and deleting folders, and all user maintenance actions to administrators.

- Keep the number of administrators to a minimum in order to keep your server secure.

- If you want to force the user to use the descriptive name (the name you entered in the Name text box), clear the Can Use Any Name check box in the Miscellaneous section. If you leave this check box selected, as it is by default, the user can log in under any name they choose.

6. Click the Save button to save the new user account and to close the New User dialog box.

Creating a Guest Account

If your server will be public, you'll probably want to create a guest account as well. (If your server is private and invitation-only, you'll have no need of a guest account.) As you'll have noticed from your use of HotLine Client, most guest accounts are extremely limited in what they can do. This is partly because restricting your guests' potential for damage is good for security and partly because HotLine Server by default grants few privileges to the guest account.

To create a guest account, follow the procedure for creating a new account described in the previous section, but assign the account the login name **guest**. Modify the default set of guest privileges if you want, and then click the Save button to save the account.

Log out as admin, then try logging into your server on the guest account. Make sure that the account works as you expect it to, and that its privileges are wide enough to let each guest get a picture of what your server offers and why they might want to get a regular account on it.

Modifying a User Account

To modify a user account you've created:

1. Click the Open User button on the HotLine Client Toolbar to display the Open User dialog box (shown in Figure 8.83).

Figure 8.83

The Open User dialog box

2. Enter the login name of the user account in the text box and click the Open button. HotLine Server displays the account in the Edit User dialog box (shown in Figure 8.84). You'll notice that this dialog box bears a strong family resemblance to the New User dialog box.

Figure 8.84

Use the Edit User dialog box to modify the permissions for a user account—and to delete a user account.

3. Change the permissions for the user account as appropriate.

4. Click the Save button to save the changes to the user account and to close the Edit User dialog box.

Deleting a User Account

To delete a user account, open the user account in the Edit User dialog box as described in the previous section. Then click the Delete button. HotLine Server displays the Delete User dialog box (shown in Figure 8.85) to confirm the deletion. Click the Delete button.

Figure 8.85

HotLine Server checks that you want to delete the user account.

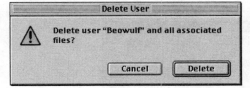

Dealing with Miscreants

If you make your server an even semi-public forum, you'll get some people on it who will misbehave. When they do so, you can take several actions:

☠ Castigate them verbally

☠ Kick them off your server

☠ Delete their account

☠ Ban them from your server

The next three subsections discuss the latter three options. (The verbal castigation I'll leave in your court.)

To take any of these actions, you need to be logged in as admin.

Kicking a User off Your Server

If a user continues to misbehave after being chastised, your first step should be to kick them off your server.

To do so:

1. Log in as admin (if you're not logged in thus already).

2. Display the Users window by clicking the Users button on the HotLine Client Toolbar, by choosing Hotline ➤ Show Online Users, or by pressing Apple+U.

3. Select the user in the user list.

4. To disconnect the user but allow them to reconnect immediately, click the Disconnect button. The user sees a Connection Closed message box (shown in Figure 8.86).

Figure 8.86

When you kick a user off your server, they see a Connection Closed message box like this.

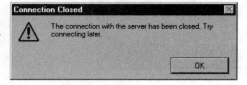

5. To disconnect the user and prevent them from reconnecting for 30 minutes, hold down the Option key and click the Disconnect button. HotLine Server displays the Ban User dialog box (shown in Figure 8.87).

Figure 8.87

When you ban a user for 30 minutes, HotLine Server displays the Ban User dialog box.

Click the Ban button to proceed. The user sees a Connection Closed dialog box (as in Figure 8.86) followed by an Administrator Message message box (shown in Figure 8.88).

If the user tries to reconnect to the server within their half hour of disgrace, they see a Server Message message box such as that shown in Figure 8.89.

Figure 8.88

The Administrator Message message box informs the user that they've been temporarily banned from the server.

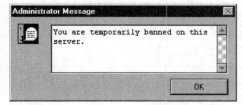

Figure 8.89

The Server Message message box lets the user know that the ban is still in effect when they try to reconnect.

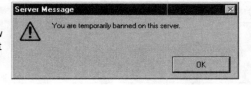

Banning a User by IP Address

If kicking a user off your server and axing their account strikes you as unsatisfyingly impermanent, you can go the extra millimeter and ban the user by IP address. Banning by IP address works better for users with fixed IP addresses than for dial-up connections (most of which are dynamically assigned an IP address from their ISP's pool each time they connect), but you'll feel a surge of godlike power anyway. (If you find a miscreant keeps coming back from a different IP address, nuke their account.)

To ban a user by IP address:

1. Click the Options button on the HotLine Server Toolbar to display the Options dialog box.

2. Click the Ban tab to display the Ban page (shown in Figure 8.90).

3. Enter the offender's IP address in the IP text box.

4. Enter any relevant information in the Info text box. For example, you might want to enter the user's name for reference or a brief note of their sins.

5. Click the Add button to add the IP address to the banned list.

6. Click the Save button to apply your changes and to close the Options dialog box.

Figure 8.90

The Ban page of the Options dialog box for Hot-Line Server

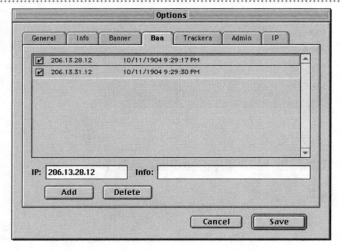

Figure 8.90

The Ban page of the Options dialog box for Hot-Line Server

Unless you've a wonderful memory for user names and IP addresses, log files can be invaluable for keeping track of offenders that you may need to ban.

Selecting a Head Admin Account

If you end up running a big server operation and create multiple admin accounts, you may at some point need to choose between them. Here's how to do so:

1. Click the Options button on the HotLine Server Toolbar to display the Options dialog box.

2. Click the Admin tab to display the Admin page (shown in Figure 8.91).

3. Click the Select button to display the Select Head Admin Account dialog box (shown in Figure 8.92).

4. To use an existing account, select the account in the list box and click the OK button. HotLine Server closes the Select Head Admin Account dialog box.

5. To create a new account, click the Create New button to display the Create New Admin Account dialog box (shown in Figure 8.93).

Figure 8.91

The Admin page of the Options dialog box for HotLine Server

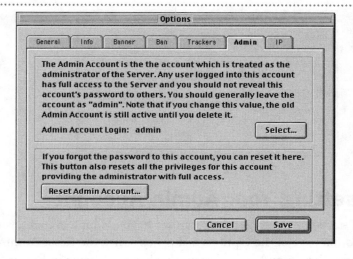

Figure 8.92

In the Select Head Admin Account dialog box, select the account to use as head admin.

6. Enter the login for the new head admin account in the Login text box, enter the password in the Password text box and the Verify Password text box, and click the Create button to create the account. HotLine Server closes the Create New Admin Account dialog box and returns you to the Options dialog box.

Figure 8.93

Alternatively, use the Create New Admin Account dialog box to create a new head admin account.

Resetting Your Admin Account

If you screw up and forget the password to your admin account, you can reset it from the Admin page of the Options dialog box. Click the Reset Admin Account button to display the Reset Admin Account dialog box (shown in Figure 8.94), enter the new password in the New Admin Password text box and the Verify New Password text box, and click the OK button.

Figure 8.94

If you forget the password to your admin account, use the Reset Admin Account dialog box to reset it.

Listing Your Server with HotLine Trackers

If you've decided to make your server public, you may want to list it with HotLine trackers so that people know about it. (Your other options are to let it advertise itself by word of mouth or to plug it on newsgroups or chat channels.) You can register with up to five trackers at a time; if you find you're not getting as much attention as you want, you may need to drop some trackers and sign up with others. You'll find details of trackers at the HotLine Communications Web site (**www.bigredh.com**).

To list your server with HotLine trackers:

1. Click the Options button on the HotLine Server Toolbar to display the Options dialog box.

2. Click the Trackers tab to display the Trackers page (shown in Figure 8.95).

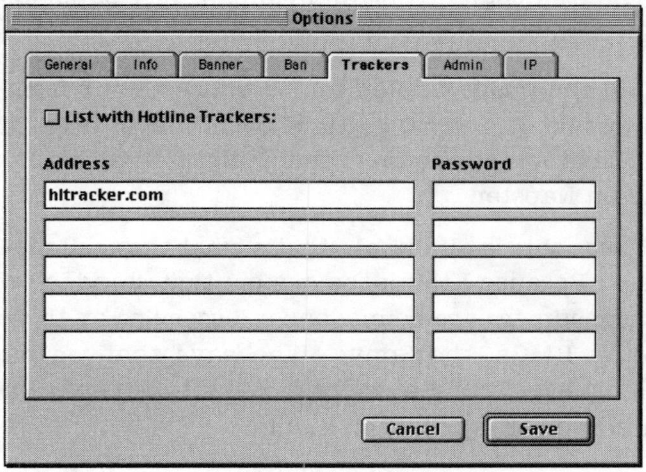

Figure 8.95

The Trackers page of the Options dialog box for Hot-Line Server

3. Select the List with HotLine Trackers check box.

4. Enter the address of each tracker in the Address text box and its password (if it uses one) in the Password text box.

5. Click the Save button to apply your changes.

Up Next

This chapter discussed the key tools that the professional digital pirates use to exchange files securely with one another: NetMeeting for Windows and HotLine for the Mac. Both NetMeeting and HotLine are designed for legitimate uses, but they happen to lend themselves to digital piracy just as easily.

That's it for the tools. The next chapter discusses the future of digital piracy, the future of digital content, and the future of P2P file-sharing. Read on, Macduff!

A Pirate Speaks: The Revolutionary Music Pirate

I don't consider myself a pirate so much as I consider myself a revolutionary.

I download all the music I listen to. I download stuff from Napster. I burn CDs. I just bought an 80-gig hard drive that's three-quarters full already; I'll have to get another soon. I digitized all my old CDs and put them up on Napster.

Although I guess this is all illegal—that's what they tell me—I do it for a good reason: Because I think the system that stands now is wrong. I think that consumers are being done a disservice by these huge corporations—the BMGs, the Sonys. Who says that we have to buy albums? It's not even fair that we're forced into buying 15 songs when we only want two songs out of an album.

The Internet makes it possible for these recording companies to sell their products to benefit the consumer. If I only want to download one song from a CD, I should be able to do that. If I want to download the entire album, I should be able to do that too. Maybe they could give me a bonus or a discount if I downloaded the entire CD. Maybe they charge me $2 for one track, $3 for two tracks—whatever pricing scale works. It seems as though they have the opportunity to be fair to the consumer now, with the Internet—and they're not doing that. They want to preserve their domination, their monopoly on sales. And it's just not fair.

I consider myself one of those people who can help break down the system. I feel like a revolutionary. I feel like things have got to change.

A Pirate Speaks: The Revolutionary Music Pirate (*continued*)

The Internet allows us to change. It allows a fair and equitable distribution. It allows consumers to pick and choose what they like. Why should I be limited to whatever music companies want to print? There are hundreds of CDs that are out of print that I'd like to have, but they're not available any more. I just think that they should make everything available for download and let us download individual songs. I think it would be good for them; I think it would be good for the industry; I think it would be good for everybody, especially the consumer.

And so what I do right now is, I don't buy CDs any more. The record companies have the means to sell us tracks individually, and they don't do it. They have the means, instead of charging $16 for a CD, of charging $1 a track for 16 tracks. They aren't doing that, and I think that's the only fair way of doing things.

So the way it stands right now, I encourage everybody to download stuff, burn their own CDs, take the CDs that they have and make them available on Napster for everybody else until the music industry gets the hint, until they start tailoring their sales to the consumer. It's happened in the retail sales, where the company with the best offerings to the consumer is the one that survives, and that's the way it should be in the music industry too. But because these huge conglomerates dominate the market, they can force us to buy things that we don't want to buy at prices that are way too high.

We have a chance now with the Internet to be revolutionaries. So I say, boycott the CDs, boycott the industry, steal as much as you possibly can, because that's the only way we're going to bring about change that's fair for everybody.

chapter 9

The Future of Piracy, Digital Content, and P2P

Featuring

This chapter attempts to wrap up the book by discussing the future of piracy, the future of digital content, and the future of P2P and information-sharing on the Net.

I say "attempts" because, despite my best efforts, I'm betting I'll be wrong in about two-thirds of what I say. I've performed five Tarot spreads, examined the leaves in several cups of tea, and dug my hands through the entrails of several live chickens—but what they say isn't clear. So far, the Internet has comprehensively defeated every attempt by soothsayers and sages to predict how it will evolve. Doubtless it will likewise defeat my feeble efforts at prophecy—but I offer them nonetheless.

(I was kidding about the chickens. They were dead, and the only entrails they had were a few pretending to be giblets. All these presaged—and correctly—was that I would need to remember to take out the trash come garbage day.)

Digital Piracy Forever

Whatever else happens, digital piracy will continue. Short of disassembling the Internet, there's no way the authorities can wipe out digital piracy.

Not that they won't try. In the next few years, we're likely to see new legislation intended to protect copyright further. Such legislation will be designed to build on the NET Act and DMCA and will seek to limit the rights of consumers by extending the rights of content producers and distributors. We'll also see new technologies that take advantage of the anti-circumvention measures in the DMCA. And we'll see new, probably illegal technologies that crack the protective technologies.

That digital piracy will continue seems certain. Much less certain, though, are the forms that digital piracy will take. Here's where the crystal ball gets murky.

Going Underground: Post-Napster P2P Technologies Take Over

As discussed a little later in this chapter, Napster seems doomed either to mutate into a corporate shadow of its former, much-loved self in pursuit of legitimacy and profits or to be nuked into oblivion by an onslaught of high-megaton lawyers.

Shed a tear and spend a moment of silence. Now wipe your eye. Even if Napster gets nuked, post-Napster P2P technologies will rise quickly to rule the resulting empire of insects and grass. Will rise? They're there already: As you saw in Chapter 7, "Post-Napster Technologies," audioGnome offers a fuller Napster experience without the central network of servers that makes Napster itself vulnerable to the authorities. Gnutella provides a bombproof peer-to-peer network that can be used to share just about any file. Freenet was designed specifically so that it cannot be shut down without an enormous amount of effort. And these three technologies are most likely only the visible tip of the P2P iceberg.

Bandwidth, Bandwidth Everywhere...

As you saw in Chapter 1, "Digital Piracy 101," one of the crucial factors that enabled wide-scale piracy was an increase in bandwidth. This increase was crucial because it enabled people to download large files in timeframes of minutes rather than hours or days.

At this writing, bandwidth is borderline acceptable for many people in the U.S. and Canada. Cable and DSL connections are available to about a third of households in the United States and Canada—mostly those living within cannon-shot of a small, medium, or giant–economy-size city. ISDN connections are available to a slightly wider area. Satellite connections are available to most anyone willing to pay for them and suffer their attendant disadvantages (such as needing to use a phone line for upstream data transfer and unfair fair access policies). A fortunate few have fiber and are dumbstruck at their luck. Everyone else is stuck with dial-up connections of 56K or less and is more or less resigned to putting up with the squeals of modems mating for a year or two longer.

It's hardly controversial to say that bandwidth will continue to improve. It has to, for several reasons:

Convergence   Gone (almost) are the old days when the wretched consumer paid separate bills for their telephone, for cable television, and Internet access. The savvy and amalgamated providers of the 21st century aim to sell you all of the above in one delightful bundle. Hell, some electric companies would like to sell you telephony, Internet access, and cable television over their power lines along with your electricity.

Consumer demand   Because all connected consumers crave almost infinite amounts of bandwidth, it's a very saleable commodity.

The Holy Grail   Not to be religious, but the Holy Grail of high-resolution video on demand to the home seems attainable in the near-ish future. Video on demand is expected to stimulate a huge increase in consumer spending on entertainment, not all of it on pornography.

So bandwidth will continue to improve—but it cannot improve soon enough for most users. It's hard to imagine having too much bandwidth or paying too little for it.

In the U.S., the technologies that deliver this increased bandwidth will essentially be more of the same: The meek shall inherit fiber-optics to their new residences, the sheep will enjoy their cable and DSL, and the goats will suffer through ISDN, dial-up, and the FAPs of satellite providers.

In other areas of the world, such as Europe, broadband wireless connectivity promises fast connections without needing to worry about the crucial "last mile" of cable or telephone wire to the home. Wireless connectivity is especially promising for roving business professionals, schools and campuses, and anyone who likes to move their laptop computer around the house. But if wireless providers can deliver fast and affordable access across large markets before wired providers can provide an analogous service, the wireless providers may be able to sail to windward of the wired and blow them out of the water.

Music

Here's what's likely to happen with music.

MP3 Remains Big for the Foreseeable Future

Despite the best efforts of the music industry to agree on a secure, high-quality audio format and force their customers to use it, MP3 will remain a major part (if not the dominant part) of the digital-audio scene.

Here's why:

- ☠ MP3 gives the consumer near-total freedom to do what they want with their music. While files in some other digital-audio formats are locked to a particular computer, an MP3 file is freely portable. Given widely available hardware, you can play MP3 files on your PC, on your home stereo, in your car, or when you're on the move.

- ☠ MP3 gives high-enough audio quality for about 95 percent of consumers. Secure digital-audio formats already boast higher audio quality than MP3, but their attendant disadvantages for the consumer make them unattractive compared to MP3. For example, some secure formats lock a track to the computer on which it is created, so that you can't play it from another computer or load it on a portable player. Other formats can be created only with expensive and complex tools that are not available to the general public.

- ☠ MP3 files are small enough to be portable. Some other digital-audio formats (such as a2b) offer smaller file sizes than MP3 together with similar or higher audio quality, but the difference in file size is not enough to make consumers forsake the freedom of MP3 for a restricted format.

- ☠ A huge amount of music is available now in MP3 format, and more music is encoded to MP3 files every day.

- ☠ Napster may mutate into a paid service with limited content, but post-Napster P2P technologies make all music in MP3 format available to anyone with an Internet connection.

- ☠ You can create your own MP3 files easily using a PC or a custom hardware device, whereas with secure digital-audio formats, it can be expensive, difficult, or even impossible to create your own files.

- ☠ Any audio file released in a secure format is likely to be cracked and encoded to MP3 almost immediately.

Music on a Subscription Basis

The future may involve customers getting music (and perhaps other content) on a subscription basis. The main thrust towards this is the Napster–Bertelsmann deal, by which Napster appears to be moving toward delivering music on a subscription basis.

The New Napster

At first sight, the new Napster service hinted at by Napster, Inc. and Bertelsmann has a certain appeal. On the face of it, all-you-can-eat music downloads for a small but regular fee ($5 a month was mentioned) could prove interesting to a number of Napster users. But there are a couple of fat maggots in the ointment:

- ☠ First, it seems likely that the entire framework of Napster will change. Instead of downloading files from other users, Napster users will download the files from central servers. Napster will change overnight from a P2P experience to a B2C experience.

- ☠ Second, unless Napster, Inc. can pull off some truly stunning deals with other record companies and artists, the selection of music available on the new service will be severely limited. If the new Napster service is limited to the Bertelsmann catalog, extensive though that catalog is, the service will die very quickly.

That said, there's a more positive side to it. Central servers should provide several advantages, including a higher (or more standardized) quality of music files, constant availability, and better performance. Less materially, the music files will be legal to possess, so users won't need to fear the copyright police. Presumably the downloads will be secure, so users won't be able to share them with other people. It's not clear how freely users will be able to use the files (on the computer they used to download them or on portable players as well?), but the suggestion has been that the files would be downloaded and stored on the user's computer rather than streamed on demand.

If the new Napster goes ahead, I predict that free and unstoppable post-Napster services such as audioGnome and Gnutella will pick up much of the Napster user base.

Subscription Music on Central Servers

Another possibility for music on a subscription basis has been receiving some attention recently. Under this model, the consumer pays for a subscription to a panoply of music stored on central servers operated by some friendly and probably horrendously rich media company. The consumer can access the music from wherever they are with the use of any convenient device, from a mobile phone to a TV to a computer.

The consumer is usually assumed to play the music via streaming rather than downloading it and saving it to any form of storage. The files would be encrypted in some way to prevent the casual user from saving the files, so the only copies would be available online. The consumer would be able to create and save favorites and playlists so that they could quickly access the music they liked.

This model is clearly attractive to the media companies for several reasons:

- First, the content is notionally secure. In practice, any consumer will be able to create slightly lower-quality files by recording the stream, and anyone prepared to fiddle with software will be able to hijack the audio stream at (or before) the sound card and record a full-quality digital version of that. But never mind—in theory, the content is secure.

- Second, the media companies receive a constant stream of money from the subscriptions. These subscriptions start off low as the media companies have to compete with each other, but sooner or later the media companies gobble each other up (or AOL buys them). Then the winner gets to enjoy the next best thing to a monopoly and can gradually rack up the fees.

- Third, the media companies enjoy drastically reduced costs. Instead of having to spend tens of millions of dollars on creating physical media, trucking them all over the world, and mulching the losers into landfill, they just have to run a few colossal server farms located somewhere inexpensive (Virginia if the winner is AOL, Bavaria if it's Bertelsmann, South Dakota for anyone else).

- Fourth, the media companies get a fantastic wealth of statistics on their customers—what they listen to, how often they listen to the tracks, and where they are at the time. (That mobile phone will be giving your location every second—hell, they do that already.) If the super-server model works, you'd doubt that the media companies would try to sell their customers the same music on physical media as well. (You *would* doubt that, wouldn't you?) But without question the media companies would hit their customers with all sorts of special offers related to the music they listen to.

But it's hard to see this model working in the real world and the foreseeable future. The first problem is bandwidth. This model requires enormous amounts of bandwidth to be constantly available. The consumers would want high-fidelity audio—better quality than radio, let's assume—and they would want instant access to it at any second of the day or night from every device they'd been told would work. The bandwidth isn't universally available now and won't be for a while, and the technology is far from robust enough to deliver the reliability that consumers will want.

The second problem is that the model assumes that consumers will take to using the devices supplied or approved by the media company rather than the devices they already have. Can you see the pitch? "Just throw out your Walkman, Discman, and MP3 player, and upgrade your mobile phone and your satellite dish!" Look around you, and you'll see plenty of people still enjoying their music on vinyl and cassettes. Even of those who have moved on to digital media (such as CDs and DVDs), many will prefer to stick with the physical media that they know and trust.

The third problem is that MP3 and other digital audio formats will still be around. At this writing, MP3 already dominates the digital audio scene and is still gaining velocity because it gives users high enough audio quality and total control over how they listen to their music. Even supposing that another digital audio format overtakes MP3 in the next few years, that format will be an even tougher nut for the subscription model to crack.

Big Five Nosedive

The Big Five record companies (Sony, Warner, EMI, Columbia, and Bertelsmann) are facing the transition from music being sold on physical media (primarily CDs and cassettes) to music being sold digitally. At this writing, none of the Big Five is well positioned to ride out the transition, let alone benefit from it. While Napster and post-Napster P2P technologies appear to have contributed to an increase in CD sales, it seems highly doubtful that this effect will last.

To be fair, it's hard to see how the Big Five record companies can respond sensibly to the threat posed by the MP3 file format and Napster, audioGnome, Freenet, and other P2P file-sharing technologies—but had they been less complacent about their position in the mid to late 1990s, they might have evolved a workable digital-audio policy by now.

In perhaps the best position—certainly the most innovative position—is Bertelsmann. In October 2000, Bertelsmann made an historic deal with Napster, Inc.: Bertelsmann would drop its copyright-infringement lawsuit against Napster, Inc. and take a stake in Napster, which would develop a new, secure Napster service for providing authorized music online under a subscription model. At this writing, the other Four were considering deals with Napster, Inc.

That Four, though, might soon be Three. In November 2000, Bertelsmann made a bid for EMI. If this succeeds, it will boost the appeal of the new Napster service, though the service will need the participation of most if not all major record companies in order to appeal to the consumer.

Free, Advertising-Supported Music

Good news for music fans is that they'll see an increasing amount of advertising-supported music. The ad-supported model has been around for a while on the Web: It started with textual content supported by banner ads of varying degrees of subtlety and intrusiveness and is rapidly spreading to music: Witness the number of artists who judge it wise (or expedient) to give away a number of tracks via sites such as MP3.com.

Driven by the growing force of P2P technologies, MP3 is spreading faster than a firestorm in New Mexico. And as a result, artists and some record companies are finding that music is far less saleable than it used to be. At this writing, CDs are still selling in historic (if not heroic) quantities, but this is partly because people are so used to buying CDs that they're slow to realize that digital audio can provide a quick and clean escape from physical media.

But once that realization sinks in, the record companies' current business model starts looking like roadkill. If people can get music for free in digital format, that same music becomes a tougher sell than bibles at an atheists' convention. The music may still be saleable on physical media (say, CDs), but you have to give people a reason to prefer paying for the physical medium. One way of doing this might be to spruce up the CD (or whatever) with designs, holograms, and the modern equivalent of the guitar-shaped 7" singles of the 1980s. Another way might be to package each CD with an attractive widget such as a T-shirt. But of course, neither option exactly enhances the record company's bottom line, where the pain is already starting to make itself known.

Failing this type of gimmick, the challenge becomes to create a business model in which the music is free but the artists (and perhaps the record companies) make money in another way. At this writing, some enterprising artists are using MP3 and P2P to fuel demand for concert tickets, T-shirts, baseball caps, and other souvenirs—but these artists are mostly the guys who have shirked the shackles offered by the record companies.

Movies, Video and DVD, and TV

Here's what's likely to happen with movies, video and DVD, and TV.

Digital Video Killed the Movie Star

Well—maybe. Actually, rather the opposite. There's every sign that movies will continue to thrive at least as much as they currently do. The better studios will prosper, particularly those able to adapt to shooting movies with digital cameras and using the Internet to promote them. *The Blair Witch Project* remains perhaps the best halfway-recent example of successful Internet promotion, but Mike Figgis' *Timecode* arguably provides a better example of the advantages of digital cameras.

Until projectors become incredibly inexpensive, the movie theater will remain the premier way of getting your brains blown out by thunderous THX blasts. The best efforts of pirates notwithstanding, it seems likely that the studios and the movie theaters will keep their security sewn up tight enough to prevent quality copies of newly released movies from being circulated. By maintaining a staged release schedule (movie theaters; pay per view; DVD and video; premium TV channels; non–premium TV channels), the movie studios can continue to milk each movie for as much as possible.

The theater stage of release is mostly secure. The pay-per-view stage is acceptably secure (though this will change as better digital video capturing technologies become widespread). As soon as a movie is released on DVD or broadcast digitally, however, all security bets are off. The DMCA notwithstanding, the DeCSS cat is now thoroughly out of the bag, and DVD-ripping software is widely available. So all DVD releases will be ripped as quickly as all CD releases. As bandwidth increases, video file-sharing will become more commonplace. If Joe and Jane Public have enough bandwidth and storage space to download and keep movies, the future for DVD sales looks uncertain. Just as P2P technologies are threatening the market for CDs, they will threaten the market for DVDs.

Outdated, poor quality, and despicably analog though it is, videotape will be around for a long time to come because VCRs and videotapes are ubiquitous and deeply dug into the fabric of life. Most households in the U.S. and Canada have a VCR and anything from a handful to a cupboardful of video cassettes; a good number have video cameras as well. Even if video-digitizing technologies become inexpensive and widely available, few people will bother to digitize their tapes, preferring to stick with the simplicity of the existing machinery.

TV and Movies on Demand

At the moment, we're seeing a gradual movement away from programmed TV towards customer choice. This movement will accelerate rapidly as soon as high-resolution video on demand becomes practical and affordable.

Once video on demand is available, we'll see a struggle between the media companies and consumers. As with music content, it seems likely that the media companies will try to shunt customers towards purchasing content and storing video content on centralized servers online, where the media companies can keep an eye on it and track each usage of it. However, customers will continue to prefer to store content locally so that they can access it immediately and without being monitored by the content provider or supplier.

On the consumer's side are the new time-shifting technologies such as TiVo, which essentially acts like an intelligent digital video recorder on steroids. On the media companies' side are the limitations and "features" built into those technologies. For example, most digital recorders will be set up so that the user cannot easily export the programs they've recorded (for example, to a PC for sharing or extra storage), and most are designed to report back to the media companies on what the consumer has watched, giving them valuable marketing information.

Ad-Free TV?

Tech-regret moment: TiVo was originally designed to offer consumers an ad-skip function. This was engineered out of it at the request of the financial backers, who didn't want to alienate their advertisers by appearing to deliver a product that would kill advertising. Instead, TiVo offers a 30-second skip, which works well for ads in 30-second increments.

But even without the ad-skip function, TiVo threatens advertising-supported TV. Because TiVo lets the user time-shift programs both in the conventional manner and while they're still in progress (for example, by pausing the show and then catching up to the real-time broadcast by skipping the ads), it enables the user to avoid all advertising. If such digital recorders become widespread, as they may well do when prices drop, they may threaten the whole model of advertising-supported TV.

Graphics and Digital Piracy

As mentioned in Chapter 1, the effect that digital piracy is having on the graphical arts is hard to gauge. While P2P technologies will doubtless continue to be used to share graphics, especially pornography, it's unlikely that this field will grow as quickly as video or to the size of music.

Books: The Fall of the House of Gutenberg?

As you saw in Chapter 1, books are far less vulnerable than audio or video to digital piracy because of the time and effort involved in extracting their text (and pictures, if there are any) cleanly from the pages. Moreover, barring a great transformation on the part of readers and *pace* Microsoft and their ClearType technology for improving text on LCD screens, paper remains the best medium for reading a whole bunch of words comfortably. Books are also portable and convenient.

E-books such as the eBooks from Gemstar promise benefits to those prepared to read on screen: the capacity to carry the equivalent of 50lb of books in a single portable device, the capability to do full-text searching, and the ability to place and access bookmarks. But the relative difficulty of getting the books you want in electronic format and loading them onto the device means that e-books will continue to be a specialty market for a number of years. Getting used to reading on screen is another hurdle, but most people who have persevered with this find it tolerable or better. Hey, it's just another paradigm shift. Another couple of generations and books may seem pretty weird.

As mentioned earlier, the Web has provided a large amount of advertising-supported text content. This is likely to continue.

Software and Digital Piracy

As discussed in Chapter 1, software has been heavily affected by digital piracy for a number of years, and the effect has grown because many users are now using more software and because P2P technologies and CD recorders have made it easier than ever before to pirate software. This piracy seems sure to continue.

At the same time, freeware and advertising-supported software will continue to grow. Linux is huge already and gaining in market share every week in both business and home settings.

At this writing, the use of advertising in software is mostly confined to shareware products that flash ads at you until you register them. (If you've been lucky enough to miss this trend and want to see it, check out the popular download manager Go!Zilla.) For the shareware developers, the advertising works in two ways: First, they're subsidized for users who refuse to register even under provocation, and second, the advertising goads many users into registering in order to preserve their sanity.

Veni, Vidi, Trasferari

As Caesar didn't say: I came, I saw, I downloaded.

Thanks for reading this book. I hope you've found it useful, and that things hadn't changed to an unrecognizable extent between this book's going to press and your reading it.

I'll see you around online. I'm the one sharing only legal files. <g>

A Pirate Speaks: The Book Pirate

I love books. I've got thousands. But I like to read online.

I think the days of e-books are coming. I personally own three Palm Pilots—a V, a III, a IIIc—and I use my IIIc with its white background and black type as an e-book. I read a lot of books on it. I use a program called CSpotRun that has a great scrolling feature on it. I'll just prop my Palm up during a big meeting or at a table in a restaurant and set it to auto-scroll, and read whole books at a time. I've read Shakespeare plays, I've read modern novels, I've read books of poetry—it really doesn't matter, all of that stuff reads quite well. I set the font on the bold setting and set the scroll speed to my own personal speed, and that's that.

I think pretty soon this will all get more and more sophisticated. I'll probably buy an iPaq because the resolution on that thing is beautiful— it's as close to an e-reader as I can get. I can put a couple of megabytes of add-on memory into it, and it'll be the perfect e-reader. I know that Microsoft is working on an e-reader as well, too. That might be worth looking at even if it doesn't live up to their hype.

I almost always got my e-texts from Gutenberg (www.gutenberg.net). Gutenberg has an enormous amount of public-domain books that have been scanned or typed in and are now available as ASCII files or RTF files. But recently I've been finding more and more copyrighted books online—books like science-fiction books, Star Wars scripts, Clifford Simak novels, Robert Heinlein novels, things like that. Even computer books are coming online now—*The Idiot's Guide to Linux*, for example, *Zen and the Art of the Internet*—more and more all the time.

It's really easy to find all these books. You simply get on one of the many servers that's available—including Napster, because most of these copy-righted books are packaged in Wrapster format, so that people who use Napster or one of the downloading programs can pull them down as they would music. All they have to do is unwrap them at the other end.

A Pirate Speaks: The Book Pirate

Anyway, the best way to do it is to get a program like audioGnome or Napigator and list all the servers that are available and connect to as many as possible. Then type in the Search field **ebook**, and you'll literally turn up hundreds and hundreds of packages. All the Tolkien books are there. The great thing is, it's only a megabyte file for all the *Lord of the Rings* books—1.2MB. All the Heinlein novels are coming online. All the books by Tom Clancy and Larry Niven are now available. All of those copyrighted materials are now appearing as text and HTML files.

It's funny. There are probably places on the Net that offer books for sale, but you know what, I *own* all these books, and I just like to read them on my Pilot. So I'll get copyrighted books and read them, and I really don't feel compelled to pay for them because I've already paid for the hard copies, or I had them at one time. And the things that are in the public domain—well, I don't have to worry about that at all. All of Shakespeare, all of Twain, all of Poe. How is downloading these files any different from taking books out of the library?

More and more books will be coming available online as scanning and OCR technology gets better. Copyrighted book pirating is only going to increase. I'm a little ambivalent about this. A good e-reader technology might stop the stealing. I think that when the e-book machine that Microsoft talks about—that notebook-type pad—comes out and they start selling books for it, that books will become a lot less expensive than they are now. The publishers won't have to print, bind, warehouse, and distribute their books anymore. Just edit them and put them online. They'll be able to pass along all that savings to the consumer—it may even lead to a new Golden Age of reading. With auto-scrolling, changeable fonts, and intuitive interfaces, the next generation of e-readers will be as convenient and ubiquitous as wallets. Hey, that's funny: Maybe knowledge will *really* become the currency of the future.

Anyway, I'm looking forward to it when the e-book/e-reader thing happens in a big way. In the meantime, I'll continue downloading whatever is available off of Napster and off of these sites and reading them at my leisure.

Glossary of Piracy

Note: Words that appear in **boldface** are defined elsewhere in this glossary.

a2b

A proprietary, encrypted, and secure format for compressed audio. a2b was created by AT&T and claims better compression and sound quality than **MP3**.

AAC

The abbreviation for **Advanced Audio Codec**.

ADC

The abbreviation for **analog-to-digital converter**.

adidasLAN

A European term for **sneakernet**.

Advanced Audio Codec

A powerful **codec** that produces great sound and supports up to 48 channels, but it is not yet widely available in an ISO-compliant implementation. Abbreviated to *AAC*.

AHRA

The abbreviation for the **Audio Home Recording Act** of 1992.

AIFF

A standard format for uncompressed **PCM** audio. AIFF is typically used on the Macintosh.

Amiga

An early personal computer with multimedia capabilities.

amplified speakers

Speakers that contain their own amplifier or amplifiers. Usually (with consumer models), only one speaker in the set contains the amplifier.

analog signal

A continuously variable waveform. (For example, sound is a continuously variable waveform in air; changes in air pressure define the signal. Signals coming out of a sound card or amplifier output are also analog signals, but their information is carried as variations in voltage.)

analog-to-digital converter

Sound circuitry that converts an analog signal into a digital signal. For example, a sound card converts the input from an analog source (such as a microphone or a record player) to a digital signal in order to record it as an **MP3** file. Abbreviated to *ADC*.

ATRAC3

A secure and encrypted format for compressed audio created by Sony. ATRAC3 is used in **MiniDisc** players and Sony portable players such as the VAIO Music Clip and the Memory Stick Walkman.

Audio Home Recording Act

An act passed in 1992 and intended to clarify the rights and wrongs of home recording with then-current and forthcoming technologies (which included digital audio recording methods such as digital audiotape). Abbreviated to *AHRA*.

bandwidth

A measure of the amount of data that a communications channel (for example, a phone line, a network line, or a **cable modem**) can transmit per second.

basic rate interface

An **ISDN** configuration that has two bearer channels and one signaling channel (data channel).

bearer channel

A 64Kbps channel in an ISDN line.

Berne Convention

The most important of the international copyright treaties. The 100+ member countries of the Berne Convention, which include almost all the industrialized nations, agree to implement copyright protection for copyright holders who are nationals of the other member countries.

Big Five

A term used, either with or without respect, to refer to the five largest record companies: Sony, Universal, Warner, EMI, and Bertelsmann.

bitrate

The number of bits per second used to store encoded information. Bitrates are measured in kilobits per second (Kbps). A bitrate of 128Kbps is generally considered to provide almost–CD-quality sound. Most **MP3 encoders** can encode at either a **constant bitrate** (CBR) or a **variable bitrate** (VBR).

bit-rot

The degeneration of the data stored on a **CD**. Bit-rot can render an audio CD unplayable and a data CD unreadable.

BRI

The abbreviation for **basic rate interface**.

broadcast streaming audio

Streaming audio broadcast across a network or the Internet in real time. Also known as *Internet radio*.

BSA

The abbreviation for the **Business Software Alliance**.

Business Software Alliance

An international body that represents leading software and e-commerce developers in 65 countries, acts as a voice for the software industry, and fights software piracy. Abbreviated to *BSA*. Its Web site is at **www.bsa.org**.

cable modem

A device that receives and transmits data through the cabling of a cable TV system. Technically, a cable modem is *not* a modem (because it does not modulate and demodulate the signal), but the name was catchy enough to stick.

cartoonz

A term for illegal cartoons.

CBR

The abbreviation for **constant bitrate**.

CD

Compact disc. A digital audio format designed primarily for audio distribution. Audio CDs contain two channels of uncompressed digital audio recorded at 44.1KHz.

CDDB

The Compact Disc Database, an online database of CD information (including artist name, CD name, and track names). By submitting the unique CD ID number to CDDB, a ripper, player, or jukebox can retrieve the information associated with the CD.

CD-quality audio

Audio sampled at a sampling rate of 44.1KHz and a sampling precision of 16 bits. CD-quality audio is considered perfect for human hearing because the amount of information (frequency and dynamic range) it provides is enough that most people cannot hear anything missing from the audio.

CD-ROM

The abbreviation for *CD read-only memory*.

CIR

The abbreviation for **committed information rate**.

circuit switched

A connection in which a single path between endpoints exists for the full duration of the connection. For example, a normal telephone call is circuit switched: When you place a call, the telephone system establishes a connection to the number you dialed. That connection persists until you or your victim hang up. Contrast to **packet switched**.

clipping

A form of audio distortion that can occur if you overload your sound card's audio circuits. Clipping is characterized by the circuits' inability to correctly handle the amplitude of the signal. When seen on an oscilloscope, the tops and bottoms of the waveforms are flatted or "clipped" off.

codec

Software or hardware for encoding and decoding an audio signal. (This term is condensed from the term *coder/decoder*.)

committed information rate

The minimum data rate guaranteed to be available on a connection such as a **cable modem** or a frame relay circuit. Abbreviated to *CIR*.

cone

The component of a speaker that produces sound. Also sometimes called a *driver*.

constant bitrate

One method of encoding **MP3** files, by using the same **bitrate** throughout the file rather than varying the bitrate to optimize the sound. Abbreviated to *CBR*. Compare to **variable bitrate** (VBR).

Content Scrambling System

A form of encryption used to protect the contents of **DVDs** from being read by unauthorized hardware or software. Abbreviated to *CSS*.

CRC

The abbreviation for **cyclic redundancy check**.

CSS

The abbreviation for **Content Scrambling System**.

cyclic redundancy check

A type of error check that computes a checksum to verify data integrity. Abbreviated to *CRC*.

DAC

The acronym for **digital-to-analog converter**.

DAT

The abbreviation (or, to some, the acronym) for digital audio tape.

data channel

Another term for the signaling channel in an **ISDN** line.

DCC

The abbreviation for **digital compact cassette**.

DeCSS

A utility that defeats the **Content Scrambling System** used to protect the contents of DVDs and writes the encrypted files from the DVD to unencrypted files on a hard drive.

digital audio

Audio that is stored in a digitized format rather than in an analog format.

digital compact cassette

A Philips competitor for **DAT**, digital compact cassette never really caught on. Philips ceased production of digital compact cassette technology in 1996. Abbreviated to *DCC*.

digital signal processor

A category of chip for manipulating and altering sound. Abbreviated to *DSP*.

digital subscriber line

A technology for high-speed transmission of data over standard copper telephone lines. Abbreviated to *DSL*.

digital-to-analog converter

Sound circuitry that converts a digital signal into an analog signal. For example, a sound card typically converts an **MP3** file (which is digital) to an analog signal for outputting through speakers or headphones. The acronym is *DAC*.

downsample

To decrease the **bitrate** (and thus the size) of an audio signal.

driver

Another term for a **cone** in a speaker.

DSL

The abbreviation for **digital subscriber line**.

DSP

The abbreviation for **digital signal processor**.

dual-line modem

A modem that can bond two telephone lines together to produce a faster aggregate connection. Also called a *shotgun modem*.

DVD

The abbreviation for *digital versatile disc* or *digital video disc*, depending on whom you believe. A DVD can store up to 2.3GB on each of its two sides, giving a total capacity of 4.6GB.

DVD-CCA

The abbreviation for the **DVD-Copy Control Association**.

DVD-Copy Control Association

A body that oversees the copy protection on **DVDs** and licenses hardware and software players with encryption keys to decrypt the files on DVDs. Abbreviated to *DVD-CCA*.

DVD-RAM

A writable form of **DVD**.

EFF

The abbreviation for the **Electronic Frontier Foundation**.

Electronic Frontier Foundation

An organization dedicated to "protecting rights and promoting freedom in the electronic frontier." Abbreviated to *EFF*. The EFF (**www.eff.org**) gets involved in cases that may affect people's free expression, digital identity, and privacy. For example, the EFF fought the **MPAA**'s attempt to prevent the distribution of the **DeCSS** source code.

encoder

Hardware or software for creating an **MP3** file from an audio stream.

fair access policy

A policy by which some Internet access providers, typically satellite services, reserve the right to throttle back a user's download speed if the user continuously runs it at full capacity. Most users affected by fair access policies consider them poorly named. The acronym for fair access policy is *FAP*.

fair use

A provision in the Copyright Act that lets you use a portion of a copyrighted work "for purposes such as criticism, comment, news reporting, teaching (including multiple copies for classroom use), scholarship, or research" without infringing copyright. Fair use does not allow the unauthorized sharing of copyrighted intellectual property (for example, **MP3** files).

FAP

The acronym for **fair access policy**.

flikz

A term for pirated movies, pornographic or otherwise.

Fraunhofer

Fraunhofer Institute for Integrated Circuits IIS-A. The German company that created the **MP3** encoding method.

handle

On an audio CD, an electronic pointer to the audio.

home theater

A sound setup that produces **surround sound** by using a 5.1 setup (five satellite speakers with a powered subwoofer) or a 7.1 setup (seven satellite speakers with a powered subwoofer) to deliver realistic sound effects and positional audio.

icecast

A server for **streaming audio**.

IFPI

The abbreviation for the **International Federation of Phonographic Industries**.

International Federation of Phonographic Industries

An international industry body for the audio-recording and -distribution industry. Abbreviated to *IPFI*.

Internet broadcasting

Broadcasting an audio stream across the Internet. Also called *webcasting*.

Internet radio

Another term for **broadcast streaming audio**.

Internet relay chat

A global network of servers that enable users to chat in real time. Abbreviated to *IRC*.

IRC

The abbreviation for **Internet relay chat**.

ISDN

The abbreviation for *Integrated Services Digital Network*, a digital telephone line that's not as fast as a **DSL** but can be implemented over longer distances from the telephone company's central office.

jukebox

An application for organizing and playing **MP3** and other audio files.

line-level output signal

An analog signal output by a line-out jack (for example, on a sound card) that is compatible with standard line-level inputs such as those on a home stereo amplifier or cassette deck.

Liquid Audio

A digital-audio format used by a number of online music sites, including the Internet Underground Musical Archive. Liquid Audio delivers impressive audio quality and provides security features, but it has not yet achieved widespread use.

lossless compression

Compression that does not remove information from the source. The opposite of lossless compression is **lossy compression**.

lossy compression

Compression that removes information from the source in order to reduce its size. The opposite of lossy compression is **lossless compression**.

malware

A general term for software designed to have a bad effect on your computer.

MCU

The abbreviation for **multipoint control unit**.

MiniDisc

A digital audio storage medium designed to provide optimum quality with extreme portability. MiniDiscs use the proprietary **ATRAC3** compression format to store compressed audio.

Mjuice

An encrypted **MP3** format that provides the same audio quality as MP3 but lets the creator create a copy-protected version of a track that can be played back any number of times on a registered user's player but not at all on an unregistered player. Mjuice files can also contain an expiration date.

Motion Picture Association of America

With its international counterpart, the Motion Picture Association (MPA; www .mpaa.org), the Motion Picture Association of America (www.mpaa.org) acts as the voice of the American motion picture industry, home video industry, and television industry. Abbreviated to *MPAA*.

MP3

A file format for storing compressed digital audio on computers. The name refers to MPEG-1 Layer III compression and MPEG-2 Layer III compression.

MP3.com

One of the major Web sites for **MP3** music, software, and information.

MP3z

Illegal **MP3** files. Compare to **warez**.

MP4

The informal abbreviation for the MP4 Structured Audio Format, a successor to **MP3** that's currently under development.

MPAA

The abbreviation for the **Motion Picture Association of America**.

MPEG

The Moving Picture Experts Group, a working group of the International Standards Organization (ISO) and the International Engineering Consortium (IEC) in charge of developing "international standards for compression, decompression, processing, and coded representation of moving pictures, audio, and their combination." Pronounced *em-peg*.

multipoint control unit

Telephone hardware used for videoconferencing and collaboration. Abbreviated to *MCU*.

muzik

A term for pirated music, often in **MP3** format (**mp3z**).

Napster

A very popular protocol and software for **peer-to-peer** sharing of **MP3** files.

National Information Infrastructure

A U.S. administration project intended (according to the Information Infrastructure Executive Order of 1993) to provide for "the integration of hardware, software, and skills that will make it easy and affordable to connect people with each other, with computers, and with a vast array of services and information resources." Its mission includes protecting intellectual property rights, reexamining and strengthening copyright laws in the U.S. and internationally, and applying intellectual property rights and copyrights to "all forms of information in the electronic environment." Abbreviated to *NII*.

Network News Transport Protocol

The protocol used for Internet **newsgroups**. Abbreviated to *NNTP*.

newsgroups

A loose agglomeration of discussion areas based on the **Network News Transport Protocol**. A newsgroup consists of the messages (and sometimes attachments) that people post to the list.

NII

The abbreviation for **National Information Infrastructure**.

NNTP

The abbreviation for **Network News Transport Protocol**.

on-demand streaming audio

An audio stream that the listener can start and stop at his or her convenience. Compare to **broadcast streaming audio**.

online service provider

A term used by the **World Intellectual Property Organization** to describe providers of online services. The term is loosely defined and is abbreviated to *OSP*.

open headphones

Circumaural headphones that expose the back of the headphone diaphragm to the air, providing better sound but admitting more ambient noise. Contrast to **sealed headphones**.

OpenMG

A proprietary copyright-protection technology developed by Sony Corporation. OpenMG is **SDMI**-compliant and conforms to the Portable Device Specification version 1.0.

OpenMG MP3

A proprietary secure audio format developed by Sony. Despite the name, OpenMG MP3 files are not open.

OpenNap

A network of servers attached to the **Napster** network but not run by Napster, Inc.

OSP

The abbreviation for **online service provider**.

P2P

The abbreviation for **peer-to-peer**.

packet switched

(Of a network or connection) In which packets of information are sent across a shared medium rather than across a dedicated medium (as in a circuit-switched connection). Each packet in the transmission may take a different path than its predecessor. Packets are reassembled into order at the destination. Contrast to **circuit switched**.

passive speakers

Unpowered speakers, typically used with an amplifier.

PCM

The abbreviation for **pulse code modulation**.

PDA

The abbreviation for *personal digital assistant*, a small (typically hand-held) electronic device for storing and organizing information.

peak output

The maximum wattage that an audio component (such as an amplifier or speakers) can deliver momentarily. Also known as *peak power*. Contrast with **root mean square watts**.

peer-to-peer

A term used to describe technologies that let users share files with each other. For example, **Napster** and audioGnome are peer-to-peer file-sharing technologies. Abbreviated to *P2P* and also known as *person-to-person*.

personal use

A provision of the Audio Home Recording Act (AHRA) of 1992 that allows users of digital audio recording devices to make copies of copyrighted works on other media. For example, if you buy a CD, you can record it onto MiniDisc so that you can listen to it in your MiniDisc player.

person-to-person

Another term for **peer-to-peer**.

PGP

The abbreviation and best-known name for **Pretty Good Privacy**, a popular encryption program (www.pgp.com).

ping time

The amount of time that it takes for a packet of information to get from your computer to the host computer and back. A longer ping time usually means there are more hops (stages) in the connection between your computer and the host. The more hops in a connection, the more Internet resources are involved and the slower the connection will typically be.

place-shifting

Using technology to enable you to watch or listen to a work (broadcast or static) in a different place from the medium in which you received it. For example, if you record **MP3** files of the tracks from an LP so that you can load the files on your Rio or Nomad and go jogging with them, you've place-shifted them.

playlist

A file that contains the names (and, if necessary, paths) of a list of audio files. You can use playlists to organize groups of tracks that you want to treat as single units. Playlists are text files (so you can create them using a simple text editor such as Notepad in Windows) saved under an extension such as M3U or PLS. Most **MP3** players, **jukeboxes**, and organizers include playlist-editing capabilities.

plug-in

An add-in component that provides additional features for a software application.

post

Another term for a message posted to a **newsgroup**.

pressed CD

A prerecorded audio or data **CD** (as opposed to a recordable CD), pressed in a mold from a master CD.

Pretty Good Privacy

The full name of the encryption abbreviated to, and usually referred to as, **PGP**.

Project Gutenberg

A project for creating e-texts (electronic editions) of documents in the **public domain** in order to make them freely available to all computer users. The Project Gutenberg Web site is at `www.gutenberg.net`.

proxy server

A computer that relays information, stores frequently accessed information in its cache, and applies filters to requests. Proxy servers are typically used to connect a network (for example, a company network or a college network) to the Internet or to another network.

public domain

The public domain comprises all works that are (or are no longer) protected by copyright. "Public domain" and "in the public domain" are used interchangeably.

pulse code modulation

A standard format for uncompressed audio, used (among other uses) for data stored on audio CDs. Abbreviated to *PCM*.

QDesign

A digital-audio format created by QDesign Corporation. To create QDesign files, you use the QDesign Music Codec (QDMC). Unlike **MP3** codecs, which apply a standardized set of audio filters to the audio they encode, the QDMC creates custom audio filters on the fly for each signal encoded. This makes for a slower encoding process than for MP3, but it produces more accurate results, even at low bitrates. The QDesign encoder can create both QDesign files and MP3 files, and it stores its native files in **QuickTime** format.

QuickTime

Best known as a video format, QuickTime is also an effective format for audio-only files. The easiest way to create QuickTime files is to use the **QDesign** codec.

ratio site

An Internet site (usually an FTP site) that lets you download files only after you've uploaded some files to the site. Typically, a ratio site allows you to download files in some ratio to the number of files you upload.

RealAudio

A digital-audio format created by RealNetworks. Though best known and most widely used for streaming audio, RealAudio is also a viable audio-storage format, providing near–CD-quality sound at **bitrates** lower than **MP3** requires.

RIAA

The abbreviation and most widely used term for the *Recording Industry Association of America,* a trade association that represents the interests of record companies and the artists signed to them. In fighting music piracy, the RIAA has sued **Napster**, Inc. and **MP3.com**.

Rio

A series of portable **MP3** players developed by Diamond Multimedia.

ripper

A program that extracts the audio data from a **CD**.

ripper/player/jukebox

An application that combines a **ripper**, an **encoder**, a player, and **jukebox** capabilities. Examples of ripper/player/jukeboxes include MusicMatch Jukebox (for Windows and the Macintosh), RealJukebox (for Windows), and SoundJam MP (for the Macintosh).

RMS watts

The abbreviation for **root mean square watts**.

root mean square watts

The wattage that an audio component (such as an amplifier or speakers) can deliver continuously. Abbreviated to *RMS watts*. Contrast with **peak output**.

sampling

The process of examining the patterns of a sound to determine its characteristics and to convert it from an analog format into a digital format. Sampling creates a pattern of data points for the audio that are saved to a digital file. The more data points there are (sampling rate) and the larger the range of values available to represent the signal (sampling precision), the closer the audio sounds to its original.

sampling precision

The amount of information about the individual sample that is saved to the audio file. **CDs** use a **sampling** precision of 16 bits (2 bytes) per second; most people encoding **MP3** files use this sampling precision as well.

sampling rate

The frequency with which sound is examined in **sampling**. Audio sampling rates are typically measured in kilohertz (kHz). For example, CD-quality audio is sampled at 44.1 kHz.

sampling resolution

Another term for **sampling precision**.

SCMS

The abbreviation for **Serial Copy Management System**.

SDMI

The abbreviation for **Secure Digital Music Initiative**.

Secure Digital Music Initiative

A forum of more than 180 companies and organizations interested in developing a "voluntary, open framework for playing, storing, and distributing digital music in a protected form." The companies and organizations involved include the recording industry, agencies, distributors and retailers, consumer electronics companies, information technology companies, computer hardware manufacturers, and **MP3** hardware and software companies. Abbreviated to *SDMI*.

Serial Copy Management System

A serial copy control system that allows the user to create first-generation digital copies of prerecorded audio works but prevents the user from creating subsequent-generation (serial) digital copies. For example, a **MiniDisc** recorder lets you create a first-generation digital copy of a track by recording it from a **CD**, but you cannot then create subsequent digital copies from that track. Abbreviated to *SCMS*.

shotgun modem

Another term for **dual-line modem**.

SHOUTcast

A server for **streaming audio**.

SIAA

The abbreviation for the **Software & Information Industry Association**.

skin

A graphical look that you can apply to an **MP3** player or **jukebox**.

sneakernet

Networking accomplished by walking files on physical media from point A to point B; a retrofitted pun on "Ethernet." In Europe, sneakernet is sometimes called *adidasLAN*.

Software & Information Industry Association

An industry association that "represents the common business interests of the computer software and digital content industries" formed by the merger in January 1999 of the **Software Publishers Association** (SPA) and the Information Industry Association (IIA). Abbreviated to *SIAA*.

Software Publishers Association

One of the industry associations that merged into the **Software & Information Industry Association**.

sound pressure level

A measure of the air vibrations making up sound, expressed in decibels. The "loudness" (or volume) of a sound is often expressed in terms of its sound pressure level. Abbreviated to *SPL*.

SPA

The abbreviation (not acronym) for the **Software Publishers Association**.

space-shifting

Another term for **place-shifting**.

SPL

The abbreviation for **sound pressure level**.

streaming audio

An audio-delivery technique in which playback occurs while the audio is being downloaded rather than after the download is complete. Typically, streaming audio files are not saved to disk after being played. This makes streaming audio analogous to broadcasting the audio rather than distributing copies of it, thus avoiding many legal issues.

subwoofer

A speaker designed to produce bass and very low-frequency sounds. A subwoofer is usually designed for placement on the floor.

surround sound

A sound setup that uses four or five speakers to produce the effect of the listener being surrounded by the sound source.

T1

A fast dedicated phone line typically used for business. A T1 delivers a constant 1.5 million bits per second (Mbps).

T3

A very fast dedicated phone line used for business. A T3 delivers a constant 45 million bits per second (Mbps).

tag

A container in an **MP3** file (or another digital-audio file) with various slots to hold pieces of information about the file, such as the artist's name and the track title.

time-shifting

Using a recorder to enable you to watch or listen to a broadcast at a later time than it was transmitted. For example, if you videotape (or TiVo) a program so that you can watch it later, you've time-shifted it. See also **place-shifting**.

TLA

The abbreviation for *three-letter acronym*. It's unfortunate that TLA isn't a true acronym (in which the initials must form a pronounceable word), and even more unfortunate that the computer world is rapidly running out of TLAs. Four-letter acronyms (or abbreviations) have proven to have far less appeal than TLAs.

Trojan horse

A virus, worm, or other piece of **malware** that comes disguised as, attached to, or hidden in an attractive program or file.

tweeter

A speaker designed to reproduce treble (high-frequency) sounds.

TwinVQ

The acronym for Transform-domain Weighted Interleave Vector Quantization Format, a digital-audio format that provides better compression and equal or greater sound quality to **MP3**.

upload cap

An artificially imposed limitation to the upload speed on a connection such as a cable modem. The limitation is artificial in that it is imposed by the service provider to prevent a user from hogging bandwidth rather than by a limitation of the connection. Also referred to as *upload speed cap*.

variable bitrate

A method of encoding information to an **MP3** file by varying the bitrate to optimize the sound. Abbreviated to *VBR*. Compare to **constant bitrate** (CBR).

VBR

The abbreviation for **variable bitrate**.

VirtualPC

Software that lets a Macintosh run a virtual PC through emulation. VirtualPC is created by Connectix Corporation (`www.connectix.com`).

visualization

A graphical display in a **MP3** player or **jukebox,** in which the graphics are triggered by the audio being played.

VMWare

Software that provides a virtual PC through emulation. At this writing, VMWare (from VMWare, Inc.; `www.vmware.com`) runs on Linux, Windows NT, and Windows 2000. For computer-emulation software for the Mac, see **VirtualPC**.

VQF

The file extension for **TwinVQ** files and, by association, the generic term for those files.

warez

Pirated software. See also **MP3z**.

WARM

The acronym for **Write And Read Multiple**.

WAV

A standard format for uncompressed **PCM** audio. Most WAV files are PCM files with a WAV header.

webcasting

Another term for **Internet broadcasting**.

Windows Media Technologies

A digital-audio format developed by Microsoft. Windows Media Technologies 4 has a secure compression scheme called MS Audio that claims to surpass **MP3** in both compression and music quality. The main player for Windows Media Architecture files is Windows Media Player, which is included with every version of Windows for the PC and some versions of Windows for PDA and hand-held devices.

WIPO

The acronym for **World Intellectual Property Organization**.

WMA

The abbreviation and file-format extension for Windows Media Architecture, which is part of the **Windows Media Technologies** family. WMA files use the Advanced Streaming Format file format.

woofer

A speaker designed to reproduce bass (low-frequency) sounds.

World Intellectual Property Organization

An international body "dedicated to promoting the use and protection of works of the human spirit" by applying intellectual property laws. The abbreviation is *WIPO* and its Web site is at www.wipo.org.

WORM

The acronym for **Write Once, Read Multiple**.

Write And Read Multiple

Media, such as CD-RW and **DVD-RAM**, that can be written to multiple times as well as read multiple times. The acronym is *WARM*.

Write Once, Read Multiple

Media, such as CD-R and DVD-R, that can be written to only once but read multiple times. The acronym is *WORM*.

Index

Note to the Reader: Throughout this index **boldfaced** page numbers indicate primary discussions of a topic. *Italicized* page numbers indicate illustrations.

INTERNET PIRACY RESOURCE GUIDE

Item	Description	URL
Other P2P Technologies		
NetMeeting	Collaboration, remote-control, and file-sharing application	www.microsoft.com
Spinfrenzy.com	P2P technology	www.spinfrenzy.com
Utilities		
AutoFTP	Download-scheduling utility	www.primasoft.com
BlackICE Defender	Firewall software	www.networkice.com
CuteFTP	Graphical FTP client	www.cuteftp.com
Free Agent	Newsreader	www.forteinc.com
GetRight	Download-scheduling utility	www.getright.com
Java Runtime Environment (JRE)	Java software required to run Freenet clients	java.sun.com
LeakTest	Online utility for testing your computer's vulnerability	www.grc.com
PGP	Encryption software	www.pgp.com
ShieldsUP!	Online utility for testing your computer's vulnerability	www.grc.com
VirtualPC	PC-emulation software for the Macintosh	www.connectix.com
VMWare	PC-emulation software for Windows NT, 2000, and Linux	www.vmware.com
Zone Alarm	Firewall software	www.zonealarm.com
Information Resources		
American Society of Composers, Authors, and Publishers (ASCAP)	Licensing agencies for broadcasting	www.ascap.com
Broadcast Music, Inc. (BMI)	Licensing agency that represents the public performance copyright interest for more than three million musical works	www.bmi.com